The 49th Paradox

THE 49TH PARADOX

Canada in North America

RICHARD GWYN

McClelland and Stewart

McClelland and Stewart Limited
The Canadian Publishers
25 Hollinger Road
Toronto, Ontario
M4B 3G2

Canadian Cataloguing in Publication Data

Gwyn, Richard, 1934–

   The 49th paradox

Bibliography: p.
Includes index.

ISBN 0-7710-3733-3

1. Canada – Relations – United States. 2. United
States – Relations – Canada. 3. Canada – Foreign
economic relations – United States. 4. United
States – Foreign economic relations – Canada.
5. Nationalism – Canada. I. Title.

FC249.G95 1985   327.71073   C85-099527-2
F1029.5.U6G95 1985

Printed and bound in Canada

Contents

Part Six: The Way We Are

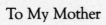

To My Mother

Foreword

This book is neither a Lament for a Nation nor a valediction for nationalism. Instead, it is an attempt to begin a search for something new. Since it is different from most books written by political reporters, different indeed from other books of my own, some explanation of its nature and structure may be in order.

The structure of the book is circular. It describes Canada-U.S. relations in the round. Library shelves buckle beneath the studies, tomes, reports on the subject. Each of these, though, addresses only a single aspect. I have taken a stereoscopic view, peering at Canada-U.S. relations in all its dimensions, political, cultural, economic, commercial, and historic, beginning with the Loyalists, who began it all. Any other view, I believe, would be unfocused. To comprehend the "Star Wars" issue of today, for instance, it is necessary to remember that throughout our history we've had to cope with periodic "loyalty calls" from the centre of the empire to which we were attached, first Britain, now the United States. In another dimension of the relationship, the issue of free trade, or of "enhanced trade" (whatever that is), makes little sense if considered in isolation from international economic developments, hence the chapter, "The Global Marketplace and the Nation-State," in which Canada-U.S. relations as such are scarcely mentioned.

The nature of the book is argumentative. A colleague warned me against this. As part of the research, I interviewed Robert Fulford of *Saturday Night* magazine. We argued and exchanged ideas. Later, Fulford sent me a copy of the introduction he wrote to the 1982 book, *Canada, A Landscape Portrait*. "When they arrive in Canada, political ideas change. The harsh demand and the urgent appeal are dissipated by the size of the country," he wrote. "For this reason, Canada offers an especially frustrating life to intellectuals, whose training is usually based on European or American models. They almost break their swords. They discover that Canadians can't or won't make hard decisions; that every idea approved of in one part of

9

Canada is cancelled out by another part." This warning is entirely sound. Two factors have given me confidence to ignore it. One is that these pages contain no "harsh demand" or "urgent appeal" but only, if the trick is brought off, a kind of insidious temptation. The other is that week in, week out, Fulford waves his own sword around, and when last spotted was still in breath.

The argument advanced in the book has to do with a possible new nationalist agenda. Its outline will unfold from chapter to chapter. One point can be made here as a kind of clearing of the throat. The prime characteristic of nationalism, the pan-Canadian version no differently from the Quebec one, was that it was inward-looking and defensive. Yet the wellspring of nationalism lay in a caring about the country. So the question is whether the spirit can be revived, but this time looking outward.

Two considerations prompted me to write this kind of book. The first was a pragmatic calculation that Canada-U.S. relations would be a hot subject in 1985. The second, a personal imperative, was that I wanted to understand the subject myself. I wanted, in other words, to understand my own country. Since the Loyalists joined the *Canadiens* in the northern wilderness in 1784, Canadian politics has revolved around just two axes: English-French relations; Canada-U.S. relations. It is this second axis that will dominate and define Canadian politics, almost certainly, for the balance of this century. In this sense, the book has served me as a kind of voyage of intellectual discovery, into Canada's present, obviously, but no less into our past because we are what we were, and also, if more tentatively, into our future. I hope that readers will share in these discoveries, sometimes making them for the first time as I did, in other instances finding amid the "stand-alone" facts in the text a point of departure for their own discoveries.

One discovery in particular was the paradox of the 49th parallel. It was chosen as the boundary line pretty much arbitrarily and accidentally – and indeed might have been drawn across the continent at the 54° 40′ mark had enough Americans really been prepared to fight. Anyway, geography and economics obviously designed the continent to be occupied by just one nation. Yet the 49th parallel functions as a true continental divide, both physically and psychically. On our side, rivers flow northward toward the Arctic other than those, like the Columbia and the Skeena, that flow into the Pacific, while on the far side the rivers flow southward.

The divide that matters is psychic. The nub of my argument is contained in the three chapters grouped in Part Three under the title, "The Other North Americans." The heading suggests the thesis. Through most of its history, Canada has survived despite the odds by consciously aspiring to no higher status than that of being a "not-America." This was a canny, tortoise-like strategy, if scarcely a creative or a courageous one. Yet it worked. We hung on, and eventually we grew up. At some time after the Second World War, when Britain ceased to be able to function as a guarantor of Canada's status as a "not-America," we made the rite of passage from semi-nation to full one. The sound barrier was breached. The great dare was taken, and was achieved.

Canadians are no longer "not-Americans." Here, so I believe, truly lies *The 49th Paradox*. We have evolved into a people who are as fully North American as are Americans, and yet who, because of our political culture, are now a quite distinct kind of North American. Conventionally, nations are sorted out from each other by their language, their dress, their customs, their styles of Morris dances. But the worst way to look at North America is in a rearview mirror. Here, as the place where the future always happens first, two nations have evolved that are utterly alike in almost all of their externals and yet are utterly unalike in their political cultures so that they are as distinct from each other as are the Germans from the French, say, even though both are Europeans just as Canadians and Americans are both North Americans.

This thesis, argued out in "The Other North Americans" section but presaged in earlier chapters and reaffirmed in succeeding ones, may be wrong. I would be surprised – disappointed indeed – if some scholars don't take several shots at it. But the opposed opinions may jell into an antithesis, and out of the contest of ideas may emerge a synthesis. This, if it happens, would be the start of something new.

To anticipate, although not to forestall, justified criticism, two qualifications about the book need to be stated in advance. The first is that Canadian-American relations are considered here largely through the prism of English Canadian-American relations. As the descendants, psychically if not genealogically, of the Loyalists, the losers of the Revolution, the counter-revolutionaries, English-speaking

11

Canadians, to title them correctly, occupy the front line of trenches along the border.

Quebecers, though, have no historic quarrel with Americans. Through much of their history, they were affected by the U.S. only at secondhand, through American capital and technology. From 1960 to 1980, Quebecers turned inward, working out their collective destiny among themselves, interacting with the outside world largely through the persona of Pierre Elliott Trudeau. But they never doubted that they were North Americans. Revealingly, Pierre Vallières titled his tirade against wrongs done to Quebecers, *Les Negres blancs d'Amerique*. The Parti Québécois government may have wanted to separate from the rest of Canada but it wanted to get as close as it could to the U.S.: in 1983, the PQ espoused free trade with the U.S., the first provincial government to do so. In an interview, *Le Devoir* editor Lise Bissonette commented, "Quebec does not so much have a French culture that happens to exist in North America as it shares the common culture of the continent which it happens to express in French. The fact of speaking French and of having inherited the French intellectual tradition does make us different, but in daily values we are wholly North American." Quebecers thus share few of the hang-ups about Americans that infect and inhibit English Canadians. Typically, a 1982 CROP Poll found that 77 per cent of Quebecers considered American influence "beneficial" compared to 66 per cent of English Canadians. English Canadians will never rid themselves of their hang-ups except by ridding themselves of their country.

The other justified criticism that can be made of this book is that it skips lightly over what is by far the most important aspect of Canadian-American relations. Overwhelmingly, these relations involve people interacting with each other in their private and professional lives. Canadians and Americans intermarry, visit friends and members of each other's extended families, hopscotch across the border up the rungs of the ladder of their particular company or institution, go to college in one or the other country, go south to escape the northern cold or come north to escape the southern summer sun and cities.

The reason for the institutional bias of the book is obvious: to have explored and described all these personal and professional relationships would have required a tome three times this size. Yet they are a vital aspect of the whole. These personal relationships fix limits to the institutional disagreements and confrontations. Canada and the U.S. are never going to go to war with each other, will always be allies, will always look at the outside world from the same, liberal, democratic premises, will always be, under the skin, good neighbours.

To close on a personal note. Tucked out of sight in between the lines are my own biases. Each topic is presented with enough facts and quotations from those who have travelled parts of this way before for readers to form their own judgements. But I have added my own "top-spin" as we say in the reporters' trade. I cannot help this: even if I'd tried not to, the green letters that formed so magically on my word-processor screen would have assembled themselves into certain predetermined patterns.

Those patterns were determined by my experience. I began life as a Brit, just survival-savvy enough when I arrived, aged twenty, in Canada in the mid-1950s to know that I had to force back the word "colony" each time it slid toward the tip of my tongue. I didn't really come to Canada at all, but, like many immigrants then, came to a part of America that for reasons not worth examining, let alone trying to understand, was much easier to get into than the real America. I didn't really come to Canada until 1967, the year of the Centennial and of Expo. That's when I became a Canadian citizen. That's when, in other words, I decided I wanted to live in Canada, not in America. Most of my career since then has been spent in Ottawa. It's fashionable to bash Ottawa, and it has certainly grown fat and sleek and unlike most of the rest of Canada. It has two redeeming qualities for a Canada-watcher, though. Everyone comes there from everywhere, at some time or other, even if only to bash Ottawa at federal-provincial conferences. As well, because Ottawa is so unlike the rest of Canada, quite a few of those who live here, many more than is generally recognized, invest a good deal of energy and time in trying to experience the rest of Canada, if only by travelling across it on periodic "parish tours." Here, I got lucky. My editor, also my wife, and my love, is a Newfoundlander. Through her, and through a book about Joey Smallwood, I came to be accepted as a kind of extended citizen of that society. Newfoundland is one of a kind, and of a very precious kind. What matters here is that being connected to Newfoundland while living in Ottawa meant being connected to Canada.

The other bias I bring to this work is that of a Canadian nationalist. It would be pretty hard to write political columns for The Toronto Star for a dozen years and not be a nationalist. It would be impossible to have been executive assistant to Eric Kierans, as I was in 1968-70 during a stint on the other side of the green baize doors, and not be a nationalist. Often, the *curriculum vitae* of nationalists start with the negatives, "I am not anti-American" as the first, "I am not narrow" as the second, and, often, "I am not negative" as the third. To hell with all of that. This curious country is never going to be, as Pierre Trudeau once prophesied, "a brilliant prototype for the building of tomorrow's civilization." But it has figured out how to fashion a very agreeable and an exceptionally civil lifestyle for its citizens from which others could learn some lessons if they came and looked and listened.

This society is now under strain. The Americans have found their second wind. Their mood today is assertive, cocky, exuberant. The New Patriotism inspires them to cheer chauvinistically for their Olympic athletes; also to take a poke at Grenada; and perhaps one day to take a poke at Nicaragua. Here, by contrast, nationalism has passed its peak, both in its appeal to the public and in its inner self-confidence. Doubts about our economic future are widespread. At the same time, an economic gap is opening up along the border. If it widens too far, it could draw south many of Canada's best and brightest. So we need to find ourselves again, as we did in a quite different context during the crisis of national unity. This book attempts to describe a new direction in which we might go collectively.

Richard Gwyn
Ottawa
August 1, 1985

Part One
The Way We Were

Our past speaks to our present. Most of what is happening today between Canada and the U.S. has happened before, or is happening as a result of what once did or did not happen. Free trade, for example, is an issue today because Canadians once rejected it, in the Reciprocity Election of 1911. That election confirmed Sir John A. Macdonald's National Policy of 1879, projecting down to today the legacy of a protectionist, inward-looking economy composed preponderantly of multinational subsidiaries vaulted in over the tariff walls and of government enterprises created to fill the spaces left by an absent Canadian entrepreneurial class.

Nor is the debate about the United States' Strategic Defence Initiative, or "Star Wars," a new one. In its first form it occurred at the turn of the century when Sir Wilfrid Laurier answered Britain's call to send troops to South Africa, even at the cost of losing his protégé Henri Bourassa. Like feudal barons, the imperial powers – first the British, today the Americans – periodically summon up their yeomen for their crusades. The unchanging decision that "dependencies" such as Canada have to make is when to say yes to pay their dues and when to say no for the sake of some larger imperative.

Beginning with the Loyalists, to whom Canadians owe the existence of Canada itself, the three opening chapters chronicle Canadian history as seen from the perspective of cross-border relations down to 1957, the dividing line between historic and contemporary Canada. Over that time, just one fundamental change has occurred in Canada-U.S. relations. Britain once provided a counterweight. Since the 1950s, Canada has been on its own.

Chapter One
Yanks and Tories

"The dream of Tory origins
Is full of lies and blanks,
Though what remains when it is gone
To prove that we're not Yanks?"

Civil Elegies, Dennis Lee

Near the end of his life in 1815, Richard Cartwright, Loyalist leader, a prosperous merchant and miller, a councillor of the assembly of Upper Canada, brother-in-law to Laura Secord, wrote what amounted to a political will. He reviewed his own and his colony's accomplishments and found them exceedingly good: "extensive and well-cultivated farms abounding in all the substantial comforts of life ... guarded by the wisest laws and equally and impartially administered." Then he summed up: "It must gladden the heart of our venerable sovereign to know that his paternal care of his loyal American subjects, settled in this remote corner of his empire, has been crowned with such complete success."*

Until their bicentenary, in 1984, the Loyalists had slipped to the outer edge of the consciousness of Canadians. They were remembered, if at all, with more than a trace of derisory embarrassment as counter-revolutionary elitists who handed down to us as a leaden legacy their habits of deference to authority and of timorous conservatism. Least attractively of all, they were remembered as having been losers.

In Cartwright's long epistle, written to the newspaper at Kingston, one word that he used unaffectedly now jumps off the page. This is the word "American." He was an American. So were all the Loyalists. So were the immigrants who poured across the border

---

* Quoted in CBC Radio's *Ideas* program, "Richard Cartwright and the Roots of Canadian Conservatism," broadcast in June, 1985, and written and narrated by David Cayley.

after learning about the land the Loyalists had cleared in Upper Canada and who, by the time of the War of 1812, constituted a majority in the colony.

The single most important characteristic of the Loyalists was that they were American. Often, this has been treated as being of small account. All of the attention has been given to the Loyalists' monarchical conservatism and to its defining effect upon their successors. In fact, a good case can be made that Canada's conservatism, while it may have originated in the circumstance of the society having missed out on both the American and the French Revolutions, really derives from the fact that Canada, almost uniquely among Western nations, missed out on the far more radicalizing experience of the Industrial Revolution; Canada only really became industrialized during the Second World War, by which time the antidote of the welfare state had been invented.

About 50,000 Loyalists left America after Britain sued for peace. Almost all of them stayed in America. This is to say that they moved to its nearest available equivalent, Canada, rather than to either of the two alternate locations, Britain and the West Indies. Those who did leave America did so with deep sadness. "I earnestly wish to spend the remainder of my Days in America," Sir William Pepperrell, former governor of Massachusetts, wrote to a friend from England where he had settled. "I love the Country, I love the People."* Perhaps understandably, American historians rather than Canadian ones have most often identified this enduring Americanness of the Loyalists. David Bell, as an exception, has written that "The Loyalists resembled fairly closely the persecutors from whom they fled.... As a result, the Loyalists were deprived of the opportunity of erecting their values – which were virtually identical to those of the Americans – into a national identity."**

Once in Canada, the Loyalists set out to recreate, not a corner of Britain, but a better America. Edward Winslow, the founder of New Brunswick, looked about him and saw "an immense multitude,

---

* In a certain way, Pepperrell did come back to America. When U.S. troops moved to Newfoundland in 1941, the site for their base just outside St. John's was named, by some inspired official, Fort Pepperrell, on the strength of a connection between Pepperrell's descendants and a distinguished Newfoundland family, the Outerbridges.

** See David Bell, "The Loyalist Tradition in Canada," in J.M. Bumsted, ed., *Canadian History Before Confederation* (Georgetown, 1972).

not of dissolute vagrants such as commonly make the first efforts to settle new countries, but gentlemen of education, farmers formerly independent, and reputable mechanics." Winslow then added, "By Heaven, we will be the envy of the American states."

It is exceedingly difficult to know the political ideas that motivated the Loyalists. Few of them wrote much. They harboured no poets or philosophers. Their silence is remarkable in contrast to the extraordinary outpouring, so original and so eloquent, that the American rebels, turned into patriots, produced. Nor was there a Loyalist leader to compare, remotely, with Thomas Jefferson, Benjamin Franklin, John Adams, Patrick Henry, or George Washington, a company indeed for whom there are few equals in Western history.

Some things can be said about the Loyalists with confidence. They were not all "Tories" (the label given them by the patriots). One American historian has called them "conscious minorities." There were blacks and Indians, both convinced they would fare far better under British than American justice; Palatine mercenaries; Scottish Highlanders recently emigrated (including Flora MacDonald of Bonnie Prince Charlie fame); tenant farmers from New York state, glad to escape their landlords; Dutch from Pennsylvania; and, of course, the stereotypical Loyalists, Anglican clergymen, merchants, colonial officials.

In certain ways, the new America of the north was less hierarchical than that of the south. It had no black underclass. It had no established aristocracy, as in the Deep South. It had no great estates – a proposal by some Tory-style Loyalists that large estates be created was angrily rejected by ordinary Loyalists – and so all its farmers answered to themselves and not to landlords. It wasn't populist, as was America, but it was democratic; the soil was just too hard for the British class system to take root.

As the American historian Robert Middlekauff has written, the Loyalists "shared the revolutionaries' beliefs in the rights of the individual." Where they differed was in believing that these rights could be best protected by established British institutions and customs rather than by what Cartwright called "the affectation of equality" or by what another Loyalist called "the madness of the multitude." The attraction to the Loyalists was neither the king himself – George III being distinctly unappealing (decidedly so to a Flora MacDonald) –

nor the idea of being part of the British Empire, which then scarcely existed. It was rather the *idea* of an America that could become the America that once had been; an America governed by British ideas, from appointed judges to an established church, rather than by higgledy-piggledy, pork-barrelling, mass democracy. As Loyalist Reverend Mather Byles put it, "Better to be ruled by one tyrant three thousand miles away than by three thousand tyrants a mile away."

They were certainly counter-revolutionaries, convinced that out of one revolution would come another, as it had in France and as it would in the U.S. in the form of the Civil War. In place of revolution, their guiding rule was peace, order, and good government. Revolutions, like those of 1837-38, they dealt with harshly, particularly that of William Lyon Mackenzie, who issued a "republican" manifesto demanding the abolition of such heresies as elected judges, universal suffrage, and titles.*

Good government, though, meant government *for* the people, if not actually by the people, since, as Governor Winslow commented sadly, "Our gentlemen have all become potato farmers and our shoemakers are preparing to legislate."** Thus it meant activist government, as in the building of the Welland Canal, so that by the 1840s, for all that it was ruled by the bewhiskered Family Compact, the colony of Upper Canada was proportionately more deeply in debt than is Canada today. The Loyalists took their political ideals from Burke rather than from Locke and Hobbes; above all they would have agreed with Burke that "Every virtue and prudent act is founded on compromise and barter." But the purse-lipped prudery commonly attributed to them is much more the product of the later waves of Calvinist Scots.

In two crucial senses, we are today what the Loyalists once were. They opened up Upper Canada, now Ontario, thus creating a society quite separate from that of the *Canadiens* of Lower Canada. Between these two colonies there was little communion, making it inevitable that Lord Durham would one day find "two nations warring in the bosom of a single state."

---

* Even so, Mackenzie returned from exile in the U.S., won election to the Assembly of Upper Canada, and declared that having experienced the two systems he was certain that British justice was far superior to the American variety.

** Quoted in Christopher Moore, *The Loyalists*.

And they defined for their descendants the national goal of building in the top half of the continent a better America. An impossible dream, of course, given geography and climate, yet not an unimaginable dream if the success of a society is not measured by the number of its missiles. Because of the Loyalists, a competitiveness between the two Americas has been handed down across the generations. Few Americans, of course, are aware the contest exists. But the competitiveness was there from the beginning. John Graves Simcoe, first lieutenant-governor of Upper Canada, described his new colony as "a dagger pointed at the heart of America." The competitiveness exists today: one of the reasons for the popularity of Pierre Trudeau's peace initiative of 1983-84 had to have been that he was seen by Canadians to be showing Americans a better way than theirs to achieve peace in the world.

The American historian Bartlett Brebner has written that "Perhaps the most striking thing about Canada is that it is not part of the United States." In the beginning, it was a very close thing. Having conquered New France in 1759 Britain almost gave it up for sugar-rich Guadeloupe. Had she done so, there would have been no "other" America for the Loyalists to go to.

It has been said often that Canada was created by the U.S., a sort of rib extruded from the side of the American Revolution. True, but so is the reverse. By conquering New France, Britain removed the threat to the Thirteen Colonies that justified its standing army here; aware of restiveness in the colonies, Britain maintained its army – the Indians provided the necessary excuse – but imposed taxes to pay for its costs.

During the American Revolution, Canada caused the revolutionaries their first defeat. In 1775, the Continental Congress dispatched a resolution northwards that "your unmerited degradation has engaged the most unfeigned pity of your neighbours," and when that invitation to union evoked no response, sent one of its best generals, Benedict Arnold, to capture Quebec by way of an overland march from the mouth of the Kennebec River in Maine that was perhaps the greatest military march of the eighteenth century. Arnold had too few troops, and the Canadiens neither helped him nor hindered him. (Their clergy were loyal to the crown, but they found this loyalty harder to sustain when France allied itself with the revolutionaries.)

The revolutionaries, by now patriots, remained hopeful. The articles of union of the Thirteen Colonies declared Canada "entitled to all the advantages of this union" by simple request, as applied to no other territories. Once the war was won, Congress sent Franklin, Adams, and John Jay to London to negotiate, among other things, the transfer to the new United States of all the northern colonies. No calculation of the worth of these "few acres of snow" entered into Britain's decision to refuse the request; probably, a contemporary "Falklands Factor" made it impossible for British politicians to give up what had been held at the cost of so much blood.

"The axes of this loyal band dispelled the forest gloom/And in the howling wilderness did make a garden bloom," wrote Cartwright in an out-of-character attempt at versification. Out of opposites, the "Frockcoat and moccasin," in Douglas LePan's phrase, the "stringency and the nobility of the primal encounter" between highly civilized settlers and the raw nature of the north, in the words of George Grant, was forged the sceptical stoicism, the wary romanticism, that now define the Canadian character.

Northernness is Canada's most nearly distinctive quality. Surprisingly few other countries share it: the Scandinavian ones, Iceland, Russia. While this northernness oppressed the early Canadians physically, it also elevated them spiritually. The first Canadian nationalists, the Canada Firsters of the 1870s, saw in northernness the well-spring of a new nationality. "May not our snow and frost give us what is of more value than gold or silver, a healthy, hardy, virtuous, dominant race," wrote the essayist Robert Haliburton. Another Canada Firster, William Foster, made the inevitable cross-border comparison between the "more manly, more real" northerners and the "weak, marrow-bones superstition of an effeminate South." We still today stand on guard for The True North Strong and Free.

Yet the idea of Canada surviving was absurd. It was too small, too distant, too northern. It ought to have been obliterated in the War of 1812, but the Americans were inept, and more important militarily, half-hearted. Retrospectively, a fair amount of wishful thinking has been invested into that war. Despite the writings of some revisionists, Upper Canadians, most of them being recently arrived Americans, didn't hurl themselves at the invaders. In the judgement of the British commander, General Brock, the local population was "thoroughly bad"; he had to hang several of them for treason.

But the scare from the south turned the colony inward and stratified and hardened it. It's at this point that the Loyalists became the elitist counter-revolutionaries of memory. In *Gardens, Covenants and Exiles*, Dennis Duffy writes that the War of 1812 turned Loyalism into "a straight-jacket for the colony," that it left Upper Canada "an imperial headland jutting upon a republican sea." Canada turned away from America – until 1812 there had been considerable cross-border commercial and personal contact, as the Loyalists kept in touch with their American Tory equivalents, the Federalists – and turned back toward Britain. Canada turned back to the past, that is to say.

In fact, the U.S. wasn't that much of a threat. Why bother to try to annex Canada? went the prevailing official attitude, for it was bound to come to its senses and sue for entry eventually. Through the first half of the nineteenth century, the U.S. was in any event preoccupied with political nation-building, the settlement of internal accounts that eventually had to be settled by the Civil War. Thereafter, it was preoccupied by extending itself to its western limits and by economic nation-building. To do this the U.S. erected a high tariff wall to protect its industries. The consequence, particularly after the U.S. cancelled its Reciprocity Treaty with Canada in 1866, was to force Canadian businessmen to turn back to Britain in search of markets. American economic nationalism thus underwrote Canadian political independence.

During these years, Britain, and not the U.S., constituted the most considerable threat to Canada's continued existence. Following the War of Independence, Britain had handed over to the U.S. all of the territory west of the Ohio River, formerly part of Quebec, even though no American troops had set foot there. This, and the later cession to the U.S. of Oregon, signalled that Britain accepted that all of the continent belonged to the U.S.* Canada, meanwhile, was bottled up because all of the lands west of Upper Canada had been

---

* A strong suggestion of this is provided by the fact that the peace terms after the War of Independence contained no provision for the Loyalists. It was the local British army, in New York, and not the British politicians, who made it possible for the Loyalists to move to Canada. Once the Loyalists had actually arrived in Canada the British government was exceptionally generous in its grants of land – largely at the expense of the Six Nations Confederacy.

23

given over to the Hudson's Bay Company.

Britain's attitude was understandable. Canada cost money for the maintenance of troops, and while an important source of timber for the navy, it provided only a minor market for British goods. In 1846, Britain, confident of its mercantile superiority and acting as all such industrial leaders do, adopted free trade – naturally, without consulting its colonies. Overnight, Canada lost its principal market. A group of Montreal merchants issued a proclamation calling for union with the U.S. They attracted little support, but to prevent a recurrence Governor Lord Elgin, in 1854, negotiated a reciprocity treaty with the U.S. Its purpose, Elgin told his secretary, was to "quiet the people of Canada and prevent their annexation." Elgin's reason for fearing annexation, though, was that it would "disturb the balance of power within the Union" – to the disadvantage of the South with which Britain was allied, commercially and emotionally, and later, if secretly, militarily.

Up to and past Confederation in 1867, official British opinion held that Canada's annexation was inevitable, and certainly not worth resisting at the price of offending as powerful a nation as the U.S. John A. Macdonald complained that the bill to create the new Dominion of Canada received as little attention at Westminster as "a private bill uniting two or three parishes."

Britain only began to be interested in Canada when it began to be interested in its empire. That didn't happen until the 1870s when the "Little Englander," Gladstone, was replaced by the "Big Englander," Disraeli; suddenly, the British became passionately interested in, and jingoistic about, the Cairo-to-Capetown chain of colonies that Rhodes was forging for them in Africa, with India as the jewel in their crown, and with Canada and its "unseizable virginity," in Rudyard Kipling's phrase, as the northern star. This new imperial order was brought to Ottawa in 1872 by Governor General the Earl of Dufferin. Before leaving London, a friend advised him "to make it your business to get rid of the Dominion." Dufferin's reply, prefiguring Winston Churchill's famous comment about the empire itself, was: "I certainly did not intend to be handed down to history as the Governor General who had lost Canada."*

By then, Canada had survived for almost a century. Just by existing for that long it had begun to generate within itself the possibility

---

* Quoted in Sandra Gwyn, *The Private Capital* (Toronto, 1984).

of permanent existence. That accomplishment Canadians owe to the Loyalists.

This accomplishment in nation-building was a truly extraordinary one. As early as the War of 1812 the Loyalists were a minority in their new land, amounting to perhaps a quarter of the population of Upper Canada. Thereafter, following the Napoleonic Wars, they were swamped by waves of immigrants from Britain and Ireland. Today, as the historian J.M.S. Careless commented on the CBC program, *Ideas*, "Loyalism [has] almost gone down the drain except for its own little circles of the faithful who keep the flame alight, but who really only represent ancestor worship." Or perhaps to be fleetingly recalled by a Mazo de la Roche novel picked up by chance from the shelf in a summer cottage.

The nation the Loyalists created was a curious non-nation, without founding myths or founding heroes, without any universalist concept of citizenship, and without a dream other than that of recreating the America that once had been. Yet the flame lit by the Loyalists, and quite unknown to them also kept burning quietly by the *Canadiens*, has never gone out. They deserve to be remembered, not as flag-waving, top-hat, High Tories, but as a breed a bit gentler than that, more nuanced, more *Canadian*.

Since the Loyalists themselves wrote so little, other more recent writers will have to say it for them. Charles Taylor sums up his book, *Radical Tories*, published in 1982, this way: "Initially pessimistic, I have grown more sanguine. For I found a conservative heritage which is far from moribund and which relates directly to our present needs. It is also very much our own tradition, for it is neither mired in nostalgic anglophilia nor obsessed with the contemporary American fad of revolutionary consciousness. Popular and even radical, it has a particularly Canadian twang."

In 1965, George Grant published one of the most influential of all the literary products of Canadian nationalism, *Lament for a Nation*. Reread today, much of what Grant wrote seems dated – his judgement, for instance, that the defeat of the Diefenbaker government in 1963 represented "the last gasp of Canadian nationalism ... the strident swan-song of that hope."

But Grant relit the flame. After elegy comes celebration. "Here was a crazy old philosopher of religion at McMaster University and

25

he woke up half our generation," Jim Laxer, a university student in the 1960s, now an economist at York University and formerly research director for the NDP, has recalled of his own reaction to *Lament for a Nation*. "He was saying Canada was dead, and by saying it he was creating the country."

Chapter Two
The Flag and the Plume

"Standing alone, it might be, gentlemen, that the lion and the lamb would lie down together. But as has been said, the lamb would be inside the lion."

John A. Macdonald

The first half century after Confederation was the era of the giants. John A. Macdonald and Wilfrid Laurier were both larger than life. More unusual still for Canadian prime ministers, each held ideas about the character of the nation, and about its future, that reached beyond the daily run of Canadian life. Their opposed visions of Canada are still being argued out today, unresolved and probably unresolvable.

Macdonald's central idea was that of a high-tariff National Policy. Its purpose was to create not merely manufacturing industries, and therefore jobs, but to create also "a union in interest, a union in trade, a union in feeling." Laurier's counter-balancing central idea was reciprocity, or free trade. Trade created by protectionism, in his view, "was not a natural trade" and reduced Canadians to commercial colonials, "deterred from the spirit of enterprise."

These ideas, and the subsidiary sentiments that each held, were not always in opposition and, indeed, often amounted to different ways of saying the same thing. To say that Macdonald stood for the Old Flag and the British Connection, and Laurier for the white plume of a bilingual, independent Canada would be to distort grossly the aspirations of both men and to infect history with today's perceptions and prejudices. When Macdonald remarked, "A British subject I was born, a British subject I will die," he was saying that this was the one way he could be certain of living as a Canadian. In the 1880s, when Imperial Federation became faddish, Macdonald opposed it, recognizing that Canadian MPs, if elected to an Imperial Parliament at Westminster, would sit there invisible and impotent – but implicated. He hanged Louis Riel, but his attitude toward French Canadians is best expressed in his famous line, "Treat them as a free people, and they will behave as a free people generally do." He read French fluently enough to be able to discuss all the racy new novels with George Etienne Cartier. Confederation was his and Cartier's shared vision.

Laurier was certainly more sceptical about the British connection. As a Quebecer, he knew only too well that burgeoning imperialism, with its dismissive distrust of everything not British, would drive a wedge between French and English Canadians and pose as great a threat to the nation as annexation from the south. Yet, thanks to the influence of his close friend Emilie Lavergne, the mistress of his mind and perhaps also of his flesh, Laurier was also more than a bit of an Anglophile. If Macdonald revered British institutions, Laurier came to admire the British style, particularly the potent, unwritten code of fair play. Each time he went to London, he dazzled the duchesses and allowed them to dazzle him. "Weak men's heads are turned in a single evening," he remarked, "and there are few who can resist long." After Riel was hanged, he shouted from a platform that had he been born on the banks of the Saskatchewan, he, too, would have "shouldered a musket." Yet he broke with the Quebec nationalists, led by his one-time protégé Henri Bourassa; he sent troops to South Africa and created a navy to help the mother country on the eve of the First World War. All of which proves that Canada really is a hard country to lead, except by guile.

Ultimately, what truly divided Macdonald and Laurier was neither their economic strategies nor their political tactics but the differences within their own natures. Both were visionaries. But the vision of Macdonald, though paradoxically the bolder one, since he took part in the creation of the country and then extended it from sea to sea, was informed by a deep-rooted scepticism, or pessimism, or realism, about what Canadians were capable of. He was the paternalist father-figure. At Confederation, he judged that it would be a century before the new country could "stand on its feet."

Laurier was a native optimist, a man, in his own description, of the "sunny way." His role was that of a cheerleader. He believed, or said he did, that the "twentieth century will belong to Canada." (Laurier, it must also be said, was luckier than Macdonald. His term coincided with the longest boom in Canadian history except for the twenty years following the Second World War.)

On the matter at hand, the National Policy versus reciprocity, two comments by each are particularly revealing. In 1884, Macdonald discussed free trade with his colleague Charles Tupper and commented, "Our manufacturers are too young and too weak. Ten years hence, they might agree they would gain by the opening of a market of 60 million. But they would be crushed right now." Laurier, in 1888, discussed the same subject. Canadian manufacturers could compete if they tried, he said, "But if you put them on their legs, they moan piteously that they are too weak to stand."

In one critical sense, all these arguments were like intellectual balloons bobbing around in a vacuum. For Canadians to decide either to accept free trade or to reject it, the United States would first have to offer it. No offer was made or considered seriously in Washington until after the turn of the century, when William Howard Taft became president.* American protectionism thus nurtured Canadian protectionist nationalism. One of the few Americans who understood just how self-defeating this policy was to the cause of continental union was the economist Henry George, author of the "Single Tax" concept. He wrote in 1886: "We may annex Canada to all intents and purposes whenever we throw down the tariff wall we have built around ourselves. Whether the Canadians choose to maintain a separate Parliament and pay a British lordling for keeping up a mock court at Rideau Hall need not in the slightest concern us.... The intimate relations that would come of unrestrained commerce would soon obliterate the boundary line." Luckily for Canadian economic nationalists, American politicians of the nineteenth century didn't read economic essays.

Macdonald's economic nationalism thus began as a defensive response to nationalism south of the border. In 1866, angered by British support for the South during the Civil War, and by similar Canadian popular sentiments, the United States abruptly cancelled the Reciprocity Treaty of 1854 that Lord Elgin had negotiated. As a further sign of disapproval, President Andrew Johnson made a conspicuous point

---

* In 1874, the government of Alexander Mackenzie did negotiate a limited reciprocity pact, but this was subsequently rejected by the U.S. Senate.

29

of not sending a congratulatory telegram to the new nation on July 1, 1867. The Fenian Brotherhood, displaced Irishmen looking for Union Jacks to tear down, was able to raid across the border with suspicious ease. For a time, in fact, Macdonald worried that the now idle Union Army might be kept busy by being dispatched northward.* Instead, the republic applied its energies to pushing its frontiers westward.

During the dozen years of reciprocity, Canadians had come to rely on the vast market to the south, had welcomed as new citizens many Yankee entrepreneurs, and had switched from the pound sterling to the dollar. All of a sudden, Canadians were isolated, all the more because Britain by now had converted to free trade so that Canadian lumber had lost out to the cheaper and closer lumber of the Baltic.

Macdonald's answer to the American push westward was the impossible dream of the Canadian Pacific Railway. The National Policy was his answer to the closing of the U.S. market. It was also a despairing attempt to staunch the hemorrhaging away of Canada's population: between 1871 and 1900, more than two million Canadians, native-born and newly arrived immigrants, as many of these as landed, moved across the border to the incredible new industrial cities burgeoning all over the American landscape: Chicago, Philadelphia, Boston, Cleveland, Cincinnati, Baltimore, New York.

Macdonald's timing could scarcely have been better. He began working out the new policy in the mid-1870s, during his post-Pacific Scandal years as Opposition Leader, at precisely the same time that Britain's attitudes toward her colonies were undergoing a dramatic change.** Disraeli's arrival in power in 1874 ushered in the new era of aggressive imperialism. At Rideau Hall, between 1872 and 1878, Lord Dufferin served as Dizzy's aggressive proconsul in the west. In 1878, when Macdonald swept back to power, the stage was set for the National Policy. The new imperialism stirred Canadians to a sense of belonging to a larger, globe-girdling whole. Further,

---

* Until the 1870s, the gauge of Canadian railways was set at five feet, six inches, to impede a northward flow of Union troops in railway cars designed to run on tracks four feet, eight and one-half inches wide.

** Time and again, Britain deferred to U.S. interests – over timber, over fishing, over boundaries – over Canadian interests. British ambassadors in Washington were especially one-sided because, as Macdonald noted shrewdly, "There is always a desire on his part to make his future residence in Washington as pleasant as possible."

as the nation began sliding into the nineteenth century's precursor to the Great Depression, Canadians were willing to take a risk on something new.

The new policy came into the world lustily, in Finance Minister Tilley's budget of March 14, 1879. The glory and the rhetoric belonged to Macdonald. Only the CPR inspired him to higher flights of oratory. "We have no manufacturers here," he said. "We have no working-people, our working-people have gone off to the U.S. These Canadian artisans are adding to the strength, to the power and to the wealth of a foreign nation instead of adding to ours. . . ." Thus, "The time has come when the people of this Dominion have to declare whether Canada is for Canadians, or whether it is to be a pasture for cows to be sent to England, whether every appliance of civilization should be manufactured within her boundaries for our own use, or whether we shall remain hewers of wood and drawers of water."

Macdonald's high tariffs did what they were supposed to do. New manufacturing plants were created and old ones expanded, particularly in Montreal. The southward flow of people began to slacken. Just as Macdonald had hoped, the union became increasingly "a union in trade and in interests." Yet, if Canada gained as a whole, parts of it lost. The small Maritime manufacturing plants were closed and "rationalized" by Montreal financiers. The farmers of southwestern Ontario complained that they had to pay high prices for their equipment with no compensating gain in access to a larger market.

For most of a decade, such complaints lacked a political outlet, not least because Liberal leader Edward Blake, a lawyer with close links to the Toronto business community, was himself protectionist-minded. Then, on June 23, 1887, Laurier, very reluctantly, took over the leadership to allow Blake to retire. The next four years, during which Laurier and Macdonald confronted each other directly, amount to a golden age in Canadian politics, made lustrous by the clash of ideas as well as of personalities.

On August 2, 1887, less than six weeks after assuming the leadership, Laurier committed the Liberals to dismantling the National Policy and replacing it with free trade. "Any kind of reciprocity with the people of the United States would be to the advantage of Canada," he told an audience of 3,000 *Canadiens* assembled for a political picnic at Somerset, in Quebec's Eastern Townships. "I may say this – it is my actual policy – that the time has come to abandon the policy

31

of retaliation, to show the American people that we are brothers, and to hold out our hand to them with due respect for the duties we owe to our Mother Country."

Laurier was forty-five that summer, with his reputation yet to build. "He will never make a leader, he has not enough of the devil in him," one of his backbenchers complained to a journalist. Yet, that early, he showed the stuff of greatness. In that same speech in Somerset, he challenged his listeners to share his own ideal of a bilingual, bicultural nation. "Our common country is not confined to the province of Quebec," he said. "Our country is wherever the British flag flies in America."

Laurier's ideas about the benefits of reciprocity came not from himself but from the party's finance critic, Richard Cartwright,* known as the "Blue Knight of Ruin" for his hectoring about the nation's bleak economic future unless it converted to free trade. By the spring of 1888, the Liberals had formally committed themselves to a policy of "Unrestricted Reciprocity," encompassing free trade with the United States in both agricultural and manufactured products but stopping short of the formal customs union implied by the label "Commercial Union."** In Parliament, Laurier's oratory matched Macdonald's. The National Policy was an expensive and cumbersome imposition, he argued. "What trade we have between east and west is not a natural trade but is due entirely to the fact that the country pays the freight. You cannot legislate against nature." Daringly, almost recklessly, he pushed on. "To pretend that our colonial allegiance demands from us that we should be deterred from the spirit of enterprise ... I deny. Colonies are destined to become nations as it is the destiny of a child to become a man.... The time is coming when the present relations of Great Britain and Canada must either become closer or be severed altogether."

Laurier's policy inspired opposition within his party. Former Prime Minister Alexander Mackenzie called it "one of the stupidest mistakes

---

* Nephew to the Loyalist leader, Richard Cartwright, quoted in Chapter One.

** The Conservatives cleverly accused the Liberals of advancing Commercial Union, or a full customs union, as a precursor to full political union. To compound the confusion, the Conservatives, in order to appease the farmers, claimed themselves to support "reciprocity" or free trade in natural products, knowing full well that the U.S. would never agree to this. Such verbal gamesmanship aside, the Liberals wanted free trade, and the Conservatives, high protective tariffs.

ever made by any section of our party." Blake opposed it, fearing that political union would be the inevitable result. Nor did it help that 1887 was the golden anniversary of Queen Victoria's reign. To mark the occasion, a group of Toronto businessmen-patriots formed a Canadian branch of the Imperial Federation League and imported, as their first guest speaker, Joseph Chamberlain, later to become Colonial Secretary, who spoke ferociously against reciprocity.

For three years Canadians debated reciprocity versus the National Policy – in the Commons, in the newspapers, in their parlours. The best analysis was never made public. In October, 1887, Governor General Lord Lansdowne wrote a memorandum to the Colonial Secretary that remains, a century later, one of the most succinct and penetrating analyses ever made of the benefits and costs of a Canada-U.S. free trade pact.

"In its strictly commercial aspect," wrote Lansdowne, "there appears to be no room for doubt that Commercial Union would be greatly to the advantage of the people of the Dominion." With remarkable astuteness, Lansdowne identified "the people" as the beneficiaries. There would be more jobs for them and the price of goods would be lower, if to the detriment of some businessmen's profits.

Lansdowne then turned to the negatives. "The centre of political activity in regard to all commercial questions affecting the North American continent would inevitably be at Washington," he wrote. "Congress would be the arbiter of the commercial destinies of the Dominion and the Canadian Parliament would find itself comparatively impotent to effect any changes which it might desire in the interests of its own country." Expressing a now-dated concern, he worried that Commercial Union would "tend towards the estrangement of Canada from the mother country." Then, displaying a generosity for which he deserves to be better remembered than by a park named after him in a capital city that he in fact detested (and soon afterwards left for India), Lansdowne urged that Britain not oppose Commercial Union "on purely selfish grounds" if Canadians "decided freely" that was what they wanted.

Laurier had committed the cardinal political sin of seizing onto the right idea at the wrong time. For Canadians, the opportunity to "decide freely" came with the election of March, 1891. The contest wasn't even close. By now, the tide of imperialism was in full flood. "We worked the loyalty cry for all it was worth and it carried the day," Macdonald remarked afterwards. As disastrous for Laurier was that he couldn't deliver what he was promising. The U.S. showed not the slightest interest in reciprocity; indeed, in 1890 it had raised its tariffs even higher – the so-called McKinley tariff – giving Macdonald the chance to claim that the Yankees were trying "to starve Canada into submission."

The election was really about Macdonald. At seventy-six, the lion was old. But he was still a lion. "His eyes were tired and disillusioned but his mouth was firm with strength and humour," in the magnificent description of the historian Donald Creighton in *The Old Chieftain*. "There was no bitterness, no mere shrewdness, no cunning in the small deceptions of his face. He offered no apologies, he suffered no vain regrets." This, and that iconic troika, "The Old Leader, the Old Flag, the Old Policy," was more than enough.

Three months later, Macdonald was dead. Another five years passed before Laurier replaced him in power. Another fifteen years went by before Laurier, in his own last hurrah in 1911, offered the nation another version of his vision, this time with a reciprocity agreement already in his coat pocket. The years between provided little in the way of clarity or constructive thinking, but much by way of chatter.

The Imperial Federalists continued to wrap themselves in the Union Jack. If their objectives were unclear, other than that the colonies should rally round the mother country in time of need, their voices were loud and reached a crescendo during the last flag-bedecked years of the old century. History has long consigned these super patriots to the "out" basket, and they were narrow-minded and bigoted. As Henri Bourassa, founder of *Le Devoir*, understood, perhaps even better than Laurier, imperialism was the wedge that divided the two Canadas. "The French Canadian has found that the pledges of equality of rights ... given to him by the Fathers of Confederation have hardly been kept up," wrote Bourassa in a prophetic article of 1912. Annexation no longer seemed the worst of fates. "He has ceased to look upon it as the worst danger to his creed and nationality," Bourassa continued, since "his English-speaking fellow citizens do not entertain ardent feelings of gratitude towards him, nor even a spirit of justice."

But the Imperial Federalists do deserve to be remembered for one attribute. They were Canada's first internationalists. "An independent

Canada means this," said the Conservative MP R.B. Bennett, later to become Prime Minister. "We Canadians are afraid of the responsibilities of empire, the white man's burden." Stephen Leacock said it best: "I am an imperialist because I will not be a colonialist." His problem, the canker in the red rose of imperialism, was that Britain wanted Canadians to remain forever colonials.

One consequence of all the flag-waving was that for the first time a number of Americans started to consider annexation seriously, as a way to rid the continent of its last Union Jack. The phrase Manifest Destiny had been coined in the 1840s to justify the Yankee takeover of the northern half of Mexico. Few Americans of that era were very much interested in Canada's ice and snow. "All we do *not* want," wrote the newspaper editor James Gordon Bennett, "is that Canada should join us." Even those Americans who did think about absorbing Canada assumed it would happen not by force, but osmotically, through the quiet persuasion of geography and economics. "I am not in favour of artificial stimulants," wrote President Rutherford B. Hayes in 1879. "Properly, and in order, and with due regard for the feelings of Great Britain, the two countries should come under one government."

Non-political observers were of the same opinion. On a visit to Canada in 1880, the poet Walt Whitman recorded that the country was "growing up, forming a hardy, democratic, intelligent ... good-natured race." Sooner or later, Canada would form "two or three grand states, equal and independent with the rest of the American union." But it wasn't until 1893, and the founding of the National Continental Union League, that a formal public lobby for political union emerged. The League's base was in New York, and its members included Teddy Roosevelt, such tycoons as John Jacob Astor, Jay Gould, and Andrew Carnegie, plus a transplanted Canadian businessman named Erastus Wiman, who founded the Canadian Club of New York and who once described his native land as "an eelskin of a country." The intellectual energy of the movement was centred in Toronto, in the person of its honorary secretary, Goldwin Smith, the "Sage of the Grange."

Smith was an unlikely annexationist. Nature and circumstances seemed to have designed him to be an Imperial Federalist. An old Etonian, a former Regius Professor of History at Oxford turned leisured man of letters, he'd fetched up in Toronto in the 1870s to marry fortune in the form of a Family Compact widow who also owned the house from which he took his title. The sheer banality of colonial politics exasperated Smith. "In this country," he lamented in his most famous line, "what is there for Conservatives to conserve, or for Reformers to reform?" After toying with the nationalist ideas of the Canada Firsters, his eyes turned southward. In *Canada and the Canadian Question*, he lectured the colonials that their only salvation was union with the Great Republic. "Canadian nationalism being a lost cause, the ultimate union of Canada with the U.S. appears now to be morally certain."

Though possessed of a first-rank mind, Smith's crankiness cost him his audience. Thus, few noticed his shrewd analysis of Britain's half-hearted advancement of Canadian interests at the Alaska Boundary Tribunal of 1904. It was absurd, wrote Smith, to expect the British to risk "mortal conflict with a powerful nation of their own race" for the sake of a "belt of territory on the other side of the Atlantic which they could not point out on a map." Canada, in other words, could only rely upon herself.

All of this amounted to no more than offstage noises, not least because Washington remained totally uninterested in reciprocity. Laurier, by now, was also little interested. Just as he came to power in 1896, the economy turned around. Not until 1909 and the arrival in the White House of William Howard Taft, a kind of part-time Canadian, would the free-trade dream be rekindled.

"Most likely no U.S. President loved Canadian soil so much as William Howard Taft," writes Lawrence Martin in *The Presidents and the Prime Ministers*. For thirty-eight years, until he died in 1930, this politician from Ohio spent his summers at Murray Bay on the St. Lawrence. The villagers loved him, called him *le petit juge*, traded tall stories with him. On the day of his death, they lit candles for him.

During these years, Taft came also to love the *idea* of Canada. The phrase "special relationship" can be traced back to him. "These two countries, touching each other for more than three thousand miles, have common interests in trade, require special interests in legislation and administration which are not involved in the relations of the United States with nations beyond the seas," he said in 1909, after a meeting with Governor General Earl Grey and Finance Minister W.S. Fielding in Albany, New York.

During that Albany meeting, some time was spent discussing the delicate matter of possible new tariff arrangements between the two countries. A Canada-U.S. trade pact, Taft recorded afterwards in his diary, could be "the most important measure of my administration." The unimaginable was happening: after a half-century of looking only at itself, the U.S. was once more looking northward and benignly accepting Canada as a co-occupant of the continent, almost entirely because of Taft's largeness of spirit. Canadians, for their part, were equally receptive. The Alaska Boundary dispute had been forgotten surprisingly quickly. An International Joint Commission was established to regulate international waters. The "brotherly" spirit of which Laurier had spoken twenty years earlier was being realized. U.S. branch plants – Singer Sewing Machines, General Electric, Westinghouse, Coca-Cola, Pratt and Whitney – were springing up all over the country. During the first decade of the new century, half a million Americans poured into the new western provinces to stake their claims in "the last, best west."

Discussions began in Washington in the fall of 1910. By January, these had burgeoned into formal negotiations, headed on the Canadian side by Fielding. To Laurier, receiving coded telegrams almost daily, the news was hard to credit. Taft had out-argued his protectionist fellow Republicans. He had gone even further and got the Republicans to agree to an offer of almost unbelievable generosity: cross-border trade in "natural" products would be virtually free; most U.S. tariffs on manufactured goods would be reduced. But most Canadian manufacturing tariffs would remain (including, as had always irritated Washington, certain ones favourable to Britain). On January 21, 1911, Fielding cabled, "Negotiations concluded today." He returned immediately to Ottawa and on January 26 told an astonished Commons what he and Laurier had accomplished.

The Reciprocity Agreement of 1911 was unquestionably the best continental economic deal ever offered to Canada. Fielding's speech was received by the opposition Conservatives in gloomy silence. Their leader, Robert Borden, could think of almost nothing to say and described the mood of his caucus as one of "deep dejection." If implemented, the deal would have transformed Canadian economic history. It offered the prospect of displacing branch plants, inherently inefficient because designed only to serve the domestic market, by Canadian-owned, internationally competitive plants. Whether this would have happened is hypothetical. But that this could have happened is demonstrated by the example of Sweden.

Through the nineteenth century, Sweden's circumstances were remarkably similar to those of Canada. It, too, was a peripheral resource nation, suffering a severe loss of population and completely overshadowed by Germany. Like Canada, Sweden opted for high protective tariffs. Consciously, though, Sweden looked outward. As Glen Williams has written in *Not for Export*, it "borrowed foreign manufacturing technologies and techniques; copied, assimilated and adapted them; and rapidly came up with a number of innovations and inventions that were competitive on world markets – dairy separators, ball bearings, diesel engines, primus stoves . . . ." By 1917, Sweden was exporting four times as much as it imported and had developed a design and engineering foundation that today is the basis for Volvos, Saabs, SKF bearings, Bofers guns, Ikea furniture. Sweden, in short, had an industrial strategy.

Equally, of course, the 1911 agreement could have transformed Canadian political history. Taft was uneasily aware of this, without in the least wanting it to happen. "The amount of Canadian products we would take would produce a current of business between western Canada and the United States that would make Canada only an adjunct to the United States," he wrote privately to his predecessor, Teddy Roosevelt. He added, with scrupulous honesty, "I see this as an argument made against reciprocity in Canada, and I think it is a good one."

Whether reciprocity would have turned Canada into an economically mature nation or ended its political existence is one of the great historical unknowns. The trouble was that by the winter of 1910-11 Laurier himself had become an aging lion. He possessed all his grace and wit and his natural quality of command. But he had now to harbour his energies. When colleagues urged him to call an election immediately, he hesitated, as if trying to postpone the arduous grind of campaigning. He made excuses: he had to attend the coronation of George V in April; it might be wise to wait to see whether the measure passed Congress; it would be wrong not to allow a full debate in Parliament.

Only once did Laurier unleash his full oratorical energies. He remained silent during the Commons debate until March 3, 1911. His speech then was perhaps the most eloquent statement about Canadian-American relations that has ever been delivered. "There may be a spectacle, perhaps nobler yet than the spectacle of a united continent, a spectacle which would astound the world by its novelty and grandeur. The spectacle of two peoples living side by side along a frontier nearly 4,000 miles long with not a cannon, not a gun, facing across it from either side, but living in harmony, in mutual confidence, and with no other rivalry than a generous emulation in commerce and the arts of peace."

While Laurier procrastinated, opposition gathered. "Bust the damn thing," pronounced William Van Horne of the CPR. The Canadian Manufacturers' Association, many of whose members represented multinationals, began churning out pamphlets and, in an irony no one noticed, coined the slogan, "No Truck or Trade with the Yankees," for the benefit of its Yankee members. (The *Grain Growers' Guide* declared smartly that another CMA slogan, "Canada for Canadians," meant "Canada for 2,500 Canadians.") T.A. Russell, general manager of the Canadian Cycle and Motor Company, inveighed against "the folly of the graingrowers' contention that they suffer unduly from the tariff"; the *Financial Post* praised the branch plants and declared, "The existence of our moderate tariff against U.S. manufacturers has been instrumental in many cases in bringing us these industries." By the summer, in a phrase not then part of the political vocabulary, Laurier had lost momentum.

Though bogged down in the Commons, the draft agreement raced through Congress. The House of Representatives approved it by 268 to 89; the Senate by 53 to 7. But Congress is not controllable by a president, perhaps not even by God. "I am for it," declared Missouri Representative Champ Clark, soon to become Speaker, and proceeded to give his reasons: "I hope to see the day when the American flag will float over every square foot of the British North American possessions clear to the North Pole.... I do not have any doubt whatever that the day is not far distant when Great Britain will see all her North American possessions become a part of this Republic. That is the way things are tending now." Hastily, Taft issued a statement. "No thought of political annexation or union was in the minds of negotiators on either side. Canada is now, and will remain, a political unit." Later, in a public speech, he declared, "Talk of annexation is bosh."

By the time Laurier called the election, on July 29, the damage was done. A later phrase of Taft's, that Canada was at "the parting of the ways," helped to revive fears that Canada had to choose between its mother country and the New World. It all came down in the end, not to reciprocity, yes or no, nor to whether the gain of larger markets was worth the loss of branch plants, for such things never stir the soul, but to the Flag against the Plume – the Union Jack against Laurier's call, invoking Henry of Navarre, to "follow my white plume." The ghosts of the Loyalists, the ghost of Macdonald, against the magic of Laurier. Canadians loved him; on election night, September 21, the tears that Laurier shed in private, in a Quebec City hotel suite, with his wife Zoe beside him now, were by no means the only ones shed when Canadians realized what they had done.*

But history – the Old Flag, the Old Policy – had been too strong. "It is her own soul that Canada risks today," Rudyard Kipling, poet of Empire, telegraphed from England on the eve of the election. Behind these sentiments was the inarticulate conviction that Canada, even if smaller and weaker, was the equal of the mighty U.S., or might become so. Perhaps the most eloquent expression of the way so many Canadians felt, all the more because it was so innocent, came from the Ojibway poet, Pauline Johnson:

> The Yankee to the south of us
> Must south of us remain
> For not a man dare lift a hand
> Against the men who brag
> That they were born in Canada,
> Beneath the British flag.

So it was over. Laurier went into opposition, there to remain until his death in 1919. The issue of reciprocity recurred many times thereafter, in different forms and guises, without any politician again daring to use the word, or its modern equivalent, "free trade." But the era of the giants was over.

---

* Canadian election results never yield to easy, let alone logical, analysis. Laurier lost heavily in his own Quebec where the nationalists had formed an "unholy alliance" with the Orange Tories to oppose his Navy Bill. Another factor was the defection of Laurier's chief western lieutenant, Clifford Sifton, probably the result of some obscure personal rancour, because Sifton had been a strong free trader.

Chapter Three
No Fences Makes Good Neighbours

"William Lyon Mackenzie King
He never tells us a goddamn thing."

White House press corps ditty

Having made up their minds never to truck or trade with the Yankees, Canadians thereafter trucked and traded with them contentedly for half a century. From 1911 until 1957, the start-line of the development of contemporary Canadian nationalism, Canada and the U.S. lived side by side in greater intimacy and in greater trust than any two nations in the world have probably ever done before or since. To describe the phenomenon, Franklin Roosevelt enunciated his "good neighbour policy."* To enlarge upon it, Winston Churchill coined the sonorous phrase, now a cliché, about the "undefended border."**

That era of amiability is long gone, but it is not forgotten. When Prime Minister Mulroney talks about "refurbishing the relationship" he is expressing at least implicitly an expectation that those times of confident cordiality can be brought back again. Mulroney's particular perspectives have been shaped by personal experience of those days when the border wasn't defended because there was no need to defend it. At a press conference on December 14, 1984,

---

* On Armistice Day 1935, Roosevelt declared: "Between Canada and the United States exists a neighbourliness, a genuine friendship, which over a century has dispelled every parting rift." In 1964, President Lyndon Johnson used almost the same language: "Canada is such a close neighbour and such a good neighbour.... Our problems are kind of like problems in a home town."

** Speaking to the Canada Club in London on April 20, 1939, Churchill said: "That long frontier from the Atlantic to the Pacific Ocean, guarded only by neighbourly respect, is an example to every country and a pattern for the future of the world."

41

Mulroney was asked about criticism by economic nationalists of his policy of welcoming foreign investment. In reply, he took reporters on a trip down his own memory lane: "I come from a town where the paper mill was built by the *Chicago Tribune*, the grain elevator was built by Cargill, and the aluminum plant was built by British Aluminum. Had it not been for that investment, my father, and I and all my friends on the North Shore would not have had the opportunities that we have had."

Mackenzie King would have said the same thing, or, as an even more cautious politician than Mulroney, would probably have only said it to himself in his diary. He forged a personal friendship with President Franklin Roosevelt, equalled in its intimacy only by that between Mulroney and President Reagan. He, too, was accused of selling out Canada, or, as was the currency of political abuse in those days, of selling out King and Commonwealth.

Given all that's happened since, it's difficult to recreate the temper of those times. But the attitudes seemed then natural, and inevitable. Canada needed the United States: as a raw agricultural colony undergoing industrialization, it needed technology, capital, and managerial know-how. The U.S. possessed all these elements of industrial alchemy; Britain, after the First World War, no longer did. All these assets crossed the border seemingly cost-free in political terms. The U.S. wasn't a threat. In between the wars it was isolationist; during the Second World War, Canada and the U.S. were the closest of allies; after it, they both thought pretty much the same way about the Cold War and equally about internationalism, performing as diplomatic partners during that uniquely creative period of the forties when so many of the institutions that still govern international relations – the UN, the IMF, GATT, the World Bank, even the Montreal-based International Civil Aviation Organization – were created.

There were some premonitory rumblings of Canadian nationalism. In the 1930s Graham Spry cajoled a Conservative government into creating the CBC with the war cry, "It's the States or the state." A few scholars, Harold Innis, Donald Creighton, and a youthful George Grant, began worrying in the 1940s that Canada, without anyone noticing let alone caring, was slipping irrecoverably into the American commercial and cultural orbits. By the early fifties Canadian diplomats were concerned that the "North Atlantic triangle" had become unbalanced because Britain's reach had become so short.

These fledgling nationalists had no constituency. The continentalists not only had the power, they had the proof that their policies worked. Canada did achieve industrialization, sort of, and took off on a post-war boom the like of which had never been seen before, nor will be seen again. And while all this was happening, Canadians remained Canadians. This is the part of the memory of those times that still influences our own times.

During this half century, Americans discovered Canada. More than a million came north during the first two decades of the twentieth century. To most of these immigrants, Canada was a northern treasure house of unbroken, cultivatable land. To an increasing number of businessmen it was a treasure house of hydro power, lumber and pulp and newsprint, minerals and metals. Canada provided as well a hard-working, undemanding work force, which was almost as valuable.

Other Americans came to places like Baie Comeau and Murray Bay and Tadoussac to hunt, to fish, to camp, to while away the summers, and they did all this in the company of other Americans exactly like themselves. The literary critic Edmund Wilson has remembered growing up thinking of Canada as a "gigantic wildlife reserve situated conveniently next door." Those who didn't come learned about Canada from the more than 200 one-reelers and B-movies churned out by Hollywood, *Darcy of the Northwest Mounted*, *Girl of the North Woods*, and above all, of course, *Rose Marie*, learning that Canada was a wide, cold land peopled by clean-jawed Mounties who always got their man and by virtuous girls who always got their Mountie.

Canadians similarly discovered the United States. By the early twenties, American investment topped British investment. Such American magazines as *Ladies' Home Journal*, *Saturday Evening Post*, and *McCall's* all sold well over 100,000 copies against 80,000 for *Maclean's*. American music became the music of Canadians, through KDKA Pittsburgh, KOA Denver, WLW Cincinnati; a 1932 poll revealed that 98 per cent of Canadians listened to U.S. radio stations. The new American culture of the silver screen became Canadian culture, and so did its heroes, Charlie Chaplin, Douglas Fairbanks, Pola Negri, and Mary Pickford (Canada's own, of course). Canadian businessmen started going to "international" conventions of Rotarians, Elks, Shriners.

Above all, Canadians and Americans discovered that they liked each other. The critical event was the First World War. "Over there," the soldiers of the two armies realized they could relate much more easily to each other – big and a bit bovine but open, friendly, and egalitarian – than to the class-ridden British troops. Afterwards, Canadians found themselves when in Europe defending and "explaining" Americans and Americans found that there was at least one country where nobody shouted "Yankee go home."

Canadians discovered as well that they thought as Americans thought about what mattered most in life – business. "The business of America is business, and the sooner Canada lives by that rule the better off we'll be," said C.D. Howe, economic czar and therefore "Minister of Everything" from 1935 to 1957. By acting on the premise that what was good, American-style, for business was also good for Canada, Howe made Canadians, by the 1950s, the second richest people in the world but for the Americans.

Differences persisted, the easiest to spot being Canada's frayed Britishness, with a mute, invisible lump of Frenchness inside it. As economically laggard people always do, Canadians convinced themselves they were culturally superior to the Americans, more sophisticated because closer to Europe. Canadians likewise persuaded themselves they were purer: a poll in the 1930s found that a majority of Canadian housewives believed that Hollywood movies were immoral.

No self-delusion was needed to persuade Canadians that they were less violent: there were no lynch mobs here, no St. Valentine's Day massacre. The political culture similarly was different: the witch hunts of the McCarthy period of the late forties and early fifties did touch off a northern echo, but it was, comparatively, a diminutive one. Although capitalistic conservatism remained Canada's prevailing creed to the end of the fifties, the beginnings of the welfare state here date from the mid-forties.

The first real harbinger of what would happen was provided by, of all things, the 1951 report of the Massey Commission on the Arts, Letters and Sciences. In keeping with the character of its chairman, Vincent Massey, soon to become the first native-born Governor General, the Commission's report was high-minded, orotund, earnest. Yet it went beyond simply recommending state support for native culture to suggest delicately that Canadian culture was threatened by American culture: "A vast and disproportionate amount of material from a single alien source may stifle rather than stimulate our own creative effort." The historian Frank Underhill, among others, castigated the Commission for calling Americans "aliens." Giving force to their criticism was the prevailing detestation of nationalism forged during World War Two; some of the sharpest expressions of this could be found in the pages of an obscure magazine, *Cité libre*, whose contributors included a dilettantish Montreal intellectual, Pierre Elliott Trudeau.

Except for these occasional misunderstandings, Canadians and Americans liked each other quite uncritically, trusted each other, and became more and more alike to each other. The first Canadian to really understand what was happening, to accommodate himself to it and to extract personal advantage from it, was Mackenzie King. His opponents called him a sell-out. Yet inside the chubby body of this most paradoxical of all Canadian leaders beat, intermittently, the romantic heart of an Anglophile Victorian.

Around the turn of the century, the United States became the world's greatest industrial power. The implications of American industrial supremacy to the evolution of Western civilization were as far-reaching as those caused in the seventeenth century by the shift in Europe's centre of economic gravity from Venice and Genoa and the Mediterranean to the Atlantic littoral states of Holland, France, and Britain, and potentially so again today by the shift of the world's economic centre from the Atlantic to the Pacific. Among the most minor of the implications was that Canada, inevitably, would soon exchange dependency on Britain for dependency on the U.S.

No Canadian aspiring to public life could say this then. Instead, King acted from his earliest days as if he accepted the new facts of life. After graduating from the University of Toronto in 1895, he chose to go on to the University of Chicago, and later to Harvard, rather than cross the Atlantic to collect his credentials and his career contacts.

At Chicago, King studied sociology and political economy under teachers such as Thorstein Veblen, author of *Theory of the Leisure Class*. He lived for a time at Hull House, a community development project and discussion centre, run by Jane Addams, a well-to-do lady with a lively social conscience. Amid the sweatshops and stockyards of the "hog butcher to the world," he began the research into industrial relations that he later gave wordy expression to in *Industry and Humanity*. He also fell deeply in love with an American nurse. His mother forbade this great might-have-been of his life because she was only a nurse and union with her would retard his career.

Using his talent for deferential acquaintanceship, if scarcely for friendship, King made himself the best-connected Canadian in the United States, and the one best informed about it. Among his Harvard contacts were Charles Eliot Norton, the most distinguished American scholar of the day, and Peter and Robert Gerry, sons of a millionaire who gave the word "gerrymandering" to the political vocabulary. In 1908, by which time King was a senior civil servant, President Teddy Roosevelt invited him to Washington for lunch, at the suggestion of a mutual Harvard friend, and appointed King as a kind of a personal envoy to the British government to convince it to get its ally Japan to limit the number of Japanese immigrating to the U.S. King's mission was successful.

In Ottawa, King advanced quickly, first as deputy minister of labour, and, in 1908, as Minister of Labour in Laurier's government, initiating a three-quarter-century Liberal-bureaucratic alliance. Reciprocity, about which King had political although not economic doubts, cost Laurier his government and King his own seat in 1911. Early in 1914, he accepted an offer to head a new industrial relations section of the Rockefeller Foundation. There he became the life-long friend of John D. Rockefeller, Jr., the son of the richest man in the world. In his will, Rockefeller left King $100,000. Himself archly conservative, Rockefeller came almost to worship King after he settled a murderous fifteen-month strike in a Rockefeller-owned Colorado coal mine by the device of a company union that became a model for corporate America until such sweetheart deals were banned during the New Deal.

Just before the end of the war, Rockefeller offered King a senior foundation post at a princely salary of $40,000. King declined and returned to Ottawa. Had he remained in the U.S. he would probably have become an early equivalent to later transplanted Canadians, National Security Council adviser Zbigniew Brzezinski, say, or perhaps – he was offered a full professorship at Harvard – an unwitty, unoriginal John Kenneth Galbraith. But only in Canada could King get right to the top. In 1919, following the death of Laurier, the Liberal Party was looking for a new leader. King won the convention.

Two years later, he had won the prime ministership. He never let it go, except temporarily on loan.

In *The Presidents and the Prime Ministers*, Lawrence Martin writes that Franklin Roosevelt "took the continent's two rival parts and did more than anyone to make them partners." King equally deserves the credit.

Of all Canadian leaders, King is the hardest to like – sanctimonious, self-centred, self-deceiving, with only his aching sexual loneliness providing a sympathetic point of entry into his character. Some contemporary observers, such as former Conservative leader Robert Stanfield, praise King highly as a manager of a fractious country. To other observers he was a succubus upon the Canadian body politic. In the famous lines of the late Frank Scott, "He blunted us./We had no shape/Because he never took sides,/And no sides/Because he never allowed them to take shape." Certainly, King understood unerringly the dirty little secret of Canadian politics: the leader that leads the least governs the longest.

Most of King's policies, particularly the imaginative ones like the initiation of the welfare state, can be put down as opportunistic. Welfare state initiatives, for example, permitted his party to regain the political lead over the CCF. But his most consistent policy cannot be so easily explained away. From the beginning, he sought consciously to develop a partnership with the United States. As soon as the right moment arrived, in 1935, he seized it and developed a neighbourly relationship that was without equal in the world. Before describing what King did it is necessary to describe some of the social and political context in which he did it, the most important element of this being that Canada, for a full decade after 1935, remained distinctively and defiantly *British*.

As a nation, Canada underwent a consciously protracted adolescence. Full self-government, in foreign as well as domestic affairs, was delayed until 1931 and the Statute of Westminster. Until 1947, Canadian passports carried the description "British subject" rather than "Canadian citizen." The flag took us until 1965; the constitution until 1982.

In all the "white" ex-colonies, the pace of progress toward nationhood was equally glacial. The British had a mysterious ability (so also the French) to psych out their overseas offspring. To the end of the 1950s, beside the blackboard in every classroom in English

47

Canada hung an oilskin map of the world splotched with red and pink. (The equivalent scholastic icon in Quebec was a crucifix.) Canadians knew they were members of the greatest empire since that of the Romans. To give this up to become Canadians made as much sense as it would have for civilized Gauls to give up Roman citizenship voluntarily.

The British Empire died in the mud in Flanders. Out of that slaughter was born not Canadian nationalism but Canadian patriotism, a pride in particularity. One impulse was bewildered disgust that Europe, the centre of civilization, could have produced such brutality and such stupidity. "It's Sunday morning in Flanders, but we must work today/Although our work be slaughter," Hume Wrong, a young Canadian officer and later a brilliant diplomat, wrote in 1916. The other was a dawning sense of possibility. "We are no longer humble colonials," said the painter A.Y. Jackson in 1919. "We've made armies. We can also make artists, historians, poets."

Begun so promisingly, this Canadian consciousness never flowered. Its end was limited by the nature of its beginning. The Union Jack and the Red Ensign had been the banners beneath which Canadians had marched in the two wars. So they clung to them and to the history they embodied. Canadians, in other words, looked back to Britain as it had been before it began its long slide into genteel poverty and imperial impotence. Through to the end of the 1950s, extraordinarily little of the incredible American dynamism penetrated north of the border; such Canadian cities as Toronto, Halifax, Ottawa, Winnipeg, Vancouver (Montreal being the only exception) remained Victorian relics in their architecture and in their mores and morals. In 1957, Canadians with great daring elected John Diefenbaker, our last nineteenth-century prime minister; three years later, the Americans elected John F. Kennedy.

This persistent Britishness divided the nation. English Canadians either were passively indifferent about or were actively hostile to the persistent Frenchness of French Canada. A society that denies half of its collective character cannot become a nation.

Some scholars did try, heroically, to impose logic on the illogicality of Canada and so to create a foundation for a distinctive Canadian identity. The economic historian, Harold Innis, wrote that Canada had been created, "not in spite of geography but because of it." East-west trade was natural. In his seminal The Fur Trade in Canada, published in 1930, Innis made of the St. Lawrence River Canada's equivalent of the Nile. Later he called for "persistent action at strategic points against American imperialism in all its attractive disguises."

The bard of this "Laurentian" school was Donald Creighton, arguably Canada's greateset historian and certainly its most poetic one. In *The Commercial Empire of the St. Lawrence*, he described that half-continent spanning river as "not only a great artery, it was the central truth of a religion ... a force in history, not merely because of its associations but because of its shining, ever-receding possibilities."

But Creighton's gaze was mournful as well as proud. There was, he wrote, "some primitive defect, some fundamental weakness, in the society of the St. Lawrence, in the resources which it could bring to bear on its problems.... All the deeds and episodes took on in retrospect the appearances of episodes which had been intended merely to prepare the denouement of a drama upon the last page of which there would inevitably be written the word defeat." It wasn't just that Creighton could never come to terms with French Canada; it was that in his heart he doubted whether Canada was real.

The audiences for scholars like Innis and Creighton were one-tenth those of a second-rate Chamber of Commerce luncheon speaker. Mostly, the character of this dumpy little country mirrored the character of its dumpy little leader. King shaped Canada into his own image by shaping it without any sides. He detested risks, so he permitted his countrymen none. Until the Second World War gave King and Canada no choice, he kept the world at bay by retreating into isolationism, making of Canada "a hermit kingdom" in the phrase of historian C.P. Stacey, a "fire-proof house" in King's phrase. That King, after meeting the Führer, judged that Adolf Hitler would "rank some day with Joan of Arc" is today a source of wry amusement; that his government's policy toward Jews fleeing from Hitler was "None is one too many" remains an enduring national shame.

But he kept on winning elections – twenty-two years' worth of them. All of his successors since have been tantalized by his techniques. In a brilliant insight, William Christian and Colin Campbell comment in *Political Parties and Ideologies in Canada* that King "imposed a style of politics on Canada which took such deep root that people mistook a way of practising politics for politics itself." This is King's longest-lasting legacy, and the heaviest.

49

King's substitute for internationalism was continentalism. He was Canada's first fully North American prime minister, and the only one until Mulroney.

In 1935, King convinced Canadians to choose him rather than chaos. With astonishing speed he justified their choice in one vital respect. One day after the election, he called on the American minister in Ottawa, Norman Armour, asking to be invited to meet the President. Two weeks later, King was in Washington. By the end of the meeting, three days later, he had secured the first Canada-U.S. trade agreement since the U.S., in 1866, had torn up the Reciprocity Treaty. In his diary King called it "The greatest political accomplishment of my life," neglecting to remind himself that all but the last details of the pact had been negotiated by his Conservative predecessor, R.B. Bennett.

But it was King who had got it, a trade pact that struck down many of the high duties levied by the Smoot-Hawley tariff of 1930; the new pact began the critical process of opening up the vast U.S. market to Canadian producers. He'd got it, as Bennett had failed to do, because he and Roosevelt got on so well together.*

It helped that both were Harvard men. It helped also, as Martin recounts, that Roosevelt was canny enough to produce a copy of *Industry and Humanity* and ask King to autograph it. It helped, on the other side, that Roosevelt knew Canada, or at least knew Campobello Island. What mattered mostly was that Roosevelt possessed a largeness and openness of spirit and that King, when an opening was created for him, knew enough about Americans and American politics to be able to seize it.

They became mutual admirers and political confidants, Roosevelt to King being always "Mr. President" and he to Roosevelt being always "Mackenzie."** The disparities in power and King's sycophantic nature made him distinctly the junior partner, but Roosevelt was always solicitous of his interests: before the signing of the 1940

---

* U.S. self-interest provided a stiffening to presidential cordiality. Armour had advised Roosevelt in a memorandum that high U.S. tariffs were forcing Canada to create its own industries, "to such an extent that Canada, equipped with low-priced French-Canadian and other labour, may become before long our most intensive competitor abroad."

** Winston Churchill also called King "Mackenzie," the oddity being that he and Roosevelt were the only two who did; to most of his friends, King was "Willie" and to a few old college classmates, "Rex."

Ogdensburg Defence Agreement, Roosevelt changed the document's date to coincide, at King's request, with the date of his birthday. In July, 1936, Roosevelt travelled to Canada to become the first president to meet a prime minister or his home ground – at Quebec City, the site of a meeting between two other close friends almost exactly a half-century later.

Because of the times, defence rather than trade most often knitted the two countries together. In 1938, in a speech at Queen's University, Roosevelt remarked, "I give to you my assurance that the people of the United States will not stand idly by if the domination of Canadian soil is threatened by another empire." Later, Roosevelt expressed astonishment – "What I said was so obvious" – at the importance attached to his comment. Indeed, the Joint Defence Board created by the 1940 Ogdensberg Agreement and the defence production sharing made possible by the 1941 Hyde Park Declaration merely confirmed the obvious – only the U.S. could defend Canada.

The pressures of the war drew Canada and the U.S. even closer, just as Roosevelt and King became closer personally during the period from the fall of France in 1940 to the U.S. entry into the war in 1941. At the 1943 Quebec City Conference of Roosevelt and Churchill and their generals and admirals, King got his photograph taken with them for publicity purposes, although he was excluded from the actual strategy sessions.

Roosevelt died on April 12, 1945. King's reaction was bloodless: "I seemed too exhausted and fatigued to feel any strong emotion. It all seemed like part of the day's heavy work." Lester Pearson, then ambassador in Washington, had to write the tribute on behalf of Canada.

King's relations with Harry Truman were cordial but were never close. He was getting too old to make new acquaintanceships. And he was beginning to wonder – the blame being someone else's, of course – whether Canada was not too close to the United States.

Canada emerged from the war as the second richest of nations and with a quite considerable industrial base. Yet this absolute gain made no relative difference. The U.S. had grown in the meantime from major power to a superpower in every respect, militarily, economically, financially, technologically, culturally, diplomatically. Canada was confronted by a cross-border disparity for which there was no historical precedent and one that it now had to cope with on its own.

King had become uneasy about this as early as 1943. After approving the construction of the Alaska Highway across British Columbia by the U.S. Corps of Engineers he expressed his concern about "efforts that would be made by the Americans to control developments in our country after the war and to bring Canada out of the orbit of the British Commonwealth." In a diary entry later that same year, he wrote, "With the U.S. so powerful and her investments becoming greater in Canada, we will have a great difficulty to hold our own." The Korean War broke out in mid-1950, during the last weeks of King's life. In one of his last diary entries he commented, "U.S. foreign policy at bottom is to bring Canada into as many situations affecting themselves as possible with a view to leading ultimately to the annexation of our two countries."

This analysis was sound. A report for President Truman by CBS chairman William Paley had painted a sombre – if quite inaccurate – picture of international resource shortages. Union with Canada would bring its resources permanently into the U.S. fold. Such a calculation was undoubtedly behind the remarkably generous bilateral free trade pact negotiated by senior U.S. officials through the winter of 1947-48. This pact was also, in contradiction to all his diary musings, King's last continentalist hurrah. More in keeping with King's character, he did the deal, and then undid it, in complete secrecy.

History is always rewritten first by those who make it. Lester Pearson makes only the briefest of mentions of the 1947-48 free trade pact in his own memoirs, thus avoiding the need to mention that, as deputy minister for external affairs, he strongly supported it. King, who always rewrote his own history, recorded in his diary in March, 1948, "I confess I get alarmed beyond measure at the casual way in which a few officials take it into their hands to try to settle great national policies, force the government's hands, etc." King had conveniently forgotten that he had given his approval to the negotiations the previous October. (The officials undoubtedly did hurry things along; they were also careful to protect their political rear by recommending that Canada offer free trade to Britain as a follow-up.)

In the end, nothing happened. King vetoed the draft pact. In hindsight, what is interesting is how close and how easily free trade came to happening. In the fall of 1947, two senior finance department officials, John Deutsch and Hector McKinnon, travelled to Washington with authority to negotiate "the complete elimination of tariffs." After the project failed, each side credited the other with having proposed it.*

The talks were begun in complete secrecy. Not only the public and Parliament but also most of the cabinet (except for such senior members as Finance Minister Douglas Abbott, External Affairs Minister Louis St. Laurent, and Howe) were kept in the dark. The talks sped along. The final deal was suggested by a middle-rank U.S. official, Paul Nitze, later head of arms control negotiations. It proposed full free trade but no customs union, which would be politically difficult for both sides. By early March, 1948, an agreement had been reached that included generous "transition arrangements" for Canada.**

When it was brought before him for an approval that the ministers and civil servants involved regarded almost as a formality, King said no. (Jack Pickersgill, then in King's office, seems to have been the one doubter.) As one explanation, there's the inevitable King story: he was re-reading the Book of Esther at the time and his eye fell on the line, "Every man should bear rule in his own house." In his diaries, King is alternately self-pitying – "The Tory party would make it out that from the beginning my whole vision had been to further annexation. I was really at heart anti-British. Everything opposite of the truth." – and paranoid – "The press would not grasp the details." Undoubtedly, at his age he dreaded the intensity of the public debate that would be unleashed*** and the near certainty he would have to cancel his announced intention to resign and stay on to lead the party through one more election.

The best analysis, surely, is Stacey's. In *Mackenzie King and the Atlantic Triangle* he describes King as "listening to ancestral voices,

---

* See J.L. Granatstein and Robert Cuff, *American Dollars-Canadian Prosperity: Canadian-American Economic Relations, 1945-50.*

** For the text of the draft treaty, see Appendix A.

***Since history always repeats, a 1948 equivalent to Speaker Champ Clark's destructive contribution to the 1911 Reciprocity Election was provided by *Time* magazine, which in a story in February, 1948, commented helpfully: "No matter how much the statesmen of each country might play it down for political expediency, the fact was inescapable: In effect, Canada has become an economic 49th state."

not from the spirit but from his inheritance." King, as Stacey comments, was a Victorian Canadian whose "inherited values were British, who admired British ways and coveted British approval." As old men always do, King turned his thoughts back to his youth when Victoria had been Queen; to revivify that call from the past, he had attended the marriage of Princess Elizabeth and the Duke of Edinburgh in November, 1947. For one last time, Britain decisively influenced Canadian politics.

Had King said yes, no guarantee existed that Congress would also have agreed. Probably yes: this was the era of the Marshall Plan. John Deutsch, who went on to become chairman of the Economic Council and principal of Queen's, remained convinced Canada had missed its great opportunity to decide between, as he described it in a memo at the time, "A relatively free enterprise world with the highest standard of living or a government-controlled world with a lower standard of living." However, Deutsch might have been less sanguine about the consequences of bilateral free trade had he known of a State Department memorandum of that time, subsequently made public, which declared "The proposal may offer a unique opportunity for bringing the two countries together."

Without knowing it, Canadians had been saved from a political fate worse than death. As reward for such virtue, Canadians went on to enjoy through the rest of the fifties the economic equivalent of heaven on earth.

By the end of the fifties Canada was still a place where, in Robert Fulford's phrase, "If you were good you grew out of it." Postgraduate studies still meant Cambridge, Massachusetts, or Cambridge, England, or Paris. The arts meant these places, and also New York, London, Los Angeles. For Torontonians, a fun weekend meant Buffalo.

Yet, just by being citizens of the country, Canadians had the world's envy: immigrants poured in; massive projects like the Kitimat aluminum smelter almost mocked war-devastated Europe. Canadians also had the world's respect. Pearson's 1957 Nobel Peace Prize was like an award to an entire nation for the services it had done to others. The Americans kept pouring in money. In November, 1947, Imperial Oil struck a gusher at Leduc in Alberta. There was nothing that God and nature, and the Americans, wouldn't do for Canada.

In the early summer of 1957, a strange messianic figure, eyes blazing, jowls wagging, stalked the land unfurling hyperbolic rhetoric: "This party has a sacred trust. It has an appointment today with destiny." None of it made much sense. But it felt right, felt exciting and inspirational. A political leader was actually daring to try to give Canada sides and a shape. On June 12, 1957, Canadians decided to give John Diefenbaker a chance. He failed, but out of his failure was born modern Canadian nationalism.

Part Two
The Moose That Roared

As a nation, Canada was born again in 1957. The year lies across our history like a fault-line: Diefenbaker won his first election; Pearson won his Nobel Peace Prize; Walter Gordon brought down his report on foreign ownership; and the Canada Council was established. These events, along with Quebec's Quiet Revolution, which began three years later, created the Canada of today, a society that seems to contain only a few trace elements of what Earle Birney called in the 1940s "a highschool land/deadset in adolescence."

From that year on, Canadian-American relations were redefined by a force for which there was no historical antecedent. This was the force, at first tentative and apologetic, then increasingly vocal, then rancorous, then celebratory, of Canadian nationalism.

This nationalism was always firmly rooted in pragmatism. Whenever times got tough or the price of flag-waving seemed likely to be too high, Canadians lowered their banners. This was predictable. Far more interesting was the way the minimum acceptable low-water mark of nationalist expression demanded by Canadians of their governments kept getting raised. The support for the "Canadianization" policy of the National Energy Program, once massive, was ground down by the Great Recession of 1981-82. Yet early in 1985, Decima Research warned in its confidential report to the government that "Canadians continue to support the principles of Canadianization and *limiting* foreign ownership ... an emotional commitment to economic nationalism still exists."

This persistence in the popularity of nationalism is almost as much of a puzzle as is the existence of nationalism itself in a nation that is a non-nation in any conventional construct of political science or of anthropology. Nationalism itself is an atavistic urge that arises from a homogeneous people who fear that outsiders may change them, let alone oppress them. With occasional exceptions, the feelings in Canada took the form of nationalism's milder variant – patriotism, a pride of place, a satisfaction in collective accomplishment.

This patriotism, though, came to acquire a sharp edge. By celebrating Canada, Canadians were simultaneously rejecting the United States. Americans personally were never rejected, nor was the best in the U.S., which Canadians copied and envied. What was rejected increasingly over the years was the U.S. as it was seen to have become: violent, polarized, militaristic. In one of Trudeau's first speeches as Prime Minister, he cited as Canada's most considerable threat neither Quebec separatism nor unemployment but that "violence may come to our cities from across the border." At the end of his term, although he himself was hugely unpopular, his peace initiative was enthusiastically applauded. If by the mid-1980s Canadians didn't want their border barricaded, neither did they want it left untended.

The various strands of nationalism that animated Canadian life from 1957 are separated out into economic nationalism (Chapters Four, Five, Six), foreign policy nationalism (Chapters Seven, Eight), and cultural nationalism (Chapter Nine). These are followed by a summation of nationalism's accomplishments and failures.

One last note of introduction scarcely needs to be said. Many Canadians during these years saw nothing wrong with the U.S.; most Canadians, indeed, were entranced by most aspects of American life. Nationalists were never more than a minority, if an influential one, like the feminists, say. Only in one area did the creed command majority support. In the description of Abraham Rotstein, this was "territorial nationalism": "In the inner recesses of the Canadian self-image, there remains the indelible imprint of the pioneer struggle with the land," Rotstein wrote in his 1973 collection of essays, *Precarious Homestead.* "A political sense of earned jurisdiction over a vanquished space that was, at least in principle, inviolable and sacrosanct, became the nuclear element of political identity that arose in the Canadian psyche. Economic and political jurisdiction of the homestead should be untrammeled, and any trespass or political infringement would be resisted."

Here, Rotstein saw clean through the Canadian character in a way that few of his fellow nationalists did. Of all Trudeau's early policies, none was more universally popular than the enactment of *de facto* sovereignty over the Arctic waters by way of environmental regulations following the 1969 passage of the U.S. supertanker *Manhattan.* His declaration of a 200-mile fishing and economic zone in 1977 received the same overwhelming applause. The Parti Québécois, disastrously for its purpose, failed utterly to understand why English Canadians reacted so viscerally to arguments that Quebec's separation would "tear apart/divide/rupture" the country. Territorial nationalism is today the source of public anger about acid rain, of public resistance to selling water, and of unease about the traverse through the Arctic of the U.S. Coast Guard ship *Polar Sea* in the summer of 1985.

As the "nuclear element" of Canadian political consciousness, in Rotstein's phrase, territorial nationalism derives from an understanding that the land is fragile, because so northerly. In this sense, territorial nationalism is a metaphor for the condition of the Canadian nation-state itself. Unless nurtured, neither the land nor the nation-state will survive. The various expressions of nationalism described in the succeeding chapters amount to different ways of saying this.

Chapter Four
Gentle Patriotism: Economic Nationalism, 1957-1968

"It was a shock to me, it was such a surprise. We did not get this feeling of nationalism, or whatever you want to call it."

James S. Rockefeller, Chairman, Citibank, to Commons
Finance Committee, January 27, 1967

Walter Gordon made an improbable Paul Revere, not least because he could never have brought himself to shout at passersby from the back of a horse. Gordon never rode, and he never, ever, shouted. Yet in his thoroughly Canadian way, laconic, ironic, reticent, he spread the message from 1957 on, "The Yankees are coming. The Yankees are coming." Canadians paid him little heed. His years of political power, 1963 to 1968, were years of almost unrelieved mishap. With a wry smile, he slipped into history, still writing and speaking, but using always the bloodless prose of the accountant that he was.

Gordon failed because he never answered, indeed seldom if ever bothered to try to answer, the opening question of all democratic debates, "What's in it for me?" Canadians didn't need any high-stepping analysis by, say, Harry Johnson, the Canadian-born anti-nationalist economist at the University of Chicago, to know that the answer was "Nothing." Or less than nothing. Driving out multinationals as latter-day moneychangers wouldn't merely mean an immediate loss of jobs, as was obvious, but a permanent loss, because there were no Canadian managers and entrepreneurs to take the place of the imported expertise, let alone to replace the imported capital. Gordon in effect asked Canadians to suspend their disbelief in their own businessmen. This Canadians refused to do, being far more sceptical about the competence of their capitalists than Gordon was, for all his know-how as a management consultant. They had a bird in their hand; they weren't prepared to let it go for a bird supposedly waiting in the bushes.

In conventional terms, Gordon was therefore a failure, a prophet honoured by only a few political disciples, and by rather more academics than it benefits any politician to be approved by. Yet as the years passed, Gordon became a martyr – an unusual martyr, certainly, since he greatly enjoyed his life and was immensely wealthy. A symbolic martyr, nonetheless, to that Canadian political rarity, an *idea*. Gordon expounded this idea before its time had come. But its time did come eventually and was manifested by the National Energy Policy of 1980, the most ambitious attempt at economic nation-building since the Canadian Pacific Railway. The story of the NEP belongs in another chapter. The story to be told here concerns Gordon's idea and how it was played out: why Canadians didn't listen, and why, as it turned out, they'd been listening, in a way, all along.

Gordon was to the manor born. His father, a much-decorated lieutenant colonel of the First World War, co-founded the impeccably respectable and immensely successful accountancy firm, Clarkson Gordon. One of Gordon's closest political allies, Senator Keith Davey, once described him as having been "born with a silver adding machine in his mouth." At Upper Canada College and the Royal Military College, he acquired the upper-class sheen that never left him – outward reserve, a polite, distanced manner – yet there was also within him, buried deep because it was so unacceptable in his social circles, the spirit of "a romantic Scot," as a friend, Alison Ignatieff, has remarked. Although quite unable to inspire large audiences, he inspired intense personal loyalties, so that right down to the mid-1980s, Tom Axworthy, by then Trudeau's top political aide, would mention frequently, as a badge of honour, that he'd once been a junior aide to Gordon. Gordon had a first-rate mind. His real asset was integrity. The title of Denis Smith's 1973 biography best sums up his character: *Gentle Patriot*.

Gordon joined the family firm in 1927 and did well by it, and for himself. As was seemly for someone of his class, he worked on various government commissions, full-time for part of the war; as was much less seemly, he took politics seriously enough to consider a cabinet offer in the early 1950s, rejecting it when he realized that Howe would stomp on him. It's difficult to know how he came by his ideas about economic nationalism since, typically, he says nothing about this in his memoirs. At a guess, the accountant in him spotted early the inhibiting effects of foreign ownership on Canadian industrial growth, while the "romantic Scot" provided the passion, however understated.

Gordon began his public political career with a mishap. In January, 1957, he released the preliminary report of the Royal Commission on Canada's Economic Prospects, of which he was the chairman, distilling into it his gathering unease about the effects of the massive foreign ownership of Canadian industry. Among other problems dealt with was that of the underdeveloped Maritimes. After recommending various remedies, the report suggested: "generous assistance should be given to those people who might wish to move to other parts of Canada." Cartoonists had a field day depicting Gordon, sleek and stern, tearing apart honest, horny-handed Maritime families and dragging off fathers and sons to Toronto. Gordon never entirely lived down a reputation for wanting to depopulate the East Coast.

His principal recommendations received a worse reception. They were largely ignored, press coverage centring on the fact that Howe had denounced the report. Nor was it easy to extract catchy headlines from the document, written more in the style of a thesis than a tract. While foreign ownership was large and getting larger, there was "little evidence" foreign companies hadn't acted in Canada's best interests. Nevertheless, "it seems probable that this will continue to cause concern in the country." Therefore, foreign companies should act like good corporate citizens. If they didn't "this could lead to action of an extreme kind being taken in the future." All of which is worth recalling only because it was the beginning of the beginning.

Howe's distemper was understandable. For two decades now, as economic czar, he'd been doing exactly what Canadians wanted – building the country, industrializing it, creating jobs. Only a few academics, and now, all of a sudden, Gordon, had noticed that at the same time he was selling off the country. Only once had Canadians as a whole seemed to care. In 1956, Howe had rammed through Parliament a bill to set up a company to build and operate a trans-Canada gas pipeline. The main issue had been what Diefenbaker called "trampling on the rights of Parliament." A subsidiary issue, though, had been that the principal owners of the company, and the beneficiaries of government funds, were Americans, from Texas.

Howe himself was American-born, a circumstance used against him politically, although he in fact became a Canadian at the age of twenty-seven. He was an engineer, and it was this background that largely shaped his character. His biographers, Robert Bothwell and William Kilbourn, have written that he possessed, "unquestionably, certain American qualities.... There was a largeness and a generosity, a decisiveness and a simplicity in his temperament." They commented also that he was "an utter philistine" who loved the company of the rich, "accept[ing] uncritically many of their views," and was a bit of a bully.* But for the last, Howe's beliefs were shared by just about everyone else: in the 1950s, everyone knew that what was good for business was good for everyone else and that what was best for business was that it should be left alone.

Retroactively, a mark of Cain has been attached to Howe for selling out Canada. His defence, on the rare occasion he bothered to make it, was : "The joint effect of our trade development and of our domestic development has been to provide a greater degree of economic welfare and economic security for the average individual." Here, Howe was dead right. Post-war, the Canadian economy and the incomes of its citizens grew faster even than those of the Americans, who by this time were bestriding the world like economic colossi.

The real defence of Howe's policy rests on two accomplishments, neither of which he intended. The contemporary welfare state, launched with the White Paper on Employment and Income of April, 1945, could never have been implemented without the surplus revenues created by Howe's crash industrialization.** Similarly, today's richly textured, multicultural Canada might never have existed without him. More than two million immigrants poured into the country from the end of the war to 1961. So many would never have been allowed into the "hermit kingdom" had it not been expanding. Paradoxically, a good deal of what we now are we owe to Howe and to his friends, the American capitalists.

At the time, of course, this future was unknowable. If any fancy intellectual defence for foreign capital were needed, it could be found in the writings of the distinguished Queen's University economist, W.A. Mackintosh, co-author of the White Paper. Foreign investment,

---

* See Robert Bothwell and William Kilbourn, *C.D. Howe* (Toronto, 1979).

** No matter the political label of the party in power, the succeeding forty years of Canadian economic redistribution derive from the commitment made in this White Paper that "the maintenance of a high and stable level of employment" was a "major aim of government policy" and "a great national objective."

he wrote, was the "life-blood" of a resource economy and would inevitably lift it beyond the "immature" industrialization created by high tariff walls. There was only one point about which Mackintosh seemed uncertain: when exactly, and how, this industrial maturation would take place.

Economics aside, Canadians in the 1950s were unready psychologically to listen to what Gordon was trying to say. Nationalism was not merely unfashionable then but was wholly unacceptable. A few years earlier it had produced a holocaust. This was why the historian Frank Underhill, his anglophobia quite apart, was so harsh about the 1951 Massey Commission's description of American culture as "alien." This was why the Montreal intellectual, Pierre Trudeau, was so deeply influenced by the seminal book, *Nationalism*, by Eli Kedourie, and in particular by Kedourie's observation that since nationalism was racial in its origin, "in nationalist logic . . . the union of English-Canada and French-Canada within the Canadian state is a monstrosity of nature." Trudeau's readings mattered: once he became prime minister, he regarded Gordon's economic nationalism as a threat to national unity because it would provoke, in counterpoint, Quebec nationalism. Trudeau only changed his mind once Quebec nationalism had been defeated in the referendum of 1980.

Gordon's final report was published in April, 1958. Much of it was made up of statistical tables showing how, if everything continued to go well, Canadians in twenty-five years would be a lot richer and that governments in the meantime would collect a lot of surplus revenues. He made specific recommendations about foreign investment: multinationals should offer up to 25 per cent of their shares to Canadians; should appoint more Canadians to senior positions and to their boards; should try harder to find Canadian suppliers and specialist professionals. These proposals attracted no great interest, although some commentators did Gordon the service of taking him seriously enough to point out that minority Canadian ownership amounted only to tinkering while leaving unchanged the substance of foreign control.

The response that mattered was that of the government. And the government laughed. Nine months earlier, Diefenbaker had won his unexpected victory. In one memorable shaft, he called Gordon "that Toronto taxidermist." He buried Gordon's report. One month before the final report was published, Dief had won his second victory, proportionately, the greatest political landslide in Canadian history. At the start of that campaign, in Winnipeg, on February 12, 1958, Diefenbaker had described his own dream: "A new vision. A new hope. A new soul for Canada." No one knew what this meant. But from coast to coast, Canadians understood that this messiah from the Prairies was daring them to greatness.

Since Diefenbaker was so megalomaniacal, so paranoid, and almost certainly a bit mad, it's difficult to fix him in the nationalist spectrum or in any political spectrum other than as a populist, a passionate believer in civil liberties, and a genuine hater of "They," an enemy never defined but certainly encompassing bankers, financiers, corporate tycoons, liberal intellectuals, bureaucrats, and Liberals; also many Conservatives.

Yet George Grant's description of Diefenbaker's defeat in 1963 as "the last strident swan-song of Canadian nationalism" had resonance. Liberal intellectuals – looking southward in envy, for the last time, as it would turn out – were turned on by John F. Kennedy and embarrassed at having as their own leader someone so un-with it as to style himself "Dief the Chief," so much so that they lined up against him and for Lester Pearson despite Pearson's blatant opportunism in committing the Liberals to accept nuclear warheads. (For details, see Chapter Seven.)

In his first foreign speech as Prime Minister, at Dartmouth College in September, 1957, Diefenbaker sounded a warning of "the sense of disquiet in Canada over the political implications of large-scale and continuing external ownership." His actual actions were few: the National Energy Board, created in 1959, with authority, for the first time, to regulate exports of energy; the National Oil Policy of 1961, which blocked imports from going west of the Ottawa River and so created a domestic market for domestic producers. He talked for a time about diverting 15 per cent of Canada's trade to Britain, but when Britain, then considering whether to join the European Economic Community, called Diefenbaker's bluff by offering a free-trade pact, he quickly backed down. Some of his ministers were strong nationalists, most notably Alvin Hamilton, who in 1960 reserved oil and gas licences in the Arctic for Canadian-owned companies.*

---

* During the 1963 election, Hamilton unleashed some fiery anti-American rhetoric, accusing the Kennedy administration of "treating Canada like a Central American banana republic." This brought a protest from the Guatemalan ambassador in Washington.

Diefenbaker's principal accomplishment was to turn Canadians onto their country. He made this dumpy country seem exciting, as it had to be to have turned out someone like him. He made politics exciting for the first time since Laurier. He created a sense of national momentum even if, so long as he was in power, it rode off in all directions.

By March, 1963, Diefenbaker was out and Gordon was in, as Finance Minister. He came to power knowing exactly what he wanted to do, with ambitious intentions for both economic nationalism and social reform. That Gordon could do all this, few doubted: already he'd proved his mettle by taking charge of the woebegone Liberal Party of 1958 and by transforming it, with new people like Davey, new ideas, new organization and fresh money, into Canada's first real twentieth-century political machine.

Instead, Gordon blew it. The same self-assured arrogance that had led him to preach to the public without ever bothering to learn the arts of a propagandist had also led him to become a politician without ever bothering to learn any political arts except those of the backroom and of the club room. His budget of June 13, 1963, the long-awaited exercise of his magical financial skills, was a fiasco. Inside the Commons, Diefenbaker tore it apart. On the outside, the financial community frothed. Among the demolishers, none was more effective that the president of the Montreal Stock Exchange, Eric Kierans, who soon afterwards became a provincial cabinet minister, and later, under Trudeau, a federal minister. (Later still, in 1971, Kierans blossomed forth as an economic nationalist himself, a more effective one than Gordon in some respects, partly because his analysis, about the tilt of the tax system toward the multinationals, was original, and even more because he conveyed his findings with a passion Gordon could never allow himself to indulge in.)

Gordon's budget contained two nationalist measures of great daring, and thus of great risk: a 15 per cent tax on all dividends paid by corporations to non-Canadians; a steep, almost prohibitive, 30 per cent tax on the sale of Canadian companies to non-Canadians. The stock market collapsed, and with it the budget. Within five days, Gordon had to announce that the takeover tax would be withdrawn. The tax on dividends soon followed. Having survived the budget crisis only barely, Gordon was promptly knocked down by a new crisis. On July 18, U.S. Treasury Secretary Douglas Dillon announced that to staunch an outflow of dollars a special tax was being imposed on all foreign borrowings in the American money markets. Israel and Mexico would be exempted, but Canada, although by far the heaviest borrower, would not be. Once again the stock markets crashed; so also did the Canadian dollar. To earn the exemption without which Canada, as a debtor nation, could scarcely have continued to function, Gordon had to agree that Canada's reserves of foreign exchange would thereafter be managed in "close consultation" with Washington. Showing an unusual comprehension of economics, Diefenbaker observed that this arrangement entailed "a veto with the president of the United States with regard to the expansion of Canada's economy, which is something that is not in keeping with the sovereignty of this nation." Gordon could only mutely nod assent.

Gordon had not only failed to implement his own measures, he'd also had to increase Canada's financial dependency on the U.S. in order to cope with an American protectionist measure that, as the final insult, was remarkably similar to his own proposed tax on dividends paid to non-residents. (The timing of the two events was coincidental, for in fact the U.S. balance of payments problem had been building for years.) The attention of the press, in any event, soon wandered elsewhere. The aspect of the story that lingered, however, was that economic nationalism had been shown to be impractical, even counter-productive. Gordon had hurt his own cause severely. He never, while in power, got another chance to advance it. Gordon remained as Finance Minister for another two years, present but no longer potent. Pearson never really trusted him again although he did take Gordon's advice to call a snap election in November, 1965, so as to win a majority. When Pearson emerged with only another minority, Gordon offered to resign. Pearson made no effort to dissuade him. In October, 1966, by now only an ordinary MP but with legions of supporters in the party, he and Mitchell Sharp, his successor as Finance Minister, argued the nationalist versus continentalist alternatives at a Liberal policy convention. Sharp won the vote, if not the debate.*

---

* Gordon's vote was organized for him by a young Toronto MP, Donald Macdonald, later Finance Minister in Trudeau's government, later still, in 1983-85, chairman of a royal commission on the economy that recommended, among other things, Canada-U.S. free trade. Asked how Gordon had reacted to this defection of his one-time protégé, Macdonald replied, "He's so much the gentleman that all he would say was 'I just can't talk to you about it.'"

Gordon returned to the cabinet in 1967, to the nominal portfolio of President of the Privy Council. When Pearson retired in 1968 to make way for Trudeau, so did he. He met with Trudeau, in 1971, to try to convince him about the virtues of economic nationalism and came away from their meeting despairing. That same year, he helped found, and fund, the Committee for an Independent Canada, headed by academics such as Rotstein and Mel Watkins, publishers Mel Hurtig and Jack McClelland, journalists Peter Newman and Pierre Berton, and Flora MacDonald, then aspiring to become a Conservative MP. The Committee churned out a lot of pamphlets, and it once mustered 170,000 signatures on a petition. But in those years it was national unity and not economic nationalism that everyone was concerned about. Gordon was by no means powerless: he appeared often in the pages of *The Toronto Star*, its publisher Beland Honderich being a close friend. He had scores of disciples in the Liberal Party, even if only in junior posts, such as Revenue Minister Herb Gray.

By the late 1960s, Gordon had run his nationalist race. Yet by now its pace was quickening. Others were picking up the baton, and more and more often they looked to Gordon, not as a leader, but as a symbol, a symbol of what might have been, a symbolic martyr, a symbol of integrity.

Two last aspects of Gordon's career need to be recounted before he can be consigned to his niche in history. During his term in power, the nationalists weren't routed on every front. Legislation to prohibit any new "Canadian" editions of American magazines was enacted in 1963, although because of Henry Luce's influence with Kennedy and phone calls from Washington to Ottawa, *Time* and *Reader's Digest* were allowed to continue their editions. Legislation was drafted, but never passed, to establish a Canada Development Corporation, to be funded by government but to function independently, buying up some foreign companies and lifting some Canadian ones up by their bootstraps. Most important, the Bank Act was changed as a response to a 1964 takeover of the small Mercantile Bank by New York's Citibank. In hindsight, there was less to this affair than there seemed to be at the time since Mercantile was already foreign-owned, by a Dutch group, while the Canadian chartered banks were themselves only a decade away from urging that foreign banks be allowed in as a *quid pro quo* for their own expanding foreign activities. Yet for the first time since the Second World War, an economic nationalist issue captured the attention of Canadians. This was because a bank was involved, and Canadians always pay devoted attention to banks, "our fiscal father-confessors" in Peter Newman's deft phrase.

To pique the public's attention yet further, there was a Rockefeller in the middle of the affair: Citibank Chairman James S. Rockefeller. He attracted an overflow crowd when he appeared before the Commons Finance Committee in January, 1967, to explain why, despite being warned by Gordon, still Finance Minister at the time of the takeover, and by the Bank of Canada, Citibank had barrelled ahead. The criticism he had received from the politicians, the press, and the public, said Rockefeller, "was a shock to me, it was such a surprise.... We did not get this feeling of nationalism or whatever you want to call it. We consider ourselves friendly neighbours. Honestly, it did not cross our minds." As he stumbled on ingenuously, his listeners, initially disbelieving, began to understand. Rockefeller wasn't being deceitful; he was being perfectly honest. Until he'd got into the committee room, he and Citibank hadn't realized that Canadians weren't Americans.

If the course of Canadian nationalism could be plotted as a graph, the Mercantile Bank affair would mark the moment when the line, while continuing to waver, first began to trend clearly upwards.* For the first time, Canadians received the message about the consequences of massive foreign ownership, not in their heads but in their guts.

In 1967, Gordon delivered a second, and a very different, message to the collective Canadian gut. This message was about America itself. No sooner had he returned to Pearson's cabinet than Gordon severely embarrassed the Prime Minister. From his earliest days as a minister, Gordon had been appalled both by the Vietnam War and, as much, by our complicity in it: publicly, the Pearson government said nothing about this silent partnership; privately, Canadian companies had been doing very well by making materials for the war. As Gordon has recounted in his memoirs, "I felt an urge to express my own horror and revulsion about the escalation of the war. I did not agree with

---

* Gordon, at the time of Rockefeller's appearance, was out of the cabinet but due to rejoin it shortly. From offstage he negotiated a compromise with Sharp so that the new Bank Act prohibited all further takeovers but "grandfathered" that of Citibank, giving it five years to reduce its holding to a new 25 per cent maximum.

[External Affairs Minister] Paul Martin's statements on the subject which, while sometimes hard to interpret, seemed on the whole to support the policy and actions of the U.S."

One month after he was back in the cabinet, and so had regained a certain status, Gordon delivered a speech in Ottawa (Rotstein was the principal author) in which he advocated a suspension of American bombing and a declaration of American willingness to negotiate directly with the Viet Cong. He then delivered his punchline: "I hope Canadians in all political parties, including especially Mr. Pearson and Mr. Martin, will continue to do everything in their power to press the Americans to stop the bombing. If we fail to do this, we must be prepared to share the responsibility of those whose policies and actions are destroying a poor but determined people."

Pearson was outraged at this breach of cabinet solidarity and encouraged press speculation that Gordon might be fired. Then something extraordinary happened. For the first time in his life, Gordon became genuinely popular. Thousands of Canadians wrote to him, applauding him. Gordon in fact made no more speeches on the subject. His views about war, in any form, never changed. In the summer of 1983, he and retired diplomat George Ignatieff travelled to Moscow on a private mission; one of the messages given to them by Soviet officials was that Trudeau, to whom an official invitation had already been extended personally by Mikhail Gorbachev, then Agriculture Minister, should make that visit, and soon.

In his detached way, Gordon had struck a chord. From 1967 on, nationalists widened the scope of their attacks on foreign ownership. As before, they argued that foreign capital inhibited Canadian economic development, an argument that gained in credibility as the first generation of Canadians to be educated in the mass to the level of a university degree began to look around for jobs and realized that most of the corporate ladders they might join would quickly carry them out of their own country. The nationalists added now the accusation that hand in hand with foreign capital came foreign influence, the influence, moreover, of a power turned militarist and imperialist.

By the end of the 1960s, nationalism was not in any sense a popular issue, except in Quebec in a quite different version. But it had become a respectable ideology to believe in. It had acquired, if not armies of determined supporters, at least several battalions. Above all, thanks to Gordon, nationalism had acquired emotional force and conviction.

Chapter Five
Passionate Patriotism: Economic Nationalism, 1968-1985

"The only U.S. industry that wouldn't be welcomed in Canada is Murder Inc."

Barron's Weekly, 1976

But for a few tentative beginnings in the Dirty Thirties, the influence exercised by the nationalists during the late 1960s and the 1970s marked the first time that ideology has played a major role in Canadian politics. (During this same period, the opposed ideologies of nationalism and federalism totally dominated politics in Quebec.)

A frequent criticism of the nationalists was that, as members of the middle class, they benefited themselves at the expense of the workers. Pierre Trudeau, while still a professor at the University of Montreal, made this point in the Manifesto that he and several other intellectuals, including Gerard Pelletier and Marc Lalonde, published in 1964, declaring that nationalist policies "are generally advantageous to the middle class though they run counter to the interests of the majority of the population and of the economically weak in particular."

In saying this, Trudeau was being politically astute: he'd seized the moral high ground for federalism. Yet Trudeau was only stating a commonplace. The fact is that all ideologies, from communism to neo-conservatism, express the interests and ideas of the middle class. The federalists and the continentalists, for instance, did at least as well out of their creeds as the nationalists did out of theirs. Inevitably, the proletariat and the silent majority end up paying the bulk of the freight for all ideologies.

72

The most interesting aspect of any ideology isn't so much its particular claim to absolute virtue as simply the fact that it exists. The emergence of an ideology confirms that a particular society has reached the point where its middle class has acquired sufficient size and self-confidence to exercise political leadership.

Canada reached this transformational stage somewhere around 1960. This was the year that Quebec's Quiet Revolution signalled that a new meritocratic elite was replacing the rural, religious, conservative hegemony that had held sway for two centuries. That same year, John F. Kennedy's victory stirred longings among Canadian liberal intellectuals for a northern magician of their own. Expo '67, the glory of Centennial Year, provides the clearest dividing line between old and new; as the most sophisticated and best-managed world's fair of the century, it demonstrated that a new generation of Canadians had taken charge. "What's got into our good, grey neighbours?" ran the caption of a cover story in *Look*. Soon after, Trudeau vaulted onto the stage. At last we had our magician, stylish, sassy, and sexy. He told us that we had to be prepared to pay any price, bear any burden, for bilingualism. He told us further that we were engaged in "building a brilliant prototype for the civilization of tomorrow."

Ideas like this were strange fruit in the maple tree. But the new middle class, assertive if not quite brash, was hungry for some sense of larger purpose, and the prolonged economic good times of that era coincidentally provided everyone with enough leisure to undertake such a quest. During these years, nationalism wasn't the only ideology to command the imagination of the Canadian middle class; liberalism, in the sense of extending collective standards of equity and tolerance, flourished equally well. Yet nationalism acquired a particular potency for reasons that have at least as much to do with what was happening outside Canada as with events within.

South of the border, once the Kennedys were dead, existed the spectacle of a society that seemed to be demolishing itself. As the best the U.S. could summon up to match against Trudeau there were Lyndon Johnson, coarse and crass, hauling up his shirt to show his gall-bladder scar and, after him, Richard Milhous Nixon. There were Harlem and Watts and Kent State. There were the race riots in Detroit and the police riot in Chicago at the 1968 Democratic Convention. There was Vietnam. Later, there was Watergate.

For the first time in their history, Canadians had to find political role models within their own borders. Amazingly, there were plenty of them. In hindsight, the "participatory democracy" of the early Trudeau years produced few policies of much permanent value, yet the Company of Young Canadians and ventures like Opportunities for Youth and the Local Initiatives Program represented, along with Medicare and regional equalization, a sane and, above all, a quintessentially Canadian way of doing things: a deft co-option of the opposition to avoid social polarization. Although it took us time, we would eventually come to terms with bilingualism and broaden it into multiculturalism; later still, we would learn how to revise our constitution, a test of national cohesion that only Sweden and Switzerland have managed successfully during peacetime in this century. If any more reassurance were needed that we were doing things right, American town planners and architects kept crossing the border to study Toronto and to report breathlessly that they'd found there "A City That Works."

Canadian nationalism of the late 1960s and the 1970s can only be understood by comparing the nature of the society in which it operated and that of the society next door, the one working, the other seemingly not working. Moreover, this neighbouring society was exporting its values across the border – by its dominance over Canadian industry, by its dominance over Canadian mass culture, and by its sheer magnetic appeal even when it wasn't consciously exercising it.

Perhaps the best expression of the schizophrenia that almost tore apart Canadian intellectual nationalists during this period, their rage not at the U.S. but at what the U.S. had become, coupled with an aching sense of loss, is contained in Robert Fulford's contribution to The New Romans, a collection of nationalist essays edited by the poet Al Purdy and published in 1968. "I have always been profoundly grateful that Canada shares this continent with the American people," Fulford wrote. "My first heroes were American musicians: Ellington, Armstrong, Peewee Russell, later Charlie Parker and Miles Davis. The novelists I first took seriously – Mark Twain, Hemingway, Fitzgerald, Salinger, eventually Bellow – were all American.... Now, doubts swarm all over me. Vietnam is a terrible disaster for everyone involved; the Vietnamese suffer horribly, but what may eventually be worse is that the American spirit, on which so much of the future of mankind depends, is buckling under the strain."

74

This political equivalent of a son discovering that his father is a thief reached its logical and inevitable conclusion in an April, 1975, article for *Maclean's* by the journalist Heather Robertson: "I am anti-American. There. It's said. The secret is out. I do not identify with American traditions or sympathize with American values. I feel no kinship."

Such expressions of explicit anti-Americanism were rare and were usually uttered self-doubtingly. Robertson and the other new nationalists took a middle-class pride in what was being achieved in Canada. They rejected, angrily and despairingly, what was happening in the United States. They despaired equally that these destructive values could be kept out, or indeed, that most Canadians really wanted them kept out.

Few ordinary Canadians shared the nationalists' ideas. When the popular broadcaster, Gordon Sinclair, read an "I like Americans" editorial on Toronto's CFRB in answer to Robertson's outburst, he received thousands of approving letters. Canadian businessmen still looked south to find their mentors, wanted to be like them, wanted indeed to *be* Americans. As many Canadians as ever continued to flock southward in search of sun or good times, though less and less often to Manhattan because of all the stories about muggings and rapings. Most Canadians had no sense whatever of being oppressed by "alien" values or an "alien" culture. Quite the contrary. Once cable TV provided the means, Canadians everywhere demanded every American TV signal that could be captured (pirated might be a better word) and distributed. During this period, baseball displaced Canadian football as the country's second most popular sport. Canadian cities ceased to look "Canadian," which in fact only meant that they stopped looking down at heel and dumpily Victorian and became glittering and gleamingly "Americanized," which is to say, modernized.

Every now and then, the imperative that Rotstein described as "territorial nationalism" did manage to unite the silent majority and the middle-class nationalists – as demonstrated by the popularity of Trudeau's extension of environmental regulation to the waters between the Arctic islands. But the nationalists made few attempts to capitalize on these sentiments. Often, they lost their audience by their verbal excesses – as, for instance, the fulminations about foreign-born academics by the Carleton University professor, Robin Matthews. Much worse, the nationalists seldom attempted to reach an audience beyond themselves. Many of their tracts – *Dominance and Dependency*; *Canada*

Ltd.; In Whose Interests – were composed in the self-conscious style of academics writing with their peers looking over their shoulders. If the nationalists remained a minority, it was mostly because, no differently from their patron saint, Gordon, they were too squeamish to get involved in the rough and tumble of democracy.*

Everything that rises must converge. Sometime during the late 1960s, burgeoning economic nationalism converged with burgeoning cultural nationalism to give the issue of foreign ownership an urgency that Gordon, even if he'd tried, could never have provided. Thereafter, the battle against American capital became just one more skirmish in the larger crusade to protect Canada from the political values that came in as the freight of U.S. capital.

This doubling of forces produced three significant intellectual achievements. One was *Survival*, Margaret Atwood's brilliant 1972 dissection of the character of Canadian literature, to be considered in Chapter Nine. Another was *A Nation Unaware*, published in 1974 by the iconoclastic British Columbia writer Herschel Hardin, to which references are made throughout this book. In Hardin's definition, Canada was a "public enterprise culture" with a unique aptitude, "a native genius," for managing government-owned commercial enterprises effectively.

This claim is a lot more difficult to make in the mid-1980s than it was in the mid-1970s, but Hardin's analysis, like Atwood's, served to provide nationalists with the philosophic underpinning for their central case: differences between Canada and the U.S. were integral to Canadian society rather than simply the accidents of historical circumstance.

The remaining important intellectual accomplishment of the nationalists was a group effort. It was provided by a bunch of leftish intellectuals, a ginger group within the New Democratic Party, who gave themselves the collective title, the Waffle. As a political force, this body with that refreshingly unstuffy name lasted for three years. It was born officially in 1969 when its members issued a Manifesto,

---

* Those who did go into the streets usually discovered that they greatly enjoyed it. Rotstein wryly recalls canvassing door to door in Peterborough on behalf of the Committee for an Independent Canada and being asked anxiously by one elderly lady, "Does being for an independent Canada mean being against the Queen?"

written by Jim Laxer and by University of Toronto political economist Mel Watkins, that proclaimed as its purpose the creation of "an Independent Socialist Canada." It reached its peak of influence that same year, when one-third of the delegates at the NDP's policy convention voted for Waffle-sponsored resolutions. In 1972, it was read out of the Ontario party by Stephen Lewis, son of the national leader, David Lewis; after that, it passed quickly into political oblivion.

But the Waffle left two marks on history. First, it pushed the NDP to the nationalist end of the spectrum. Traditionally, in Canada as everywhere else, the left had been anti-nationalist.* As a reinforcement to this tradition, all the major unions allied to the NDP – the autoworkers, the steelworkers, the machinists – were "international," that is, American, unions. Although the Wafflers never managed to sell themselves to the New Democrats, they did sell the party many of their ideas. From the mid-1970s on, the NDP became the most nationalist of the three parties, as was demonstrated in 1973 when it chivvied the minority Liberal government into creating Petro-Canada.

In their youthful excess and beards and sandals, the Wafflers also did a key part of the job that the Committee for an Independent Canada had been set up to do. Founded in 1971, this worthy establishment creation of Gordon's and Rotstein's busied itself with analysing the costs to Canadian society of foreign ownership. It could claim several successes – content rules for broadcasting as an example – in advancing the cause of cultural nationalism. Some of its supporters, such as Gray and Alastair Gillespie, went on to become senior cabinet ministers, at Trade and at Energy. Another sympathizer, John Shepherd, executive director of the Science Council from 1975 to 1978, imported from Britain the telling phrase "de-industrialization" to describe the phenomenon of branch plants scurrying home and minted the even more telling phrase "truncated economy" to describe Canada's condition of having lots of resources underneath and lots of bureaucrats on top but no manufacturing industry in between. But on the core economic nationalist issue of foreign ownership, the CIC's disabling handicap was never to be able

---

* In 1935, the League for Social Reconstruction, out of which was born the CCF and out of it in turn the NDP, had denounced "those who in defiance of all the evidence persist in believing that the Canadian capitalist is a different kind from the foreign, that the one is a philanthropist and the other a robber and cheat." Marx said it more succinctly, "Workers have no country."

to suggest a credible alternative.

The problem was self-evident. If foreign capitalists were to be driven out, there had to be Canadian capitalists ready and willing to take their place. Not until the late 1970s did the first few members of this breed begin to emerge – the harbinger being Bob Blair of Nova Corporation (originally Alberta Gas Trunk), who in 1976 outmanoeuvred the multinational consortium, Canadian Arctic Gas, for the right to bring natural gas from the North to U.S. markets. To the end of the decade, Canada in more than a century of existence had engendered just two entrepreneurial classes: the nineteenth-century Montreal fur traders and the post-Second World War real estate developers. Otherwise, Canadian businessmen were "a comprador class," in the vivid phrase of the sociologist Wallace Clement, agents for foreign capitalists or, in the case of those who were capitalists themselves, risk-avoiding financiers rather than risk-taking entrepreneurs.

The Wafflers understood this. Their Manifesto called for "public ownership of the means of production in the interests of the Canadian public as a whole." In *Canada Ltd: The Political Economy of Dependency*, Laxer wrote: "Canada's dependency is a function, not of geography or technology but of the nature of Canada's capitalist class." The Wafflers' remedy of public ownership of seemingly everything was, of course, utterly impractical in a North American context. Yet, just over a decade later, the Trudeau government applied precisely this remedy to the most heavily foreign-owned of all industrial sectors: energy. Pushing the National Energy Policy along was the NDP, to which most of the Wafflers had by then returned, including Laxer, as the party's research director.

From the late 1960s to the end of the 1970s, all accounts compiled by economic nationalists of the progress of economic nationalism read like an unrelieved record of failures, betrayals, sell-outs. Such gloominess did not encourage converts. Yet the nationalist audience kept on growing, or, perhaps more accurately, the constituency for the idea of an independent Canada kept on growing, as demonstrated by the findings of the Gallup Poll on public attitudes about U.S. investment:

	Enough investment now	Like to see more
1964	46%	33%

78

	Enough investment now	Like to see more
1967	60%	24%
1970	62%	25%
1972	67%	22%
1975	71%	21%
1977	69%	20%
1978	69%	23%

A much tougher question, whether Canadians would accept "a big reduction in our standard of living" as a worthwhile price to buy back majority control of Canadian companies, attracted a remarkable 46 per cent expression of support in 1970 and an astounding 58 per cent in 1975, slipping back marginally to 52 per cent in 1978.

There was no mystery to this trend in public opinion. The nationalist message was getting through, in its diagnosis if not in its prescription. By the mid-seventies, Canadians were fully informed about the extent of foreign ownership and about many of its consequences, such as attenuated research and development, minimal exports, the transfer out of the country of attractive jobs, most clearly so in the instance of the auto industry. Here are the statistics* for 1972, which in fact turned out to be the peak year for foreign ownership in Canada:

Industries	Percentage of foreign ownership
Book publishing	95%
Chemical products	82%
Construction	15%
Credit agencies	43%
Electrical products	64%
Investment companies	29%
Machinery	72%
Manufacturing	58%
Mining	67%
National Hockey League teams	86%
Paper and allied products	40%
Petroleum and coal	99%
Primary metals	55%

---

* These statistics are published annually under the Corporations and Labour Union Returns Act, CALURA.

Industries	Percentage of foreign ownership
Retail trade	21%
Rubber products	93%
Transportation equipment	87%
Wholesale trade	31%

That same year, to complete the picture, 63 per cent of all trade union members belonged to "international" unions with headquarters in the U.S., while 43 per cent of all university teachers were non-Canadians.

There was indeed nothing like it, nothing remotely like it, anywhere in the world.* Economically, Canadians were like actors performing in a rented hall in a play owned by an investor in another town. Increasingly, Canadians realized this. Increasingly, they were prepared to support a government that would try to do something about it, and as a kind of dress rehearsal for the NEP of 1980 they prevented the Clark government from privatizing Petro-Canada in 1979 as it had originally planned to do.

During this period the record was not quite as barren as the economic nationalists made out. The Canada Development Corporation had been set up at last in 1973, although it largely vanished from sight after buying an American-owned lead and zinc mine. To keep the NDP on side during his minority term, Trudeau announced a national oil policy, out of which came, in 1975, the oil and gas crown corporation, Petro-Canada. In 1976, legislation was enacted to withdraw *Time's* tax privileges, although not those of *Reader's Digest* because it was located in Montreal.

The major nationalist success was the establishment of the Foreign Investment Review Agency, FIRA, in 1974. Its genealogy could be traced back to Gordon and, more immediately, to Herb Gray, who in 1972, as Revenue Minister, published on behalf of the Trudeau government a 500-page report that told everyone more than they could possibly have wanted to know about foreign ownership. Among its endless statistics one stood out and remains as striking today as it did then: of all the increase in foreign ownership in Canada between 1945 and 1967, fully three-quarters had been funded not

---

* Except for the special case of Ireland, which in the 1970s adopted a policy of attracting foreign plants by the double-bait of tax subsidies and low wages.

by new foreign capital but by Canadians themselves, out of the retained earnings of the multinationals already operating in the country. The principal reason for this was the Canadian tax system, which favoured large companies over small ones, most of the former being multinationals, and most of the latter, Canadian-owned independents. This was history by now. The issue for the present and future was, if the foreigners weren't in fact bringing in any new money, why allow them in at all unless they could demonstrate tangible benefits?

Out of this analysis came FIRA. Takeovers of Canadian companies by foreigners and proposed new investments by outsiders would be screened to determine if they would bring "significant benefit" to Canada in terms of jobs, research and development, exports. The new agency survived for ten friendless years before it was put out of its mostly self-inflicted misery by the Mulroney government in 1985. Investors, both Canadian and foreign, saw it as a red-tape monster. Nationalists saw it as a paper tiger. Both were right, sort of.

FIRA's annual rate of approvals was about 90 per cent; in 1983, its approval rate was 97 per cent.* Nationalists kept quoting the 1975 comment of the New York financial weekly, *Barron's*: "The only U.S. industry that wouldn't be welcomed in Canada is Murder Inc." In rebuttal, businessmen pointed to the costs imposed on them by form-filling and nitpicking, even when their applications were approved. In 1979, FIRA issued a five-year report card on itself, in which it claimed to have created 50,000 jobs and $20 million worth of new research and development. These were paper accomplishments: as its officials admitted, FIRA never once checked to see whether commitments made to win approval for a takeover were actually fulfilled. Many weren't. The same day, in May, 1983, that FIRA approved the takeover of a Burlington, Ontario, company by a French firm, on the promise of new jobs, sixteen of its employees were laid off. (No firm was every prosecuted for breaking its legally binding commitments.) Some decisions were just plain dumb, as, for instance, forcing the influential *Wall Street Journal*, which thereafter had its knife out for Canada, to churn out paperwork to justify taking over a small Canadian consulting company already owned by a U.S. company that the *Journal's* subsidiary, Dow-Jones, had just bought

---

* Only in cultural fields was the rate of disapprovals high: printing and publishing (23 per cent); communications (29 per cent).

up in the U.S. In summary, FIRA was at one and the same time too fine a screen (reviewing takeovers involving as little as $50,000) and too permeable a one to do the job.

Two misconceptions about FIRA, however, need to be cleared up, mostly because they have both passed into conventional wisdom. The first is that FIRA was part of a consistent policy of the Trudeau government calling for the replacement of foreign capital by domestic capital. The Trudeau government's policy was, instead, consistently inconsistent. At the same time as it was screening foreign investors it was subsidizing them – a grant of $68 million, jointly with Ontario, to get Ford to locate a new V-8 engine plant in Ontario rather than in Ohio; a combined Ottawa-Quebec giveaway of $275 million to Bell Helicopter of Texas to set up a plant at Mirabel Airport to employ 3,000, according to the initial claim of the two governments, although in fact, as revealed by the Montreal *Gazette*, just 600 jobs were created.

Just as misleading is the conventional wisdom that FIRA frightened away foreign investors. During this period the reason that foreign capital stopped flowing in and that Canadian capital flowed out was because the economic pastures to the south were so much greener, a disparity that explains the absence of major new inflows since FIRA's disappearance. Two "objective" witnesses for the defence are handily available. In May, 1979, the U.S. ambassador in Ottawa, Thomas Enders, approvingly told a Stanford University audience that, "I can understand how Canada, relying as heavily as it does on outside investment, feels the need for having such a mechanism to ensure that its interests are identified and met." The other is a more recent U.S. ambassador to Canada, Paul Robinson, who in the spring of 1983 forthrightly described FIRA as "a lap-dog."* The foreign investors most angered by FIRA were never in fact Americans – except during the period 1980-82 when FIRA and NEP became conjoined swear words – but West Germans, who in the late seventies and early eighties poured more than $1 billion worth of investment into Canada through a loophole in the West German tax laws. They didn't like being screened because it meant spelling out their business affairs.

* Some American politicians thought highly enough of FIRA to want to copy it. In 1982, the House of Representatives Committee on Government Operations recommended: "A Foreign Direct Investment reviewing and screening agency, similar to the agencies in Canada, Mexico and in many other countries ... to extract substantial benefits for the U.S."

82

In December, 1984, Industry Minister Sinclair Stevens announced FIRA's demise and its replacement by Investment Canada. Mostly, though, Stevens had stage-managed a change in FIRA's form rather than its function. In the new order, new direct investments will no longer be automatically reviewed; takeovers of Canadian companies will be reviewed only if the amount exceeds $5 million. The number of companies being reviewed by Investment Canada will be only 10 per cent of those reviewed by FIRA, and the test for approval will be softened to "net benefit" from "significant benefit."

One week after Stevens' announcement, officials at the Canadian consulate in New York briefed financiers and investment bankers on the new legislation. One banker discomfited the officials by commenting after listening to them: "So the floor has been raised to $5 million. What's the difference? When do I do deals that small?" In dollar terms, the takeovers being examined by Investment Canada will amount to about two-thirds of those that FIRA would have examined; on demand all takeovers in the cultural and "national heritage" industries can be reviewed. In brief, if FIRA had died, the idea behind FIRA remained alive.

From the start of its life to its little-mourned end, FIRA's purpose was largely symbolic. It got into trouble because it was visible: comparable constraints on foreign investment in the U.S. are tucked into the sub-clauses of more than twenty separate statutes and regulations. In addition, FIRA got into trouble not because of what it did but because it did this so bureaucratically. As the minister responsible during the most difficult years, 1980-82, Gray handed to his critics all the ammunition they needed by personally examining every application obsessively. As always in politics, luck played a major part. FIRA coincided with a cyclical outpouring of capital, both Canadian and foreign, to which it added at most a shallow curve, but for which it served as a handy scapegoat.

FIRA's most significant contribution to the Canadian economy was one that its defenders could not mention in public. By discouraging foreign companies from bidding, it forced down the prices of Canadian companies that were up for sale. The effect was to make it easier for bright, young Canadian businessmen to acquire their first enterprises. Conversely, of course, the older businessmen selling off their concerns had a bit less to take with them into retirement in Florida.

Tom Taylor, a thirty-six-year-old owner of a Preston, Ontario, manufacturing company, who himself benefited from this process, says, "The debate about FIRA was really a debate between the generations, between those who had made their stake and wanted to cash in and those who were still trying to make it and who still had the juices to do so."

By 1980, the economic nationalists, without realizing it, had achieved their most significant success. They had sold Canadians on the idea that foreign ownership constrained the Canadian economy in a straight jacket. All that was needed was a government, and some entrepreneurs, prepared to make a break for it.

Chapter Six
Oil Wars: The National Energy Policy, 1980-1985

"Only governments can ensure that the West does not become the victim of this energy casino."

Anthony Sampson, author of *The Seven Sisters*, in July, 1979

About federalism, about bilingualism, about the constitution, Marc Lalonde and Pierre Trudeau did not so much think alike as think as if they were one person. But about other matters, each man thought as he pleased. In the early 1960s Trudeau bruised the pride of René Lévesque, then Quebec's Minister of Resources, by pointing out that nationalizing privately owned power companies would create jobs for the middle class at the expense of the working class. Lalonde disagreed: he campaigned publicly for Hydro-Québec.

The National Energy Policy of 1980 was Lalonde's personal equivalent to Hydro-Québec. About half a dozen senior officials and aides, and a couple of ministers, including Trudeau, played important parts. But the NEP was Lalonde's: it couldn't have happened without him, and because of him it happened in the particular way that it did. The NEP became the political equivalent of a bone stuck into the throat of the West, so that the Mulroney government had no political choice but to scrap it. In this sense, Lalonde was both architect of the NEP and its saboteur.

By the mid-1980s the NEP had become synonymous with self-defeating economic nationalism and with destructive bureaucratic interventionism. In the prevailing judgement, it had been an unmitigated disaster. Almost exactly a century earlier everyone had thought much the same way about the CPR, as its construction slipped far behind schedule and the company almost slid into bankruptcy. The NEP's true niche in history won't be decided for many years. The success or otherwise of the free market system created by Energy Minister Pat Carney's "Western Accord" of April, 1985, will be a major factor in determining which niche that will be.

In trying to guess whether contemporary opinion will be revised, two permanent consequences of the NEP need to be considered. Just by existing it made a return to a free market system – in theory, at least, a more economically efficient system – politically possible because during the NEP's term, 1980-85, a sufficient number of Canadian oil companies grew to a size sufficient to be able to take on the multinationals on more or less even terms. As well, the NEP fostered among Canadians a *permanent* bias in favour of Canadian ownership. "Canadians continue to support the principles of Canadianization and limiting foreign ownership," the Decima Research Group warned the Mulroney government in the spring of 1985. It concluded: "While clearly the federal government does have some room to manoeuvre on the foreign investment issue, it seems equally clear that it is still an issue which must be managed carefully."

In private, Alberta Premier Peter Lougheed once described Lalonde – this in mid-1981 when in public they were fighting tooth and claw – as "the best Minister of Energy I've ever dealt with." As doubtless impressed Lougheed, Lalonde was always on top of his briefs, founded his arguments on facts and not on rhetoric, was a workaholic, and was very, very tough. He could also be disarmingly charming, a beatific smile every now and then transforming his stern, hook-nosed visage. At other times, he could be astonishingly dumb. While Minister of Federal-Provincial Relations, he told "Newfie" jokes to reporters. In the instance of the NEP, he failed totally to comprehend western sensibilities and grievances, copying Trudeau's style of assuming that because what he was doing was "right," it would be seen to be right.

Lalonde was the son of a farmer, which gave him a rooted sense of everyday practicalities and a rather prudish attitude toward what are now known as "lifestyles," including Trudeau's. He began his political career in the late 1950s as an aide to a senior Diefenbaker minister, Davie Fulton, came to despair of Diefenbaker's ever understanding Quebec, then discovered Trudeau and became his Talleyrand. As Trudeau's chief political aide, 1968-72, Lalonde, while brilliant, magnified Trudeau's arrogance by his own arrogance. As a cabinet minister for the next half dozen years, he worked diligently to reform the social security system and to reform the constitution. He accomplished neither. In defeat in 1979, he, like Trudeau, read the press "obituaries," realized the historians would be harsh, and, also like Trudeau, returned to power determined to rewrite history.

While in opposition during the Clark government of 1979, Lalonde was energy critic. Influenced by his nationalist colleague, Herb Gray, he began to conceive of a dramatic new energy policy. It took shape under the pressure of the election campaign of early 1980: Canadianization; a "made-in-Canada" oil price kept below the then-soaring world price as a boost to industry, particularly in central Canada; new taxes to recapture surplus revenues from the overwhelmingly foreign-owned energy industry.

The election victory gave Lalonde his chance. More significant, victory in the Quebec referendum of May 20, 1980, liberated him. He knew he would face ferocious opposition. What his opponents didn't realize was that for Lalonde, after two decades of fighting Quebec separatists and FLQ terrorists, these new battles would be about the equivalent of being transferred from the Russian front to the North African one.

The oil and gas industry is engagingly crazy. More than it's about the mining of hydrocarbons, it's about the mining of money: large oil companies allocate more of their talents to drilling holes in the tax system than in the ground; small companies spend more time looking for gullible investors than for oil and gas; the glamorous independent oilmen of folklore are about as important to the industry as a whole as family farmers are to agribusiness. And yet, in a way, the myths are real. The oil culture, the culture of Texas and of *Dallas*, envelops everyone in the business, from Norwegians in the North Sea to Egyptians in the Red Sea. It's a swaggering, J.R. Ewing-style culture. Multimillion-dollar deals really are done on a handshake. Oilmen may rely on lawyers and accountants, but they truly revere the "great oil finders" amongst them. As in the case of those airlines whose chief executives were once test pilots, there's a mystique about those oilmen who, before climbing to the top of the corporate ladder, have actually done the real work out in the field as geologists, physicists, engineers, roughnecks on the rigs.

Through the 1970s the oil industry progressed from being merely crazy to being right out of its gourd. Thanks to some Arabs who'd learned about cartels at the Harvard Business School, it was no longer necessary to mine money, simply to shovel it up. Albertans who in 1970 owned no more than a scrub quarter section and a pickup truck, were paper multimillionaires by 1980, though in fact far more made their fortune by flipping real estate in Calgary than by wildcatting in the Western Sedimentary Basin. Just when the craziness began to subside, and when some experts were beginning to say that, come to think of it, there was a lot of supply around, the Shah fell. Night after night, westerners saw on their TV screens the baleful, zealotic stare of the Ayatollah Khomeini: he really did hope we would freeze in the dark before we went on to burn in hell.

That half decade of hysteria defined much that followed. Lalonde and his officials were, in hindsight, naive to assume that oil prices would rise forever. Oilmen, and all their bankers, were, however, equally naive; among the experts the only real argument was whether, as collateral for all those loans to Dome Petroleum and to Mexico and Nigeria, oil would reach $100 a barrel by 1990 or not until 2001. As a result, oil companies kept on buying each other up at inflated prices and kept on inflating their own costs by offering hiring bonuses to freshly graduated geologists and engineers and by bidding up land prices like matrons gone giddy at an antique auction.

Not all the oil companies were quite that naive. The smart ones took their windfall profits and hid them – out of the oil industry itself. Through 1978-80, at a time when President Jimmy Carter was talking about an impending "national catastrophe" unless Americans consumed less and the oil companies produced more, Standard Oil bought up Kennecott Mines for $1 billion, Exxon spent $1.2 billion on an electric motor company and another $2 billion buying up high-tech firms, Mobil bought the department store chain, Montgomery Ward, for $1.5 billion.

The most eloquent justification for the NEP was provided two weeks after it was announced, when Imperial Oil president Jack Armstrong gave a speech at a November, 1980, conference in New York he had obviously prepared long in advance but was too careless or too confident to bother to change. "The aggressive program of diversification we have pursued for a number of years means that we don't have all our eggs in one basket," he said. Having redeployed its profits, Imperial was now among "the top ten mineral exploration companies in North America" with interests in coal, uranium, metals, and petrochemicals. For Imperial, this strategy made perfect corporate sense. For Canadians it meant that the more we paid for oil, the more of Canada the various multinationals would buy up with the profits Canadians handed them at the pump. (Shell Canada excitedly bought up "electronic office" companies.)

The Harvard economist Robert Reich has divided multinationals into two groups: "national multinationals," like those of the Japanese, which, wherever they go in the world, perform there in the best interests of Japan as well as of themselves, and "real multinationals," that is, most American multinationals, which have no loyalties except to their corporate selves.

Through the 1960s and 1970s, a certain myth developed about American multinationals, best expressed in the title of Jean-Jacques Servan-Schreiber's book, *Le Defi American*. They came to be seen either as global octopi or, as in Allende's Chile, almost as extensions of the CIA. But in fact, Americans are homebodies. In corporations like General Electric, say, the fast track for rising executives is at head office, not overseas. With a few exceptions, such as IBM and Coca-Cola, the only "real" American multinationals are the mining and petroleum ones, and only because these need to control their sources of supply.

In this sense, George Ball, former U.S. Undersecretary of State, was guilty not so much of rudeness as of misperception when he made the famous comment in his 1968 memoir, *The Discipline of Power*, that "Canada is fighting a rearguard action against the inevitable. . . . The struggle is bound to be a difficult one, and I suspect, over the years, a losing one. . . . Sooner or later, commercial imperatives will bring about free movement of all goods back and forth across our long border. The result will be substantial economic integration, which will require for its full realization a progressively expanding area of political cohesion." As an analysis of the problems of maintaining Canada's sovereignty, this was routine stuff. The interesting aspect of Ball's thesis was his bias, revealed in 1967 in an article in *Fortune*: "While the structure of the multi-national corporation is a modern concept, designed to meet the requirements of the modern age, the nation-state is a very old-fashioned idea and badly adapted to serve the needs of our complex world." Multinationals, in other words, would soon become substitutes for nation-states. Herein lay the core of the NEP: a battle between two types

89

of social organisms. Ball's misperception was to assume that the multinationals were more efficient and more powerful.*

In the Canadian context, the oil multinationals can be divided among the "good" ones, like Imperial and Shell, which operate semi-autonomously and plough back their profits, if not always into oil, and the "red telephone companies" as they're known, like Mobil and Texaco, whose executives jump to orders from south of the border. Mobil Canada, for example, wanted to explore the Hibernia field off Newfoundland in 1976 but the parent company had better uses for the money and postponed exploration until 1978.

These, however, are differences of degree more than of kind. "Multinationals can never be good corporate citizens. The most they can ever be is good corporate guests," says John Bulloch, president of the Canadian Federation of Independent Businesses. Some have made honourable efforts to blend into the local background. Several manufacturing multinationals have developed "world product mandates" – Canadian General Electric in airfoils, Westinghouse Canada in gas turbines – and now export, worldwide, one-quarter and more of their output. (CGE's airfoil plant at Bromont, Quebec, is one of the most advanced on the continent in the extent of its automation and in the sophistication of its labour-management relations.) As to whether multinationals do more or less research and development than equivalent Canadian companies, the evidence is mixed. A 1984 study for the federal government by University of New Brunswick economist D.C. McCharles concludes, however, that multinationals export proportionately far less than Canadian companies (other than in intra-company trade in components with their parents) and "are not using world product mandate strategies to any great degree."

Whether they perform as good corporate guests or as make-it-on-the-run transients, the central fact about multinational companies is that the corporate strings on which they exist are always held somewhere outside the country. Every now and then, the strings are tugged: in the late 1960s, the oil multinationals all but shut down

---

* At a seminar on Canada-U.S. relations organized by the Brookings Institute in April, 1984, Ball revised, to a degree, his prediction of Canada's inevitable demise, but revealingly anchored his new analysis on American domestic interests: "I was not advocating such a course of action. In fact, I think that very few Canadians would want this to happen, once they examined all the implications, principally because it would upset the political balance in a way that would mean the rewriting of American politics."

in Alberta in order to shift their resources to Alaska's Prudhoe Bay.

Often the problem isn't so much that strings are being pulled elsewhere as that attitudes are being shaped elsewhere. Two books about the NEP, *Controlling Interest* by David Crane and *The Politics of Energy* by Bruce Doern and Glen Toner, recount how the multinationals invariably favoured the American suppliers and specialists they had always dealt with. To persuade Gulf Canada to allow Canadian companies even to bid on its Arctic projects took two years of endless haggling by Industry Minister Gray and his officials. By 1980, not a single oil refinery or petrochemical plant in Canada had been built by Canadian consulting engineering companies.

The fact that the NEP forced most of the multinationals – Texaco and Mobil simply bunkered down and went on behaving as they always have – to act like good corporate guests was one of its major accomplishments. It achieved this, essentially, by scaring the hell out of them. One of the unanswered questions about the new Western Accord is whether the multinationals have really learned their lesson or whether, after playing possum for a couple of years, they'll go back to dancing at the end of their strings.

The draftsmen of the NEP were an interesting blend of idealists and political opportunists. Their objectives were complex and contradictory. It was hard sometimes to tell whether Canadianization was a noble end in itself or just a politically popular means by which Ottawa could scoop up revenues that would otherwise have stayed with the oil companies or have gone to the provinces.

Two comments can be made with reasonable certainty. The NEP draftsmen were an exceptionally bright lot. In the top tier were Trudeau, Lalonde, and Allan MacEachen, then Finance Minister. Under them, on one side, were civil servants Mickey Cohen and Ed Clark, the deputy and assistant deputy ministers of energy, and Petro-Canada's executive vice-president, Joel Bell; on another side were the political aides, Jim Coutts and Tom Axworthy in Trudeau's office and Mike Phelps in Lalonde's.*

The NEP, further, was an idea whose time appeared to have come.

* The Mulroney government dismissed Clark and Bell from their public service posts and accepted Strong's resignation from Petro-Canada. Cohen was highly regarded by the new government but resigned, as deputy minister of finance, in August, 1985.

In the last pre-NEP year, 1979, multinationals accounted for 82 per cent of Canadian oil production; among the top ten largest companies, the single Canadian-owned firm was the crown company, Petro-Canada. During the preceding three decades going back to the first discovery at Leduc, in 1947, 303 Canadian oil independents had been bought up by multinationals. The times, however, were changing. Little noticed elsewhere until Peter Foster celebrated them in his 1979 book, *The Blue-Eyed Sheiks*, a genuine entrepreneurial class was taking shape in Alberta.

The most serious defect of Lalonde and the NEP planners was that they didn't understand this new breed. They expected the entrepreneurs to support the NEP because its new scheme of direct grants favoured Canadian-owned companies over the multinationals. But the small independents damned the NEP almost unanimously. Many fled across the border to try their luck in the free enterprise ground of the U.S.*

One problem was technical. The independents were gas producers and Alberta was their stamping ground. The NEP, though, was concerned with increasing oil production, by the lure of direct grants, in the "Canada Lands" of the North and offshore. The real problem, though, was cultural. The independents identified with the multi-national bureaucracies, even though they were unlike them, because both belonged to the magical oil industry. Government intervention, however well intentioned, threatened their heroic self-image.

Lalonde learned a lot during the NEP. He learned, and later applied the lesson as Finance Minister, that commercial creativity is driven by what Keynes called "the animal spirits" of businessmen, a driving force that is crude but energetic. Even in 1980, he did not misread *all* of the oil industry. By then, for the first time, some increasingly sophisticated Canadian companies of medium size had also begun to emerge – Husky, Norcen, Dome, Home Oil, Canterra. These, and Petro-Canada, could be the building blocks of a truly Canadian oil and gas industry, one that would always be here and that could use Canada as a base from which to reach out internationally, to China, Indonesia, Australia, in a way that multinational branch plants could not.

It was an American, ironically, who best understood this nation-

---

* Known as "snowbirds," most of these exiles, lacking contacts and knowledge of the local geology, lost their shirts.

building dream. In a report sent to the clients of New York-based MultiNational Strategies Inc. early in 1981, Stephen Blank observed that "the 'old' [Canadian] nationalists, composed of intellectuals, trade union leaders and left-wing politicians," while "not without influence" had had little effect on government policies "because [they] offered no realistic alternative to foreign ownership." Blank continued: "The new nationalists are a new generation of Canadian entrepreneurs whose economic ambitions are highly competitive with foreign firms.... They worry little about cultural domination. They are not anti-American. They are concerned about political and economic power, however, and they mean to acquire it."

Bob Blair, the head of Nova Corporation, a shy visionary and a dual nationalist, every bit as fervent an Albertan as a Canadian, is the best-known example of this breed. While gazing out at the Rockies from his penthouse office on the top of Nova's Calgary tower, Blair is given to making such statements as: "I fail to see why a multinational cannot have its headquarters here and be competitive worldwide." Dome Petroleum's Jack Gallagher and Bill Richards, even though they both eventually high-rolled themselves out the game, were of the same stripe. As important were the non-petroleum types like Larry Clark of Spar Aerospace (the builder of the Canadarm for NASA), Walter Light of Northern Telecom, Raymond Royer of Bombardier, Mike Cowpland and Terry Matthews of Mitel, and, later, Frank Stronach of Magna International. They and others – the list each year grew longer and younger – represented the long-missing link in the equations of the economic nationalists. If the multinationals were driven out, a generation of Canadian entrepreneurs was at least beginning to emerge and to offer the promise of being able to take the place of the "compradors" and the corporate guests.

The trouble with this dream was that it ran head-on into an opposing dream. In the 1970s, Alberta had ceased to be Tomorrow Country. The future was now. Just as Canadian nationalists wanted to repatriate power and interesting jobs from Americans, so the new elites of the West wanted to repatriate those same things from Toronto, Ottawa, and Montreal.

If economic nationalists looked to Lalonde as their champion, then westerners looked to Alberta Premier Peter Lougheed. Although he was by no means Lalonde's match intellectually, Lougheed was every bit as tough, as thorough in mastering his briefs, possibly even more stubborn, and unquestionably an abler politician. In his response to the NEP, Lougheed brilliantly invoked "territorial nationalism," this in the heart of homestead country, by declaring that Ottawa was "coming into our house and occupying the living-room." He gave a credibility to critics of the NEP they would never have had otherwise. He raised the stakes until the cost of the NEP became that of dividing the country. Lougheed's tactics were self-interested, yet they served a larger purpose. By the Western Accord of 1985, westerners won themselves the same kind of psychic victory that Quebecers had won when they elected the Parti Québécois in 1976. Thereafter, it became possible for westerners to enter Confederation fully for the first time, just as Quebecers have done. As for Lougheed, his job for his people done, he announced in June, 1985, that he would retire.

The odd aspect of all of this is that the NEP's intellectual origins can be traced back to the West. In June, 1975, Allan Blakeney announced the most dramatic policy of his eight-year term as New Democrat Premier of Saskatchewan. One-half of the U.S.-owned potash industry, then enjoying windfall profits that the provincial government found impossible to tax, would be nationalized; to maximize the local scientific and executive jobs, a new crown company for potash would be created.

The potash takeover attracted little attention because the mineral is unglamorous. But it was the NEP writ small. In turn, its intellectual origins can be traced back to the former Trudeau minister, Eric Kierans. Possessed of that political rarity, a genuinely original mind, if at times an erratic one, Kierans had ploughed through Statistics Canada reports while Postmaster-General and had concluded that, because of the tax system, Canadians were paying multinationals to buy up everything in sight. Kierans quit the cabinet when the Ottawa economic establishment rejected his analysis. His ideas were picked up by the NDP in its "Corporate Welfare Bums" campaign in the 1972 election. Kierans himself set out his ideas in a long article in the *Canadian Forum* of April, 1972: a flat-tax of 35 per cent, with no loopholes, for Canadian-owned corporations while foreign ones paid the same rate as in their home country; simultaneously, a warning to the multinationals that unless they maximized their benefits to

Canada, "(Their) intransigence could easily lead to nationalization." A passionate and appealing fighter, Kierans became a standard-bearer for economic nationalism. He was at his most eloquent in his 1983 CBC Massey Lecture series in which he warned that "the logicians of the world enterprises [multinationals] refuse to recognize that nations are autonomous enterprises."

The specific ideas for the NEP were developed during the spring of 1980. Among Lalonde's most daring proposed policy options was the immediate nationalization of a major multinational. This was turned down by a three-to-two vote among the government's big five: Trudeau, MacEachen, and Privy Council Clerk Michael Pitfield voted no; Coutts supported Lalonde.

Trudeau, by now preoccupied by the constitutional battles, thereafter played little part in the NEP. He did cool down an angry President Reagan when they met at the White House in July, 1981, by cannily pointing out, "This program is as important to me as your tax [cut] plan is to you. Like you, I just won an election on it." Trudeau's only other direct contribution to the NEP was quirky and harmful. The part of the NEP that most angered Washington was the provision that Petro-Canada would acquire a 25 per cent share or "back-in" of discoveries made in the Canada Lands. By the winter Lalonde had concluded that the back-in was politically indefensible because it was retroactive. He recommended it be dropped. Trudeau said no. He wasn't resisting pressure from Washington or from the oil industry, though; instead, he was applying pressure to Jack Gallagher of Dome (affected by the back-in no less than the multinationals), who had annoyed him by his incessant lobbying.

Lalonde announced the National Energy Policy on October 28, 1980. Much of it, in particular the parts about prices and revenue-sharing, was incomprehensible. But the essentials were perfectly clear. The target was 50 per cent Canadian ownership by 1990. Petro-Canada would undertake "one or two large acquisitions" and be helped to grow further by the back-in. To assist privately owned Canadian companies to grow in parallel, the existing system of tax incentives, which benefited the large multinationals over small Canadian companies, would be replaced by direct grants (Petroleum Incentive Program, or PIP grants) to be given in disproportionate amounts to companies with the largest Canadian ownership.*

Everyone hated it. Independents started moving rigs south of the border, taking good care that TV cameras were on hand to record their passage. The multinationals announced they would have to cancel planned mega-projects. Lougheed went on television to declare he would be cutting back oil supplies to the East.

Everyone hated the NEP, that is except the people.

In April, 1981, the Canadian Petroleum Association, composed mostly of multinationals, commissioned Decima Research to survey public opinion. An incredible 84 per cent of Canadians supported Canadianization. More incredible still, 61 per cent thought that the Canadian-ownership goal should be higher and should be targeted earlier. Of all of Trudeau's policies, only his peace initiative of 1983-84 received a higher rating. For the first time perhaps since the 1911 Reciprocity Election, Canadians had declared unequivocally they wanted their economy to be their own. This was the supreme, shining moment of Canadian economic nationalism: each takeover – of Petro-Fina by Petro-Canada for $1.5 billion (the Auditor-General later said the real cost was over $2 billion), of Hudson's Bay Oil and Gas, U.S.-owned despite its name, by Dome, and of Aquitaine, renamed Canterra, by CDC – was like another victorious communiqué from the front.

This can-do mood was washed away by the Great Recession of 1981-82. The NEP was blamed for the collapse of the oil industry (the real cause was the collapse in oil prices), and, entirely accurately, was also blamed for the hemorrhaging away of foreign capital. Some $7 billion poured out in the first six months of 1981, forcing MacEachen to advise the banks not to loan any more money for takeovers of multinationals. Support for the NEP was also eroded by Canadians' rising concern that it was magnifying the regional discord already created by Trudeau's attempt to revise the constitution.

But since the support for Canadian control was once palpable, and it hasn't vanished since, it's worth trying to comprehend it. One of the seeming paradoxes about the issue of foreign ownership is that Canadians became progressively more assertive as foreign owner-

---

* The least comprehensible aspect of the NEP, but the aspect most important for Ottawa's revenue purposes, was the PGRT, Petroleum and Gas Revenue Tax, worth about $2 billion, which unlike all other taxes was not on net taxable income nor even on income but on sales, off the bottom as it were rather than off the top.

ship declined. Canada reached its nadir of economic colonization in 1972, as these statistics* of the proportion of total non-financial industrial assets held by foreigners show:

1968	34%
1971	37%
1976	30%
1980	27%
1981	25.4%
1982	24.6%

At this rate, foreign ownership may be below one-fifth by the end of the 1980s.

The public's eagerness to see the oil industry Canadianized is easy to explain. Essentially, Canadians regarded the multinationals as liars. To the dismay of oil executives, but equally to the dismay of policy planners and high-minded conservationists, Canadians from 1973 on refused to believe that the oil crisis was a real crisis rather than one manufactured by the oil companies. They were delighted to see their nation-state take them on, as after all Saudi Arabia, Venezuela, Mexico, the Arab Gulf states, and Libya had all done by this time.

Canadians were also cocky during those years, engagingly so since the trait itself is un-Canadian, but dangerously so since much of it rested on an illusion. In the 1970s Canadians knew that, among industrial nations, only this country and Britain were or could be self-sufficient in oil. Simultaneously, because of worldwide inflation, the selling prices of all our commodities, from minerals to wheat, went sky-high. Thus Canadians came to believe that this country was somehow uniquely untouchable and self-generating. They were thus prepared to see their government take risks on their behalf. Then, with the recession of 1981-82, Canadians came back down to earth. Mulroney's greatest challenge may not be to restore the economy, which will either achieve this condition or fail to do so mostly by itself, but to restore some of that lost national self-confidence, grounded this time in reality.

---

* These statistics are from CALURA reports. Since they concern actual ownership rather than control they understate the extent of external influence. As well, foreign-owned assets tend to be more productive: in 1981, while foreigners owned 25 per cent of industrial assets these branch plants accounted for 29 per cent of industry sales and for 35 per cent of industry profits.

The most novel aspect of that pre-recession mood of bounciness was that Canadians were looking over the border without blinking. The very fact that Canadianization and the back-in, and separately FIRA, were so unpopular in Washington made them all the more popular here.

Because of the changing of the presidential guard following Jimmy Carter's defeat in 1980, reaction in Washington to the NEP was slow in coming. When Reagan met Trudeau in Ottawa in March, 1981, he didn't mention the subject. Soon afterward, the volleys came northward.

By far the best account of this period is contained in *Canada and the Reagan Challenge* by Stephen Clarkson.* Drawing on inside information, he recounts the relentless pressure applied on Ottawa by Washington through the fall and early winter of 1981, until a key Canadian-American meeting in Ottawa on December 16, 1981, at which, Clarkson reports, the mandarinate "decided to fight back." He identifies this as "a turning point in the tension." Until then, Clarkson's view of the ebb and flow of Canadian fortunes is conveyed by his subtitles: "Collapse on the Rideau" and "After Appeasement, More Demands."

Beyond any doubt, the American pressure was relentless. Secretary of State Alexander Haig's first note of protest, in March, 1981, was so intemperate that he withdrew it and replaced it with a milder version. Canadian ministers were bombarded by letters from their American opposite numbers, complaining not only about the NEP but about Canada's overall trade and economic policies. Signals were sent north, through officials and through leaks to American reporters, about a "hit list" of retaliatory measures, from opening up the Auto Pact to discriminatory tax measures, to threats to bar Canadians from bidding for oil leases on federal lands.

Lest anyone think they were kidding, the Americans said it all over again in public. Ambassador Bill Brock, the special trade representative, called Canadians "book-burners"; Meyer Rashish, Undersecretary for State, said Canada-U.S. relations were "sliding dangerously close to crisis." Ambassador Paul Robinson informed Canadians that their government's only bigger blunders than in energy were in defence. The *Wall Street Journal* denounced the NEP as

---

* First published in 1982; updated edition in 1985.

"xenophobic nationalism." The *New York Times* ran an editorial page article that ended, "Let them freeze in the dark." Brock dropped Canada from a list of invitees to an international trade conference in Florida (eventually, he was persuaded to invite Trade Minister Ed Lumley). At the U.S.'s insistence, the FIRA legislation, by then six years old, was referred to GATT for a decision on its legality.*

All of which was a lot to cope with. Yet despite Clarkson's "Collapse on the Rideau" thesis, it's remarkable how little ground was given up. Petro-Canada's right to a free 25 per cent share of new discoveries – essentially another form of royalty – was ineptly drafted; the concession to Washington that Petro-Canada would pay for this share was simple justice, but in substance was trivial. The original plan to give Canadian firms a preference on mega-projects was scrapped, but it was maintained in another form through the "industrial benefits" required of oil companies as a condition for PIP grants. Clarkson points out that Ottawa's plans to expand FIRA's authority and the excited talk about "NEP-ing" other industries came to nothing. But the real problem lay elsewhere. "We knew we had to act fast that summer [1980] because our political tails were up and we couldn't cope with too much more after the constitution," recalls Tom Axworthy, then Trudeau's chief aide. "The trouble was, the NEP was ready but the industrial strategy, including the expanded FIRA, wasn't. The chance for it never came again."

Industry Minister Herb Gray had been charged with responsibility for developing an industrial strategy. Notorious for his obsession with details, he spent too long at it. By the time Gray presented his ideas to cabinet, at a special policy session at Lake Louise, Alberta, in September, 1980, all of the available funds had already been allocated. Not that Gray should take all the blame for failing to come up with an industrial strategy. After a dozen years of effort dating back to Industry Minister Jean-Luc Pepin in the early 1970s, no one yet has sighted that probably mythical beast.

A case can be made that Ottawa listened too little to Washington rather than listened too much. A key American concern was that the NEP set a protectionist precedent that, "if unchallenged, would be likely to encourage other countries to adopt similar measures,"

---

* GATT ruled in July, 1983, that FIRA, although legal by international law, could not compel companies to abide by rules, such as local purchasing, that did not also apply to Canadian companies.

99

as Robert Hormats, Assistant Secretary of State, put it in a speech. This concern was a valid one. The Trudeau government was almost blithely indifferent to American public opinion throughout the life of the NEP. Lalonde made only a couple of speeches about it south of the border, and Trudeau none at all.

Far from buckling under American pressure, however, the NEP collapsed under its own dead weight. It was too bureaucratic. It was too divisive politically. In any event, the slide in oil prices made it unsustainable: the tax schedules and the pricing system had to be continually revised, and Dome had to be rescued from its takeover spree. Lalonde and his officials and aides had behaved like gamblers in a casino staking everything on one throw of the dice, and using the taxpayers' money to do this. For their version of the NEP to succeed, oil prices would have had to go on shooting up forever.

By early 1982, with the Great Recession scything down companies and individuals, Canadians had lost interest in any economic ideology but that of personal survival. The Gallup Poll reported that the proportion of Canadians who "would like to see more" foreign investment had jumped to 36 per cent from 21 per cent in 1981.

Pat Carney put the NEP out of its misery on April 25, 1985. The PGRT tax that the West and the oil industry so detested would be phased out by 1989; world prices would determine Canadian prices; the PIP grants would be replaced by conventional tax incentives. Oil companies gained about $2 billion a year, a loss in Ottawa's revenues partly made up by the two cents a litre tax on gasoline imposed in the May, 1985, budget. Above all, the invisible hand of the market replaced the benign but bureaucratic hands of government. The continental free market, moreover, would be the new determinant of behaviour. Imports and exports of oil and gas could move freely across the border – as considerable an advance toward bilateral free trade as the Auto Pact although, curiously, this fundamental policy change attracted little public attention.

Carney in her own way was gambling almost as much as Lalonde. Unless world oil prices stayed level – some experts forecast a drop from $29 U.S. to as low as $20 a barrel – the oil industry would be unable to perform as "an engine of economic growth," in Carney's phrase. Carney was gambling also that the multinationals, who stood to gain about two-thirds of the revenues handed over by Ottawa, had learned their lesson and would pour their profits back into the ground rather than re-routing them into acquisitions or across the border. She was gambling, lastly, that Canadian oil companies had grown up enough to be able to cope with the challenge, both from the multinationals and from a true market system.

All these gambles have a common denominator. No government could have undertaken them unless the NEP had first paved the way by making it possible for Dome and Home and Canterra and Husky and Norcen, let alone Petro-Canada, to grow up. In August, 1985, Gulf Canada joined the "family" by being bought up by the Reichmann brothers of Toronto. This takeover increased to 46 per cent from the previous 40 per cent the share of the total industry in Canada owned by Canadians; almost certainly, Lalonde's original target of a half share by 1990 will be met ahead of schedule.

Now that the NEP is history, it can be seen in perspective. The cross-border sound and fury died quickly away. Indeed, the "refurbishing" of the relationship that Mulroney understandably claims as his in fact began two years before he achieved power. Part of the memory that lingered in Washington about the NEP was a positive one. As Charles Doran of Johns Hopkins University, probably the best informed of all Canada-watchers, remarked in an interview for this book, "There's absolutely no doubt that Trudeau got the message through that Canada is different. Not just a different country but a different kind of country. You'd have to credit the NEP and the rest for part of that. Americans like risk-takers. They saw Trudeau as a risk-taker, so they liked him even if they didn't like his policies." Another Canada-watcher, George Carver of Georgetown University, commented, again in an interview: "Canada is now accepted as a fact of life. Not as a good thing or a bad thing but as a thing we have to live with."

In another perspective, the NEP may not have caused the Canadian oil industry any consequential difficulties at all. Cross-border statistics in the spring of 1985, before the Western Accord, provide the best comparison. In Houston, then, the office vacancy rate was 20 per cent; in Calgary it was 12 per cent. Through 1984, the last full year of the NEP, exploration drilling in Canada reached a new all-time high of 9,600 wells.* Lastly, the NEP may have put the oil companies'

---

* Oil company profits in 1984 doubled to $3.7 billion; this was one-fifth of all the profits earned by all Canadian companies.

101

money to better use than they could have, or at least would have. Because of the NEP, Shell Canada cancelled its Alsands mega-project; had this been proceeded with, it would have seen Shell today trying to sell oil half again as expensive as the world price. South of the border, moreover, all the companies that had used their profits to "diversify" were wishing that they hadn't. Exxon, for instance, has sold off its high-tech companies, and Mobil has put its Montgomery Ward chain up for sale after suffering a $500 million loss.

The most important perspective is contained within the minds of Canadians. Told incessantly that the NEP had been a "disaster," Canadians stubbornly refused to believe it. They refused to believe, it turned out, that the NEP's foundation idea, Canadianization, was the wrong idea. In a Decima Research poll, taken in December, 1984, Canadians gave a 58 per cent to 21 per cent preference to Canadian companies on the test of "providing secure jobs." Conversely, while multinationals had a wide edge in perceived profitability, the likelihood that these profits would leave Canada was the most commonly cited drawback of foreign ownership. Intriguingly and indeed puzzlingly, these negative attitudes toward foreign ownership were in every instance higher than in Decima's last poll on the subject in December, 1982.

Perhaps the highest praise ever given to the NEP came in March, 1985, one month before it was buried, from Armstrong's successor as head of Imperial Oil, Donald McIvor. "Assuming that nationalism is dead is a mistake," McIvor warned his shareholders. "It's got a dent in it, but it isn't dead."

102

Chapter Seven
Diplomatic Distinctions: Foreign Policy, 1957-1968

"Diefenbaker tried, in relations with the U.S., to be a sort of pocket de Gaulle. It didn't work. We have not the will, or the means, to be sufficiently exorbitant."

Charles Ritchie, *Storm Signals*, diary entry for July 1, 1963

It's an anomaly of Canada-U.S. relations that most of the serious disputes between the two countries have been caused not by something that was happening in either country but by something that was happening in, or to, a third country – Cuba, Vietnam, the Soviet Union in respect particularly of arms control matters, and, today, Central America. The various bilateral economic squabbles, from fish to lumber to autos, certainly matter. Yet none of them stick in the memory. Most Canadians, if asked about the Nixon "shock" of 1971, would probably guess it had something to do with Watergate rather than with an import surcharge; many could probably reply correctly that the "Bomarc affair" of a decade earlier, 1962, had something to do with the Americans getting mad at Diefenbaker.

Foreign policy disputes are not merely sharper and nastier than economic disputes, but they usually unfold by themselves independent of any trade and financial disagreements on the go at the same time. Politicians and officials at Ottawa constantly fear, indeed are almost mesmerized by "linkage"; angering Washington in matters diplomatic, goes the rubric, will bring retribution on fish or lumber or autos. Evidence of this ever happening is remarkably scant. Probably the most sulphurous meeting ever between leaders was the dressing down President Lyndon Johnson gave Lester Pearson following his April, 1965, speech suggesting a halt to the bombing of North Vietnam; yet Johnson never raised the subject of retaliation, even indirectly. Conversely, the May, 1963, meeting between Pearson and President

Kennedy at Hyannisport was the most cordial of all post-war encounters until that between Mulroney and President Ronald Reagan; yet just three months later, Washington sideswiped Canada, while exempting Israel and Mexico, with a punitive tax on foreign borrowings on Wall Street.

Trudeau's last term, 1980-84, does provide a partial exception. Trudeau angered Washington both coming and going by the National Energy Policy and his peace initiative. Threats of retaliation – abrogation of the Auto Pact – were made, and Canada was poor-mouthed among American businessmen. Yet during this period, Canadian exports to the U.S. almost doubled, the fastest rate of increase in two decades; in 1984, Canada enjoyed an unprecedented $20 billion surplus in trade with the U.S.

All canny politicians operate on the rule that in politics there are no permanent friendships or enmities, only temporary alliances of coincidentally common interests. This rule applies equally in international politics. At the same time as Canada and the U.S. may have opposing interests in, say, arms control, they may have common interests in mutual trade liberalization. Anger stirred up in Washington on the one subject won't necessarily affect the calculation made there of U.S. self-interests in the other. In part, this is because Washington functions like a multiple-armed Hindu god with each member of the body politic waving disconnectedly. Mostly, it's because *real politik* is the rule there: trade liberalization remains a desirable end in itself even if Canadian squeamishness on defence matters, say, is an irritant.

Canadian politicians either do not believe this or guess it to be true but would just as soon not test out the theory. The possibility of economic retaliation is cited constantly as a justification for diplomatic inaction. The explanation for this willing suspension of belief lies in Ottawa, not in Washington. The fear, self-invented or real, of U.S. economic retaliation provides Canadian governments with an excuse to avoid diplomatic initiatives of which the real risk is failure and international embarrassment rather than fewer exports of fish or lumber or automobiles. Perhaps the best example is Canada's repeated refusal to join the Organization of American States (OAS) on the grounds that it would involve Canada in confrontations with the U.S.; instead, the reason for looking the other way is almost certainly a disinclination to get involved in such obdurate hemispheric problems as internal revolutions and continent-wide poverty.

Trade and economic disputes are the daily currency of cross-border relations. They amount to far more than small change. Yet they have been curiously ephemeral. Canada secured an exemption from the 1963 tax on foreign borrowings within a week; Nixon lifted the "shock" of his 10 per cent surcharge on imports four months after he had imposed it. The NEP and FIRA sent thunder rolling across the border throughout 1981, yet by mid-1982 the two foreign ministers, MacEachen and Shultz, were consorting comfortably.

Economic disputes are ephemeral because it is in the interests of the U.S. that they be so, while Canada's interests are obvious. The cross-border dependency is mutual: if three-quarters of Canadian exports go south, one-fifth of American exports come north. Most Americans have no idea of this, indeed have little idea of Canada at all.* Official Washington, however, is fully aware that while the U.S. could blow the Canadian economy apart by retaliatory measures – cancellation of the Auto Pact being a favoured threat, employed by both Nixon and Reagan – it would at the same time shoot itself in the foot. U.S. multinationals function here as "hostages": harsh measures imposed on Canada by Washington would provoke harsh measures by Ottawa against them. Similarly, arbitrary trade actions against Canadian fish or lumber would hurt American consumers of those products.

None of this is to say that Canadian worries about U.S. trade actions are misplaced. Whenever the U.S. figures out what its economic interests are, it has the power to enforce them. Nor is "linkage" imaginary. Washington officials talk to each other and develop a common mindset, a negative one toward Canada in general during 1980-84, a positive one since Mulroney's accession to power. But the principal inhibitor of Canadian diplomatic enterprise is lack of political will in Ottawa.

Diplomatic practicalities and economic exigencies aside, foreign policy amounts to the external expression of the inner aspirations of a people. It's the way a society tells the rest of the world about itself. The foreign policies of Canada and the United States are different

---

* A survey done by Market Opinion Research in December, 1984, for the Canadian embassy in Washington revealed that most Americans thought, as did Nixon back in 1971, that Japan was the U.S.'s largest trading partner. More disconcerting, most Americans thought that Canada provided a market for U.S. goods of about the same size as major European countries.

because the two societies are different, so different, indeed, that the two countries perform abroad as rivals. Canadians are generally reluctant to admit this; Americans are almost wholly unaware of it. There are, of course, significant similarities between the two countries. Canada and the U.S. are both Western, democratic, affluent, and above all, both are North American nations.

The differences, though, are profound. Canada is a "peaceable kingdom"; the U.S. is a messianic republic. Canadians believe in compromise, and search constantly, incessantly, for the common denominator between opposed interests; Americans believe in competition, and in winning. The overarching difference in foreign policy behaviour is that the U.S. is a superpower, with worldwide responsibilities and duties and temptations. Canada is a middle power, militarily minuscule, and able to be friendly to everyone because we bear no responsibility for anyone. Americans are involved in the world whether they want to be or not; Canadians are involved by choice.* The abiding temptation to Canadians, the direct opposite of that of Americans today, is isolationism. The temptation to allow others, Americans in particular, to man the pumps on behalf of the free world, and of Canada, is never that far below the surface of the Canadian consciousness.

The poet Douglas Le Pan has described Canada as "a country without a mythology." There are no decapitated kings or glorious civil wars or revolutions in our history. We don't even celebrate the birthday of our Founding Father, John A. Macdonald; as a perverse substitute, we celebrate the birthday of a monarch who never came here, Queen Victoria.

But Le Pan was too pessimistic. Lester Pearson fabricated a mythology for Canada. His bow tie, his self-deprecating wit, and his Nobel Peace Prize are all embedded in our collective psyche.

As well as being skilled, adroit, and charming, Pearson was lucky. During the "Golden Years" of Pearsonian diplomacy, from the end

---

* Charles Doran of Johns Hopkins University makes the interesting observation: "Canadians would make better imperialists than Americans. We're too guilt-ridden. Our constitution and our political culture are all about resisting power. Your whole governing system is based on a frank recognition of power as a fact of life."

106

of the Second World War up to around 1957, Europe was devastated while Asia and Africa had yet to be de-colonized. Later, pushing our luck, we pursued what has been called "pseudo-Pearsonianism," arrogating to ourselves the role of international honest broker and sounding, as we lectured others about virtue, more and more like a global nanny. It was to end this overreach that Trudeau in 1970 proclaimed that our foreign policy would henceforth be based on "national self-interest." The new mood was set by the tart observation in Trudeau's foreign policy paper: "to be liked and to be regarded as good fellows are not ends in themselves; they are a reflection of but not a substitute for policy."

But the Pearsonian myth got to Trudeau, one of the rare occasions when the felt rather than the expressly articulated wishes of the Canadian people forced him to change his policies. By the mid-1970s, he was expounding the doctrine of international "sharing"; later he held up his end of the North-South dialogue; later still he pursued peace across three continents.

Mulroney, a politician more attentive by far than Trudeau, picked up the signals on his antenna much more quickly. Soon after taking office, he made the most widely applauded appointment of his term so far by naming former Ontario New Democrat leader Stephen Lewis as ambassador to the United Nations, and in tandem named a peace activist, former Conservative MP Douglas Roche, as ambassador for disarmament.

The Pearsonian myth is durable because he summed up in his persona, or was seen to sum up, all the attributes that Canadians like to present to the world: helpful, reasonable, wishing to dominate no one economically let alone militarily, and performing, if not as an honest broker, then as a source of disinterested, offstage advice to those looking for it. It's not a role out of which history, which is about decapitated kings and glorious revolutions, is made. But it's an honourable role. It's the role that comes naturally to Canadians and always will. And it's a quite different role from the one the U.S. plays as a superpower, and always will play as the particular kind of society it is.

As long as the Cold War remained hot, these differences remained inconsequential. We were allies in a lethal contest and thought the same way about the enemy. NATO indeed was a Canadian initiative, one of those our diplomats were proudest of.* In *Indochina, Roots of Complicity,* James Eayrs recounts that it was "regular procedure" for Canadian members of the International Control Commission of the 1950s to send copies of their reports about conditions in North Vietnam to American officials, at times before sending them to Ottawa.

During this period, Canadian diplomacy was directed at two objectives, both of which were achieved: to extend the rule of law by creating international institutions such as the United Nations, GATT, the World Bank, and to use these institutions, as Pearson described it in his memoirs, "to escape the danger of a too-exclusively continental relationship [with the U.S.], without forfeiting the political and economic advantages of that inevitable and vitally important relationship." This diplomatic strategy neatly combined idealism and self-interest: by doing good unto others, Canada did good unto itself. NATO was the best example. It got the U.S. involved, permanently, in Europe, in contrast to what had happened after the First World War, but it also provided European allies for Canadians to march beside. With uncommon prescience, Pearson wanted some Norwegian troops to be stationed in the Arctic so that Canadians would not be alone up there and invisible among all the Americans. Washington vetoed the proposal: Canada's North was considered its "home" territory.

As the 1950s progressed, as the Russians failed to roll west and as Western Europe recovered, Canadian scepticism about the Cold War grew, fed by doubts about the "brinkmanship" of Secretary of State John Foster Dulles and by the coarse fanaticism of Senator Joseph McCarthy. Eisenhower's parting comment about the potential danger of the "military-industrial complex" suggested other motives for the continued international rivalry. Ironically, though, it was the most popular, in Canada, of all post-war presidents who drove a wedge between the foreign policies of the two nations. By his inaugural challenge, "We will bear any burden, pay any price," John F. Kennedy revived a Cold War that seemed to be settling down into competitive co-existence. Canadians loved Kennedy, but they didn't care at all for the new Cold War.

---

* The intellectual author of the idea for NATO was in fact the U.S. historian Bartlett Brebner, who advanced it in his book, *The North Atlantic Triangle* (New Haven, 1945).

Pearson had foreseen that this would happen. "The days of easy relations are over," he had said as far back as April, 1951, in a speech that raised eyebrows in Washington. "Our preoccupation is no longer whether the U.S. will discharge her international responsibilities but how she will do it, and whether the rest of us will be involved."

Two harbingers of future bilateral difficulties had by now taken place. On the outbreak of the Korean War in 1950, the U.S. invited Canada to send troops, taking for granted, much as Britain used to do, that they would be sent. Both St. Laurent, then Prime Minister, and Pearson were sceptical about the commitment. Only volunteers were sent, some 22,000 Canadians in all, a contribution that is still remembered gratefully in South Korea. Also at this time, Canada had been on the point of recognizing the new People's Republic of China, as Britain and Sweden had done. Because of Korea, the moment passed and did not reoccur for another two decades, in October, 1970, when Trudeau seized the moment to do it, one year before Nixon's historic visit to Peking. (The U.S. raised no objections to the Canadian initiative, limiting its expressions of concern to questions about future diplomatic relations between Canada and Taiwan, which in fact were ended abruptly.)*

Once in power, Kennedy quickly showed what he'd meant by the phrase "pay any price," first in the Bay of Pigs in Cuba, then in the dispatch of "advisers" to South Vietnam. Canadian concern about this assertive militarism was muted, though. The cross-border difficulties, which before long emerged, happened mostly because of personality rather than policy.

In *The Presidents and the Prime Ministers*, Lawrence Martin describes vividly the misunderstandings and then the open personal warfare between Kennedy – young, glamorous, witty, but also cocky and contemptuous – and Diefenbaker – old, cranky, jealous, but also in his confused way trying to express an international perspective more nuanced than the simple, winner-take-all view of the courtiers manning the ramparts of Camelot. The best expression of that perspective was provided by a 1961 speech given at Geneva not long after the

---

* Very adroitly, Trudeau pledged to recognize China during the 1968 election campaign. Thereafter, this became a "sacred trust" that he had no choice but to fulfil.

Bay of Pigs fiasco by External Affairs Minister Howard Green: "The more Cuba is pushed, the greater will become her reliance on Soviet Russia." Green, an innocent, a pacifist, and an idealist, outraged Kennedy's men; he did so again later by refusing to break off diplomatic relations with Havana despite Washington's pressure.

A couple of additional details can be added to Martin's account. To help defeat Diefenbaker in the 1963 election, Kennedy not only loaned the Liberals his personal pollster, Lou Harris, but phoned Pearson himself several times with campaign advice – an intervention that, had it been known at the time, would have won the election for Diefenbaker. In his recently published memoir *History on the Run*, Knowlton Nash, then a reporter in Washington, recounts that Robert Kennedy once told him: "There were only two people my brother really hated, Sukharno [the Indonesian dictator] and Diefenbaker."

The actual 1962-63 confrontation between Kennedy and Diefenbaker over whether to arm Canadian planes and missiles with nuclear warheads prefigured the issue of Star Wars in the 1980s in a way that is striking. The underlying cause was a radical change in armaments technology. Unable to match the size of the conscript armies of the Soviet block, NATO in the mid-1950s found the solution in the new technology of miniaturized nuclear warheads: installed on "battlefield" nuclear missiles in Europe, these devices, so went the theory, could halt a conventional Soviet attack without precipitating an all-out, intercontinental nuclear exchange. Best of all, nuclear warheads were a lot cheaper than tank and infantry divisions.

To do their bit, Canadian forces in Europe acquired Honest John ground missiles and Starfighter fighter-bombers, both designed to use nuclear warheads.* But Diefenbaker, influenced by Green and by an emerging peace movement led by the Voice of Women, refused to install the nuclear warheads. To keep them from toppling over, the warheads of the Honest Johns had to be stuffed with sand. Back home, the Diefenbaker government acquired two batteries of Bomarc missiles and bought Voodoo interceptor planes, both of which were again designed to use nuclear warheads. These also remained virginal.

In almost everything Diefenbaker did, farce was inseparable from tragedy. In this instance, tragedy probably played the larger part.

---

* The Starfighters were in fact perfectly capable of using conventional warheads. To force Diefenbaker's hand, the Canadian Air Force "designed out" the planes' conventional capability, and, as J.L. Granatstein recounts in *Man of Influence* (Deneau, 1981), refused to answer Diefenbaker's questions on the subject.

Diefenbaker indeed offered Washington a reasonable compromise: nuclear weapons for our forces in Europe, justified as part of the general NATO strategy, but conventional ones at home where our own writ was sovereign. In their cocky way, Kennedy's people refused the offer. Diefenbaker, further, was dead right to describe the Bomarcs, nuclearized or not, as useless; Defence Secretary Robert McNamara later confirmed this in testimony before a Congressional Committee, declaring that the only military value of the Bomarcs was that the Russians might waste some of their missiles on them.

The real figure of tragedy in the affair was not Diefenbaker, except to the extent that he went down to defeat, but Pearson. In order to force an election he was bound to win, he broke faith with his own past and committed the Liberals to accepting nuclear warheads; Trudeau, who was then almost on the point of becoming a Liberal, denounced Pearson as a "de-frocked priest of peace." Collectively, Canadians performed like the chorus in a tragedy: so dazzled, nationalist or not, by Kennedy's glamour and so embarrassed by Diefenbaker that they wouldn't listen to what he was trying to say. So Diefenbaker went down, and the nuclear warheads went in, for another two decades until July, 1984, when the last one in Canada was phased out just after Trudeau himself stepped off the stage.

One last piece of background is needed. In May, 1958, after delaying for a year, Diefenbaker formally signed the NORAD agreement that, just as Pearson had feared, linked Canadian and U.S. air defence systems indissolubly. The rub here was that Pearson himself had negotiated the agreement, leaving it behind as part of the detritus of the St. Laurent government after its defeat in June, 1957. The next year, though, it was Diefenbaker himself who negotiated and signed the Defence Production Sharing Agreement, which has integrated the defence industries of the two countries by ensuring that each country buys roughly the same amount of defence material from the other.* This agreement was the reason why Canada was so successful a profiteer during the Vietnam War and the reason why

---

* Many of the most successful Canadian bidders for U.S. defence contracts are U.S. branch plants, like Litton Industries, to whom their parents steer contracts, such as those for the guidance systems for cruise missiles. With these exceptions, most of the contracts awarded to Canadian companies tend to be low-tech ones, as, for instance, the berets of the famous Green Berets. To the end of 1984, Canada was in deficit on cross-border contracts by $1.6 billion, largely because of recent heavy equipment orders by the Canadian Armed Forces.

the Pearson and Trudeau governments were so reticent about criticizing U.S. policy in Vietnam. In the beginning, however, Diefenbaker's problem was that the NORAD agreement left him with almost no options: if the U.S. decreed that nuclear weapons were needed to defend North America, then Canada either agreed or broke the agreement.

On October 22, 1962, President Kennedy went on television to accuse the Russians of having committed a "reckless and provocative threat to world peace" by secretly installing medium-range missiles in Cuba. He announced a naval blockade of the island; for a week the world held its breath as Soviet freighters, loaded with more missiles, neared the line of American destroyers. Instantly, all the Western leaders, even de Gaulle, proclaimed their support. All but Diefenbaker. In the Commons, following the advice of his top foreign policy official, Norman Robertson,* he sounded sceptical: "The only way the world can secure the facts would be through an independent inspection." He declined to put Canadian forces on full alert, although they went on it anyway on orders from NORAD headquarters in Colorado. Not until three days had passed did Diefenbaker join the parade: "We intend to support the U.S. and our allies in this situation," he said.

Canadians never forgave Diefenbaker for this shameful indecision during the moment of the supreme trial of the Western alliance. Although the details of the personal difficulties between the two leaders weren't then fully known, it was obvious that Diefenbaker had been motivated more by personal jealousy and paranoia than by any logical analysis of American and Soviet military intentions. The immediate consequence, after Khrushchev backed down and removed the missiles, was to make Kennedy look like a shining prince and Diefenbaker look like a clown. The succeeding consequence was to rob Diefenbaker of any credibility when he tried to argue, through the winter of 1962-63, that nuclear warheads were not needed in Canada, as opposed to overseas with the Canadian forces in Europe. (A third consequence was to demonstrate just how ruthless an American government can be when it makes up its mind to be. From the Cuban missile crisis onwards, Kennedy made the defeat

---

* See Granatstein, A Man of Influence.

of the Diefenbaker government a prime objective of his foreign policy. In a phrase not then in use, he "de-stabilized it.")

At a private session during a NATO ministerial meeting in Paris on December 14, 1962, the Kennedy government rejected Diefenbaker's compromise offer – nuclear warheads for the Canadian forces in Europe and those for Canadian forces at home to be stored in the U.S. and flown north in a crisis. The American team declared that this was technically impossible; in fact, to have flown the warheads north to Canadian bases would have taken just one hour. On January 3, 1963, U.S. General Lauris Norstad, the retiring NATO commander, passed through Ottawa; in answer to reporters' questions, he declared that Canada was committed to nuclear weapons and without them would be letting down its allies. Pearson, as if on cue, reversed Liberal Party policy.

On January 25, Diefenbaker delivered a speech in the Commons that attempted to concoct common ground between his "hawks," such as Defence Minister Douglas Harkness, and his "doves," such as Howard Green. Instead, because it was so confused, this effort opened up a black hole into which, first, several ministers including Harkness jumped, and into which his government soon afterwards fell. To make certain it went down, the State Department, on January 30, issued a statement that is probably without parallel in Canada-U.S. relations: this statement in effect called Diefenbaker a liar, declaring, as if the direct opposite hadn't happened at the Paris meeting a month earlier, "the Canadian Government has not as yet proposed any arrangement sufficiently practical to contribute effectively to North American defence." In a later memorandum to then President Lyndon Johnson, McGeorge Bundy, National Security Adviser to him and to Kennedy, gloated: "I knocked over the Diefenbaker government with one incautious press release."

As he went down, Diefenbaker tried to drag the temple walls down with him. He raged against the Americans and turned to his own advantage a *Newsweek* cover story on him, masterminded by its editor Ben Bradlee at Kennedy's instigation, that lampooned him viciously, comparing his features to "those of a grotesque gargoyle." He let it out that Kennedy, during their first meeting in Ottawa in May, 1961, had left behind him on the table a memorandum advising him to "push" Canada into joining the OAS, and in the margin of which he had scribbled, in a reference to Diefenbaker, "S.O.B."* It made no difference: Canadians didn't believe anything Diefenbaker said, and they loved Kennedy, the last President they would love.

Canadian intellectuals, entranced by Kennedy, were delighted to see Diefenbaker gone. There was, however, one dissenter. Charles Ritchie, then ambassador in Washington, still found time to record entries in his diaries that were published in *Storm Signals*. "I admire them within limits," he wrote of the New Frontiersmen, "but mistrust the application of the business computer to international affairs, particularly when it is allied to power and to love of power." At the height of the crisis, Diefenbaker ostentatiously ordered Ritchie back to Ottawa as a signal of his displeasure. Slyly, Ritchie argued, "No one will miss me," and came back reluctantly. But in his diary, Ritchie recorded his real feelings: "Deep down, I feel satisfaction at hearing the Canadian government finally lash out at the omniscience and unconscious arrogance of Washington."

At Hyannisport in May, 1963, Kennedy and Pearson "refurbished" the relationship. That July 1, Ritchie wrote, for his own eyes, an elegant elegy for his country: "Can our country survive as an independent, united sovereign state – a reality, not a fiction? Or must we fall into the embrace of the U.S.A.? We struggle in the net, make fumbling attempts to find our way out, but all the time getting deeper in, in terms both of our defence and of the control of our economy. Diefenbaker tried, in relations with the U.S., to be a sort of pocket de Gaulle. It didn't work. We have not the will, or the means, to be sufficiently exorbitant."

In one of their exchanges during the Hyannisport meeting, Kennedy asked Pearson what he should do about Vietnam. Pearson replied that he thought the Americans should get out. Kennedy responded: "Any fool knows that. The question is how." Pearson loved recounting this anecdote. Like so many of his self-deprecating stories it didn't deprecate him at all. Instead, it showed him discussing the highest affairs of state with the American leader in complete candour and

---

* As Martin reports, Diefenbaker was quite correct about the "push" part, except that it was routine for aides to give a president such advice about national self-interest in advance of a meeting with another leader. The "S.O.B." part was pure fantasy, though, one of the many fantasies with which Diefenbaker's mind was so richly endowed.

with a mutual understanding of political realities.

In his memoirs, Pearson spoke proudly of his five years in power: "I am happy to say there was no breach in our relations with the U.S. during my period as Prime Minister." This analysis doesn't seem to accord with the facts, for during this period Walter Gordon was enacting nationalist economic measures, and Washington, whether by coincidence or in counterpoint, failed to exempt Canada from its 1963 tax on foreign borrowings. In fact, in 1965, in an attempt to restore amicability, two ex-ambassadors, the American Livingston Merchant and the Canadian Arnold Heeney, were appointed to study the problem. Their recommendation, "Wherever possible, divergent views of the two governments should be expressed, and if possible resolved, in private," was promptly dumped on by the nationalists and ignored by everyone else.

Yet Pearson was near enough to being right. Canadian commentators, such as Lawrence Martin, have recorded almost lovingly Lyndon Johnson's angry-bull response to Pearson's speech at Temple University in Philadelphia on April 2, 1965. There, Pearson had said with painful circumspection that "There does appear to be at least a possibility that a suspension of such air strikes against North Vietnam, at the right time, might provide the Hanoi authorities with an opportunity, if they wish to take it, to inject some flexibility into their policy." Having been invited to lunch at Camp David the next day, transported by a helicopter made instantly available, Pearson was subjected to being grabbed by the lapels, told "You pissed on my rug," and compelled to sit through an evening-long harangue that continued the next morning. All those details have passed into Canadian folklore, enshrining the memory of Johnsonian coarseness and of Pearsonian bravery.

There is, however, a good deal of sentimentality in this folklore. Pearson himself never held Johnson's behaviour against him, indeed sympathized with him for the fearful pressure he was under. Johnson was outraged not by what Pearson said – domestic critics, such as Senator Fulbright, had been far bolder – but that he, whom Johnson so respected as an international statesman, should have said it in Johnson's backyard. In his memoirs, Pearson commented coolly: "We would have been pretty angry, I suppose, if any member of the American government had spoken, in Canada, on Canadian government policy as I had spoken in Philadelphia."

The important aspect about Pearson's speech in Philadelphia – he

115

was receiving a World Peace Award and so had to say something about the subject – was that it was the *only* time he spoke out publicly against the Vietnam War; even then, following their Camp David meeting, he sent Johnson a long and almost deferential letter. The preponderant evidence is that Pearson's real intended audience at Philadelphia was the Canadian voters, whom he hoped to influence in advance of an upcoming election and who were becoming increasingly disgusted both by the war and by their government for saying nothing about it.

The comparison Pearson makes in his memoirs between Johnson's reaction to his speech and that of Canadians to comments by a U.S. president "in Canada, on government policy" amount to a rationalization of his own silence. The comparison is inapt. Almost all U.S. foreign policy deeply affects its allies; the reverse is seldom the case. Thus America's allies have, or ought to have, a stake in its foreign policy decisions. Washington seldom concedes this, of course, and never accepted the claim Trudeau made during his peace initiative that Canada, although not at the U.S.-Russia armaments bargaining table, nevertheless had a right to express its opinions and to have these listened to seriously.*

Since the Vietnam War was so horrendous, and since Canadians increasingly viewed it as such, Pearson's silence provokes the double question of why he kept silent and why Canadians allowed him to do so.

One explanation is to be found in the reaction to the Philadelphia speech by Pearson's External Affairs Minister, Paul Martin, who read a draft of it in advance. Martin threatened to resign. His reasoning was that the speech would end Canada's influence in Washington, and as a result Canada would lose all influence in Hanoi since the North Vietnamese were only interested in talking to Canadians if they knew that the Americans listened to us. The problem with this reasoning – shared by the Mulroney government today – is, of course, its circularity: if silence is the necessary price of influence in

---

* Australia provides an example of just how difficult it is for a satellite to be heard in an imperial capital. Australia sent troops to Vietnam, and indeed kept them on after the Americans had gone. Its prime minister, Harold Holt, proclaimed on a trip to Washington, "All the way with LBJ," yet earned himself no say in the American councils of war. Canada and Australia and others were similarly overlooked by the U.S. and Britain during the Second World War; all satellites hover in low orbits.

Washington, then the price of silence is to be taken for granted and so to have no influence.

As for the silence of Canadians, Pearson's personality explains a good deal of it. He was an international giant, the winner of the Nobel Peace Prize. To Canadians, it was just not imaginable Pearson would not be pursuing peace, and if he was not doing it publicly then he must surely be doing it in private. During Pearson's term, Canadians' attitudes did change in one important respect. Whenever they looked south, Canadians more and more often beheld what they saw in horror: Vietnam; the assassinations of the Kennedys, first Jack and then Bobby, and of Martin Luther King; the revelations about the CIA. Thus, when Trudeau passed the greater part of his term acting as if the United States didn't exist, Canadians were more than prepared to maintain the pretence themselves.

Chapter Eight
Diplomatic Distinctions:
Foreign Policy, 1968–1984

"My God, he's going to Peking."

Comment by Canadian Press reporter Ed Stewart after reading press release issued by the Prime Minister's staff in New Delhi, November 25, 1983

Through most of Trudeau's term, Canadians turned their attention away not only from the U.S. but from the entire world. We spent the better part of a decade and a half staring fixedly at our own navels. A span of seventeen years passed between debates on foreign policy in the Commons. Defence came close to being treated as a national joke. Newspapers closed their foreign bureaus, Canadian Press scaling down its London office from ten reporters to one. The membership of such organizations as the Canadian Institute for International Affairs shrank, and aged. Universities replaced programs of international studies with Canadian studies programs. The topics that Canadians cared about during this long span of time were: What does Quebec really want? Why are the Albertans so upset? And, more positively: How might surplus government revenues best be reapplied to extending social services, to improving educational facilities, to developing the arts?

Trudeau's contributions to foreign policy in general, and to Canada-U.S. relations in particular, can only be judged within this context. If he did little, Canadians asked little of him, except to do us proud in foreign capitals, even though there were complaints each time he left the country.

During the early part of this period, Canada's foreign policy was distorted by circumstances over which neither Trudeau nor Canadians had control. For the first time since the U.S. stopped glancing acquisitively northward in the nineteenth century, Canada had a genuine international foe. In 1967, Charles de Gaulle came to Montreal and pronounced benediction upon Quebec separatists: *Vive le Québec libre!* So long as de Gaulle remained in power, France did all it could – diplomatic recognition; money; secretive emissaries – to promote, if not the breakup of Canada, then the liberation of Quebec. Not until Quebec's international aspirations had been contained could Trudeau really devote himself to foreign affairs in the conventional sense.

This aside, Trudeau's contributions to foreign policy were mostly erratic, if not dilettantish, particularly regarding U.S. affairs. He waited almost until the end of his years in office to fulfil his potential by his peace initiative of 1983-84. Whatever this effort may have done for peace, it did a great deal for Canadians. It made them feel proud. It made them turn their gaze from their navels to the wide world outside. One of the many puzzles about the volatility of public opinion today is that the instant a leader pointed Canadians back toward internationalism, they followed and then kept on going in the same direction.

Trudeau started out, in his 1970 Foreign Policy Review, by proclaiming the new doctrine of "national self-interest." Trade mattered more than waving the flag. Our diplomats were told to earn their national-unity keep by becoming bilingual and by doing battle with France over Quebec's attempts to secure a separate international identity.

Then the Pearsonian myth got to him. Trudeau, inclined in that direction anyway from his years as an international scholar-gypsy, took up the cause of the Third World. Almost alone among Western leaders, he believed in the North-South dialogue. He talked eloquently about "international sharing" and increased foreign aid past the $1 billion mark, all the while taking good care to maintain rigidly protectionist measures on clothing, textiles, footwear. Later, in 1978, he delivered a brilliant speech at the United Nations advocating a "strategy of suffocation" that would slow the arms race by halting research into new arms systems. Eventually, he would tour the world in pursuit of peace.

In one respect, Trudeau re-oriented Canada's international posture in a dramatic way that Canadians didn't fully realize until he took that posture to its logical conclusion by criticizing both superpowers during his peace initiative. Pearson's 1964 White Paper on Defence had referred to Canada and the U.S. as "partners" in the defence of the continent. Trudeau's 1970 version, while just as barren of fresh policies, referred only to "co-operation" in defence, subtly implying a certain drawing apart. More explicitly, Trudeau's 1970 foreign policy paper declared: "World powers can no longer be grouped in clearly identifiable, ideological camps." It was no longer, therefore, "The U.S., right or wrong," nor, conversely, Russia as invariably wrong just because it was Russia.

This even-handedness was in a sense less daring than it seemed. It provided Trudeau with an intellectual excuse not to get involved, an attitude he had acquired while coming of age in the immediate post-war years when the prevailing internationalist ideas had been equally those of the rule of international law and, contradictorily, the doctrine of "spheres of influence." Trudeau disappointed many Canadians by his lack of emotion about the Soviet invasion of Czechoslovakia and, years later, the military takeover and outlawing of Solidarity in Poland in the early 1980s; he angered others by being just as cool about what the U.S. was doing in its backyard of Central America and in its rented property in Vietnam. This quasi-isolationism was reflected in Trudeau's 1969 cutback of Canada's contribution to NATO by half and his decision to stand back from further peacekeeping ventures.

Perhaps the most daring expression of Trudeau's even-handedness, and one that demonstrated also the prevailing Canadian sentiment, was Canada's open-door policy toward American draft dodgers and deserters. Many entered illegally; few could claim to be refugees. Some 50,000 came, and none were turned back, in a kind of contemporary equivalent to the nineteenth-century Underground Railway for blacks. About half eventually returned home under the various amnesties, but they and those who remained contributed significantly to a Canadian consciousness of a southern society in decay.

As a subject for foreign policy as such, the U.S. interested Trudeau little during this early period. The "mouse and elephant" quote that he whipped off after his first visit to the White House has passed into the Canadian political vocabulary. In fact, an inventive reporter added the diminutive animal to Trudeau's actual words, which were, "Living next door to you is in some ways like sleeping with an elephant. No matter how friendly and even-tempered the beast, one is affected by every twitch and grunt." That said, he dropped the subject. Then the elephant twitched. In reply, out popped the Third Option

On August 15, 1971, Nixon had announced, without warning, a 10 per cent surcharge on all imports to head off an exchange crisis by keeping dollars at home. The reaction in Ottawa was panic: calculations of the job losses ranged up to 100,000. Trudeau remained not only calm but comatose. He was vacationing in the Adriatic with his new bride. When External Affairs Minister Mitchell Sharp reached him, he declined to fly back. Instead, ministers and officials flew to Washington to argue for an exemption. Demonstrating that he was unaware why one might be necessary, Nixon referred to Japan as "our largest trading partner." The meetings were angry and tense – although to spoil a good story, Deputy Finance Minister Simon Reisman did not stub out his cigar on Treasury Secretary John Connally's desk, a piece of furniture that once had belonged to Alexander Hamilton, but only spilled some ash on it accidentally.*

By the end of December, worldwide pressure had persuaded Nixon to scrap the surcharge on imports, although he had achieved what was probably his real objective of winning international agreement to devalue the dollar. Even before this, estimates of Canadian job losses had dwindled to below 40,000. Trudeau during this period remained out of touch with events, though he did go to Washington early in December and emerged to baffle reporters with the "fantastic" news that Nixon had told him that Canada was after all the U.S.'s largest trading partner and that he was aware of the damage U.S. actions could do.

Even so, the shock of what came to be known as the "Nixon shock" profoundly affected attitudes in Ottawa. It had "brutally broken the custom of according special treatment to Canada," wrote Trudeau's personal foreign affairs adviser, Ivan Head, in the January, 1972, issue of *Foreign Affairs*. The question now became, if indeed the "special relationship" no longer existed, what could replace it?

In fact, neither Trudeau nor any of his ministers went as far as pronouncing that the "special relationship" had passed into history.

---

* Reisman might well have stubbed his cigar on Connally's desk had he known the full story. Connally, a bluff bully, in his original package of measures for dealing with the foreign exchange crisis had included unilateral abrogation of the Auto Pact, and this was cited in the official press release. Only arguments made by the State Department that to scrap an international agreement would be to put the U.S. into international contempt convinced a very reluctant Connally.

Its epitaph was pronounced instead by Nixon in what was certainly, no matter what else can be said about him, the most insightful comment about Canada-U.S. relations made by any president. Speaking to a joint session of Parliament in Ottawa in April, 1972, Nixon remarked:

> Through the years our speeches on such occasions have often centred on the decades of unbroken friendship we have enjoyed and our four thousand miles of undefended frontier. In focusing on our peaceful borders and our peaceful history, they have tended to gloss over the fact that there are real problems between us. They have tended to create the false impression that our two countries are essentially alike. It is time for Canadians and Americans to move beyond the sentimental rhetoric of the past. It is time for us to recognize that we have very separate identities; that we have significant differences; and that nobody's interests are furthered when these realities are obscured.

No easier a leader to scan than Trudeau himself, crooked and coarse – "that asshole Trudeau," he intoned into one of his Oval Office microphones* – Nixon in international affairs was one of the most innovative of all post-war presidents.

One of the many oddities of Trudeau's 1970 Foreign Policy Review was that it dealt with Canada-U.S. relations by not mentioning them. A separate report was promised "because of the importance of the subject." It never appeared. Instead, in the fall of 1972, in the magazine *International Perspectives*, published by External Affairs, there appeared a long article signed by its minister, Mitchell Sharp.

The inspiration for Sharp's article had come one year earlier. The specific idea for a Third Option was tossed out by a middle-rank External Affairs official, David Lee, at a meeting of officials just one week after Nixon's 1971 "shock." Eventually, it was fleshed out into a departmental document that was submitted to cabinet. There it halted. Most ministers supported the idea of a Third Option, but they recognized that no plan to decrease Canada's economic dependence on the U.S. made any sense without a coherent national industrial

---

* While they were never in the least easy with each other, Nixon and Trudeau maintained a wary mutual respect. Trudeau's relations with Nixon's successors, both Gerald Ford and Jimmy Carter, were cordial and close. He and Reagan, however, might as well have been beings from different planets.

strategy to back it up. Since there was no industrial strategy in sight, the cabinet concluded that the document could not be issued under the government's imprimatur. Instead, Sharp published it under his own name, by way of *International Perspectives*. As a member of a "rational government," Sharp solemnly identified in his article three alternative options. Two of these were made of straw: first, "To maintain more or less our present relationship with the U.S."; second, "[To] move deliberately toward a closer relationship with the U.S."

The real option was the Third Option: to develop new economic and political ties with other countries as part of "a comprehensive, long-term strategy to develop and strengthen the Canadian economy and other aspects of Canadian life, and in the process to reduce the present Canadian vulnerability [to the U.S.]." In the rather laboured analysis that led up to this predestined conclusion, there was one observation as pertinent today as in 1972. Among its criticisms of the Second Option of closer relations with the U.S., the article noted: "The experience of free trade areas suggests that ... they tend towards full customs and economic union as a matter of course.... A Canada-U.S. free trade area would be almost certain to do likewise."

Before implementing the Third Option, Trudeau first had to regain a majority. Having achieved this in 1974, he set off for Europe the following winter in pursuit of what was described as a "contractual link" with the European Economic Community. No one in Brussels, after signing this "contract," could explain what it meant, nor could anyone say why Conservative leader Robert Stanfield wasn't quite correct to call it "a big bag of fog." Fitful attempts were made to create some new transatlantic ties. Canada joined the European Space Agency; the cabinet tried, unsuccessfully, to bully Air Canada into buying the European Airbus rather than DC-10s. Despite the best efforts of "Europeanists" in the government, the Third Option thereafter faded quickly away.

During the period of the Third Option – Trudeau, during his last term, 1980-84, acted as if it had never existed – Canada-U.S. trade increased proportionately rather than declined. Yet those critics of the Third Option who have made much of this tend to overstate their case: trade everywhere has grown fastest intraregionally, within Western Europe, within Eastern Europe, within Southeast Asia, within North America.

Perhaps the best comment about the Third Option has been made by Charles Doran of Johns Hopkins University: "It was the right option for a country in Canada's situation of always having to push against the weight of U.S. influence, like Sisyphus. The mistake wasn't in trying to develop 'counter-weights' to U.S. influence; the mistake was in thinking that the Europeans and the Japanese were in the least interested in helping to provide them when all they wanted from Canada was cheap resources."

Doran's comment is a useful corrective to the conventional analysis that Trudeau's cutback by half of Canada's NATO contribution caused the Europeans to fail to respond to the Third Option. (France in fact had pulled right of NATO.) More to the point, this interpretation implies that different approaches might have made the Third Option, or variations of it, work. In the end, the Third Option can be credited with just one accomplishment. It demonstrated, finally and conclusively, that Canada cannot count on any country to help it "create counterweights to the overwhelming presence of the United States," as Trudeau described the policy's purpose in 1975; Canada cannot depend on any country, this is to say, except itself.

The state of Canada-U.S. relations during Trudeau's last term, 1980-84, is without historical parallel. Twice, in the case of the National Energy Policy and in the case of Trudeau's peace initiative of 1983-84, Canadians in effect told Americans to go to hell. Never before have Canadians been so bold about risking economic retaliation. Yet right afterwards, in pragmatic counterpoint, they elected a government committed to "good relations, super relations" with the U.S.

By no means all Canadians supported either of these initiatives. The NEP in particular, as related in Chapter Six, attracted vociferous opposition at home – from westerners, from the oil industry, from businessmen in general; many Canadians during this period used each trip across the border to reassure Americans that they didn't at all agree with Trudeau's interventionist economic nationalism. Not all Americans, however, were impressed by these protestations. Willis Armstrong, a savvy old retired State Department hand, observed to a 1983 seminar on Canada-U.S. relations, "People keep telling me they don't agree with Trudeau's policies, but someone up there must because they've elected him for fourteen years."

In the first years of the 1980s, Canadian attitudes were conditioned by a widespread mistrust of Reagan. He won in 1980 by promising to "make America stand tall again," meaning by this that Americans should put their trust in a strong defence and in "the magic of the marketplace." Not until 1983-84 was the strength of the American recovery appreciated in Canada, and in particular the widening of the gap in the relative performance of the two economies. Thereafter, attitudes toward Reagan changed to a kind of rueful admiration. About the military aspects of Reagan's policies, few Canadians had any doubts where they stood: a poll taken late in 1983 by Decima Research revealed that 85 per cent of Canadians supported Trudeau's peace initiative, one of the highest approval ratings of any policy of any government in modern times; when questioned more closely, most Canadians said they doubted that Trudeau could have any effect on the superpowers but that they wanted him to go on trying because, as the most frequent comment Decima received, "it's the right thing to do."

During this period, the U.S. exercised some of the "linkage" so long dreaded in Ottawa. Such links, though, were never as simple as "B" as a retaliation for "A." The U.S. Senate's 1981 rejection of the East Coast Fisheries Treaty, for instance, had little if anything to do with Canada, almost everything to do with log-rolling among senators. The Reagan administration's 1982 rejection of a Canadian joint-action plan on acid rain again reflected domestic political tensions rather than cross-border ones. During this period Shultz and MacEachen started the quarterly bilateral meetings that continue today, and Washington responded enthusiastically to Ottawa's tentative initiative on sectoral free trade.

Nevertheless, a prevailing negativism toward Canada did exist, much of it directed at Trudeau personally. In Reagan's Washington, Trudeau acquired a reputation as flighty and irresponsible. Reagan's praetorian guard bitterly resented Trudeau's barely concealed contempt for Reagan's intellectual powers. Almost recklessly, he sometimes made no attempt to hide his feelings. At a press conference following the 1982 economic summit at Versailles, when Reagan stumbled while answering a question, Trudeau muttered loudly enough to be heard, "Ask Al," implying that Reagan needed Secretary of State Al Haig to provide the answers.

Negativism toward Canada also derived from two other American sources. Reagan's aides and neo-conservative Republicans thought that Canada had gone "socialist"; U.S. businessmen worried about their investments. Here, the most frequent expression was found in the editorial pages of the *Wall Street Journal*. Yet a third source emanated from Canada. Canadian businessmen, provincial politicians and officials, and even some federal officials often astounded their American listeners by the viciousness with which they denounced their own country, or at least their elected government and its leader. Mulroney, just by getting elected, changed all that. But for a time some of Canada's worst enemies were, sadly, Canadians.

Specific consequences of this negativism are hard to identify. Businessmen simply switched off. New Brunswick Premier Richard Hatfield remembers flying to Texas to try to sell provincial bonds, being rejected, and then being told by the president of the Texas School Board Pension Fund, "Didn't your prime minister once paddle to Cuba?" In Washington, officials no longer gave Canadian concerns the same sympathetic attention as before, confident that someone up the line would nod approvingly.

These rumbles in Washington and in Wall Street produced thunderclaps in Ottawa. The Trudeau government became increasingly defensive, trying to deny that it had knocked over a set of dominoes: poor cross-border relations leading to the recession and on to mass unemployment. In order to prove its innocence, to Canadian voters at least as much as to Washington politicians, the government had no political choice but to surrender hostages. Cabinet approved the 1983 policy paper that proposed sectoral free trade talks largely to show to the public that it could still get on with Washington. By far the most important hostage was the cruise missile: the very fact that so many Canadians protested testing the cruise over Canada increased its value as a peace signal sent to Washington.

Defence analyst Gwynne Dyer, Newfoundland-born and now living in London, describes the cruise missile tests as "a Pentagon loyalty call." He means by this that the U.S. Air Force was relatively indifferent whether the missiles were tested over the Canadian prairies instead of over the Dakotas, but Canadian involvement represented a useful show of Western military solidarity.

The AGM-86B cruise missiles are designed to be launched, roughly over the North Pole, by B-52 bombers, and then to fly to targets in Soviet Russia 1,500 miles away, hugging the ground to escape radar detection. They are exceedingly difficult to identify and to knock down. They are also exceedingly accurate, and though, because relatively slow, not a first-strike weapon they constitute an ideal near-first-strike weapon to be aimed at communication and command centres. (The Russians have, or are believed to have, cruder versions.) Canada's significance to the cruise was that it happened to have the same flat, featureless territory as, in the delicate official phrase, "the Eurasian land mass in the high latitudes."

On July 15, 1983, External Affairs Minister Allan MacEachen announced that the cabinet had formally agreed to operational testing and evaluation of unarmed cruise missiles, with the principal testing site to be the Canadian Forces base at Suffield Range, Alberta.* This was just two months before Trudeau set up an interdepartmental task force to develop plans for a peace initiative.

During the preceding eighteen months, the cabinet had devoted more time to debating cruise missiles than any other single issue during Trudeau's entire term other than the constitution. The doves were led by Don Johnston and Lloyd Axworthy, both senior ministers. But the dove who mattered most was Trudeau himself. To the amazement of his ministers, he allowed the subject to be brought back time and again, and each time it came up on the agenda he allowed the doves to express their opinions at length. The reason for the amazement of the others was that they knew the result was a *fait accompli*. So also did Trudeau. But old memories – having called Pearson a "de-frocked priest of peace" – coupled with his own life-long detestation of war in general and of nuclear war in particular, kept tugging at him; so did, more urgently, his rising concern about the seemingly inevitable U.S.-U.S.S.R. confrontation that would follow the planned deployment later that year of U.S. cruise and Pershing missiles in Europe. (One emotional tug in the other direction was a personal appeal by his friend, former West German Chancellor Helmut Schmidt, the author of the original idea for installing cruise and Pershing missiles in Europe as a response to Soviet SS-20s.)

The *fait accompli* had been accomplished at least two years earlier. According to documents later obtained under the Freedom of Information Act by the *Montreal Gazette*, discussions at the official level began as early as 1980. The same documents reveal that at his meeting with Reagan back in December, 1981, Trudeau had

---

* The first flight was undertaken in March, 1984, with the missile attached to a B-52. The first "solo" flight by a cruise missile over the Primrose Lake range took place in February, 1985. The agreement allows the U.S. to conduct up to six flights a year through 1988.

"agreed in principle" to the tests, long before the agonized debates in cabinet. In between, a strictly technical document about joint Canada-U.S. weapons testing had been brought before cabinet in June, 1981, and had been given routine approval by the cabinet during the same week that everyone's attention was focused on the annual economic summit of the leading Western powers then being held near Ottawa.

"It got past us," recalls Tom Axworthy, who was then Trudeau's senior aide. "By the time the cabinet got around to focusing on it, it was too late." The cruise missile testing didn't become a political issue in Canada until the winter of 1982, following the incredible rally of half a million people in New York the previous June organized by the Freeze Now movement. By then, the cabinet was committed but for the formalities. To have cancelled the agreement at that late stage would have caused a cross-border rift at least as serious as the one precipitated by the 1962 Cuban missile crisis. On the heels of the NEP, another row with Washington was the last thing Trudeau could afford politically. So he temporized and allowed the cabinet debates to go on and on, knowing all the while how they would end.*

During the cruise missile affair, Trudeau was consistently testy. He lashed out at his critics, calling them "hypocrites" for being willing to be defended by the U.S. nuclear deterrent yet unwilling to make any contribution to that deterrent. He got especially testy at those who pointed out that the tests contradicted his 1978 "suffocation" speech at the United Nations. He tried to hide behind the shield of alliance solidarity, claiming that the missile-testing represented a Canadian contribution to the defence of Europe, although the Alberta cruise missiles were of a quite different order, being strategic missiles to be used by the U.S. Air Force.

Trudeau has never enjoyed being on the defensive. His peace mission provided him, through one last conjurer's twirl, the chance to go back onto the offensive – as an emissary for peace.

Among the millions, if not billions, of words written about the debate

---

* All the negotiations about the cruise, from 1980 on, were of course conducted in complete secrecy. Simultaneously, and again without Canadians being told, negotiations were also under way to develop what came to be known as the North Warning System, or a new northern radar network.

over nuclear weapons, perhaps the most insightful and the freshest were those used by Freeman Dyson in his 1984 book, *Weapons and Hope*, when he described the two sides as "victims and warriors" rather than as stereotypical good guys and bad guys. Dyson explained: "The military establishment looks on the peace movement as a collection of ignorant people meddling in a business they do not understand, while the peace movement looks on the military establishment as a collection of misguided people protected by bureaucratic formality from all contact with human realities."

Trudeau's peace initiative amounted to an exercise in bridge-building between those two sides. He himself was a politician in power, with access to all kinds of experts and to privileged information. He never played to the gallery, nor except right near the end of his mission said anything that was in any way "irresponsible." Yet he came to embody the hopes of the victims, in Canada and elsewhere. He was trying to do *something*, at a time when the U.S. and the Soviet Union were doing nothing except "shouting at each other," in his own phrase, and either deploying more missiles or threatening to deploy more.

This isn't the place to recount in detail Trudeau's peace initiative. Its main elements are, in any event, familiar: Trudeau's response, "We are at the brink of the abyss," to the Soviet shooting down of Korean Airlines flight 007 over the Sea of Japan in September, 1983; his extraordinary public debate with Margaret Thatcher, she arguing the Russians could not be trusted, he that they had to be, during her visit to Canada later that month; his announcement, early in October, of the formation of a special peace task force, and his inauguration of his initiative at a minor-league conference at Guelph that same month; his tour of Europe in November, which yielded little; his modest success at the Commonwealth Conference in New Delhi; his dramatic "air dash" to Peking in the middle of the conference, which suddenly gave credibility to his entire mission; his December meeting with Reagan at the White House; his trip to Eastern Europe in January, including, as the first Western prime minister to do so, a visit to East Berlin for talks with Prime Minister Hoenecker, during which he began to open doors long shuttered by the omnipresence of the Russians. Then, finally, in February, his long-delayed – delayed too long to be effective – trip to Moscow for Yuri Andropov's funeral.*

---

* A detailed account was published in *Saturday Night* magazine in May, 1984, written jointly by the author and Sandra Gwyn.

Historians will have to judge how much effect Trudeau had in moderating East-West tensions. They did moderate slightly, but they may have been due to moderate anyway. The aspect of particular relevance here is the effect of Trudeau's peace initiative on Canada-U.S. relations. In one sense, this was dramatic; in another sense it was inconsequential.

Throughout Trudeau's peace initiative, American official opinion ranged from uneasy to outraged. During a dinner in Washington, Lawrence Eagleburger, undersecretary of state for political affairs, blurted out that Trudeau's conduct was "akin to pot-induced behaviour by an erratic leftie." At a routine Canada-U.S. conference in New York a couple of officials from the U.S. Defence and State departments sufficiently forgot the presence of reporters to declare that Canada, by its minimal military effort, had lost the right to posture about peace. Trudeau denounced them as "Pentagon pipsqueaks." In Washington, officials sought out reporters to tell them that Trudeau's initiative was "a loose cannon," "a shot across our bows."

Yet Trudeau could not be denied. He was too senior an international statesman to be ignored and far too formidable a dialectician to be engaged lightly. The simple fact is that most American public figures were a bit afraid of Trudeau. Thus, Washington granted Trudeau what he wanted: a personal meeting with Reagan in the White House. For the media, this encounter was a disappointment. Reporters had assumed the two would collide; instead, Trudeau and Reagan emerged from their December 15 meeting with smiles almost as broad as those of Reagan and Mulroney after the Shamrock Summit.

Of all Canadian prime ministers since Mackenzie King, Trudeau understood Americans the least and made the least effort to try to understand them. Official trips aside, he scarcely knew the country other than for its ski slopes and its Manhattan discos. He himself, as Joe Clark once observed deftly, wasn't so much a North American as a European who happened to grow up in Canada. Put more straightforwardly, Trudeau was a snob about Americans.

For his encounter with Reagan, however, Trudeau (coached by the ambassador in Washington, Allan Gotlieb) applied his formidable intellect to the problem at hand. He devised a brilliant strategy. Rather than arguing with Reagan about nuclear weapons, which would have only caused the President to retreat to the protective cover of crackerbarrel anecdotes, he engaged him in a discussion about public relations, and riveted the attention of the Great Communicator by telling him he was failing to get across his true quality as a man of peace. Immediately after his encounter with Trudeau, Reagan gave two *Time* magazine reporters the "scoop" that he would never again call Russia "an evil empire."

This was a major accomplishment. Commonly, Canadian prime ministers have tried to influence U.S. foreign policy by quiet diplomacy. This technique, though, leaves no track behind it to show whether any impression has in fact been made.* Trudeau had followed the high-wire route of public diplomacy. Quite deliberately, he didn't at any time criticize either U.S. or NATO nuclear strategies. But simply by saying that *both* superpowers were in part to blame, he was directly challenging U.S. sensibilities – quite aside from the fact that everyone in Washington hoped he'd just shut up about peace. Thus Trudeau got Canada into the nuclear action even though, since we had no nuclear weapons, we could claim little "right" to say anything at all. (In a disheartening paradox, Canada's very lack of nuclear weapons leaves it with no bargaining chips to offer up in any arms control deal.)

The truth about arms control is, and always has been, that any U.S.-U.S.S.R. agreement will in the end, and throughout most of the negotiating, be a deal between the U.S. and the Soviet Union alone. Trudeau didn't challenge this reality. But he did demand a right for small powers like Canada to be heard, critically but constructively. He expressed the *leitmotiv* of his peace initiative during the state dinner for Thatcher at the Harbour Castle Hotel in Toronto on September 27, 1983. Replying directly to a hawkish speech that Thatcher had just given, Trudeau said: "We must get involved. We must not yield to the temptation that because we are not at the bargaining table, we cannot be blamed for what happens there."

Trudeau's concept was rejected by Washington at the start of his peace initiative and at its conclusion, and it is rejected today no less emphatically. Empires want their dependencies to provide cannon fodder, not generals back at headquarters. The best illustration of

---

* In *In the Interests of Peace: Canada and Vietnam 1954–73*, Douglas Ross makes the claim that by quiet diplomacy Pearson strengthened President Johnson's hand against those hawks who wanted to resort to nuclear weapons. This presupposes, though, that these hawks weren't products of Johnson's fertile imagination conjured up by him to persuade allies such as Pearson that he, Johnson, was really a moderate.

131

this is provided by the fate of what was by far the best of the specific tension-reducing proposals that Trudeau carried with him as talking points while he toured the international capitals. This was the idea for a ban on the development of weapons systems that could destroy high-altitude satellites. The inventiveness in this proposal lay in the fact that neither side was yet working on such systems and so would be giving nothing up, and since high-altitude communication satellites would have to be destroyed in any pre-emptive first strike, both sides would have an assurance that a surprise attack by the other was unfeasible. In the spring of 1984, Trudeau planned to table a draft A-SAT ban treaty at the Geneva Disarmament Conference due to meet that fall. Washington protested: it would distract from and thus would slow down the direct U.S.-U.S.S.R. disarmament talks then in prospect. Trudeau, who by now had already announced his retirement, agreed reluctantly. Washington's real reason was revealed in a comment by a senior U.S. official to a Canadian opposite number: "You'd be playing in our game."

If Trudeau gained little ground in the area he cared about most, he scored a singular victory in an area he probably cared about only marginally yet which today still influences Canada-U.S. relations decisively. On the age-old principle that the squeaky wheel gets the oil, Trudeau got the U.S. to pay attention to Canada. "I'm not sure I agreed with any of Trudeau's policies, but I have to say I like him," comments George Carver, once with the CIA and now a professor at Georgetown University. "A lot of Americans liked him: we like people who are daring and who take risks." In the opinion of Charles Doran, "The irony is that it's because of Trudeau that Mulroney can do what he's doing. Trudeau made the American elite, although not the public at large, aware that Canada really is a different country. Because that's established, it's become possible for Mulroney to move the two countries closer together."

Trudeau made one other difference by his peace initiative. He turned Canadians' attention back to the world. And he revived the Pearsonian myth. The myth may now be no more than a memory of a mythical "golden" time when Canada, by luck as well as by skill, exercised a quite disproportionate international influence that can never be recaptured. Yet myths matter. Without them, a nation cannot sustain.

Chapter Nine
From Massey to Masse: Cultural Nationalism, 1957-1985

"Canadians are desperate for a Keats."

Leonard Cohen

"I've been wondering if others have the same feeling that I have about Canadian cultural life at the moment," wrote Rosemary Sullivan, a professor of English and editor of a collection of writings by Canadian women, in the July, 1984, issue of *This Magazine*, a small, leftist, nationalist monthly. As if heresies are best committed on the run, Sullivan moved immediately to her point. "It seems to me we've fallen into a slump. It's not just the impact of the recession.... There's something deeper at issue. We've become tired of 'Canadian' culture, a little bored with talking about national cultural issues."

In an interview for this book, the playwright Rick Salutin, also a regular contributor to *This Magazine*, went further: "Sullivan's right, and I'm glad of it. It gets people like me out of a box. For far too long, we've invested too much time in creative cultural apologetics, either being cheerleaders for Canadian culture, or being doomsayers about it."

Until the 1960s, Canada was a culturally underdeveloped nation. There'd been, back in the twenties, the Group of Seven and Emily Carr. In 1948, there'd been *Le Refus Global*, the manifesto – Make Way for What is Needed! – by which Paul-Emile Borduas and a group of other Quebec artists liberated themselves from the dead hand of the past. In the 1950s, there were Glenn Gould and Lois Marshall. Not least, in the era when E.J. Pratt, Frye, Innis, and Donald Creighton were all teachers, there was the intellectual flowering of the University of Toronto, now just a memory. Yet except for such occasional blooms, the environment was an enemy of artistic promise.

Then, all of a sudden, a society that had never produced much but wheat and lumber and hockey players and Mounties was turning out painters, sculptors, musicians, writers, and poets. The catalytic year was 1967. By then, the Canada Council had been sowing its seed on pre-Cambrian rocks for a decade, and some of these seeds had taken root and started to bud. Centennial Year and Expo '67 gave the government an excuse to build a lot of arts centres and to commission works to impress the visitors. The success of Expo gave Canadian artists respectability: they had done their country proud, and now it owed them a chance to make a living. Indeed, except for resource ones, Canada's first two world-class industries were both artistic ones: Expo '67 and the Stratford Festival.

As an industry, as federal cultural officials came increasingly to favour describing their charge, the arts enjoyed a growth rate through the 1970s for which there were few equals in an economy then suffering "de-industrialization." At the start of the decade there were five professional dance companies in Canada; at its end there were twenty-three. The number of professional theatres increased sixfold, to 121, and half of their productions were Canadian. The number of professional visual artists more than tripled, to 7,950, and that of writers and editors had almost doubled, to 28,755. The number of publishing houses had more than doubled, to eighty-nine, almost three-quarters of them now Canadian-owned. The bottom line of the cultural industry may still have been written in red, but the numbers in all the lines above were incomparably larger than they had ever been.

We still hadn't produced a Keats. But by 1982 Northrop Frye could write in *Divisions on a Ground* that "Canadian literature since 1960 has become a real literature and is recognized as such all over the world." There were Margaret Atwood and Margaret Laurence and Marie-Claire Blais and Adele Weisman and Alice Munro, who explained as the cause of their commonality, "As the subject race, women are tougher than men." There were also Timothy Findley and Robertson Davies and Hubert Aquin and Rudy Wiebe; there was Mordecai Richler still, and, as there had always been, Morley Callaghan and Hugh MacLennan. The 1985 edition of the *Oxford Companion to English Literature* failed, in 1,154 pages, to find space for a single contemporary Canadian writer, but an English-literature university textbook published in West Germany contained twenty-two stories, of which twelve were American, six Canadian, three British, and one by a New Zealander.

Collective theatre, so vital and inventive in the 1970s, a distinctively Canadian development in which Toronto's Theatre Passe Muraille gave birth to grassroots companies in St. John's, Saskatoon, Vancouver, and even in Ottawa, had by the 1980s passed its productive peak. At the same time, painters and sculptors – Harold Town, Christopher Pratt, Jack Shadbolt, Alex Colville, Yves Gaucher, Michael Snow – who had raised the first banner of Canadian art as far back as the fifties, were themselves getting into their fifties and beyond. The baton had been picked up by playwrights – David French, David Fennario, Carol Bolt, George Ryga, Andy Jones, Michel Tremblay, Sharon Pollock, Judith Thompson, Salutin. The symphony orchestras of Montreal, Toronto, and the National Arts Centre at Ottawa were being applauded in Europe, in the U.S., in Asia. At Stratford, with its Gilbert and Sullivan spectacles, and at Niagara-on-the-Lake, with the Shaw Festival and its *Cyrano de Bergerac*, there was a new quality of depth and assurance. Artistic fashions come and go; creative juices here or there dry up before bursting out again. But by the mid-eighties there was a self-confidence, the stuff of permanence to artistic life in Canada.

So why the talk of "a slump"? There were government cutbacks, but these only nicked the arts and scarcely scratched the surface of the CBC. There was the new Communications Minister, Marcel Masse, eager to be photographed handing out cheques to artists and reluctant to understand what the "arm's length" principle, which doesn't translate into the other official language, meant. These, though, were just political bumps and grinds.

More debilitating, certainly, had been the collapse of the Canadian film industry, not into a slump but into a spread-eagled surrender to Hollywood. After the promise of *Why Shoot the Teacher?* and *Who Has Seen the Wind* and *Outrageous* and *Mon Oncle Antoine* and *J.A. Martin, Photographe*, and *Les Ordres* and *Kamouraska*, and after hundreds of millions of dollars in subsidies and tax write-offs, there had come *Porky's* and *Meatballs*. And after them, there had come *Porky's II*. Meanwhile, out of Australia, had come *My Brilliant Career* and *Picnic at Hanging Rock* and *Breaker Morant* and *Gallipoli*, and then, as the ultimate, unnerving put-down, *Smash Palace* and *Sylvia* from New Zealand. Nor had we produced a Canadian equivalent to Australia's Nobel-winning novelist, Patrick White.

Yet we had Atwood and Munro and Richler and Findley and the rest. CBC Radio was beyond question the second best in the world. Many of Canada's best actors and filmmakers still went south, or crossed the Atlantic, but some came back to try to do here what they could do nowhere else, like Ted Kotcheff, to direct *Joshua Then and Now*, while others, like the director Robin Phillips and the conductor Charles Dutoit, came because the opportunities were better here than anywhere else.

The pop-psychology phrase "mid-life crisis" may explain the talk of a slump better than any deeper analysis. By the early 1980s, the ideology of nationalism had dominated the public debate about culture for two decades. The argument of "nation-building" had served artists well: it had shaken loose a lot of government money. But many individual artists had paid a high personal price: they had expended an enormous amount of time and energy in "creative cultural apologetics," in everything from performing as nationalist spokesmen to writing briefs to governments, to organizing groups to present those briefs. Now nationalism had gone as far as it could go. It had helped to lever into existence, and to sustain, even if often only at the commercial margin, all those performing arts companies and painters and writers. But Canada's popular culture of movies, TV soaps, magazines, and popular music was as American as it had ever been, more American than ever, in fact. If nationalism had gone as far as it could, then Canadian artists were on their own from here on in. Their organizing principle would have to be the pursuit of excellence for its own sake rather than the measure of "good for Canada." Excellence cannot be defined, but every artist understands what it is to the tips of his or her own nerve-ends, and understands also that pursuing excellence is the most daunting and solitary journey of all.

Two markers can be pointed out to show the new direction that Canadian artists are taking. One is a recent work of literary criticism. The other is an insight provided during an interview for this book.

Bruce Powe is twenty-nine, and *A Climate Charged*, published in 1984, is his first book. It's an inventive, exuberant work in which Powe takes on the icons of Canadian literature, including its Godfather, the critic Frye, and its Earth Mother, Atwood. Powe doesn't only indulge in youthful invective. He praises the poet Irving Layton's "destructive vulnerability" and Margaret Laurence for her "feeling, hard won and real." He lovingly portrays Marshall McLuhan, of whom he was once a student: "The world is in ruins and to read its runes the writer must become available to its tensions and adopt an appropriate style." But he is harsh about Frye: "My charge that Frye ignores individuality and personality pertains to his disregard for the specificity of voice in a poem or novel.... For Frye, reality is a construct, a feat of the imagination, that which human beings 'have no business with'." As for Atwood: "Impassioned, wild, unexpected, epic and merry are not adjectives you could apply to her work, but controlled, careful, elegant, witty, and (yes), sometimes beautiful, are. She is important, but not for the reasons given by fawning journalists.... Atwood's popularity as a novelist-poet-critic is a useful indicator of the values of current fiction, criticism and best-sellerdom."

Powe's criticisms are open to criticism. By putting down Atwood's "best-sellerdom" he's failed to notice that, since best-sellerdom *is* our contemporary culture, she's positioned her finger right over society's pulse. A *Climate Charged* serves as a marker less in itself than in its context. Powe takes for granted that the killingly kind, love and maple syrup standards of "Can-Lit" are irrelevant to the responsibilities of a Canadian literary critic. So equally did reviewers of Powe's book. Unlike the extravagant attack upon Atwood's seminal analysis of Canadian literature, *Survival*, by the nationalist Robin Matthews in 1972,* no reviewers criticized Powe for his abandonment of Can-Lit apologetics.

The other marker was set down in an interview by Robert Fulford, editor of *Saturday Night*. Fulford, who has surveyed Canada's cultural scene since the late fifties, commented on how much has been accomplished: "We have reached a stage where it is possible to make a play, say, that is important only in Canada and for it to be accepted as valid rather than for us having to wait for it to be justified for us by success in New York or London. We've created a platform in this country upon which our artists can perform. It isn't a large platform and it has a lot of holes in it, the failure of our films and

---

* The ultra-nationalist point Matthews was trying to make was made for him in the spring of 1985 by the English professors at Simon Fraser University who voted to reject him as an exchange professor because they found his nationalist views "disturbing."

of our TV drama as examples. But the platform does exist, and we can now stand upon it and look out beyond our own borders."

Fulford then pointed to the gaping hole in the middle of the Canadian artistic platform. "The great lack in Canadian culture has been its inability to think originally about the United States. It's the great empty space in our thinking. If de Tocqueville were alive today, he ought to be a Canadian."

For Canada to have as yet produced no single creative genius is the luck of the genealogical draw: a Mozart is as likely to be found in Saskatoon as in Salzburg. But the failure of Canadian artists and intellectuals to think originally about the United States – other than in one respect to be described later – represents a collective failure of imagination and nerve. Living in North America and yet not being Americans, Canadian artists ought to have performed like a "Distant Early Warning Line," in McLuhan's phrase, sensing the future before it happened and communicating their sensibility through the medium of cultural artifacts. By failing to do this, Canadian artists have failed their public.

Some exceptions do exist: Atwood's "best-sellerdom" novels; the satire of SCTV that plays upon American nerve-ends; the explorations on film by Michael Snow and Bruce Elder of the effect upon language and upon visual perceptions of American film and TV.

If Canadian artists move now to take up positions along the Distant Early Warning Line across which the future will fly, they will have broken the last of their colonial bonds. Colonials are always schizophrenics. The heart pounds with local pride; the head informs that excellence is happening somewhere else. Strikingly, no Canadian painter or poet had anything original to say about either the First or the Second World War, nor about the decline of empire even though its down-going redefined us. (The first important Canadian artistic statements to come out of the Great War – Findley's novel, The Wars, and John Gray's play, Billy Bishop Goes to War – appeared more than half a century after the events they described.) The same phenomenon can be observed within Canada: the West, for all that it shakes its fist at Toronto, has yet to say anything original, not so much about the metropolis itself, which is understandable, as about the relationship between a hinterland and a metropolis. For Canadian artists, America now constitutes the ultimate challenge; it is a variation of the theme of pursuing excellence wherever it leads.

Coming to terms with America may be more difficult for Canadian artists than for those of any other nation. They have spent the last two decades rejecting it. And in doing that they were always rejecting a part of themselves and of their audience.

In any archives of Canadian cultural nationalism, the key source document is the collection of essays and poems noted earlier, *The New Romans*, edited by the poet Al Purdy and published in 1968. All of the major names of the day are there – Richler, Stephen Vizinczey, Hugh Garner, Peter Newman, Fulford – and many who were then little known – Atwood, Michael Ondaatje, George Bowering. Many of them today would wince at what they wrote, but that would be revisionism. They wrote what they felt then, about Vietnam, about the race riots, about the murdered President. They wrote, angrily, despairingly, about how *their* metropolis had become a charnel house.

In an "open letter," Farley Mowat advised his son to "voluntarily enlist in the legions of the Eagle" in order to be "rewarded with citizenship in the Master State, although this would require that you reject all you have heretofore been taught to believe is good in man"; by doing this his son would have "something you never had before – a verifiable nationality." Raymond Souster, gentle and reclusive, wrote: "America/ You seem to be dying/ America/ Moving across the forty-ninth parallel each day a stronger, more death-laden stench." Purdy's own introduction expresses the double self-doubt of so many Canadian artists: that Americans wouldn't care or notice what they said; that most Canadians wouldn't either: "All this book may do is register a sullen protest, a belated yap, from a captive dog.... I think this book will be amusing to those citizens of a second-class nation who are unable to comprehend their own subservience. But for some Canadians the book will not be amusing."

Many Canadians found this kind of anti-Americanism embarrassing and offensive. What critics failed to appreciate was that this anti-Americanism was a Canadian echo of American anti-Americanism. It had crossed the border as a cultural import through the writings of Norman Mailer and James Baldwin and others. Among the most popular of the features in *The Georgia Straight*, the counter-culture paper published in Vancouver in the 1970s, were articles by such American counter-culturists as Allan Ginsberg, Jerry Rubin, and Herbert Marcuse. In their attacks on America, Canadian artists and intellectuals were repeating what many Americans had already said themselves about their society, more angrily, more despairingly, and usually more eloquently.

In attacking America, even derivatively, Canadian artists were at the same time attacking themselves. Atwood has recalled of her youth, "Canada for us was not-America; the comics were news bulletins of the action going on across the border which we could watch but not join." Fulford has written, "Some large part of the furniture of my mind and imagination has always been clearly stamped 'Made in the U.S.A.'" Salutin, who went straight to Brandeis University from high school in the sixties, has written, "It never occurred to me to stay. Canada was like a huge wet dream."

Salutin came back in the late sixties, excited by Trudeau and disgusted by the U.S. as it was then becoming. Yet Canadian artists still could not escape their schizophrenia. In Frye's description, "It is hard for him to visualize either the audience in front of him or the audience behind him out of which his imagination has grown."

As nationalism gathered strength from the late sixties on, Canadian artists tried increasingly to weld themselves to a uniquely Canadian audience, informing it about itself and in return commanding its imagination. It amounted to an attempt by Canadian artists to repatriate themselves to their own public, with nationalism as their connecting instrument. In those nationalist battles Canadian artists gained some victories: Canadian content requirements for TV and radio (in the latter instance creating the foundation for a Canadian pop music industry); the withdrawal of tax privileges from *Time*; the disallowance for tax purposes of commercials placed by Canadian companies on U.S. border TV stations (it generated about $50 million in additional revenue for Canadian TV stations, none of it, discernibly, reapplied to Canadian programming); and, by far the most important of all, the increase in spending on culture by all governments, which reached more than $2 billion a year by the early 1980s. They also suffered defeats: the sell-out of the film industry; the collapse of pay TV.

But in the crucial contest, for command of the popular imagination of Canadians, artists gained almost no victories at all. "We must sing our own songs, dream our own dreams," author Pierre Berton told the Senate Committee on the Mass Media in 1970. But in the early 1980s, no differently from the early 1960s, the culture of most Canadians was American culture. The American mass culture, the world's first populist commercial culture – its songs, its dances, its

140

music, its movies and TV soaps, its mass journalism, and also its automobiles, jeans, junk food, commercialized sports, and Disneyland – was indistinguishably Canada's culture. In 1978, then CBC president Al Johnson complained that "Most of our kids know more about the Alamo than they know about Batoche or Chrysler's Farm. They know more about Davey Crockett than they do about Louis Riel." McLuhan understood far better what was going on: "Canadians don't see American cultural domination because it's the environment, and the environment is always invisible."

Today, English Canadians watch U.S. television programs (including those carried on Canadian channels) for about three-quarters of their viewing time. They watch American drama about 97 per cent of the time that they watch drama. Only the occasional Canadian movie, such as *Duddy Kravitz* (provided that American-Canadian movies like *Porky's* aren't counted), attracts more than cult audiences. A careful scrutiny would be needed to tell the differences between magazine stands in Toronto and in New York. If interrogated about their preferences for American TV, movies, and magazines, most Canadians would be surprised by the question itself and would reply that what they were doing was watching movies and TV and reading magazines. To most Canadians, these cultural artifacts have no national content; their content is their own daily life, equally its fantasies and its realities.

Canadian artists thus never escaped being marginal to their own society. This is the logical conclusion to be drawn from the evidence. Instead, the wholly illogical has happened: Canadian artists have become integral to Canadian society.

It all began to happen because a couple of millionaires died simultaneously in the mid-1950s before they could arrange to protect their estates from the taxman. Out of this windfall came the money to endow the Canada Council, set up in 1957 with a unique status as "not an agent of Her Majesty," and, for a time, able to generate enough interest on its endowment to fund itself.

This, of course, was a British idea. In those years, the Brits were everywhere: Peter Dwyer, a graduate of MI5 (his last case was the Gouzenko affair) as the soul and guiding spirit at the Canada Council; Alan Jarvis, British-trained, at the National Gallery; Celia Franca at the National Ballet; the Anglophiliac Vincent Massey, whose royal commission had recommended the creation of the Canada Council; and before all of them, John Grierson at the National Film Board.

Their ideas, strongly supported by others such as Père George-Henri Lévesque and Maurice Lamontagne, amounted to the last political lesson Canada learned from the far side of the Atlantic. In fact, there were two lessons: first, that artistic expression is integral to nationhood, that a nation without a distinctive culture is not a nation at all; second, that artists matter as artists, not as aspirant entrepreneurs. As such, it becomes the responsibility of the state to try to meet not simply an artist's financial needs but his or her artistic needs. Those lessons became conjoined into one: subsidies would be provided to artists, but at "arm's length," so that decisions about grants would be made by the artists themselves – by the peers of the applicants – rather than by the state or by its intervening agency.

Two exemplars of this system already existed in the late 1950s, both also borrowed from Britain. One was the National Film Board. The other was the CBC, its creation justified by Graham Spry's famous cry, "It's the state or The States." The Canada Council, though, extended the system and Canadianized it. Over time, as its budget grew, the Council became dependent on the government for annual grants, just as all other crown corporations are. But it continued to dispense these funds as if they belonged to the artists rather than either to the government or to the Council.

This respect for artists by a particular agency, and later by others, helped to inspire a generalized public respect for artists. The Council, which, quite remarkably for the 1950s, was bilingual from the start, also found a way to maintain a balance between two quite contradictory Canadian definitions of excellence: regional diversity and excellence for its own sake. In a way that is most mysterious – other agencies discovered the same formula – the Council managed to be regional enough to satisfy the regionalists and demanding enough in its standards to satisfy those who recognized no standards but excellence. No way exists to describe how this trick is managed, except that a remarkable number of Canadian institutions understand it without a line about it being contained in their terms of reference.

In a North American society, where money is the measure of most things (an alternative measure of achievement is celebrity status), those who cannot make it in the marketplace, as most artists cannot, are bound to be marginal. Instead, quite extraordinarily in a society where historically they hadn't been so much marginal as invisible, artists in Canada came to be accepted as full citizens. It helped, of course, that governments came to appreciate artists' value as ambassadors, particularly at a time when Canada had so few commercial and technological ones. (The same motive prompted the extensive subsidization of athletes.) But the fact is that during this period major Canadian artists, a Karen Kain or a Maureen Forrester, came to be accorded a public respect far higher than that accorded to businessmen, say, and perhaps exceeded only by truly popular performers, such as athletes. Canadian artists repaid in kind the dues paid them by the state: their accomplishments, the plaudits for a Kain or a Forrester or the Montreal Symphony Orchestra, or the Oscars awarded to NFB documentaries, became a source of collective pride. These accomplishments told the outside world that Canada existed, and they sent the same message back to Canadians.

Public sponsorship of that most private of all activities – artistic expression – is bound to lead to contradictory results. In *Marginal Notes*, Salutin makes the intriguing point: "The institutions (Canada Council, CBC, NFB, National Arts Centre, etc.) exist not just to support but to create and at the extreme to substitute for culture. They have become cultural objects in themselves." Institutions created to catalyze artistic expression can institutionalize it: certainly, a number of artists became quasi-bureaucrats themselves, concocting grant applications with many of the same skills as corporate lobbyists. As well, the system demanded more of a political and bureaucratic nature than was reasonable. Mutually reinforcing each other, the urge of bureaucrats to build empires and of politicians to get their names in the papers led first to the redefinition of the arts as "cultural industries," and then to an attempt to bring the Canada Council and other agencies within the reach of bureaucratic direction. The most direct attack came from the minister responsible, Marcel Masse. His determination to end the "arm's length" principle and to replace it with political direction and selection led, in July, 1985, to Canada Council Director Tim Porteous warning publicly, right after he'd been told he was to be fired, that the Council was "in danger of being seriously damaged, or destroyed." At least for the record, Mulroney committed himself to the arm's length principle. This story is for another book.* The

---

* A handy illustration of "arms' length" is the NFB's 1984 release, *Le Dernier Glacier*, It recreates the death of the mining town of Schefferville, Quebec, closed down by Iron Ore of Canada during the term of its president, Brian Mulroney. He in fact comes out of it looking pretty good.

aspect that's relevant here is that at risk is a system that now is uniquely Canadian.

Since popular culture in Canada is American culture, Canadian culture has never been able to aspire to a status other than that of a minority culture. The one exception, and even this is arguable, was in Quebec during its extraordinary, but brief, period of emotional togetherness.

Almost all artists are in fact elitist – Shakespeare being the exception that comes handily to everyone's mind. What is interesting instead about Canadian art is how large a minority it reaches. The claim by the Department of Communications that more Canadians attend cultural events than athletic events is misleading: vast numbers of Canadians follow sports on TV. But it is true that CBC Radio FM and AM is available everywhere, as its U.S. equivalent, Public Radio, is not, that performing companies and art organizations tour almost constantly, and that there are now an almost unbelievable 1,500 museums and art galleries across the country.

It is true also that the minority audience for Canadian cultural artifacts keeps growing: in the pre-Christmas sales season, close to one-half of the books on the best-seller list are by Canadian authors (only a dozen American novelists, in a market ten times larger, can top the hardcover sales of Atwood and Richler); CBC-TV's The Journal attracts a daily audience of a million and a quarter. Toronto supports more professional theatre companies, forty-two, even if many are impecunious, than any North American city but New York. Most successful Canadian painters have lost interest in exhibiting in the U.S. – except to add a line to their credits – because they can sell all they can produce at higher prices at home.

When he was Communications Minister in the early seventies, Gerard Pelletier proclaimed the doctrine of "decentralization and democratization," an out-of-character policy to emerge from so elitist a government. But in the years since, Canadian culture has certainly become decentralized (there were, in 1971, one-quarter the number of art galleries and museums of today), and if not exactly democratized, it has been broadened from a minority culture into one that is generally available. If Canadians became Americans, the aspects of their nationality they would miss most would be Medicare, the Pearsonian myth, the tradition of public civility and tolerance, and their access to the arts. Canadian arts aren't central to Canadian society, neither are they marginal to it; they are an integral part of it.

In its character Canadian art has been thoroughly Canadian, analytic rather than imaginative, nuanced rather than declarative. It always has been this way. The art historian Jeremy Adamson, who has assembled an exhibition of nineteenth-century Canadian and American paintings of Niagara Falls, that ultimate commonality between the two societies, comments, "On our side, you get discreet, topographical watercolours, and on their side, a messianic approach; they really believed that if you listened to the falls you heard the voice of God."

One of the best descriptions of the character of Canadian art was that of the critic Neil Compton, who wrote in a 1970 *festschrift* for historian Frank Underhill: "There have been no great works of art or literature, no breath-taking feats of speculative philosophy, no daring technical innovations. Canadians excel in the more sober pursuits, scholarship, criticism, applied technology and the interpretive arts." Compton went on to remark that Canadian artistic energies were being "channelled into arts which involve processes of mediation, communications and interpretation, scholarship, journalism, criticism, radio, TV, cinema and the performing arts."

The documentary tradition in Canadian art can be traced back to Grierson at the Film Board, and before him back to the Group of Seven. It is manifest today in the strength of radio and TV public affairs programming, in the quality of magazine writing (little though there is of it), and in the abundance of non-fiction writers who, as in the case of Peter Newman and Pierre Berton, limit themselves exclusively to Canada as if this was the only audience that would really appreciate their chronicles, in contrast to fiction writers who reach out to a wider world. In a different form, the documentary tradition manifests itself in the way those Canadian artists who've made the deepest marks on the world – Glenn Gould, Jon Vickers, Oscar Peterson, Melissa Hayden – have done so as performers rather than as creators.

There is a practical explanation for this. Canada is hard on artists because it is so easy a society. Stephen Lack, a Canadian painter now living in New York, has commented: "Living on the East Side, you see people dying in the street. You go back to Canada and everyone is comfortable." It is hard for happy families to have a history.

The discomfort Canada provides to artists, as grit to an oyster, is an impersonal discomfort that doesn't so much stimulate the imagination as freeze it. The finest analytic work of the nationalists undoubtedly was Atwood's *Survival*. Published in 1972, it caused a "click" of recognition just as Grant's *Lament* had done a decade earlier. She wrote of the "intolerable anxiety" that suffused Canadian writing. If the thematic symbol for American writing was "The Frontier" and that of British writing "The Island," its Canadian equivalent was "Survival/La Survivance" – survival amid a hostile frigid land, and survival amid two societies that were as fragile as the land itself:

> A preoccupation with one's survival is necessarily also a preoccupation with the obstacles to survival. In earlier writers these obstacles are external – the land, the climate and so forth. In later writers, they are no longer obstacles to physical survival but obstacles to what we may call spiritual survival, to life as anything more than a minimally human being.... a character is paralyzed by terror (either of what he thinks is threatening him from the outside, or of elements in his own nature that threaten him from within). It may even be life itself that he fears.

In a summary of her analysis that passed into the Canadian vocabulary and helped to magnify the condition she diagnosed, Atwood wrote that characters in Canadian literature "survive, but just barely. They are born losers, failing to do anything but keep alive."

A decade and a bit later, Canada and Canadian culture are both still alive. So it's worth turning to the two questions Atwood posed in the last two lines of her book:

"Have we survived?"

"If so, what happens *after* Survival?"

Atwood's answer to her own question was to go on being a writer and to produce some of her finest works, such as *Life Before Man*. She's reached out for excellence and has grasped it.

Another way in which Canadian artists now may reach out toward excellence is suggested by a remarkable book, written by Concordia professor Arthur Kroker, titled *Technology and the Canadian Mind: Innis/McLuhan/Grant* and published in 1984. "Canada's principal contribution to North American thought consists of a highly original, comprehensive and eloquent discourse on technology," declares Kroker, who then sets out to establish his ambitious thesis. Kroker's writing is dense and demanding. Every now and then, though, he sends a line soaring off the page: "For Canadian thinkers, technological society jeopardizes at a fundamental level the received traditions of western culture, and makes of our fate as Northern Americans a journey, almost a skywalk into an unknown future." And again: "Politics can now be so cynical just because it is shadowed by the logic of exterminism; ethical questions concerning human reproduction are screened out by rapid advances in human engineering; video-rock has become the most dynamic literature of the last decades of the twentieth century."

To summarize is invariably to trivialize, especially in the instance of an analyst as complex and at times as contradictory as Kroker. His core argument, though, is that Canadians, being at one and the same time heirs of the "received traditions of western culture" and yet also North Americans, have evolved "a Canadian discourse [that] is neither the American way nor the European way but an oppositional culture.... a restless oscillation between the pragmatic will to live at all costs of the Americans and a searing lament for what has been suppressed by the modern, technical order."

In making his point, Kroker stretches it. Of his three "highly original, comprehensive" technological thinkers, only McLuhan is known beyond Canada's borders, his reputation now beginning to rise again after undergoing the inevitable post-chic fall. Nevertheless, technological analysis has been a consistent theme in the Canadian intellectual tradition. Abraham Rotstein's 1972 collection of economic nationalist essays, Precarious Homestead, includes an eloquent tribute to Robert Owen, the nineteenth-century British textile millionaire turned utopian, who "focussed unerringly on the central feature of the coming age – machine and society." In an almost prototypical Canadian symbiosis, Gutenberg Two, a collection of essays about technology and society, was edited jointly by a novelist, Dave Godfrey, and a federal assistant deputy minister of communications, Douglas Parkhill.

Today, the technology that dominates our psyche even more than that of computers or genetic engineering is the Bomb. Here, Kroker reaches his intellectual and literary zenith: "With the smell of exterminism in the air, we have reached a fantastic cusp of human history. In the most practical and terrifying sense, we are now either at the end of history or, just possibly, are at the beginning of all things. Literally, if we are to survive as a species, it will be due in no small part to the terrible fact that the sheer extremity of the threat posed to the human species by the new technologies will have forced a dramatic re-evaluation of human ethics." One Canadian who may be able to move this analysis a step further is Derek de Kerckhove of the University of Toronto. He sees the Bomb as "not the destroyer but the transformer"; it has, in his terms, "Cancelled war. Generals hate the Bomb because it has taken war away from them and given it to the politicians."

Perhaps a Kroker or a de Kerckhove will fill up that "lack" in Canadian culture of original thinking about the United States, which is to say about mankind's contemporary condition. More simply, Canadian artists may go on extending and reinforcing the "platform" they have built during the past couple of decades, together with Canadians as taxpayers and as consumers of art. What has been achieved is neither incandescent creativity nor popular culture but an integration of Canadian culture into contemporary Canadian society. It is time, though, for us to produce at least one *Breaker Morant.*

Chapter Ten
Nationalism: Elegy and Epilogue

"The oldest and most tenacious tradition in our communal memory centres around our determination not to become Americans.... One can never tell what will be the next occasion on which we'll gird up our loins and save ourselves once again from the United States. One can only predict with confidence that the occasion will come."

Frank Underhill, *In Search of Canadian Liberalism* (1961)

For two decades, from the early sixties to the early eighties, Canadian nationalists girded up their loins and went off to do battle. The NEP was their single major victory. Most of their other successes, from FIRA to Canadian content for radio and TV, amounted to hard-won skirmishes. One victory, the subsidies for Canadian-made films, turned out to be not even Pyrrhic but a rout.

The 1981-82 recession changed Canadian attitudes. The new government of 1984 radically changed Canada's policies. Canada was "open for business again." The cross-border relationship was to be "refurbished" to one of "good relations, super relations." Out went FIRA and the NEP. In came a smiling, beaming Investment Canada and a continental, free-market, energy market. Scheduled next was some form of free or "freer" or "enhanced" trade. The idea of exporting water, the ultimate expression of "territorial nationalism" once unmentionable, became a part, if a small part, of the public agenda: Quebec Liberal leader Robert Bourassa published a book, *Power From the North*, proposing the ultimate mega-project – damming up the fresh waters flowing into James Bay and carrying them, at a cost of around $100 billion, down to the U.S.*

---

* Former Deputy Finance Minister Simon Reisman publicly advocated that Canada bargain sales of water for a free trade pact tilted in its favour. The idea was clever, but too clever: it would overload the political system. It is also questionable whether the U.S. is interested in buying water as opposed to creating more of its own by desalination. It is even more questionable whether it is in Canada's interest to provide rival Sun Belt manufacturers with the water they need to keep on expanding.

In response, there was the Council of Canadians. After one press conference it largely lapsed into silence. If Canadian cultural nationalists were in a "slump," so equally were the economic nationalists. Their formulas were familiar, and frayed. In *Rebuilding from Within*, published by the Canadian Institute for Economic Policy, Rotstein offered more government spending, "made-in-Canada" interest rates (made lower, by fiat, that is), protectionism, and import substitution.

Canadians looked the other way. In 1984, Gallup reported that only 50 per cent of Canadians believed that no more U.S. investment was needed, as against a 67 per cent negative rating in 1981, the peak year of support for the NEP. In the winter of 1984-85, the Canadian Manufacturers' Association polled its members about comprehensive free trade; close to three-quarters said "yes" compared to a dead heat in 1980 of one-third for, one-third against, and one-third "don't know." Royal commission chairman Donald Macdonald, once an ardent nationalist, declared that Canada had to take a "leap of faith" into free trade. Eric Kierans, the golden oldie among the nationalists, sold his company, Canadian Adhesives, to a U.S. manufacturer. Marc Lalonde, retired from politics as a Montreal corporate lawyer, found himself giving advice to Chevron.

Nationalism has run its course, for the time being. It's worth considering some of its stumbles and some of its leaps forward.

The most serious criticism that can be made of the cultural nationalists is that they produced no single work of the imagination comparable to Hugh MacLennan's *Two Solitudes*; out of all that energy, something of the same order – Timothy Findley's *The Wars* perhaps comes closest – ought to have appeared. The most serious criticism that can be made of the economic nationalists is that they seemed to have only one song, an unending dirge about foreign ownership. One exception was Jim Laxer; in 1984, in a stinging indictment of "obsolete economic policies" of the NDP of which he had recently been research director, the one-time Waffler began to try to come to terms with the post-bureaucratic entrepreneurial economy. Cultural nationalists are going to have to attempt the same kind of imaginative leap: the new technology of VCRs, pay TV, and direct broadcast satellites has made bureaucratic-style content regulations virtually obsolete.

A consequential criticism of all the nationalists is that many of them didn't understand their own country, and that some didn't try. In Canada, as Northrop Frye has written, "identity is local." Often, identity is expressed by a province; at times by a region within a province, as for instance Cape Breton Island within Nova Scotia; at times by a particular community, such as the coal-mining town of Glace Bay rather than the next-door steel city of Sydney. This aspect of Canada exasperates intellectual absolutists, and the nationalists could never come to terms with it. Most of them lived in Toronto and Ottawa, and those that didn't physically did so spiritually. By treating as somehow disloyal those Canadians who did not agree with them because of their regional perspectives, the nationalists deepened the country's divisions. In particular, they helped to widen the fracture between East and West.

In this respect, the nationalists may have been guilty only of wish fulfilment, of wanting Canadians to possess an overarching identity since without it their nationalism was ultimately hollow. Perhaps their sin was only the venial one of being ahead of their time. Through the 1960s and 1970s, all of the regions, Quebec, the West, the Maritimes, Newfoundland, were as doubting about their identities as Canadians were collectively. That mood has changed. Modernization, as it turned out, had not made Quebec indistinguishable from the rest of the country, nor Newfoundland, nor the West. The notion of a pan-Canadian identity no longer threatens regional identities. Whether such an identity in fact exists is the subject for the succeeding section.

Most of the other criticisms made of the nationalists deserve to be mentioned only to be dismissed. Some of them did well personally out of their creed, but the anti-nationalists or continentalists didn't exactly fare badly either. The nationalists were at times shrill and strident, such as the painters and sculptors who chained themselves to the railings outside the Art Gallery of Ontario to protest the appointment of an Amerian as curator. All pioneers have to shout to be heard – the first feminists, for instance, or the early Quebec nationalists – and sometimes shout to drown out their own self-doubts.

The great accomplishment of the nationalists was that they manned the ramparts and held them. In 1968, George Ball wrote, "Canada is fighting a rearguard action against the inevitable." The inevitable hasn't happened; Ball himself now thinks it will never happen. This time he's right.

151

The nationalists cared. Although historical precursors can be dug out of the archives, they were the first generation of Canadians to care about the *idea* of Canada; to believe, that is, there was something about this curious peripheral society that resided in itself rather than in the accident of it being a bit of leftover Britain in North America or of it being a bit of America that wasn't quite American. In the same way that women today owe a profound debt to the feminists of the early 1960s, however much they may now sometimes wince at some of their excesses, so do Canadians of today and of tomorrow owe a debt to the nationalists of the sixties and seventies.

The nationalists also scored more victories than the formal record suggests, or than they themselves, often predisposed to pessimism, allowed themselves to celebrate. Canadians themselves, rarely in a flag-waving way, have also come to care about the *idea* of a Canada that controls its own destiny. Not in a long time has a government been more sensitive to public opinion than is the Mulroney government. In opposition, it had ridiculed economic nationalism. After six months in government it was beginning to sidle over to the other side of the fence.

As noted earlier, there was rather less to the change in regulation of foreign investment than Industry Minister Sinclair Stevens suggested by his early rhetoric. In dollar terms, two-thirds of FIRA's workload remains reviewable. Stevens and Energy Minister Pat Carney engaged in a major behind-the-scenes effort to ensure that Gulf Canada passed into Canadian hands.* Communications Minister Marcel Masse, even if only to win back his cultural constituency, announced that a policy would be developed to Canadianize the publishing industry. Over time, the government's calls for "free" or "enhanced" trade have become progressively softer and softer.

Probably the most precise measures of public opinion today are those complied by Decima Research of Toronto, not least because it sends its reports to the Prime Minister's Office in Ottawa. According to Decima's surveys in the spring of 1985, Canadians believed overwhelmingly (77 per cent) that Canada's best interests were served by "closer" relations with the United States, and believed as strongly

---

* The irony about the "open-for-business" policy is that Canada no longer needs foreign capital. According to a truly original analysis by Toronto financial consultant Nuala Beck, Canada, late in 1984, racked up the largest total capital surplus in its history – $3.4 billion. Canada still needs outsiders for their ideas, technology, and access to external markets, but not any longer for their money.

(72 per cent) that these relations were improving. Further, those who "agreed totally" with the proposition that the government should enact legislation to encourage greater Canadian ownership of industry had declined to 34 per cent from a high of 61 per cent in 1980.

These attitudes were pragmatic, self-interested, calculating. Embedded within them, however, was a stubborn streak of romanticism, or maybe of a different but no less pragmatic calculation of self-interest. Asked whether Canada should pursue an independent foreign policy "even if it means disagreeing with the United States," 75 per cent said "yes." More revealing, perhaps, was the response to a kind of "Third Option" question. Asked whether Canada should "concentrate" on the U.S. or broaden its relations with other countries even at the expense of intimate cross-border relations, Canadians opted for the rest of the world over the U.S. by a margin of 38 per cent to 31 per cent. At the same time as Canadians wanted to get closer to the U.S., but not too close, they remained curiously ambivalent about foreign ownership. Decima reported that Canadians believed that Canadian firms were more likely to create jobs while foreign ones were more likely to create profits but then to take these out of the country. In its spring, 1985, quarterly report, Decima summed up its findings: "The government could face a problem in the future should the current approach to the pursuit of an enhanced Canada-U.S. economic and trade relationship not produce concrete initiatives in the areas of greatest importance to Canadians. This would particularly be the case if a perception grows that Canada is getting too close to the U.S. on defence."

Economics and technology and popular culture will progressively make the boundary line across North America more permeable. Somewhere along it, Canadians still want to draw a line. This collective urge, and even more so the nation's ability still to exercise it, is the legacy of the nationalists. They held the ramparts; they even began to build inside it a "platform" from which Canadians can look out at the world, and can learn from it.

Part Three
The Other North Americans

In a long article on Canada for the *New York Times Magazine* published in 1983, the newspaper's Ottawa correspondent, Michael Kaufman, recounted his observations during a coast-to-coast tour. "There are no slums. There are no graffiti. There is no litter.... Parks are used both day and night." He then expressed his own judgement about what he had seen: "I have a high regard for the pervasive comfort Canada has bestowed on its citizens. Yet if forced to choose, I would stick to our own messier arrangements, of liberty, pervasive freedom and personal responsibility."

This was a fair summation of the different ways by which the citizens of the two societies of North America have chosen to order social relationships among themselves. One consequential quarrel can be picked with it, though: Kaufman took for granted that "liberty" and "freedom" are constrained on the northern side of the border – so that people don't mug and rape each other in parks – but are unconstrained on its southern side.

Instead, Canadians and Americans interpret the ideals of freedom and liberty differently. Allowing bag ladies the freedom to starve or allowing individuals to be bankrupted for life for lack of medical insurance imposes severe constraints on their freedom. More subtly, since no northern equivalent to the American Dream exists, Canadians possess the freedom not to be Canadians but to be almost anything they choose to be in a bilingual, multicultural, regionalized country. This said, American messiness is unquestionably creative. The homosexual leader, Sister Boom-Boom, roller-skating around the Democratic Convention in San Francisco, would probably, if in Canada, have been ticketed for jaywalking.

Which system is superior is neither here nor there. The point instead is that the two social systems are different, including that an equal rights constitutional clause now exists north of the border but not south of it. The proposition considered in the next three chapters is that, although when looked at quickly, Canada and the

U.S. appear to be two North American peas in a pod, instead, from a common soil they have grown into two quite different social organisms.

Chapter Eleven
The Politics of Liberalism, the Culture of Red Tories

"To be a North American is an amazing and enthralling fate."

George Grant, *Technology and Empire*

Liberalism has been described as decency institutionalized. Exactly who said this is unknown; perhaps no one person can lay claim and the insight was tossed out during some forgotten late night conversation over the lees of a last bottle of wine. But no matter who said it, or how it was concocted, the phrase describes the essence of Canada's political culture. Only rarely, in a handful of statements uttered by Macdonald, by Laurier, by Diefenbaker, by Trudeau, and even these have to be winnowed out of a lot of dross, has our politics been set in flight toward some larger purpose, some half-glimpsed vision. Mostly, it's about brokering between interest groups, about the apportionment of patronage, and about the exigencies of re-election.

Yet, while politics in Canada seldom rises high, it seldom falls below a widely recognized and fiercely insisted upon standard of decency, or of "civility," to use Prime Minister Brian Mulroney's favourite word. There is a way of doing things that is fitting, like a code of conduct among members of a club. Dissent is tolerated and differences are accepted as an inevitable and, indeed, a creative condition of life. If a Parliamentary Committee on UnCanadian Activities were ever to be established, it would never proceed beyond its first executive session. Problems are to be resolved by compromise, which allows everyone to claim a share of the solution, rather than by confrontation, which singles out the winners from the losers. The process, the way things are done, matters as much as the product.

No Canadian politician could bring a convention bellowing to its feet by proclaiming that extremism in the defence of *anything* was not a vice.

In Canadian public debates, the two words most frequently used are "fairness" and "equity"; whoever can first accuse an opponent of failing to meet those standards wins the debate. For the better part of a half-century, the *leitmotiv*, the sustaining purpose of Canadian governments, has been to make the lives of Canadians fairer and more equitable, more just, seemly. Canada was founded on the principle of allegiance to the crown, rather than on the principle of a social contract between its citizens, as in the United States. Since then, Canadians have in effect made a new social contract with their government: the government maintained the extensive powers it had acquired during the Second World War in exchange for guaranteeing institutionalized decency for everyone. Such institutionalization has taken many forms: Medicare and social safety nets, regional equalization, bilingualism and multiculturalism, the Charter of Rights and Freedoms, an immigration policy that is culture-blind and colour-blind, and, as the newest and least-developed aspect of collective decency, land claim settlements and self-rule systems for native peoples. At some moment during the last forty or so years, Canadians rewrote their history. A rigid and fearfully conservative society, characterized by a belated and timid experiment with the New Deal and by a policy toward Jewish refugees that "none is one too many," transformed itself into perhaps the most liberal society in the world, and certainly into one that in the North American context is *sui generis*.

In its liberalism Canada is much more akin to a number of European nations, particularly those along Europe's northern littoral fringe, than it is to its North American neighbour. Except in the vital matter of immigration, countries such as Sweden, Denmark, Holland, and Britain (though rather less so nowadays) are as much committed as is Canada to advancing the contemporary liberal ideals of collective equity and equality. European countries, however, are no longer useful role models. Whether liberal or conservative, they exist in a state of *being* in which the values and aspirations of each new generation are shaped by those of its predecessors, like a layer of alluvial silt falling on the contours of a delta. Canada is a society in a state of *becoming*, a "New Society" in the famous phrase of the American political scientist Louis Hartz, still incomplete, still shaping itself.

This is the "amazing and enthralling fate" that Canadians share with Americans, and with Australians. (South Africa and Latin America are also new societies but their mutability has been immobilized by the religions their pioneers brought with them from the Old World – or it was in the case of Latin America until very recently, when another absolutist religion, Marxist-Leninism, crossed the Atlantic.)

The true transatlantic divide was the First World War. Canadians and Americans and Australians were involved in it but were not implicated by it. The final casualty of the mud of Flanders was the nineteenth-century idea of progress, of the belief in the possibility of human perfectibility. In Europe, the collapse of conviction produced the narcissism of the 1920s and the authoritarianism of the 1930s, and today a more measured, amused cynicism. Canadians and Americans remain naifs, Australians less so, their expectations constrained perhaps by the realism engendered by their working-class origins. We North Americans are perhaps the last people in the world to believe that progress is possible, the difference being that Canadians and Americans are trying to achieve it in quite different ways.

Since liberalism, in both its classic nineteenth-century individualistic sense and in its contemporary redistributive or reformist sense, presupposes a belief in the possibility of human perfectibility, and since, quite aside from theological debates about original sin, humans manifestly are not perfectible – indeed would die of ennui if they ever achieved that state – liberalism amounts to an ideological castle grounded upon sand. All ideologies share this defect. The idealism of Marxism has decayed into bureaucratic authoritarianism. The hopeful expectation of American conservatives that "trickle-down" economics will actually trickle down to the poor will undoubtedly be dashed by the reality of human greed; the test of Reaganomics will come, not today, while the economy is expanding, but tomorrow when the society is polarized. Perhaps more to the point, the alternative to living by the dictates of one ideology or another – in some state of hopefulness – is to live by the rule of *raison d'état*, in which the end of the exercise of power justifies the means. This morally uncluttered approach does have its appeal, although it's worth remembering that the role model for its inventor, Niccolo Machiavelli, was Cesare Borgia. In any event, Canadians and Americans are both just too guilt-ridden, from whatever obscure sources that guilt flows, to accept *raisons d'état* as a standard for political conduct. Both need some moral justification – "international honest broker"; "protector of the free world" – for their actions.

There is, however, a fundamental difference in the way that Canadians and Americans pursue the mythical Holy Grail of progress. Americans regard collective progress with extreme scepticism, yet contradictorily regard individual perfectibility as wholly plausible. This is why the powers of the American state are constrained and its various parts consciously designed to act in opposition to each other. It is equally the reason why Americans possess "inalienable rights" and why the memory of Jeffersonian democracy, or of informed populism, has so powerful a hold on the contemporary American imagination.

Canadian expectations are the direct reverse. It is taken for granted here that the state, for all its periodic inefficiencies, will cause the society to progress for the benefit of all the individuals in it; Canadians therefore yield to the state the absolutist authority of the supremacy of Parliament, and until the Charter of Rights and Freedoms they possessed almost no constitutional rights at all. But while Canadians place their trust in government, they withhold their trust from each other. In *The American Character*, Denis Brogan remarks on the "absence of jealousy" toward the wealthy by Americans who are down and out; those who fail accept that they did so despite a reasonable chance to succeed, and accept also that they will benefit from the accomplishments of those who do succeed. By contrast, envy of success is one of the most evident of Canadian social traits, sharpened by a conviction not simply that success if achieved in Canada cannot be for real, but also that if success is somehow achieved here it had to have been done at the expense of other Canadians.

The ultimate yielding to the authority of the state by Canadians occurred during the imposition of the War Measures Act in response to the FLQ kidnappings of October, 1970. The shock of the discovery that history in its crudest, most violent form could burst in upon the peaceable kingdom explains in part the popularity of the suspension of civil liberties by the War Measures Act. So does, within some unadmitted layer of the English-Canadian psyche at that time, a satisfaction at seeing Quebecers being disciplined. The root explanation has to be that Canadians agreed with Trudeau's diagnosis, that to protect the liberties of individuals it was necessary for the

160

state to temporarily suspend those liberties.

Even the most sympathetic of American observers of Canada, such as the scholar Edgar Friedenberg and the journalist Andrew Malcolm, have found this kind of willing suspension of disbelief in government baffling and deeply disturbing. Their unease is understandable, and in the instance of the FLQ crisis was shared by Canadian civil libertarians. Yet their perspective is off-centre, like that of Canadian critics of American society who fail to make the connection between the opposition of American citizens to the Vietnam War, which they cheered, and the opposition of other American citizens to gun control legislation, which they wholly deplore.

Seven months after using the War Measures Act, the same government that enacted it almost brought into force a Charter of Rights, at the Victoria Conference of First Ministers of June, 1971, and was later able to enact a successor to that Charter, by then grown incomparably more ambitious. This 1982 Charter of Rights and Freedoms contains perhaps the most expressive of all the differences between the two political cultures. Included in it, reinserted into it by overwhelming public pressure after the politicians had log-rolled it out for their convenience, is an equal rights clause, the same clause, virtually, that the American women's movement has failed to achieve, for all its far greater intellectual vigour and public activism.

In the end, no elaborate analysis is needed to explain the persistence of Canadians' belief in the state. They believe that the state is *their* state. And it is. Certainly since the early 1940s, the Canadian state has been doing exactly what Canadians wanted it do to – moving their society toward the liberal ideals of greater equity, fairness, and tolerance. At times, as in the adoption of a colour-blind immigration policy, this has happened by osmosis, by some unacknowledged social consensus probably catalyzed by a recognition of the value to the economy of the energy of immigrants but never stated publicly since to do so would be to admit that the previous immigration policy had been racist, as it had been. At other times, as in the restoration of an unqualified equal rights clause to the Charter of Rights and Freedoms, it has happened as a response to an explicit declaration by the public of its definition of fairness and equity. In whatever ways it has happened, it has happened. No criteria exist to determine whether Canada today is or is not the most liberal political culture in the world. Beyond any doubt, it is one of the most liberal. In no doubt at all is that, within the environment of North America, this liberalism makes Canada as different from its neighbour as do, within Europe, say, all the inherited differences of speech and dress and social custom and which, conventionally, serve as the boundary lines between one society and another.

A word is in order here about the way that words are used here. Throughout, "liberal" is used in the way everyone now uses it – quite often indeed as a term of abuse – in the sense of being synonymous with progressive or reformist or redistributive or welfarist. Those liberals who aren't Liberals sometimes refer to themselves as "small 'l' liberals," a coy disclaimer that inspired the comment from one British politician, "Small 'l.' At which end?"

Scholars will be properly appalled. This usage is almost the direct opposite of the word's original meaning, derived from Locke and Hobbes, of a society founded on the principles of individualism and of egalitarianism. In his seminal *The Liberal Tradition in America*, Hartz used the word in its original, classical meaning and took for granted that every reader would understand this. So, though, did the conservative critic Emmett Tyrrell take for granted that everyone would understand that his 1984 polemic, *The Liberal Crackup*, was about too many bureaucrats and too much government spending rather than about the decline of American entrepreneurship.

Words change. Once, "gay cavalier" meant a womanizer. Conservatism now is generally used to mean what liberalism once was used to mean. Much in the way that George Orwell once subdivided the British class system into categories such as "lower upper class" and "upper middle class," so it is possible to further subdivide conservatism into mutants such as neo-conservatism, the New Right, populism. Broadly and roughly, in popular parlance, all usages involve giving primacy to individualism – and to the "magic of the market-place."

Liberalism, in its modern sense, means interposing the state between the marketplace and the citizens. It has come to be regarded as synonymous with Big Government, the original connecting link being that liberals committed themselves to Big Government to combat the market power of Big Business and Big Labour; an obvious intellectual challenge for liberals is to come to terms with the contemporary reality that for most citizens most of the time in a well-fed late twentieth-century society, Big Government is more oppressive – a hectoring "nanny state" – than Big Business ever was, let alone the *papier-mâché* tiger of Big Labour.*

As used in this chapter and elsewhere in this book, the meanings intended by the terms "liberalism" and "conservatism" can be simply stated. Liberals make their choices between available policies on the basis of the tests of "fairness" and "equity," or they try to; conservatives make their choices on the basis of "freedom" and "efficiency." Those differences constitute in turn the essential difference between the two political cultures of North America; each is groping its way toward progress, but each is approaching it along quite different paths.

A last explanatory note is almost certainly unnecessary: as defined here, Canadians' prevailing political culture of liberalism has nothing whatever to do with the formal ideologies – such as they are – of Canada's alternate governing parties, the Liberals and the Conservatives. Of the two present leaders, John Turner is the more conservative and Mulroney is the more liberal, certainly by instinct. While the Conservative Party does attract to it more ideological conservatives, this certainly wasn't true during the contest between Diefenbaker and St. Laurent, and it is worth noting that the three most liberal-minded external affairs ministers of the last quarter century have all been Conservatives – Howard Green, Flora MacDonald, Joe Clark. Predictably, John A. Macdonald figured out how to square the circle; his official designation was Liberal-Conservative.

Two objections can be made to this definition of Canadian political culture as being prevailingly liberal, and to liberalism in turn being the source of our distinctiveness as a North American society. The first objection derives from common sense, fortified by ample evidence: Canadian politics, far from being defined by a liberal ideology, is defined by the absence of any ideology at all. In this argument, pragmatism, opportunism, and the sheer impossibility of ever getting all the regions to agree to anything at the same time have boiled down whatever fragments of conservatism, liberalism,

---

* Liberalism in this sense is almost synonymous with "social democracy," but that European term doesn't transplant well in North America, although New Democrats apply this term to themselves, or occasionally, more daringly, call themselves "democratic socialists."

and socialism survived the transatlantic crossing into a homogeneous if quite palatable stew.

"Bland works," former Ontario Premier Bill Davis, the most successful of his breed in modern times, replied to a reporter who inquired why he was so boring a public personality. Author Christina McCall once memorably compared the ideology of the Liberals to "silly putty." More to the point, however, it was not until the Conservatives had acquired the same malleability that Canadians again trusted them with a majority government. If it is true that no Canadian politician would ever propose extremism as a solution to anything – Trudeau, as the least Canadian of all politicians, serves at times as an exception to the rule – it is also true that no Canadian politician would attempt the grandeur of lines like, "We hold these truths to be self-evident, that all men are created equal, that they are endowed by their creator with certain and inalienable rights"; still less would a Canadian politician be so intemperate as to tell bankers, "Thou shalt not crucify mankind upon a cross of gold." It would be unseemly, perhaps even be unfair to the bankers.

Some of this is circumstantial. Politics has become tele-politics. The medium filters out all messages except symbolic, impressionistic ones. One "photo opportunity" is worth a 10,000-word Speech from the Throne. As well, in all affluent, middle-class societies, all political parties move to the centre because that's where everybody, being middle class, is. Lastly, while Canada is not in any way the "difficult country to govern" it is often claimed to be, since it is inherently orderly, democratic, and affluent, it is an almost impossible country to lead.

Saying that successive Canadian governments have stayed safely in the centre is to say only that Canadian governments have done exactly what Canadians have wanted them to do. It is the character of the centre rather than its popularity with all parties aspiring to power that matters. "Redistribution in one form or another is a leading principle of Canadian society and is rarely questioned because to question it is to question the existence of Canada itself," Herschel Hardin wrote in A Nation Unaware. Since the White Paper on Employment and Income of 1945 Canadian politics has amounted to a continuous exercise in redistribution: through public services such as Medicare and hospital insurance; through geo-economics as in regional equalization; through income sharing, by means of devices like unemployment insurance and old-age pensions; through grants to artists and athletes who would not otherwise survive in the marketplace; through virtually tuition-free post-secondary education; and, most recently, through affirmative action programs such as those for women, native people, and the handicapped, and of which the first was the accelerated promotion of francophones in the federal civil service. No wonder Canadians trust government; it's been a friend in need to most of them.*

There is a solid core of pragmatism to Canadians' view of the purposes of redistribution. The Conservative pollster Allan Gregg, for instance, believes that the test Canadians apply in their judgements of public policies isn't so much that of "fairness" as that of "a dislike of meanness." Gregg's polls show that Canadians are fully prepared to deal harshly with individuals who rip off unemployment and welfare, yet they are equally prepared for payments to individuals who really need them to be increased.

The mettle of the Canadian political culture of liberalism is being tested now by its ability to discriminate. There is no more surplus wealth to redistribute; at the same time, the bills of yesteryear are overdue to be paid. The Mulroney government may have missed its great opportunity in its budget of May, 1985. A public readiness to accept restraint existed palpably through the winter of 1984-85. It was not seized upon. Instead, in a bungled attempt to reduce the deficit by raising taxes in small amounts from all sources, the government offended Canadian perceptions of fairness, or provoked the public's dislike of meanness, by de-indexing the pensions of the poorest of Canadians.

The other objection that can be made to this description of Canadian political culture as distinctively liberal is a more scholarly one. Its starting point would be Hartz's classic work, *The Liberal Tradition in America*, in which he set out the thesis that all new societies are "fragments" of the Old World societies from which they had sprung, so that their political culture "congealed" into the ideology prevailing in the original society at the time of their breakaway. In Hartz's analysis,

---

* More than one Canadian in two receives all or the greater part of his or her income from government. This calculation takes in all public servants, active or retired, including those at government-funded institutions such as universities and hospitals, all pensioners with limited private means, all those on unemployment insurance or welfare, veterans, many native people. It excludes employees in industries such as textiles and fishing that get by on government subsidies.

the congealed, or permanent, political culture equally of Canada and the U.S. is that of classic liberalism, or Whiggery, or business liberalism – conservatism in today's vocabulary – since this was the dominant ideology in Britain at the end of the eighteenth century. To Canada, Hartz allowed only the marginal distinction of possessing certain "Tory traces" brought north by the Loyalists.

Succeeding scholars have accentuated the importance of this Tory tradition. Canadians' distinctiveness lies in our condition of being "counter-revolutionaries," a term first coined by Harold Innis. At times lovingly, as by Creighton and Grant, at other times in exasperation, as for instance by Friedenberg – "Canadian society is deficient, not in respect for law but in respect for liberty" – and at other times with clinical precision, as by the University of California sociologist Seymour Lipset, these commentators have chronicled Canada's differences as being those of a hierarchical, transplanted monarchy in contrast to the neighbouring egalitarian, self-invented republic.

Lipset's work is so voluminous, dating from his 1965 essay, *Revolution and Counter-Revolution: The United States and Canada*, and extending to a lengthy paper he delivered at a November, 1984, conference held in Harriman, New York, that his ideas deserve an extended look.* He describes Canada as a "more conservative, traditional, law-abiding, statist and elitist society than the United States," and substantiates this by opinion surveys and other data showing that Canadians are more trusting of governments but also more readily abdicate to them responsibility for charity and volunteer work.** Lipset states also that Canadians are far less inclined to take commercial or financial risks, are far more inclined to obey the law, and are more inclined to believe in policemen rather than in the victims of police violence.

According to Lipset, the reason for these Toryish traits is that Canada "is a nation created by defeated nationalities which tried to institutionalize and memorialize the traditional value of cultures

---

* Lipset's intimate knowledge of Canada dates back to the 1940s when he studied at the University of Toronto, receiving his doctorate for a study of the CCF in Saskatchewan, subsequently published as *Agrarian Socialism* (Berkeley, 1950).

** An excellent analysis of the trade-off between state charity and individual charity is contained in Samuel A. Martin's *An Essential Grace*. He notes that Sweden, the most socialized, or liberalized, of all societies has the lowest level of volunteer charity. Canada ranks about midway up the Western table on both counts.

overthrown in battle" – anti-democratic, anti-materialist clericalism in the instance of Quebec, anti-republican elitism in the instance of the Loyalists.

This surely is attributing too much to the Loyalists. Calvinist Scots should bear the blame for many of the purse-lipped, risk-avoidance habits of modern Canadians. Sheer northernness helped perpetuate Canada's conservatism: for revolutions to succeed, mobs have to be prepared to gather at the barricades, an activity not encouraged by sub-zero temperatures. Just as potent as inhibitors of radicalism have been Canada's long-delayed industrialization and the similar tardy arrival of mass immigration, both of which happened here about three-quarters of a century later than in the U.S. A last influence, although nowadays unfashionable to cite, has been Canada's quality of Britishness, which lingered until relatively recently. The studied reticence that amounts almost to squeamishness about intruding on the privacy of others; the tradition of public service as a personal duty; the favoured style of ironic self-deprecation in public debate: these are "distinctively" Canadian qualities only in that they are distinctive in North America. Blessedly, the British class system failed to survive the sea passage; the occasional traces of it that made it across got blown away in winter storms which, come to think of it, are probably the greatest social leveller of all, as evidenced further by the egalitarianism of the Scandinavians and the Scots. But Canada does owe its character as a private, Sony-Walkman kind of culture to the influence of the British.

The real drawback to this analysis, though, is that it spends too much time looking backward at Canada as it used to be. Thus, while it is interesting to observe that Americans, in full pursuit of Jeffersonian democracy, acquired universal male suffrage in 1840 and Canadians resisted such an extravagance until 1898, or that American democratic political conventions date from 1832 and the Canadian equivalents only from 1918, the contemporary relevance of such cross-border comparisons is questionable. It isn't easy to find in the Canada of today – urban, secular, liberal, multicultural, bilingual – much that could have been predicted as likely to emerge from the Canada that existed as recently as a half century ago – rural, conservative, hier-archical, and monocultural (Quebec then was hidden from sight). The old Canada hasn't vanished. But it has been transmuted, certainly in its cities, into a new form by a society that is still in a state of becoming rather than of being, and which in the future will become something else again – manifestly a more multicoloured society, for instance.

Near the end of his 1984 paper, Lipset attempts to come to terms with the mutability of his target. He comments that "My main modification of prior formulations" is that "Canadians are now more supportive of redistributive equalitarianism than Americans ... are more liberal than Americans with respect to sexual morality" and "now view their country as more 'leftist' or liberal in its institutions and international objectives than the United States." This is another way of saying that sometime, somehow, we ceased being Tories, obsessed with having lost the Revolutionary War, and became liberals committed to trying to build a fair society, even though, being Canadians, we are building it in a very conservative way.

While it's fairly easy to characterize the Canada of today as a liberal society, it isn't easy to identify exactly when and how it made the transition to this state from that of being a conservative agrarian society with, secreted inside it, a quasi-feudal Quebec. Modernization and urbanization, which weaken traditional ties, account for a good deal of the change but leave much of it unexplained since those forces have likewise been at work in the U.S. and have affected it quite differently.

Ronald Reagan's victory in 1980 has often been called a revolution. In fact, it was less that than a restoration. By his appeal to patriotism and to traditional values, Reagan restored the U.S. to its natural conservatism or classic business liberalism. For Americans to abandon that creed, briefly so in historical terms, required them to have been shocked out of the true faith by the catastrophe of the Depression and then, following the Eisenhower interregnum, to have been seduced back to the new liberal faith by the glamour of John F. Kennedy.

Even during their long term out of power, from 1960 to 1980,* American conservatives were never that far from power. Their candidate, Barry Goldwater, won the Republican nomination in 1964 and Reagan was a serious contender for it in 1976. While in the political wilderness, conservatives remained well watered. They possessed the resources, not merely financial but also intellectual, to

---

* Among interim Republican presidents, Nixon for instance lost his conservative credentials when he proclaimed: "We are all Keynesians now."

168

publish magazines such as *Commentary* and to staff such high-calibre think tanks as The Heritage Foundation, the Hoover Institute, and the Georgetown School of Strategic and International studies (out of which came Jeane Kirkpatrick). And while liberals generally dominated the eastern media establishment, the influential *Wall Street Journal* provided a platform for conservative thought.

The cross-border contrast is striking. At the 1976 Progressive Conservative leadership convention, one of the country's few intellectual neo-conservative politicians, Sinclair Stevens, felt it necessary to protest that he was really only a "cuddly Conservative." At the 1983 Conservative convention, the two right-wing candidates, Peter Pocklington and John Gamble, gathered between them less than 5 per cent of the votes. A survey of Canadian neo-conservative students published late in 1984 by political scientists Neil Nevitte and Roger Gibbons found that while such students were sceptical of government and had "little interest in reducing the income gap between rich and poor," few wanted government to actually shrink, most favoured gun control, and a majority opposed the testing of the cruise missile. From coast to coast, the single source of intellectual conservative analysis is the Fraser Institute think tank of Vancouver. Its director, Michael Walker, the son of a Newfoundland coalminer, has issued some provocative studies of the counter-productive effects of rent controls and affirmative action programs and of the consequences of too much government and high taxes. Even so, the Fraser Institute has been infected by the bug of fairness: its studies have also criticized social programs, such as unemployment insurance, for providing the largest payments to those with the highest incomes.

The gap between the two political cultures of North America was perhaps most dramatically demonstrated in the fall of 1984. On November 4, Americans re-elected Reagan by a landslide: "You haven't seen anything yet," he declared. Two months earlier, Canadians elected, also in a landslide, the most liberal of all conservative leaders in the Western world; ever since, Mulroney hasn't stopped talking about "fairness." He likes to be liked, certainly; he also knows what Canadians like to hear.

One source of contemporary Canadian liberalism has been identified by a Canadian scholar, Gad Horowitz, daring enough to challenge the thesis of Hartz that Canada's political culture constitutes American

169

business liberalism moderated by certain "Tory traces."

After a bit more than a century of effort, Canadians can claim to have minted just two political insights with a certain originality to them. One was the declaration of the Royal Commission on Bilingualism and Biculturalism that Canada was composed of two co-equal majorities, English Canadians being the "majority majority" and French Canadians being a "minority majority" and so having the right to determine linguistic and cultural conditions in their homeland. This represented an evolutionary step – a thoroughly liberal step, in fact – beyond the states' rights argument of "concurrent majorities" developed by the nineteenth-century American politician John C. Calhoun.

Canada's other claim to political originality resides in the phrase "Red Tory." It was coined by McGill University political scientist Horowitz in his 1967 essay, *Conservativism, Liberalism and Socialism in Canada*. Predictably, some other academics doubt that any such animal exists. "The Red Tory is a myth," concluded Rod Preece in a 1977 article for the *Canadian Journal of Political and Social Theory*. This judgement would come as a surprise to those who have styled themselves as Red Tories, the MacDonalds, Flora and David, Gordon Fairweather, David Crombie (also Mulroney, at the 1976 leadership convention), and, coming toward the centre from the other direction, Senator Eugene Forsey, one-time research director for the CCF, and former Ontario NDP leader Stephen Lewis, now ambassador to the United Nations, who has confessed, "I like Tories."

The Red Tories were never particularly Tory, in contrast to such British equivalents as the "radical Tory" aristocrats and squires, renamed "wets" by Margaret Thatcher. Certainly they were never particularly Red. They resembled many liberals in the Liberal Party yet were not like them – here lay the expression of their Toryism – in their attachment to community and to continuity. Red Toryism is currently out of fashion among Conservatives. What's interesting about it isn't that it's had to retreat into the closet but that it's so often been able to parade openly in public. Red Tories have been able to do this because they have a constituency, and a history, within the Progressive Conservative Party and within the country.

Horowitz traced the origins of Red Toryism back to the fact that, because of heavy immigration from the British Isles, Canada's political culture didn't "congeal," in Hartz's terms, until the First World War. By this time socialism had infected the Canadian body politic, like

170

a bacillus plague brought over by cloth-capped unionists. Here, despite the absence of a class system, socialists found something to fight – the Toryism of the Loyalists – unlike their counterparts in the U.S. who found themselves perversely pre-empted because that capitalist society insisted on believing that all men were equal, which is socialism's moral core. Wrote Horowitz: "In the U.S., original socialism is dead; in Canada, socialism, though far from power, is a significant political force.... The relative strength of socialism here is related to the relative strength of Toryism here."

Horowitz's political equation contains several loose ends. If Toryism is the catalyst of socialism, then egalitarian radicalism ought to have taken root in the nation's most conservative region, the Maritimes. As a socialist himself, Horowitz exaggerated the socialist character of the CCF and NDP, which in fact have been much closer to an alliance of agrarian radicals, concerned clergymen, and liberal intellectuals dissatisfied with the "silly putty" liberalism of the Liberal Party.

Yet Horowitz was onto something. Much as Atwood's *Survival* serves as a chart for Canadian literature, Horowitz's analysis provides a map, incomplete in some parts and tugged out of kilter in others, by which it becomes possible to plot out some shapes amid the bland, homogeneous stew of Canadian politics. The fact is that Canadian Conservatives and their predecessors, the Loyalist Tories, always have been a reddish lot. The Loyalists used government funds to build the Welland Canal and left the colony in proportionately far deeper debt that Canada is after several decades of redistributive liberalism. The country's first major crown corporation, Ontario Hydro, was created by a Conservative government. Perhaps the most radical economic program ever presented to Canadians, certainly in the context of the times, was Conservative Prime Minister R.B. Bennett's New Deal of 1935. It presaged, as he said forthrightly, "the end of laissez faire." If the business community detested Trudeau, it positively loathed Diefenbaker for his prairie-populist attacks on "Bay Street." It would be hard to imagine a more "liberal" election platform – the "sacred trusts" of universal social programs and fully indexed pensions framing it like ceremonial arches – than that of Mulroney in 1984.

Another root source for contemporary Canadian liberalism can be found down in church basements and inside church and chapel pulpits. At the turn of the century, the Social Gospel movement, led by such men as Josiah Strong, swept across the border. Much in the record of Canadian Protestant churches then doesn't make for pleasant reading today: they were anti-papist and anti-French. But they possessed, almost uniquely in those rude times, a social conscience. In 1906, the General Council of the Methodist Church defined as its goal, "a social order founded on the principles of the Gospel." The prairie preacher Salem Bland called for "nothing less than a transformation of the whole economic life from a basis of competition and profits to one of cooperation and service."

To an extraordinary degree, the Canadian version of the Protestant ethic turned out to be a liberal ethic. That ideal was implanted into the CCF by clergymen such as J.S. Woodsworth and Stanley Knowles and Tommy Douglas, was handed on by the latter two to the NDP where it was perpetuated through the 1970s by Catholic priests such as Andy Hogan and Bob Ogle, and is being extended into the 1980s by a new generation of socially activist clergymen, Bill Blaikie, Dan Heap, Jim Manley.

This displaced Protestant ethic also infected the first generation of the Ottawa mandarins. Pearson, Hume Wrong, Arnold Heeney, Escott Reid were all sons of the manse, as was that outsider-insider Frank Scott. Several others, O.D. Skelton, Norman Robertson, W.A. Mackintosh, were the sons of teachers, the secular equivalents of ministers in those underpaid days. Today, "bureaucrat" has acquired the same abusive value in social discourse as once attached to real estate developers. But in their heyday in the 1940s and 1950s, those Ottawa Men, in Christina McCall's generic description, set a style of public service that still endures, however much now faded and at times tarnished.

The last source of modern Canadian liberalism resides in Quebec. Until a quarter of a century ago, that society had little to recommend it, other than to harbour, unnoticed, some individuals of quite remarkable quality. Its shining contribution to Canada was simply to exist, to have survived: by doing so, Quebec helped to transform the Canada of history into the Canada of today.

The point of Quebec, really, its transformational effect upon Canada, is that if one group of Canadians can be different, then all can be different. Before a majority can acquire the habit of tolerance – no matter how slow English Canadians may have been to acquire it toward French Canadians – that majority must encounter a minority that is both different enough to be noticeable and large enough to command political attention. Those conditions applied in Canada; they did not in the United States. The cross-border differences between "mosaic" and "melting pot" are grossly overstated; those that matter are the differences in demography.

If there is any defining quality to liberalism it resides in its acceptance of the inevitability of ambiguity. A society that tolerates and even cherishes cultural and racial and regional differences cannot survive unless it accepts the constancy of ambiguity, for any single collective policy is bound to threaten some group, some minority, some region, some province. This is the lesson that Quebecers taught to all Canadians.

In searching for the moment when Canada began its transformation from a conservative society to a liberal one, two dates therefore suggest themselves. One is Diefenbaker's election victory of 1957. The other is Quebec's Quiet Revolution of 1960. The two events relate to each other and reinforce each other. Perhaps Diefenbaker's boldest idea was that all Canadians were equal, that Ukrainian Canadians and German Canadians and others should no longer be hyphenated and so be marked as second class. For French Canadians, though, "One Canada" meant a Canada in which there would be no place for them to be different. Quebec nationalism represented an attempt to redefine Canada into two nations, different but equal. Out of conflict and crisis the two opposed ideas merged into the regionalized, bilingual, multicultural, multicoloured Canada of today, where almost everyone is different but all are equal.

Such a nation can survive only by defying the laws of political gravity. Two forces sustain the parts within the whole. One is the emerging sense of Canadian patriotism that Diefenbaker first affirmed and which was triumphantly confirmed by the Quebec referendum of 1980 and by the patriation of the constitution of 1982. Canada today belongs to Canadians in a way that the Canada of history never did because Canadians themselves have now invented it. The other sustaining force is the prevailing political culture of liberalism. It, similarly, is Canadians' own invention, shared equally by Quebecers who as a result of the Quiet Revolution have become just as liberal a society as the rest of Canada. At one and the same time, Canadians have never before been so obviously North American, and yet so obviously a different kind of North American. The old Tory Loyalists and their successors made it possible for this to happen; Canadians themselves made it happen.

Chapter Twelve
La Différence

This Country in the Morning quiz: "Define the Canadian identity in a single, short sentence."

Winning entry: "As Canadian as possible, under the circumstances."

In the United States, it is almost impossible to buy an electric kettle. Winners of horse and dog shows are awarded blue ribbons while those in Canada receive red ones, even though we talk about "blue-ribbon" committees. Canadian beer has an alcohol content of 5 per cent as against the more genteel 3.2 per cent of much American brew. Andrew Malcolm's book *The Canadians* appeared in its American edition with a bright red, yellow, and green cover and in its Canadian edition with a pure white one. On the other hand, the title of Alison Gordon's chronicle of her years covering the Toronto Blue Jays, *Foul Balls*, appeared south of the border delicately abbreviated to *Foul Ball*.

Then there are the similarities. Almost all of the famous Winnipeg goldeye come from the Missouri River, and almost none of it from anywhere in Manitoba. Zenith 800 numbers can be used to phone from anywhere to anywhere in either country. The U.S. postal service charges the same rate for trans-border as for domestic mail, although Canada exercises its sovereignty and charges five cents more. A number of Canadian companies, such as AMCA International, quote only U.S. dollars in their annual reports.

The *Financial Post*'s Washington correspondent, Fred Harrison, reports that at parties Canadians divide into two groups, one in one corner discussing cross-border similarities and the other discussing dissimilarities: "we hoard them like precious jewels." One such jewel he's observed is that Washington bureaucrats talk about "opening an account" while in Ottawa the operative phrase is "opening a file."

It's a game that anyone can play. Stereotypes about nations, no differently from those about men and women, are seldom accurate, but no other way exists to discuss the subject. In a review of Malcolm's book for the *New York Times*, Margaret Atwood warned that cross-border comparisons are "fraught with peril" and then offered some of her own: "The Canadian mind-set is skeptical-ironic, the American idealistic-optimistic.... Praise an American and he'll agree with you; praise a Canadian and he'll think you're trying to sell him something."

A useful way of starting the game is to consider the possibility that there are no differences between Canadians and Americans, or none that matter. The most persuasive proponent of this thesis is Joel Garreau. In his book, *The Nine Nations of North America*, Garreau sweeps aside all national boundaries, including that of Mexico, as "pale barriers, thoroughly porous to money, immigration and ideas." In their place, he identifies "regional nations," each of which "has a particular economy; each commands a certain emotional allegiance from its citizens.... Most important, each nation has a distinct prism through which it views the world." Among his "nations" are New England, which extends north through the Maritimes, The Foundry, which encompasses the northern industrial states and southern Ontario, The Breadbasket, which unites all the grain-growing flatlands, and Ecotopia, which extends from halfway up B.C. to halfway down California. Tex-Mex takes in the rest of California and much of northern Mexico, "where mellow is no longer just a product of sun and surf but is being caused also by the softening influence of Spanish culture." The single existing political entity Garreau leaves untouched is Quebec: "Which properly speaking is a nation unto itself."

Garreau makes a few careless mistakes, such as writing "Ottawa" when he means "Ontario." But his observations are sharp and his anecdotage is lively. His core thesis is that nation-states are dinosaurs with shrivelled brains: "Washington doesn't work any more." At the same time, people are no longer as dependent on Washington as they once were, or on New York, because, thanks to TV, travel, and instant communications, "people less and less feel the need to move to metropolitan centres to lead complete lives."

Two conclusions can be drawn from Garreau's analysis. The first is that most North Americans are defined by their regional identity rather than by their national citizenship. Many of their values and attitudes and speech patterns are determined by regional characteristics, such as those of topography and climate, history (ancient or recent being the key dividing line), and type of economic activity – resource extraction, agriculture, smokestack manufacturing, high-tech. Clearly, there is a good deal to this: Saskatchewanians, say, and North Dakotans, have far more in common with each other than either have with New Yorkers or Ontarians; steelworkers in Hamilton and Cleveland speak a common language that condominium-dwellers in Toronto and Chicago would not understand.

The other conclusion, a more jarring one to Canadian autonomist sensibilities, is that the entire continent, including northern Mexico, is a single socio-economic unit; political boundaries still exist, but they have lost almost all meaning.

There is also a good deal to this second thesis. For many Canadians much of the time, the international boundary makes no more difference in a practical sense than do the provincial boundaries. On any day in January and February, there are about one million Canadians, or 4 per cent of the total population, in Florida, and also great numbers – this is one of the prime cultural distinctions between eastern and western Canadians – in Hawaii. For all these people, the U.S. has become an essential extension of their native land, for a winter week or two or year-round once they retire, except for summer visits to children and grandchildren.* According to the best estimates of the consulate in Los Angeles, there are one million first- and second-generation Canadians in the area; according to another best estimate, about three-quarters of a million Canadians are living and working illegally in the U.S. In the perception of these groups, the relationship between the southern mass of the continent and the north strip where they were born and brought up is that between metropolis and hinterland, scarcely different from the one that exists between the Maritimes and Toronto. Canadians in search of money and fun – the 175 Canadian doctors in Houston who've formed a golf club to which only Canadian doctors can belong – or in search of the chance to be excellent – as, for instance, Robert Mundell, the supply-side theoretician, once at Waterloo University, now at Columbia; or the actors and film producers; or the former

---

* Former Liberal cabinet minister Jean Chrétien has remarked: "Canadians love Canada, but not for fifty-two weeks of the year."

Avro Arrow engineers at NASA – find opportunities that just aren't available in a medium-sized society no matter how much progress it has made.

The flow northward to summer camps and cottages and national parks and fishing streams and lakes is smaller, but for these Americans Canada similarly has become an essential extension of an overcrowded country. If many Vancouverites drive south to Bellingham, Washington, and to Seattle to shop, many Detroiters drive to Windsor – drive southward, in fact, because of the geography – to be able to go to a restaurant without having to worry about losing their hubcaps or their wallets. Between 50,000 and 80,000 American draft resisters and deserters came north during the Vietnam War; about 20,000 Canadians joined in it to prove their manhood.

Thus, to a degree, we are all regionalized North Americans. In a splendid bit of invective, Peter Brimelow, a journalist who has worked in Canada and who now is in New York, has written in a report for the Manhattan Institute: "For Canadian nationalists to have been able to raise doubts about such an obvious reality when the interaction between Canada and the U.S. is so overwhelming as to amount to what Goldwin Smith called 'political fusion', is a classic case of ideological hegemony transcending material reality."

Yet the ideological hegemony persists. The Gallup Poll stopped asking Canadians whether they wanted to join the United States in the early 1950s when those answering "Yes" dropped to an insignificant 9 per cent. The occasional political attempts to convince Canadians to accept objective reality, such as former Saskatchewan Conservative leader Dick Cullver's Union Party, have passed quickly into oblivion through an intervening period of farce. (Cullver could never figure out an answer to those few Saskatchewanians who showed even the faintest glimmer of interest when they asked what would happen to Medicare.)

Over the years, many Canadians have voted for the U.S. with their feet. The number of footloose Canadians would increase significantly if the cross-border economic gap widened too far. But today, there is little difference in living standards. American incomes are higher and consumer prices are lower – at present because of the high value of the dollar but at all times because of the far more competitive business environment. Canadians, though, spend far less on health and hospital care; aren't required to spend, if they are middle class and have children, as much as $20,000 a year in private university tuition fees; spend little, by comparison risibly small amounts, on private security. Comparisons in international living standards are always iffy, but perhaps the best measure of the cross-border gap is that the average American family occupies 5.1 rooms while a Canadian family fills up exactly five rooms.*

Canadians themselves have little doubt that they've got it made. In the winter of 1984, Decima Research asked them whether they agreed or disagreed with the proposition, "Canada is the best country in the world in which to live at the present time." Just 7 per cent disagreed; 81 per cent agreed totally or strongly, a minor decline from the 85 per cent who thought the same way in the winter of 1980, even though in the meantime Canada's economic performance had fallen well behind that of the U.S.

Over and above the cross-border regional similarities, which certainly exist and which create potent north-south interconnections, there are obviously national dissimilarities. Otherwise, Canadians would have no reason to think themselves better off than their neighbours.

No one has studied the differences between the two societies more scrupulously or more voluminously than Seymour Lipset. There is little his dossier doesn't encompass.** Canadians are less prone to murder, rob, rape, and mug than are Americans. They are decidedly more relaxed about sex: 48 per cent of Canadians but only 36 per cent of Americans think premarital sex is okay, or did in 1977, and many more Canadians take a ho-hum attitude about nudes in magazines. Canadians save twice as much and are much more timid about investing in stocks or trying new consumer products. They are much readier to doff their caps to authority: the RCMP gets an approval rating of 61 per cent as compared to 45 per cent for federal law enforcement officers. They are much more dependent on governments, which take 44 per cent of the Gross National Product in

---

* This view of Canadians as a well-off lot is widely held. In advance of the 1982 economic summit in Versailles, *Paris Match* commissioned a survey to determine who among the citizens of the seven summit nations "live the most happily." West Germans, Japanese, British, French, and Americans all awarded the laurels to Canadians.

** See Lipset, "The Cultural Dimension," in *Canada and the United States*, ed. Charles Doran and John Sigler (Englewood Cliffs, N.J., 1985).

Canada as against only 37 per cent in the U.S.

There are some exceptions to these familiar national character profiles that Lipset doesn't mention. Contrary to the universal assumption, here and elsewhere, Canadians hold less life insurance than do Americans – $24,300 by each adult as against $26,400 in the U.S., according to the Canadian Life and Health Association. Nor, again despite the general belief, is the Canadian social security system uniformly superior: average disability payments are $250 a month compared to $450-500 in the U.S. In the instance of life insurance, the explanation may lie in the Canadian tax system, which by encouraging saving through RRSPs and other means, has made life insurance relatively less necessary. (Medicare has a similar effect.) Differences in the tax systems also explain why, although the level of home-ownership is the same in both countries (61 per cent here; 65 per cent there), almost one in two Canadians (45 per cent) have fully paid off their mortgages as against only one in four Americans (27 per cent), who can deduct their interest costs from taxable income. It must be added, though, that tax systems both influence people's cultural preferences and are themselves influenced by them. A further qualification that needs to be made is that Lipset, in his reckoning, doesn't fully allow for the fact that certain cross-border cultural differences are affected statistically to a significant degree by the presence in the U.S. of both a black under-class and huge numbers of illegal immigrants, neither of which exist here.*

Lipset does though make the point, as some other commentators have neglected to, that within Canada the once dramatically wide sociological differences between French and English Canadians have largely vanished. As Lipset's data show, French Canadians are now as liberal as English-speaking Canadians on redistribution issues and are more liberal, or permissive, on sexual and religious issues.

One of Lipset's most useful contributions is to record, as is often overlooked by Canadian commentators, the important cross-border religious differences. He points to the size and vigour of fundamentalist and evangelical churches in the U.S.; by comparison, "each of the three largest Canadian denominations (Catholic, Anglican, United) has something of the qualities of an *established church*." He quotes

---

* Eliminating the "black factor" doesn't eliminate cross-border cultural differences. The national rate of teen-age pregnancies in the U.S., for example, is 90 per 1,000, compared to only 60 in Canada, but among non-black American girls it is still markedly higher, at 80 per 1,000.

data showing that Americans, far more so than Canadians, believe in the devil, in Heaven, and in the applicability to them personally of the Ten Commandments. Canada's secularity is in fact the norm throughout the Western world, while the U.S.'s relative religiosity places it among a very small group of advanced countries, such as Israel, South Africa, and Poland. Within North America, this creates some of the most dramatic of cross-border differences. Canada has never had a national leader who was publicly religious in the manner of Jimmy Carter; religious leaders play no role in Canadian politics remotely comparable to those played by a Jerry Falwell or a Billy Graham, or by Reagan's personal preacher, James Robison. The portions of Canadian broadcasting that are most thoroughly "Americanized" are the TV Bible hours.

National differences, or at least distinctions, therefore exist. The question is whether these are just variations on a single North American theme, comparable to the list of cultural differences that could be compiled between Californians and Georgians, say, or whether these differences derive from some quality intrinsic to Canadian society.

Of all the differences between the two societies, the most striking is the one that has been curiously overlooked by all the analysts. This is the fact that Canadians mostly live in cities while Americans, mostly, don't.

More than one in four Canadians (29 per cent) live in metropolitan areas with a population of at least one million – Toronto, Montreal, Vancouver; only one in twelve Americans (8 per cent) live in comparable urban agglomerations. More than one in two Canadians (56 per cent) live in cities or towns with a population of at least 100,000; only one in four Americans (25 per cent) live in similar-sized cities and towns.

This oversight isn't really curious. The land is Canada; Canadians are their land. Just a glance at a map to confirm that we occupy more space than any country but Russia (the Mercator projection exaggerates its extent a bit) infuses any Canadian but a dullard with a surge of pride. Only a dullard, again, could traverse the land in the comfort of an airplane and not feel small by an appreciation of the courage and stoicism of the explorers and voyageurs and sod-hut pioneers who opened it up, and not feel also, while gazing down at its immense emptiness, a sense of wonder and doubt that any nation owning all of it yet occupying so little of it could actually survive.

The land, and the nature that envelops it, has defined Canadians and has made Canadians what they are. "From the land, Canada, must come the soul of Canada," wrote the historian Arthur Lower. Northrop Frye has written that "central to Canadian writing is the imminence of the natural world"; Margaret Atwood's thesis of survival as the central image in Canadian literature derives from her appreciation of the shock to the creative imagination of finding itself surrounded by an immense, forbidding, unconquerable terrain. The land inspired the first great Canadian artists, the Group of Seven, and soon afterwards, Emily Carr. It still inspires those who have left the country. "I still wake up some mornings in North London," author Michael Ignatieff wrote in a recent essay, "and remember slipping through the back-channels of Georgian Bay in the early-morning haze, feeling the plumb of the craft's balance down my spine and the silver drops from the lip of the paddle breaking the stillness of the lake."

The land has defined Canadians in more practical ways. Except for Quebec and Newfoundland, Canada's provinces differ little from each other in their cultures and lifestyles, far less than the individual U.S. states although that country is far more centralized politically. Geography has made Canada into a regionalized country, and so into a decentralized federation. Geography keeps Canadians apart, not just by sheer distance but by its intervening spaces – the Rockies, the emptiness of northern Ontario that cuts off the Prairies from central Canada, the upthrust of Maine that does the same to the Maritimes.

Much of the Canadian character derives from its northernness. Reticence, pragmatism, wariness of public display, and, far from least, "puritanism tempered by orgy" in William Kilbourn's wonderful phrase: all are common traits of northerners everywhere. An awareness of the fragility of civilization in a sub-Arctic environment, or just the social-levelling experience of getting splashed by a passing car, does make a people "sceptical-ironic," in Atwood's phrase. Canada unquestionably owes some of its liberalness to its northernness, for it seems to be the case that too much southern sun makes people want to worship something or somebody. One familiar northern trait Canadians have chucked off is that of dourness. A collective sense

182

of humour may be Britain's finest legacy to Canadians. Among the most advanced of art forms in Canada are those of cartooning – Bengough in the beginning, Duncan Macpherson and Aislin today – and of radio and TV political satire – the Royal Canadian Air Farce, the SCTV Network, Nancy White. If in U.S. politics wit is suspect and did in Adlai Stevenson, on the northern side of the border wit was almost enough to make John Crosbie and Jean Chrétien the opposing leaders.

Without that northern presence stretching behind it almost to the pole, however empty and largely uninhabitable, Canada would be a Chile, laid along a latitude. Yet most Canadians have put the North behind them. The North still awes those Canadians who experience it directly, and inconveniences those who experience it tangentially while shovelling out their driveways, but it no longer has them in its grip. Modern transportation and communications and everything from enclosed shopping centres to domed stadiums have reduced nature's scale; so has urbanization. To most Canadians, most of Canada has become what it once was to many Americans, "a game reserve situated convenient to us" in Edmund Wilson's phrase. They go into it to hunt, fish, canoe, hike, and, having experienced the land on their own terms, go back to their townhouses and condominiums. "The cottage," as it always is called, has become the point of contact between most Canadians and the Canadian landscape; come winter, they escape the Canadian nature in Florida or Hawaii.

Today, cities shape the Canadian character as much as the land once did. Because proportionately far more Canadians live in cities, they are in a certain sense more "Americanized" than are Americans. The new trends and fads of New York and California penetrate far more quickly through urban Canada than through rural America where, because of the climate and soil, proportionately so many more Americans live. Further, Canadian urban-dwellers are more urbanized than are those Americans who similarly live in cities. From Jefferson to Thoreau to Ronald Reagan, an American constant has been a suspicion of cities as effete, decadent, un-American. Rural life in Canada has never been similarly glamourized because so much of rural Canada is just too hard, too cold, too isolated to be lived in by choice; the Prairies have been depopulated, not by the banks or the CPR or other western demons but by farmers exercising their free choice to pass their winters in Regina or Edmonton, or Hawaii. In the U.S., making it means living outside a city, in Oak Forest rather than in Chicago, in Beverly Hills rather than in Los Angeles. In Canada, making it means living right downtown, in Toronto's Annex or in Montreal's Vieux Cité.*

Urbanization reinforces Canada's liberalness. Urban-dwellers tend to be secular and to be more readily impressed by the benefits of an activist government, of which the advantages are harder to justify in self-contained rural communities. Tolerance comes more easily to those who live in cities because they constantly encounter people who are different from themselves.

If contemporary Canada can claim any achievement that should earn it at least a paragraph in the history books, this would be the creation of contemporary urban Canada. The nature of that achievement is summed up by the slogan about Toronto that has been used so often in American architectural and town-planning magazines: "The City That Works." Toronto, although many Canadians, being Canadians, would rather not admit it, is the urban miracle of North America. It is at one and the same time dynamic and competitive and yet is civilized and sophisticated. On the continent, only New York – possibly, although arguably, San Francisco also – surpasses Toronto in its urbanity and in its cultural variety. The author Jan Morris, over from Britain on a commission for *Saturday Night*, went away ambivalent about Toronto – understandably so since her travel-writer's eye needs the raw material provided by disparities between wealth and squalor, by urban decay, and by a minimal amount of civic decadence. Even so, Morris summed up living in Toronto as like "winning second place in the Lottario of life." For a medium-sized nation stuck away on a northern fringe to have produced a metropolis that can contend for second place in an international table that includes New York, London, Paris, Rome is about the same as Canada pulling off a second, larger, and permanent Expo '67.

Canada's urban accomplishments amount to a kind of long-running Expo, and without its deficit. Other major cities, Montreal, Vancouver, Edmonton, Halifax, and, thanks to the generosity of the taxpayers, Ottawa, have achieved this same quality of unobtrusively efficient livability. A rung below, the differences between Calgary and Dallas, between Hamilton and Cleveland, and of course between Windsor

---

* Canada's most "rural" city, Calgary, is also its most "Americanized" one. Its downtown is a desert after five p.m. Everyone who can afford it has an "acreage" in the country; the most admired oilmen commute in from ranches.

and Detroit are palpable. True, many European cities are just as livable; none of them, though, have had to cope with the North American challenges of constant change and of mass in-migration by people of all kinds of cultures and races and colours. Within North America, the difference between the two societies comes down in the end to just that: Canadians have figured out how to make their cities work for them; Americans work in their cities and live outside them.

A common perception of Canadians, by themselves as well as by outsiders, is that they are nice Americans. The nice get taken for granted. They aren't exotic enough to command attention, or troublesome enough to compel it to be paid. "Americans know absolutely nothing about Canada. I think of it as an enormous curtain that goes right along the border from Maine to Washington [state] that they can't see through," comments Edith Iglauer, a *New Yorker* writer who spends half of each year in Manhattan and the other half in Garden Bay, B.C. The American media have long been famously indifferent to Canada, although in fact this attitude began to change in 1985 as *Time*, *Newsweek*, and the *Washington Post* all established new bureaus in Canada.*

This indifference irks Canadians and thoroughly distresses Canadian officials, particularly those in the embassy in Washington who conducted a massive opinion survey late in 1984 and discovered to their chagrin that most Americans think (a) that Japan is the U.S.'s largest trading partner, and (b) that Canada provides a market for U.S. goods of about the same size as major European countries.**

Some qualifications to this familiar Canadian gripe need to be set down. It's not just Canada about which Americans are indifferent but the entire world except for China and Britain, each for sentimental, if quite different, reasons. (In the Washington embassy's survey, Britain just edged out Canada in the "best friend and supporter"

---

* One instance of U.S. media indifference didn't merely irritate but cut to the quick. In May, 1985, *Life* magazine published a memorial issue on the Second World War. Although 96,000 Canadians were casualties in that contest, one of the highest proportions of all of the Allies and far higher than that of the U.S., *Life* managed to avoid a single mention of Canada's contributions in its 114 pages.

** The correct answers were: (a) Canada No. 1; Ontario No. 2; Japan No. 3. (b) The gap is about five to one.

185

contest, with no other country even in contention.)

Further, this indifference is quite benign. Bob Mathieson, an executive with AT&T in New York, describes as "almost pathological" the indifference of Americans to what is happening up at the top of their TV weather screens but then adds, "I myself, and a lot of others, find the informality, the gentleness, the relaxed atmosphere in Canada very, very refreshing." Lenny Glen, a reporter with *International Investor* in New York, says, "I think of Canada as a giant upper New York state, and I love upper New York state." This laid-back benignity is worth contrasting with the positive irritation toward Canada that is beginning to develop in Europe, and most particularly so in Britain. Among recent Fleet Street comments about the ex-colony are: "A great white waste of time"; "Of all the wet, wooden places at the end of the earth"; and "One of the nations one visits for its mountain peaks rather than its mundane people." In the newspapers of continental Europe – West Germany as perhaps the exception – Iceland could give Canada a close contest for column inches. Australia – *L'Express* magazine's "Person of the Year" for 1982 – now occupies the space in the European imagination that Canada once filled in the 1950s.

Last, and most to the point, Americans, when they do look north, do so not just benignly but with just a trace of envy. In a certain sense, Americans seem to see in Canada the America that once was. *New Yorker* movie critic Pauline Kael once identified correctly for her readers a film made in Toronto that pretended to have been made in New York: "I spotted the infelicity immediately. Everything was too clean and everyone was too polite." Stephen Blank of MultiNational Strategies of New York comments, "Your cleanliness and orderliness are a constant of amazement." He adds, "Mind you, so are your business practices. I start calling my American clients at eight a.m.; I never call Canadian ones before nine a.m." The literary agent Nancy Colbert, an American now living in Toronto, says: "Canadians have a fixed perception that Americans think of them as the frozen north, Nelson Eddy and all that. In fact, the perception is one of openness, cleanliness, freedom."

Cleanliness and orderliness and the rest aren't the stuff out of which history is made. But they do represent a certain kind of North American history. Orderliness and civility are essentially rural virtues.

186

They exist every bit as much in the towns and hamlets of New England as in comparable communities in Canada. Courtliness and a belief in the importance of protocol are much more a way of life in the U.S. South than they are anywhere in Canada: the southern "Y'all come back now" is at least as nicely mannered, if no more intended to be taken literally, as is the Canadian compulsion to say "Thank you" to everyone who has merely done his or her job – taxi drivers, store clerks, bank tellers, and, not inconceivably, burglars.

The Canadian particularity, the source of Canada's distinctiveness as a society within North America, is to have found a way to transplant these virtues of rural communities into its cities. Canadian cities today are confederations of communities rather than urban agglomerations. There is nothing like them – really – in the United States. Most Canadians live in them. This is why Canadians are different. To be nice Americans is no big deal: lots of Americans are every bit as nice. To be nice urban North Americans is almost a contradiction in terms, since North American cities are shaped, and are constantly being reshaped, by a relentless, ruthless imperative. Canadian society isn't anything like as dynamic and as creative as American society; but it works.

Chapter Thirteen
The Canadian Identity, Eh?

"In Toronto there are no classes
Only the Masseys and the masses."

B.K. Sandwell in *Saturday Night*, 1952, to mark the appointment of Vincent Massey as Governor General

If the cross-border differences described in the preceding chapter are valid and if the political culture of liberalism does indeed make Canadians unique in North America and uncommon anywhere, why then has the quest for a Canadian identity been going on so long, and getting nowhere?

The sheer fun of the game is a tempting explanation. "Canadians are forever taking the national pulse like doctors at a sick-bed," wrote Atwood in *Survival* "The aim is not to see whether the patient will live well but simply whether he will live at all." By the early 1980s, Canadians had become the world champions at collective self-analysis. As a kind of warm-up exercise, we came to terms with the paradox that Quebec was at one and the same time a nation and not a nation. From there, it was a short leap to the metamorphosis of Anglo-Saxons into "Anglo-Celts" so as to create room for the Scots and Irish. Northerners, once divided into whites and non-whites, were first reclassified into whites and natives, and then, once it was realized that some of the whites were actually black or brown (i.e., "visible minorities"), into natives and non-natives. In official reports, native peoples were solemnly called "autochthonous peoples." If a Canadian identity is ever agreed upon, this national game of psychoscrabble would be over.

A second explanation has substance. Many Canadians have long seen the concept of pan-Canadian identity as a threat to their own regional and provincial identities. Westerners resisted Trudeau's version of "national unity" no less than Quebecers resented John Diefenbaker's "un-hyphenated Canadianism." The waxing of regional confidence in the permanence of their particularities has caused this potent counterforce of the 1960s and 1970s to wane. So has the departure of the personalities who turned federal-provincial battles into a bloodless Canadian equivalent of the Wars of the Roses. Trudeau, the centralist emperor, was the first to leave the field; soon afterward, the provincial barons – René Lévesque of Quebec, Peter Lougheed of Alberta, Bill Davis of Ontario – struck their tents. Peace has broken out from coast to coast, and Mulroney is equipped with the negotiating skills to maintain it. Canada is and always will be a regionalized country, and tensions and rivalries will always remain. But the *idea* of a Canadian identity no longer menaces local identities.

Even so, the very term "pan-Canadian" continues to challenge one of the cardinal characteristics of being Canadian: people here aren't required to be Canadian in the way that all Americans are required to be American. Many instead are Alberta Canadians or Ukrainian Canadians or whatever, and only become unqualified Canadians when outside the country. Quite a few immigrants come here as a second choice to going to the U.S. Many Canadians will leave as soon as they retire, to go south to the sun or back to their homeland. Canadian citizenship is dished out without much fuss (three years' residence), and Canadians can maintain dual citizenship (many Americans here do) without difficulty.

Yet in several important respects, Canadians are more cohesive than Americans. At 25 million, the size of the population makes it relatively easy for everyone to know everyone else. "They are insufficiently strange," essayist Harry Bruce once wrote wryly of the large numbers of acquaintances-of-acquaintances encountered on a Barbados beach. As already noted, the much cherished regional differences are, but for Quebec and Newfoundland, far more muted than those in the U.S.; to an untutored ear, a Nova Scotian and a British Columbian sound pretty much alike while no training is needed to distinguish a Californian from, say, a Georgian. Regional differences in Canada aren't so much organic as they are the consequence of geographic distances and of the extent of power exercised by provincial governments.

The very fact that the country is so regionalized has prompted Canadians to work hard to compensate. Proportionately, many more Canadians travel the country on official business (all those federal-

189

provincial conferences); both the CBC and the private networks provide much more regional programming. While it's incumbent on governments to behave like good citizens, individual Canadians share this sense of coast-to-coast citizenship. The "national newspaper," the *Globe and Mail*, sells proportionately more copies outside of Toronto than the *New York Times* does outside of New York. National organizations, from the Canadian Manufacturers' Association to the Canadian Medical Association, conscientiously rotate their top executives and annual meetings among the regions.

In all these ways, Canadians have created for themselves a more considerable stake in the society as a whole than have individual Americans. They have taken hold of a share of what has to be called a Canadian Dream. It isn't comparable to the messianic American Dream, nor does it mould Canadians into anything comparable to the palpable Frenchness of all Frenchmen or Britishness of all Britishers. Yet the spirit exists.

Those who live outside a forest can often see its trees more clearly than the people inside it. In *Deference to Authority*, Edgar Friedenberg, the American philosopher now at Dalhousie University in Halifax, makes a shrewd and provocative point about multiculturalism. He regards it as something of a genteel charade. "The British, and especially the Scots, have transmitted this defence against pluralism to their heirs," writes Friedenberg. "The result is a peculiar uniformity: Foreign influences rapidly disappear and are subtly, or not so subtly, derogated if they persist. This is not, in Canada, an expression of bigotry. That is to be found here – where is it not? – but bigotry is not a Canadian social trait at any conscious level. . . . Foreigners are not rejected in Canada, but foreignness is; it is something you owe it to yourself to get over."*

Something curious is at work. Multiculturalism's official purpose has been to make the mosaic shine in all its variegated colours. Yet Canadians seem to have been able to psych out all these newcomers even though, in the way of all immigrants, many are far more energetic

---

* To some of those affected, this rejection of foreignness can be exceedingly painful. "I cannot describe the agony and the betrayal one feels hearing oneself spoken of by one's own country as being somehow exotic to its nature," wrote Calcutta-born novelist Bharati Mukherjee in 1981, not long after she became a Canadian citizen and shortly before she left for the U.S., preferring its "rough sense of justice [that] derives from slugging it out."

and purposeful than native-born sons and daughters, and even though, as first- or second-generation citizens, they now account for 40 per cent of the total population. (In Vancouver, English is the second-language of more than half of the school children.) Unless some version of a Canadian Dream has taken hold, this assimilative seductiveness of the society is inexplicable. Even immigrant Americans – Her Majesty's Yankees – get sucked in. Those who have been here for a while confess they've noticed themselves becoming quieter, more reticent, and impelled to utter many more meaningless "Thank yous." In a *Globe and Mail* article marking the tenth anniversary of the fall of Saigon, the reporter Stephen Strauss, once a draft dodger, wrote that while it had taken him time to undergo "mental Canadianization," he now found the U.S. "an exuberance to visit and a joy to leave," and that he'd even begun to feel "a sense of bonding with the Revolutionary War Tories."

Ironically, at the same time as Canadians seem to have acquired a certain capacity to seduce newcomers into acting like Canadians (whatever that behaviour in fact involves), Americans seem to be losing some of their historic certitude about the nature of being American. In a recent article, author William Pfaff remarked that one in ten Americans no longer speaks English at home (the U.S. is now the world's fifth largest Spanish-speaking nation), and that Asians, who now number four million, are the fastest-growing ethnic group. Pfaff then commented, "It is no longer possible to give a secure answer to the question, What is it to be an American?"

The Canadian Dream may be pretty pallid compared to the technicoloured American one. But, proportionately, far more Canadians share in it. Canada is a middle-class nation, by no means as equalitarian as the Scandinavian ones, but far more so than the U.S. In 1982, these were the shares of total national income received by low to upper-income families:*

	Lowest quintile	2nd quintile	3rd quintile	4th quintile	Top quintile
Canada	6.3%	12.6%	18%	24.1%	38.9%
U.S.	4.7%	11.2%	17.1%	24.3%	42.7%

* The income disparities in both countries aren't as bad as they may seem from a glance at the table. Many of those with low incomes are young people who will move up the ladder as a simple function of age and work experience.

191

Income, whether earned or received in transfers from government, isn't a full surrogate for standard of living. Non-cash income, such as Medicare (30 million Americans are without any health or hospital insurance) and public housing, would make the Canadian income distribution statistics still more comparatively equitable. This condition doesn't mean that the distribution of income in Canada is satisfactory. It does mean that many more Canadians are full citizens in the true meaning of that word.

This perspective of Canada as a middle-class society contradicts the image of Canada as an elitist society. The heirs of the Family Compact are still around, and turn up most frequently in insurance and trust companies and in establishment law firms. But the blood is getting pretty thin. In several respects, Canadians are less hierarchical than Americans. Nowadays, many of those unfortunate enough to have been sent to a private school – Upper Canada College, or Havergal or Bishop's – go to pains to pretend they were not; few Americans who went to Groton or Choate or Farmington would let other Americans forget it. With occasional exceptions, such as the Lougheeds, there are few Canadian equivalents to the ancestral American political dynasties, the Rockefellers, the Roosevelts, the Kennedys. There are no Canadian equivalents to the orgiastic displays of wealth along Park Avenue and the Hamptons, let alone of the J.R. Ewing style in Dallas and Houston. It's as if the fierce egalitarianism of Americans sanctifies the parading of inequalities that are unacceptable in a middle-class country like Canada.

Canada's old elitist image isn't inaccurate. But its character has changed. Canada has evolved into what can best be called a meritocratic elitist society. Those who have authority are still deferred to, but those who wield authority – as, for instance, deputy ministers in Ottawa – frequently started off on a Saskatchewan farm or in a Maritime villege or a crowded flat in the North End of Winnipeg.

The most important societal difference derives not from the persistence of elitism in Canada but from the absence of populism. In the U.S., since Andrew Jackson, populism has been a continuing national phenomenon. Both Jimmy Carter and Ronald Reagan ran successfully by casting themselves as the champions of "ordinary Americans" against the Washington establishment. North of the border, whenever a populist movement does flare up, as with the Créditistes in Quebec or with Social Credit in Alberta, it never extends beyond the region from which it emerged.

Any commonalities between the Canadian Dream and the American Dream cease abruptly when the subject of government is introduced. Here lies the great, subliminal, continental divide. As has been said many times, Canadians trust their government in a way that Americans find quite incomprehensible. But as has been remarked upon much less often, Canadians trust their government because they themselves, in a profound way, are a part of that government.

If there is any alchemy within the Canadian political system it resides in the fact that the opposition party is not just the opposition party but the Loyal, Official, Opposition. Those on the outs of power spend all their time trying to ridicule and to undercut those on the in. While doing this, they are not being disloyal. Instead, they are performing a function that is an integral part of the national governing process. This concept, of course, has crossed the Atlantic from Westminster. But there, it has never evolved beyond a kind of parliamentary courtliness. The reason is the British class system. A large majority of the British people simply don't trust each other.

In Canada, the absence of political ideology, let alone of a class system, makes it far easier for a government to accept the legitimacy of opposition to itself. Paradoxically, almost the last place to look for this quality of political maturity is in Parliament itself. Instead, the principle in practice is to be found within a vast and ever-expanding "extra-parliamentary opposition" through which Canadians who have grouped themselves together in support of almost any imaginable cause – women's rights, peace, the environment, native land claims, consumer protection, civil liberties, the arts – first exercise their right to be funded by government so that they can properly present their case and then exercise their right to criticize the government.

The Parti Québécois provides by far the most dramatic example of this oppositional system at work. As would have been quite unimaginable in the U.S., and in most other countries, no one challenged the right of a political party dedicated to breaking up the country to seek election, nor its right, once elected, to hold a referendum inviting one group of Canadians to decide, unilaterally, to separate from all other Canadians.

This process can amount to co-option of all opposition and to the smothering of dissent by the cloying syrup of sweet-reasonableness. One reason Canada has never produced a Ralph Nader is because the Canadian Consumers Association is so sensible and so well-endowed by government. While American feminists burned their bras, or threatened to do so, Canadian feminists wrote briefs to the Royal Commission on the Status of Women, and then helped to write its report. Canadians don't harass corporations and banks with class actions or doctors with malpractice suits (a very expensive habit of Americans, since doctors write off in their fees their annual insurance costs of $100,000 and more). Canadians didn't fight seat-belt legislation, as Americans have done almost as fiercely as they have fought gun-control legislation. Proportionately, far fewer Canadians are engaged in volunteer activities or contribute to charity, assuming that government will do it for them. Far fewer write to MPs than Americans write to and lobby congressmen.

Canadian's don't lobby and fight for their rights against government, because, in the collective perception, their government is *theirs*. They assume it is working for them. And it is enough of the time to continue being trusted. Women achieved the equal rights clause. Quebecers achieved their referendum.

The particular version of the Canadian identity advanced in this book is that Canadians are, uniquely, North Americans who have embraced the political culture of liberalism. A couple of comments can be made here about the continental aspect of that definition.

A reason why there have been so many unconsummated attempts at defining the Canadian identity is, surely, that so many of them have started out on the wrong foot – quite literally so because the first step taken has been placed in another country. To Creighton and to Grant, Canada was British North America. Later, any mention of the word "British" came to be regarded as injurious to national unity and "European" replaced it as a socially acceptable alternative. In his 1972 book, *The Canadian Identity*, the historian W.L. Morton described Canada as, "a civilization European in origin, and American in evolution."

Most times, the first step was put down south of the border. Frank Underhill wrote, "If we are eventually to satisfy ourselves that we have at last achieved a Canadian identity, it will only be when we are satisfied that we have arrived at a better American way of life than the Americans have." William Kilbourn described Canada as "An American alternative to what has happened in the U.S." Other commentators haven't merely begun their attempt to define the Canadian identity in another country, but have ended it there. Herschel

194

Hardin wrote in *A Nation Unaware* that "If the United States did not exist, neither would Canada, because there would be no outside threat to keep the diverse regions, particularly Quebec, inside Confederation." In his brilliant 1969 essay, *Limited Identities*, J.M.S. Careless wrote, "One is tempted to conclude that there could not be a Canada without the United States, and that there may not be a Canada with it."

The flaw in these analyses is that they take for granted that Canada is the sort-of-American society that it is only because it is next door to America. Surely, many of the common qualities shared by the U.S. and Canada derive from the fact that both societies occupy this particular New World continent, as "co-tenants" in the phrase of Liberal leader John Turner. The joint origins of the two societies as predominantly Anglo-Saxon and Protestant (and thereby unlike Latin American New World societies) made it inevitable each would evolve into the kind of North American-style societies – egalitarian, democratic, progressive – that both now are. The "American way of life" wasn't created only by the Americans. The continent itself can claim co-authorship. Had, for instance, the U.S. disappeared into a black hole the instant the Loyalists crossed the border, Canada would have developed on its own into pretty much the same kind of "Americanized" society that it is today. The British class system simply couldn't have survived in a raw, frontier society. The newness of everything would have put a premium on self-reliance and the space all around would have widened the ambitions of immigrants. Conversely, had the original American colonists settled in Central America, say, it's hard to imagine that less fertile and less temperate region developing into a contemporary superpower.

Canada's evolution into a mature North American society was delayed because it went into a defensive crouch and stayed there for so long. Nomenclature created its own inhibition. "North American" sounds too close to "American" for the psychic comfort of Canadians. Much might have been otherwise had the continent been named after Amerigo Vespucci's last name. Had Americans then still been known as "Americans," after the explorer's first name, Canadians would have felt no unease at being known collectively as "North Vespuccians," any more than it troubles the Germans and French and Italians to be known collectively as Europeans.

The point here isn't to try to rewrite history, but to use it to try to illuminate the present. It's a fact of life that America is the dream-factory for the entire world. It's no less a fact of life that Canadians will forever compare themselves invidiously to their giant neighbour. It's a fact, lastly, that so far as most of the world is concerned, the Americans personally invented everything in the continent, including Canada.

Those facts cannot be denied. But they need not overwhelm. Canadians happen to occupy half of the continent, parts of it for as long as have Americans. Psychically as well as physically, we can claim a co-equal share of the continent. We are neither "Europeanized North Americans" nor "quiet Americans." We are the Other North Americans.

The thesis advanced in this book won't, of course, end the debate about whether a Canadian identity exists, and if so, what it is. The thesis will have served its purpose if it renews the debate.

Why bother? The reason is, if a Canadian identity does exist it can be used as an inspiration for some collective purpose. The last comment on this subject is best left to an American. "I really want to see Canada have more clout in the U.S.," Stephen Blank of MultiNational Strategies of New York commented in an interview. "You have a quality of civility that is precious, and you have an immensely superior social system. You have, although you refuse to admit it and would rather not be told it, a civilizing mission in North America."

Part Four
The Economic Imperative

As is common among people who earn their living by selling resources, Canadians have never taken economics particularly seriously. After all, it was God and nature, not Saudi Arabians or Australians or Canadians, who put the resources into the ground in the first place. Thereafter, the value of those resources is determined more by events elsewhere – wars, depressions, booms, bumper harvests, droughts, and floods – than by the ingenuity of those who happen to live on top of the resources.

Among Canadians, this tendency to economic passivity is heightened by the massive extent of foreign ownership and by the comprador character of so many Canadian businessmen, as order-takers rather than as decision-makers.

The Great Recession shocked many Canadians out of this mood. The change could have and should have happened earlier, during the oil crises of the 1970s. But the Trudeau government deluded Canadians into believing that, somehow, we could get the world to stop while we kept our oil prices low and our incomes high.

Today's mood is more inquisitive, more demanding, more practical, and much more concerned. Canadians know that the winning lottery tickets aren't falling into our hands any longer. The three succeeding chapters try to describe the nature of the economic environment that now envelops us. These chapters provide a backdrop, and a good deal of the script as well, for the decision the Mulroney government will have to make about free trade with the U.S., which is considered in Chapter Nineteen. The point here is that free trade, if accepted, is not a panacea, and if rejected, is not a denouement; whichever decision Canadians make about this particular issue, the economic imperatives will continue to bang on our door.

Chapter Fourteen
The Global Marketplace and the Nation-State

"The lowest level of the economy, not being paralyzed
by the size of its plant or organization, is the one readiest
to adapt: it is the seedbed of inspiration, improvisation
and even innovation, although its most brilliant discoveries
sooner or later fall into the hands of capital."

Fernand Braudel, *Civilization and Capitalism*, vol. 3

Several times a month during the last year or so, groups of
industrialists, or of civil servants or politicians or bankers, from the
U.S. or Canada, others from Europe or Asia, have been driving
through the rolling hills of Marin County north of San Francisco.
Their destination is the village of Mill Valley, where they stop at
a building that used to be a post office. Once inside, they cluster
around a slim, dark-haired man named Paul Hawken, who appears
to be in his late twenties and who usually wears a faded T-shirt
and grubby jeans. They ask him to tell them about "the Next
Economy."

Hawken in fact is forty. His qualifications as an economic guru
are that he has written two books and that he's made, and tossed
away, several fortunes. Hawken's real appeal is that he's done it at
all. In the 1960s he was part of the Free Speech Movement at Berkeley;
later he did the Haight-Ashbury drug scene, staged some of the first
multi-media light shows, managed the Grateful Dead rock group,
discovered natural foods, and started the Erewhon Trading Company,
which made him a millionaire in his twenties. His first book, *The
Magic of Findhorn*, was about that astonishing community in Scotland
where they grow forty-pound vegetables in soil so thin even the gorse
bushes are stunted, and do this, apparently, by talking to the vegetables
and to predatory insects. He made $250,000 on it. He came back,
became a management consultant, joined the Stanford Research
Institute, and then wrote *The Next Economy*, which carries on its

flyleaf an encomium by a senior vice-president of the Bank of America.

Hawken believes that the old "mass economy," of mass consumption, mass production, and thereby of massive institutions, is vanishing; in its place an "informative economy" is arising in which wealth is generated by ideas – ideas about new products and services, about adaptations and variations of old products, about new ways to manufacture these products more cheaply or to service and maintain them more efficiently. His core thesis is: "The single most important trend to understand is the changing ratio between mass and information in goods and services." Lumber and metals, Canada's staple products, are high in mass; computer software and fashion designs are high in information.

Some of Hawken's best lines accompany his advice on how to survive in the Next Economy. Smart businessmen should ask "dumb" questions and "look at problems with fresh, unprofessional eyes." University students shouldn't try to become professionals, like lawyers, "a sort of vocational heading for the hills," but should study everything "from Greek to cybernetics" and so stay flexible and adaptable. Businesses should stay small, should specialize, and should treat their employees and their customers as more important than their products and their profits.

The Next Economy won't be a New Jerusalem. Job security will be something grandparents reminisce about. "There will be tremendous polarization. The rich will become richer and more outrageous than ever." Getting from here to there will be exceedingly painful for all those for whom bureaucratic tenure has meant a lifestyle and a security blanket. The compensation for ex-sixties types like Hawken will be the chance to "integrate life and work" in a small, family-run business like his own – when not functioning as a guru, he sells high-quality garden tools.

One place to find the Next Economy in action is in Peterborough, nestled in the wooded New Hampshire hills. Its population from dusk to dawn is just 4,000. During the days it swells to about 25,000. Rural yuppies account for the difference. They drive into Peterborough in Volvos and Hondas and four-wheel station wagons, to work on magazines (thirty-five of them are published here) like *Byte* and *Robotics Age* and *Yankee*, which presents to its 900,000 subscribers a kind of Norman Rockwell America of trim picket fences, smiling postmen, and fat cabbages. Or they stay in their converted farmhouses and new chalets and tap away at their desk-top personal computers, doing at the end of a telephone line what they once did in overcrowded, expensive, dirty, violent New York or Chicago or Houston. Some experts believe that at least one in five Americans will work out of their homes by the turn of the century; some new townhouses, in California and elsewhere, have been designed specifically to function as "electronic cottage industries."

Another place to find the Next Economy is in the Veneto region of Italy, stretching inland from Venice. According to international comparative statistics, Italy has long been Europe's "sick man." But almost half – 40 per cent – of its economy is underground, or unmeasured. Much of it is in the Veneto, which has 30,000 small to medium-sized family businesses turning out, among other things, many of the products that end up with a Gucci label on them. The Veneto has Italy's highest incomes and lowest unemployment rate (even without counting the unreported incomes and jobs).

The historian Fernand Braudel compares the underground economy to "a rich zone, like a layer covering the earth," and thus in direct contact with reality, unlike the layers of corporate and governmental bureaucracy above it. Hawken describes it as "the individual's response to the crisis of the mass economy" and comments that even in law-abiding societies like Holland and Switzerland it now amounts to about 20 per cent of the gross national product. (University of Alberta professors Rolf Mirus and Roger Smith have calculated that it accounts for 10 to 13 per cent of Canada's GNP.) It is certainly true, whether underground or above it, that almost all invention starts with an individual or a small group – the famous garage of the Apple computer inventors Steve Jobs and Stephen Wosniak – rather than in some bureaucratic laboratory. It's true as well, as Braudel noted, that the financiers come along and buy up these brains; on the street the saying goes, "The first gets the glamour; the second gets the profits." Mitel's progress from electronic *wunderkind* to subsidiary of giant British Telecom provides as good an example as any of this process.

Braudel in his scholarly way and Hawken in his more colloquial fashion are describing what amounts to neo-capitalism with a human face, a personalized, entrepreneurial capitalism as an alternative to the brutal "creative destruction" that the economist Joseph Schumpeter defined as capitalism's driving force. As gurus always do, Hawken pursues his line of thought too single-mindedly. He blames almost everything on oil, attributing the crack-up of the mass economy to the oil crises of the 1970s. The price of oil has fallen since, but

201

it hasn't brought the old ways back. Perhaps the mass economy's error was to have fulfilled itself. By 1980, the average American family owned two cars while 99 out of every 100 households owned a TV set, a fridge, an electric or gas stove. To find new markets, corporations had to invent new products that appealed because they were more specialized and commanded loyalty by personal service rather than just price. Simultaneously, the mass institutions, the corporate and government bureaucracies, had filled up to overflowing. So the next generation, the last of the Baby Boomers, had to set off on their own, like economic gypsies, often creating their own businesses or going into partnerships with their parents. The women's movement has changed the economy. A striking number of new small businesses now are started by women; simultaneously, young men, no longer constrained by the certainty of having to be life-long sole breadwinners, are able to try their wings in small companies or on their own, rather than having to scurry to safety in the bureaucracies.

Except for that glancing reference to "polarization," however, Hawken, like most futurologists, skips over one of the most disturbing manifestations of contemporary change. This is what the economist Barry Bluestone has called "the vanishing middle." The jobs of skilled and semi-skilled workers, in such old "mass" industries as steel, autos, and machine tools, are vanishing. The new jobs are mostly high-paid ones in high-tech* or are low-paid ones in places like McDonald's, which now has a larger payroll that U.S. Steel. Dropping out of sight down the middle is the middle-middle class, the taxpaying, front-lawn-mowing foundation of American – and Canadian – social stability.

Hawken's analysis, though, does provide a map – a three-dimensional map in contrast to Ronald Reagan's one-dimensional "magic of the marketplace" – by which it becomes possible to predict some of the terrain, most of it unfamiliar and a good deal of it downright frightening, across which all economies will have to travel. A second instructive map can easily be found: any map that shows all the countries of the world.

---

* High-tech also creates many low-paid assembly jobs, but most of these are on the far side of the Pacific.

Despite all the competition the U.S. is now encountering, the field of industrial activity in which America still clearly leads the world is that of computers. Among American electronics companies, by far the largest and most efficient is IBM. Among this company's products, by far the most successful is its IBM PC personal computer. The manufacturing cost of each unit is $860 U.S. Of this amount, three-quarters, or $625, is accounted for by components that are manufactured abroad: the monitors for the IBM PC are made in South Korea; the printer, semi-conductors, power unit, and keyboard are made in Japan; and the floppy disk drives are made in Singapore.

Hourly wages in Hong Kong are $5 and in Indonesia are eighty cents U.S., or were in 1979. The low-wage "New Japans" like South Korea, Hong Kong, Taiwan, and Singapore are now looking nervously over their shoulders at the even more undemanding and docile labour force of China as it strays ever further from the path of Marxism-Leninism. In today's global economy, the diffusion of technology and of managerial know-how makes it possible for anything to be made anywhere and then to be sold anywhere. Japanese cars are old hat. The Korean Pony was the 1984 hot-seller in Canada. A Yugoslavian "Yugo" will soon be on the market. In 1986, the first Ramcharger sports utility vehicles, made in Mexico, will go into the showrooms in North America. There are no industrial secrets any more. All patents can be bought or licensed, or can be "reverse-engineered" or copied.

In the global marketplace, goods not only move back and forth but in circles. Eastman Kodak markets copiers under its name that actually are made by Canon of Japan. Merck and Company is doing the same with drugs made by Sweden's Astral. Apartment buildings going up in Riyadh, Saudi Arabia, are being constructed out of modules manufactured in Brazil, assembled by South Korean workmen, and supervised by American engineers. Tridon of Hamilton sells windshield wipers to Japan that come back again on assembled Japanese cars; Hyundai is building a plant in Newmarket, Ontario, to make electrical components that will be sent to South Korea, to be installed in Pony Excel cars that are then shipped out to North America. In one of the most interesting of industrial shifts, some 200 American high-tech entrepreneurs have moved to Japan.

Instant communications and rapid transportation make this global interchange possible. So do corporate handshakes across the oceans. AT & T has linked up with Phillips of Holland and Olivetti of Italy,

General Motors with Nissan, General Electric with Rolls-Royce. The Airbus planes are made by companies in Britain, France, West Germany, and Spain. In response, Boeing has formed a consortium with Mitsubishi, Kawasaki, and Fuji. RCA and Sharp of Japan are jointly manufacturing communications satellites. All of the Big Three automakers own shares in Japanese and South Korean auto companies and import their models – 500,000 a year in the case of GM – to sell under their brand names. The reason for AT & T's ties with Phillips and Olivetti is to give it an opening into Europe; the same motive, in reverse, inspired British Telecom's takeover of Mitel of Kanata.

The vital ingredient of the global economy is global money. It's now available almost anywhere to do almost anything. According to the October, 1984, issue of *Euromoney*, we are witnessing the creation of "an almost global capital market" in which "the lines of demarcation between domestic and international capital markets are increasingly blurred."

Canada was in at the start of this creation. In 1983, Bell Canada Enterprises made the first true international equity offering, issuing simultaneously $273 million (U.S.) worth of shares in Canada, the U.S., and Europe. Alcan of Montreal was the second. So far, the largest international equity offering was British Telecom's sale of December, 1984, in which shares amounting to $6 billion sold simultaneously in North America, Europe, and Japan.

In a certain sense, a global financial market has long existed. There is something like three *trillion* worth of dollars, yen, francs, deutsch-marks, pounds sterling sloshing around in the Eurocurrency pool, all of it for all practical purposes unregulated by any government; it was this pool that the banks dipped into to make all those loans to Argentina and Mexico and Poland they now wish they hadn't made. But the catalyst of today's global financial marketplace is national deregulation, as governments give up on trying to regulate closely their financial industries in "the public interest," whatever that is; as a necessary consequence of this, governments cease also to protect them from foreign competition "in the national interest." Everywhere, "foreign" banks are becoming harder and harder to distinguish from local ones: Australia's Labour government has just allowed in eighteen of them (including the Royal Bank of Canada); there are now fifty-eight in Canada. Soon after the Bank of Montreal took over Chicago's Harris Bank for $500 million (U.S.), its president, Grant Reuber, declared, "We are no longer a Canadian bank but an international bank headquartered in Canada." The Royal Bank of Canada is even more internationalized: its subsidiary, Orion Bank, ranks sixth in the world in its volume ($39 billion) of international bond issues.

Behind the banks come the brokerage companies. New York's Citicorp bought up London's Vickers da Costa in 1984, which in turn has acquired a seat on the Tokyo Stock Exchange. To keep pace, Merrill Lynch has bought up a 25 per cent share of Hong Kong's Sun Hung Kai. More than fifty British and Japanese companies now trade on the New York stock exchanges. Some 200 Canadian companies trade on American exchanges; many major firms – Alcan, Seagram's, Northern Telecom – do two-thirds of their total share trading in the U.S. The London Stock Exchange, which recently voted to allow foreigners to buy majority holdings in its brokerage house members, is planning to establish a satellite-linked, twenty-four-hour-a-day trading system with the New York Stock Exchange. Both the Toronto and Montreal Stock Exchanges are linked to U.S. exchanges; Japanese brokers have bought up two dozen seats on the Chicago financial futures exchange.

The mobility of money is compressing all national economies into a global village. Because of satellites, hundreds of millions of dollars, and other currencies, can now chase the highest interest rates, and the sun, beginning in Amsterdam and London in the morning, moving in the afternoon to New York or Toronto, and ending the same evening in Tokyo or Singapore. To protect the value of export sales or purchases or loans that they've made against the yo-yoing of international currencies, companies today routinely engage in interest-rate "swaps" and currency "put" and "call" future options. The Royal Bank of Canada now does $1.5 billion worth of currency trades a year, in fifty-three currencies. (In more innocent days, Cadillac-Fairview once lost $18 million on a $27-million Swiss loan when the value of the Swiss franc soared.) Concurrently, electronic fund transfers make it much easier to move money around illegally as an alternative to stitching Kruggerands into the bottom of a suitcase: an estimated equivalent of two-thirds of the Mexico's total international debt and one-third that of Argentina's are now back in the vaults of banks in the U.S. and Switzerland, including no doubt in the vaults of many of the same banks that made the original loans.

The economic consequences of all of this are obvious enough: money can make almost anything happen almost anywhere in the globe. The political consequences are more problematic. A handy one-line summation of them is provided by Don Lenz, vice-president of Goldman Sachs in New York, a spot he's reached from beginnings in Eston, Saskatchewan: "Money is escaping national control."

The Next Economy, in which individuals hack out a livelihood in the marketplace on their own terms, and the global economy, in which production and money have been internationalized, may seem to be quite dissimilar. In fact, they are different manifestations of the same process of fundamental economic change. Conjoined into the global marketplace, these phenomena are affecting Canada profoundly. In two ways. They are transforming our economy. They are also transforming our policy. Since the bias of this book is to treat economics as a means to an end rather than as an end in itself, it is these political effects that need now to be considered.

Of all nations, Canada may be the most affected by the global marketplace. This is because Canada isn't so much a nation-state in the classic meaning of that term as a state-nation. An organic nation like, say, France could survive the disappearance of its state during wartime occupation; Poland could survive its disappearance for hundreds of years; Jews could wander the earth for 2,000 years and remain Jews. Canada's condition is quite different and can be compared only to that of some African ex-colonies and perhaps to Belgium. The Canadian state is the Canadian nation, or nations; its national instruments, such as Air Canada, the CBC, Petro-Canada, have nurtured the Canadian national identity, and almost have created it. The global marketplace eats away at the effectiveness and the authority of all states, both from without and also from within, because the state is largely irrelevant to individuals making it on their own in the marketplace. The question then becomes, can a state-nation continue as a nation when its state loses authority and effectiveness?

Trudeau, even though economics was not among his strong points, recognized the problem. On May 2, 1984, in his last official speech as Prime Minister, he spoke to the American Publishers' Association in Montreal. In the manner that had become his trademark, he said, "We really are our brothers' keeper. It is now an economic necessity that we be so, as well as a moral imperative." He then continued:

206

"Economic interdependence transcends trade barriers. It goes to the heart of our national values, and the way we structure our political system."

A year earlier, a distinguished British economist, Michael Stewart, had made the same point, but from a different perspective. In *Controlling the Economic Future: Policy Dilemmas in a Shrinking World*, Stewart observed that Keynesianism, which in its vulgar version has come to mean using deficit-financing to mop up unemployment, was "an inevitable concomitant of the existence of the nation-state." Keynesianism, in other words, can work only if nation-states are autonomous economic units; if not, the extra money pumped out will simply slip away into neighbouring states with no increase in local employment. This is what happened to President François Mitterand's 1980 attempt to prime the pump of the French economy: money left the country; the franc fell; inflation rose; and unemployment remained as high as before. Based on this example and others, Stewart concluded that "National economic sovereignty is an illusion."

Canadians have suspected for some time now that a good deal of our economic sovereignty was as illusory as our sovereignty in defence. It's been several years since many of us believed that our interest rates were set by Governor Gerald Bouey of the Bank of Canada rather than by Chairman Paul Volker of the Federal Reserve Bank in Washington, and perhaps not even by him but by the international financial marketplace. Very few now deny that as goes the U.S. economy so goes the Canadian economy, up or down. In fact, since 1983 at least one-quarter of Canada's growth – the margin between stagnation and minimal growth – has been accounted for by the increase in our exports to the U.S.

The pace of continental commonality is quickening. Deregulation in the U.S. was followed, a little more slowly and a little more softly, by regulatory reform here, first by Liberal Transport Minister Lloyd Axworthy in 1984, then more boldly by Conservative Don Mazankowski in his White Paper of July, 1985, that pledged across-the-board deregulation of airlines, railways, trucking, and shipping. A successful flat-rate tax there will undoubtedly be followed, more slowly and more softly, by tax reform here. Finance Minister Michael Wilson's May, 1985, budget amounted to an attempt, if a tentative one, to inspire here a belief in "the magic of the marketplace."

Going with the flow of the marketplace isn't a uniquely American phenomenon, although Canadians tend to regard it that way. Japan, that near-hermetic kingdom, is deregulating its financial industry (those foreign stock brokers on the Tokyo exchange) and its government-owned telecommunications giant, NTT. Belgium, one of the most centrally controlled of all European economies, is similarly deregulating its public telephone company and allowing non-Belgian companies to bid on contracts. Britain's Margaret Thatcher did all of this before anyone else: British Telecom has been sold; the $25 billion giant, British Gas, will be next on the block. The most dramatic moves toward the marketplace are those now occurring in China.

Everywhere, government is shrinking. In the process, the illusion of national economic sovereignty is shrinking. John Bulloch, president of the Canadian Federation of Independent Businesses, says: "From a small businessman's point of view, the nation-state is a fiction in a commercial sense. Our needs are local and non-institutional, or non-governmental, and our markets are either local or are international. The only businesses that really deal with the governments of nation-states are either the large national corporate bureaucracies, or, as is a bit ironic in view of the fuss the nationalists make about them, the multinational bureaucracies."

Small businesses now account for about three-quarters of all new job creation. At the same time, about two-thirds of all new jobs are in the service sector, made up of retailers and wholesalers and specialists and independents for whom governments can do little other than to get out of the way. In contrast, the traditional support systems of the nation-state, the national and the multinational corporate bureaucracies, are all frantically "down-sizing." Noranda, as an example, has shed 18,000 employees since 1981. Simultaneously, the conglomerates, the corporate darlings of the sixties and seventies, are divesting most of what they once gobbled up: ITT has $2 billion worth of assets up for sale; Mobil Oil is trying to unload the Montgomery Ward department store chain. Canada's equivalent to the conglomerates, the Blacks Conrad and Montague, have had to offer up Dominion Stores in a fire sale.

Bigness can still be beautiful on its bottom line. IBM is the most successful in its field because it is by far the biggest. Photographic film production is dominated worldwide by just three companies, Kodak, Agfa, Fuji. In May, 1985, General Motors and American Tobacco each spent $5 billion (U.S.) to buy up, respectively, Hughes Aircraft and Nabisco.

These giants, however, are governed now by the rules of the global marketplace. The new "in" word in American business is "intra-preneurship," meaning an attempt by large companies to recreate within themselves the creative entrepreneurial disorder of small companies, or what *The Economist* magazine has called "confederations of entrepreneurs." Minnesota Mining and Manufacturing (3M) actively encourages employees to spend 15 per cent of their time at the office on private projects. People's Express has an inflexible open-door office rule for all executives: no secretaries for anyone including the president; all employees do almost every job, from taking reservations to handling baggage (except, of course, for flying the planes). Quite possibly the most advanced example of "intra-preneurship" in the world can be found in Magna Industries of Markham, Ontario (see Chapter Fifteen).

An instructive example of a failure to appreciate the nature of the new global economy occurred during the February, 1985, meeting between Mulroney and Commonwealth Caribbean leaders in King-ston, Jamaica, at which Mulroney was asked for a one-way free trade deal comparable to the United States' Caribbean Basin Initiative (CBI). Apparently inadequately briefed, Mulroney failed to mention the proposal in his set speech and later said only that the idea would be "studied." The CBI is by no means yet a success, but it is beginning to create a synergy between the economies of the Caribbean and the U.S. At new plants in Jamaica and Haiti, men's and women's clothing is being sewn together from apparel fabrics that have been cut in the U.S. by lasers. In the Barbados, American Airlines facsimiles in raw data by satellite to be punched into terminals by keyboard operators paid $2 an hour. Here the U.S. benefits, just as it does on an even larger scale from the "in-bond" factories that employ 200,000 Mexicans just across the length of its southern border. This low-cost Caribbean and Mexican labour holds down U.S. domestic production costs and thus in turn improves its international competitiveness.*

It has been said often, and has been used to justify the need for a free trade pact with the U.S., that Canada almost uniquely among industrial nations is handicapped by its lack of secure access to a market of at least 100 million people, whether a multinational one

---

* Though American unions were originally hostile to the CBI, they've come to realize that plants, whether in the Caribbean or in northern Mexico, "anchor" in the U.S. manufacturing that would otherwise have moved in its entirety to the far side of the Pacific.

as in Europe or a domestic one as in the U.S. and Japan. As considerable a handicap may be Canada's lack of a trade pact with an underdeveloped region with which a symbiotic economic relationship could be developed. (Proposals to establish duty-exempt "economic zones," in Vancouver, for example, where minimum wage rules would be suspended and environmental regulations relaxed, represent an alternative technique for achieving the same objective.)

The central fact about the global economy is exactly that – it is global. To quote Bulloch once more: "If your competitor opens up a plant in Mexico or in the U.S. South you have no choice but to do the same or go under, although as a Canadian you might choose to do it with a local partner so you won't be seen to have moved jobs out of the country." (One Vancouver high-tech company, Mobile Data, recently moved its assembly plant from there to Puerto Rico in pursuit of lower wages and lower taxes.)

The economic problems created by this phenomenon resemble those of being trapped on a treadmill. As autoworker leader Bob White comments, "Those who talk about industrial restructuring to meet low-wage competition never tell the full truth. The truth is that the restructuring never ends. There will always be some new country with wage levels that we can just never hope to meet: Japan today, South Korea tomorrow, maybe Bangladesh next."

An economic answer does in fact exist, although it's not one that White's likely to favour. In a prescient report back in 1977, the International Labour Organization commented: "The process of industrial development in the Third World may now go into reverse in some areas with industrial nations recapturing the old industries thanks to the micro-processor." In this scenario, a fully automated factory can function as efficiently in Halifax as in Hong Kong; it would eliminate the comparative advantage of the "Little Dragons" by eliminating all labour costs. This nightmare of science fiction writers, and *angst* of social scientists, doesn't yet exist and probably never will. However, in Murata's new plant outside Tokyo, the overnight "graveyard" shift is operated by one man who monitors TV screens. Fujitsu-Fanuc has built, as was bound to happen eventually, a robotized plant to produce industrial robots with a "payroll" of 150 workers and thirty robots. The new micron mega-bit chips with circuit lines so fine that 200 are needed to equal the thickness of a human hair can only be manufactured by automated machinery because the presence of a human would ruin the process.

Less apocalyptically, CAD/CAM systems (Computer Aided Design/Computer Aided Manufacturing), robots, and "flexible manufacturing systems" are radically altering conventional calculations of comparative advantage. These systems can compensate for high labour costs by eliminating much of the need for labour. The new MacMillan-Bloedel plant in Chemainus, British Columbia, for instance, employs seventy workers in contrast to 600 in the old mill; its output is half as much as before but with a higher-value product and with less wastage. Further, by making possible customized "batch" production – 75 per cent of all mass production is now done in batches of fifty or less – the new technology has compensated for Canada's historic disadvantage of a small domestic market and a consequent lack of the economies of scale created by long production runs.

The political problems created by these economic developments are pretty obvious, although acceptable political answers aren't obvious in the least. The imperatives of the global economy will put at risk the livelihood of hundreds of thousands of workers and the future of towns and villages and perhaps of entire regions. Simultaneously, the marketplace economy will tend to polarize society between those who can capitalize on it and those who become "economic gypsies" moving from one temporary job to another in insecure small businesses.

These problems are not unique to Canada. Western Europe similarly is suffering seemingly permanent double-digit unemployment and has only just begun to come to terms – Britain as the pacesetter, but at a fearful social price – with the need to change its economic structure from one of integrated bureaucratic cartels to one of autonomous, competing enterprises. Change may come more easily to Canadians because in North America change is a constant rather than a novelty.

But Canada faces one problem for which there are no role models available to serve as guides. The global economy and the market economy make the nation-state progressively more porous, from within as well as from without. In Canada, uniquely, the state serves as the container of the national identity. If it becomes a sieve, as it is already doing and will do increasingly, can Canadian sensibility, the "liberal political culture," function as an alternative container, or does that culture itself depend critically on the effectiveness and authority of the Canadian state?

Jane Jacobs, the American architectural and social critic now living in Toronto, believes that the future will be defined by city-states rather than by nation-states. In *Cities and the Wealth of Nations: Principles of Economic Life*, Jacobs describes as "transactions of decline" the typical economic activities of nation-states – subsidizing industries and pump-priming by military spending – because instead of allowing new industries to be born, to innovate, and sometimes to fail, these programs smother them beneath the established corporate bureaucracies that all nation-states are so concerned to perpetuate because they are, or have been, the principal mechanisms for job-creation. As for the economic planning activity of the nation-state, it is better left unplanned, "mak[ing] itself up expediently and empirically as it goes along," writes Jacobs. In its place there will flourish natural transactions of growth – as in Italy's Veneto, as in Peterborough, New Hampshire – as individuals and small groups figure out how to "replace imports" by making themselves what they used to buy from the metropolis or by figuring out new services to sell to the metropolis.

Jacobs is a philosopher, not a politician. Aware that it's politically impractical, but following her own logic to its limit, she proposes that cities within nation-states be allowed to establish their own currency units. In one interview she advised the Canadian government to pick cities with a natural capacity for growth and to concentrate available spending on them at the expense of declining industries and regions. Since this would mean picking Toronto and abandoning the Maritimes, it will never happen. Almost sadly, she writes: "Virtually all national governments, it seems fair to say, and most citizens, would sooner decline and decay unified, true to the sacrifices by which their unity was won, than seek to prosper and develop in division."

For the foreseeable future, division as such doesn't threaten the Canadian nation-state. The threat instead may be a kind of osmotic dissolution as the global economy progressively robs national boundaries of their traditional economic value, and as, within those boundaries, job-creation comes to be accepted as the responsibility of individuals themselves, and of families and other social groups, rather than of the state. The national market won't disappear. The state will still be able to be used as a kind of nursery in which to help companies and enterprises toward the take-off point, by subsidies, by purchasing contracts, by tailor-made regulations. But inevitably, more and more Canadians will depend for their livelihood either on the global economy or on themselves; the nation-state itself won't disappear but it will become, more and more often, a kind of afterthought.

Since Canada itself is a wholly illogical political construct there's no particular reason why Canadians cannot cope with the challenge of trying to preserve a state-nation amid a global marketplace that makes most of the traditional economic functions of the state less and less relevant. It is, though, as considerable a challenge as any Canadians have ever faced. The first step toward coping with it has to be a recognition that the dilemma exists and will intensify.

Chapter Fifteen
The Canadian Economy: Poor
Little Rich Kid

"For the first 100 years after Confederation, Canada got
by on its resources. For the next seventeen years, we got
by on our credit. From now on, we're going to have to
get by on our brains."

Conservative leadership candidate Michael Wilson,
March, 1984

A charge frequently made against Prime Minister Brian Mulroney
is that because he likes to be liked he tends to tell people what
they like to hear. Every now and then, though, he puts aside his
straw hat and cane and says what he really thinks, as in an interview
published in *Fortune* magazine in March, 1985. Asked why so little
new foreign investment had come in across the border, since his
declaration that "Canada is open for business again," Mulroney
answered rhetorically: "What is so compellingly attractive about
Canada that causes us to think that anybody is going to rush in
simply because somebody says, 'I'd like to do business with you?'"
Mulroney then answered his own question: "We don't have a very
good track record. Our products have not been of the highest quality.
Our deliveries have been lacking in reliability. Our expertise has been
in large measure borrowed. Our technology has been purchased. What
the hell makes us so special?"

Once, Canadians had no doubt that we were special. We had the
resources the world needed. The phrase "limitless resources" rings
like a mantra through Canadian public debate from the turn of the
century, when Laurier, realizing their extent, predicted that the
twentieth century belonged to Canada. We didn't have much technology, or capital, or managerial know-how, but these we could buy
from next door in exchange for our resources. As late as November,
1981, a federal economic development strategy paper declared almost
gloatingly that "our rich bounty of natural resources" could be the

basis of a national mega-project strategy – this at the instant the collapse of oil prices wiped out the mega-projects.

One reason Canada is no longer special is that so many countries now are equally special: copper from Chile; newsprint from Brazil, not to mention iron ore from deposits four times as rich as those in Canada; coal from Colombia and Australia; liquefied natural gas from Indonesia, in direct competition with our own in the Japanese market. Perhaps the single most alarming economic news story of the year for Canadians was carried in the newspapers on February 25, 1985: it reported that China, for two decades our first or second largest grain customer, was seeking to sell some of its own surplus grain to North America; later stories recounted that India this year will export 500,000 tonnes of grain to Russia and Rumania.

Everywhere, underdeveloped countries are stripmining their resources to earn foreign exchange to pay their debts, and consequently they are depressing international commodity prices. The price cycle will eventually rise. Never again, though, will it rise to the heights of the late 1970s, for too many new sources of supply have been developed. More significant for the long term, exotic "new materials" are displacing the old metals and minerals. Before the end of this decade the first cars may be marketed with lightweight plastic bodies and with ceramic engines that should be able to do 125 miles to the U.S. gallon. Cans of food may be made of plastic rather than of tin or aluminum (as a side benefit, these can be heated in microwave ovens). Already, optical fibres are replacing the copper "paired-wires" of telephone cables. Canadian agriculture industry may be the hardest hit. Bio-genetics holds the promise of almost unimaginable improvements in crop yields, in all countries; new breeds of cattle that are resistant to hot-weather diseases have made Florida, where they fatten much faster than further north, the number-one cattle state in the U.S.

A good deal of the decline in Canadian specialness is entirely homegrown. Those resources are no longer limitless. The output of the Canadian forestry industry, the country's largest employer, may shrink by one-third by the end of the century because of management practices by corporations and governments – random harvesting and lack of silviculture – that are virtually criminal; Canadians have almost certainly destroyed more trees themselves than have been destroyed by the worst ravages of acid rain drifting across the border. Because of oil supply forecasts that were either extravagantly incompetent or consciously fraudulent, concocted by the multinationals but accepted passively by the officials responsible, most of the best, cheap oil in the Western Sedimentary Basin is gone; new oil from the Arctic or offshore will yield a far narrower margin of revenues to companies and to governments. Many deposits of metals and minerals have been high-graded in the same way; as serious, major resource companies, with eastern pulp and newsprint mills as perhaps the most conspicuous example, have failed to re-invest in new plant and equipment despite some of the most generous tax depreciation allowances in the Western world.

So much for our resources. Our credit has turned into a national debt of almost $200 billion. This represents a debt of about $8,000 for each Canadian adult and child. Even Finance Minister Michael Wilson's semi-tough budget of May, 1985, will add about $30 billion to that debt for each year of the next five years.*

Next, as a last resort, our brains. "Canadians are like poor little rich boys who've never had to learn to live by their wits," commented Jim Gilmour, research director of the Science Council, at a stage in the interview at which discretion – he's a Scottish immigrant – had yielded to exasperation.

Late-learners always find the going hard. The historian Michael Bliss, who is writing a history of Canadian business, doubts whether Canadians can make it. "For as far out as I can see, for the next ten or fifteen years, I am extremely pessimistic: I can see nothing ahead for us but economic decline." Bliss casts his view into a perspective that's easy to remember, if without much pleasure. He believes that Canada has alternated over the decades between one of two economic states, one being that of a "Northern Treasurehouse," as for instance around the turn of the century with the opening up of the Prairies and again during the post-Second World War boom, and the other that of a "Northern Fringe." Says Bliss: "I

---

* International comparisons aside, which always are iffy, a case can be made that Canada's debt isn't as burdensome as it seems to be since Canadians mostly owe it to each other. Further, Canadians' credit remains excellent; international banks, which after all have to put their money somewhere, would rather lend it to Canada than to Argentina, Mexico, Poland. The real cost of the deficit is that it leaves the government with no room to spur growth by a tax cut, as the economic circumstances probably warrant.

believe we are now reverting to being a Northern Fringe."

Most of the particular causes of Canada's decline from specialness are well known, and thoroughly depressing. We have the poorest productivity growth of any Western industrial nation. We have the worst strike record except Italy (there, the Supreme Court once went on strike). We have the lowest rate of research and development. We pay (and receive) almost the highest wages. Our rate of hourly output in manufacturing is about 25 per cent less than that of the U.S.* Our deficit is almost half as high again, per capita, as that of the U.S., and it is far more difficult for the government to reduce because so much of it is accounted for by social spending rather than by military spending. Our capital is hemorrhaging away, some $55 billion having moved out since 1977, in all forms, according to Bank of Nova Scotia chief economist William Mackness; indeed, one of the most disturbing of cross-border comparisons is that while investments by Japanese auto companies in the U.S. to the end of 1984 totalled $4 billion, their equivalent investment in Canada amounted to $125 million. And it goes without saying that with a few notable exceptions – Canadian Westinghouse, Pratt and Whitney, Canadian General Electric, Griffith Laboratories (its Japanese-style bread crumbs sell in Japan) – heavy foreign ownership limits the horizons of many Canadian corporations.

Other Canadian deficiencies that are less frequently commented on matter almost as much. We have one of the slowest comparative rates of growth of skilled labour – just ahead of the U.S. but half that of France, say – despite the fastest total labour force growth in the Western world. With the University of Waterloo as the shining exception,** we have a conspicuous lack of universities capable of playing the same kind of catalytic role in the generation of high-tech companies that Stanford has done for Silicon Valley and MIT for Boston's Route 128, despite the heaviest public spending on post-secondary education of any Western country but Sweden. Until very recently we have lacked any aptitude for entrepreneurship and risk-taking: proportionately half as many Canadians as Americans hold shares in public companies. And we have an equivalent lack of venture

---

* This calculation, for the year 1982, has been made by York University economist Donald Daly.

** The University of Waterloo earns larger royalties from its software programs than do Stanford and MIT, *combined.*

capitalists who command both the money and the know-how to nurture enterprises through their growing pains.

These shortcomings, and others, have been enumerated often enough by think tanks, academic economists, and spokesmen for business groups. In a search for a fresher perspective, it may be more useful to review some of the non-economic reasons that have contributed to Canada's economic decline. After all, most of the most successful contemporary economies – Japan, Singapore, South Korea, Taiwan – lack any economic assets at all, except will.

Economic decline is an almost inevitable succeeding stage of economic achievement. Britain was the first modern nation to discover that societies behave just as individuals do: the purpose of acquiring wealth is after all to enjoy it, the problem being that enjoyment precludes continuing acquisition. Most of Western Europe, having caught up to the U.S. through the 1960s and 1970s, is now showing signs of exhaustion. Even Japanese workers are apparently beginning to tire of performing like "workaholic ants," as they've been called. Daniel Bell diagnosed the social malady in his 1978 book, *The Cultural Contradictions of Capitalism*: "American capitalism has lost its traditional legitimacy which was based on a moral system of rewards derived from the Protestant sanctification of work. It has substituted a hedonism which promises material ease and luxury." The transition point probably happened around the mid-sixties. Then, "heroes of production," the grey-flannelled organization men and robber-baron tycoons, were displaced in the popular imagination by "heroes of consumption" – entertainers, celebrities, athletes.

The possession of resources increased the probability of Canada's relative economic decline. All resource-rich societies – Australia, Argentina, Canada – behave like "poor little rich kids." Most smart societies, like Taiwan and South Korea, also Singapore and Hong Kong, and also Switzerland and Austria, have no choice but to be smart. Maybe the secret of economic success is some kind of blended Sino-Puritan ethic. The exceptions among those countries that have managed to stay smart while being resource-rich are Sweden and the U.S.

The U.S. now is making a galvanic attempt to reverse its economic decline. If it succeeds, it will be one of the few societies to have done so. Success is by no means certain. For all the talk of

218

entrepreneurship and innovation, a grossly disproportionate share of American business energy is being devoted to the "paper entrepreneurship" of mergers and roll-overs and acquisitions, for it is a self-destructive truth about economic life in the U.S., and in Canada, that it is easier to make money by buying someone else's product than by inventing, developing, manufacturing, and marketing your own product. Further, despite its recent gains in competitiveness, the U.S. is still losing ground: in 1984, the U.S. went into the red for the first time, by $7 billion (U.S.), in trade in its best products – electronics.

But the U.S. has two assets going for it. One is the compulsive competitiveness of its people. The other is the magnetic tug of the American Dream. To fulfil that dream, the U.S. has to be Number One. The prospect of becoming an economic Number Two, to Japan, has seized the American imagination – the best example of this is the U.S.'s decision to take on Japan, despite its head start, in a race to be the first country to develop "fifth-generation" computers based on artificial intelligence. This race isn't yet run, but most observers guess that that contest between bred-in-the-bone American capacity to innovate and the endemic Japanese capacity to imitate will in the end turn out to be no contest.*

It's tempting to locate Canada midway between the U.S. and Western Europe on the scale of adaptability to economic change. In one sense, this would be too generous. Canada's great economic blunder, for which there is no European equivalent, was to refuse to accept the reality of the oil price increases of the 1970s. Canada thereby failed to adjust to the new economic circumstances, including the circumstances of a decline in real incomes – hence the growth in the national deficit. Likewise, no European country perpetuated Canada's dependence, psychic as well as economic, on resources as an easy out.

In another important sense, however, this judgement would be, if not too harsh, then at least misplaced. Those European countries such as Austria, Sweden, and Switzerland to which the Canadian economy has consistently been compared unfavourably – quite justifiably – are all stable societies. (They're also small societies.) Unique-

---

* The great U.S. asset isn't so much its huge domestic market of 225 million people as that it encompasses within itself the world economy. Ideas and people from all lands pour in, including from Canada. Japanese society is by contrast hostile to new people and to speculative as opposed to practical new ideas.

ly, except for the U.S. and Australia, Canada has had to cope with a rapidly expanding and an increasingly heterogeneous population, and, entirely uniquely, with the threat of national dissolution. If from the early 1960s onward Canada was allowing its economy to run down, it was at the same time building a nation, or rebuilding it. We had little time, while worrying about What Does Quebec Really Want?, to worry about where we were going economically.

Perhaps one of the most astute comments about Canada's economic miscalculations was made by a senior member of the U.S. cabinet, whom protocol requires remain anonymous since he made it during an informal conversation with the author. After a fairly lively exchange of opinions, but no meeting of minds, about the National Energy Policy, this cabinet minister commented: "Your problem is that you've politicized your economy. Your government is almost incapable of taking actual economic decisions, as opposed to political ones, to support this or that group or industry or region."

This describes the principal contemporary difference between the two North American economies. Politics certainly plays a major part in U.S. economic decision-making: a good deal of U.S. defence-spending amounts to a covert program of regional subsidies, as well as of payoffs to supportive politicians. The difference is one of scale – a multi-year study would be required to find a corporation or institution of consequence in Canada not in receipt of funds from one government or another – and one of public expectations.

The fact is, Canadians mistrust the marketplace and trust government while Americans locate their angels and devils the other way around. Each people has perceived their circumstances with considerable clarity. In the U.S., governmental power is feared and resisted. Americans assume they will work out their own destinies in the marketplace and ask only of government that it make the marketplace more evenly, and openly, competitive. Most of the examples of greater governmental interventionism south of the border than north of it are of instances where the government has stepped in to make the marketplace function more like a true marketplace – the U.S., for instance, has far more stringent anti-trust laws and far more severe requirements for corporate financial disclosure (this is why the salaries of executives of Canadian corporations are available only when these companies are listed on U.S. stock exchanges).

The Canadian distrust of the marketplace is also soundly based. Ours has never been a marketplace so much as a quasi-cartel or oligopoly. As an obvious example, we have had, until very recently, only six Canadian chartered banks, as against 14,700 in the U.S. Even more striking, 46 per cent of the shares of the companies on the Toronto Stock Exchange's 300 list are controlled by just nine families, such as the Bronfmans, the Blacks, the Reichmanns, the Southams, and among those in solitary splendour, Galen Weston, Ken Thomson, Paul Desmarais.* In Canada the 100 largest companies control 34 per cent of the total, non-financial, industrial assets; those in the U.S. control just 15 per cent. This is why Tom Kierans, vice-chairman of McLeod, Young, Weir, has warned that the "privatization" of crown corporations "may prove counterproductive to Canada's true interests" because if these are bought up by major private Canadian companies, as is most probable, the result would be to increase corporate concentration still further and make the Canadian economy even less like a marketplace. In a speech to an Institute for Research on Public Policy conference in February, 1985, Kierans, taking another bite at the corporations that feed him, declared, "I believe there to be no larger blot on the public policy record than our failure to come to terms with competition policy."** (For all practical purposes, Canada has no competition or anti-trust policy, which is unique among industrial nations.)

As is true of all cartels, the most important member, if invisible, has been the government. Until the late seventies, chartered banks were not merely protected from any foreign competition but also from any consequential domestic competition, from trust companies, investment firms, and other finance companies. Other quasi-cartels were treated as solicitously. In an interview with the author, the Canadian-born economist John Kenneth Galbraith remarked, "I've never understood this concern in Canada about multinationals being so uniquely difficult to regulate. It seems to me they are much easier to regulate than the CPR. So why isn't it regulated?"

---

* In a breach of corporate solidarity, the study that revealed this fact was undertaken by the Canadian Bankers' Association in an effort to end criticism of lack of competition among the banks by demonstrating that no greater competition existed among other Canadian industries.

** Kierans' father, Eric Kierans, the former Trudeau cabinet minister, has more forthrightly described Canadian businessmen as "the most sclerotic in the world."

The Canadian economy can be said to function like an unwritten social contract. Canadians pay high prices for goods and services because of the government-approved lack of commercial competition, but in exchange they receive from their government lower-cost and superior public services – the best example being health and hospital care, for which Canadians pay only 8.4 per cent of the Gross National Product as against a total take of 10.5 per cent south of the border. The question is whether, amid the pressures of the global marketplace, the price of that contract has become too high – on both sides of the ledger. The costs of too extensive a public sector are well known. The costs of a private sector that's too uncompetitive may need some elaboration.

In a splendid bit of invective, Mordecai Richler once described Canadian businessmen, in an article for *Harper's*, as, "Not builders but vendors, or at best circumspect investors in insurance and trust companies." He blamed this astringent timidity on the Scots. Other commentators have called Canadian businessmen "rentiers" and "compradors," or agents for absent capitalists, whether Canadian or foreign. Abraham Rotstein has remarked, "Almost uniquely among national capitalists, Canadian businessmen lack an *esprit de corps*, a collective sense of themselves."

Here, foreign ownership is a major factor. So, more subtly, is the foreignness of our corporate culture. Canadian businessmen have always looked abroad for their role models, yesterday a Stephen Wosniak, today a T. Boone Pickens, tomorrow no doubt some South Korean tycoon. Domestic role models – Bob Blair, Mike Cowpland – have emerged only very recently. Only within at the most the last half decade, and still only tentatively, have Canadian businessmen begun to make a contribution to nation-building, in contrast to Canadian artists who began paying their dues from the 1960s on and the civil service mandarins who began doing so in the 1940s and 1950s.

Another factor has been that governments have discouraged private entrepreneurs by subsidizing public entrepreneurs. Most of Canada's most successful businessmen have been those who've figured out how to get what they want out of government; it was said of former Dome Petroleum chairman Jack Gallagher, "he did his best exploration in Ottawa." In an interview for this book the senior executive for

222

a major company commented, "Sure we often applied for and got grants to do things we were going to do anyway. But if your competitors are getting them, how can you justify to your shareholders not going after them?" This practice of giveaways has nothing to do with party ideology or label. The Mulroney government has, if anything, increased the pace of the payouts – the $225 million bailout of the Canadian Commercial Bank, the $150 million worth of loan guarantees to Domtar to help finance a paper mill that was already commercially viable. Industry Minister Sinclair Stevens has declared he intends to negotiate long-term funding agreements with individual companies and industries (such as petrochemicals and autos).

If few Canadian businessmen have become celebrated entrepreneurs, they can claim in self-defence that Canadian society seldom celebrates entrepreneurs. Peter Gatien grew up in Cornwall as the son of a postman. He now owns nightclubs in New York, where he lives, and in Chicago and London; he made his first million at the age of twenty-five. He remembers of his youth: "It wasn't anything anyone said exactly or anything the media said outright, but you got the message that there were just two ways to become famous in Canada – become a hockey player or become a politician." The fact is that a society that gives primacy to "equity" over "efficiency" is also close to putting equity ahead of individual creativity.

The dividing line between past and present is marked by the Great Recession of 1981-82. As in the case of the Vietnam War for Americans, a traumatic shock, if less apocalyptic, it forced people to reassess the nature of their society. Since then, the belief in resources as a cure-all has lost its hold on the collective imagination. So, equally, has a belief in government as a cure-all; if in a less dramatic way, Canada's best and brightest turned out to have performed as ineptly as had America's best and brightest on the far side of the Pacific.

Everything hasn't changed, as demonstrated by the Mulroney government's difficulty in forging a consensus on how to spread the pain of reducing the deficit. But for the first time, economics has become a subject of popular debate, with newspapers and magazines and radio and TV scrambling to keep up with the demand for information and analysis. Because of the collective awareness of the high stakes involved, it has become possible to think the unthinkable out loud. When John Crosbie began his 1983 campaign for the Conservative leadership by calling for an "economic partnership" between Canada and the U.S. his opponents attacked him for giving up on Canada. Quickly, they changed the subject: it turned out that Conservative delegates and the public were fully prepared to consider such a proposition and gave Crosbie credit for putting it on the public agenda.

The most considerable change has involved Canadian attitudes toward entrepreneurship. What has happened has been like the breaking of a dam above which the water has been gathering for a long time. It has become apparent that during the long period that Canada has functioned like an economic cartel, it had also been transforming itself in social terms into a raucously competitive society.

Immigration has been the single most important agent of change. *The Vertical Mosaic* described by John Porter in his book of that title has long since become a horizontal mosaic even if some genteel pyramids still jut up from it. Jews were the first to move up the ladder to join the WASPs on its top rungs. Now, in a Canadian equivalent to the burst of creative energy that the nineteenth-century immigrants to the U.S. brought with them across the Atlantic, "new Canadians" of all cultures and languages and colours are racing or clambering or clawing up the ladder. In high schools, the top spot in the class now is frequently held by a Chinese Canadian, a Japanese Canadian, a Vietnamese Canadian.

Simultaneously, another infusion of creative energy is being provided by women: women are starting up new small businesses at a rate three times as fast as men. Further, for the first time since Confederation, Quebecers are turning their talents away from church and civil service to commerce: some 40 per cent of all business students in Canada are enrolled at Quebec universities. Lastly, an entire generation of young people, fully aware there is no room left for them in the bureaucracies, is moving into the labour force in search of small businesses that can employ them, and, if none are available, in search of ways to employ themselves.

Entrepreneurship isn't yet as Canadian as maple syrup. But it is taking root. Among the examples: Alfred Sung and his high fashions; Erna Tripp and her aluminum flagpoles, of which she now sells annually $100,000 worth, all self-made, from the garage of her house in Tillsonburg, Ontario, after deciding that at the age of sixty she needed a new interest in life; Don Green of Tridon in Hamilton who sells windshield wipers to Japan and signal flashers to Sweden and Hong Kong and who has expanded his payroll from 40 to 2,000; Wally Pieczonka of Burlington, Ontario, who went south with IBM and then came back to start Linear Technology, a firm that manufactures miniature amplifiers for half the hearing aids in the Western world; Erick Schmidt of Edmonton whose GSR Company makes probably the world's most advanced computer-controlled continuous laser cutters (GM uses them to cut the fabrics for its seat covers). Others include Lise Wattier of Montreal, who sells $10 million worth of her Charme et Beauté cosmetics against such competitors as Elizabeth Arden; the Taylors, Stephen and Bonnie, whose Atien line of cosmetics for men sells in Bloomingdales; Michael Bregman of Montreal who started with a single muffin stand and who now has fifty Mmmuffin outlets in the U.S. as well as a chain of French-style bakeries; the Shaver Poultry Farm of Cambridge, Ontario, which is, or claims to be, the largest in the world; Colin Kerr, who turns out 1,000 wind generators a year in Vankleek Hill, Ontario, some of which are now being installed in Inner Mongolia; George Patton of Oakville, Ontario, whose Leblanc and Royle company is among the world's top ten builders of telecommunication towers, selling from Rwanda to Riyadh; Charles Williams of Markham whose GEAC computer company has sold library systems to the Smithsonian and the National Library in Paris.

Conventionally, Canada may seem to still be stony ground for entrepreneurs. Canadians still like to keep their money in the next closest thing to a sock: our personal savings rate is one-half as high again as in the U.S.; we have too few venture capital companies, and too many conservative bankers. Not least, Canada is on the outer rim of the centres of international economic action.

On second glance, though, the prospects become more promising. No differently from other people, businessmen are attracted to places where they can walk the streets in safety, where the schools for their children are good, where individuals don't face being obliterated by medical costs, where the cultural amenities are attractive. While Canada's liberal political culture has imposed real economic costs, it has simultaneously created for Canada a new version of comparative economic advantage. Although Canadians constantly look nervously over their shoulders at the industrial competition coming across the Pacific Rim, they less often notice that tens of thousands of immigrants from those countries – ten times more would come if they could – make the journey across to Canada each year; something has to exist here that no amount of full employment assembling microchips can compensate for.

225

Bliss's concern that Canada is destined to decline to "a Northern Fringe" is in part misplaced: the global economy has no centre; thus, neither does it necessarily have any fringe. Because of communications and transportation and cost-saving technology, almost anything can be made, or can be done, anywhere. Some of the world's most advanced radio receivers for use by the oil industry and now being sold to the U.S., Britain, Norway, and South Korea are made in the Orion Electronics plant in Saulnierville, New Brunswick, on the Bay of Fundy. The largest independent fish broker in the Atlantic Provinces, Herb Davis, now lives in a leafy suburb of Ottawa and starts his working days at three a.m. making calls to East Germany, Poland, Russia, and Finland. Calgary is now the world's second centre for geophysical analysis, after Houston. Out of Winnipeg, which is as far removed from continental markets as it is possible to get, a Finnish immigrant, Peter Nygard of Tan-Jay, sells $50 million of his line of women's sportswear in the U.S. and expects to reach the $100 million mark by 1987.

A couple of further examples may establish the case that while Canada labours under economic disadvantages – weather; relative distance from major U.S. markets; a heavy load of social spending – those with brains can make it as readily here as anywhere else.

But for the word itself, which was minted by U.S. management consultant Francis Gifford Pinchot III, "intrapreneurship" is a Canadian invention, at least on a large scale. The idea behind it is that large companies should recreate the entrepreneurial conditions that exist within the best of small companies – the sense of personal responsibility and of belonging, the adaptability, the lack of fear of novelty.

Fittingly, if a trifle stagily, the most prominent object in the office of Frank Stronach, the president of Magna International of Markham, Ontario, is a bronze copy of Rodin's statue, "The Thinker." Because of the way Stronach thinks, Magna now employs more than 7,000 people and turns out close to $700 million worth of auto parts, four-fifths of which go south of the border. By 1987, Magna's sales will top $1 billion. Stronach even talks of Magna's payroll eventually reaching 80,000, and that might seem extravagant. But already every single American car manufactured on this continent contains an average of $40 worth of Magna products.

Magna's products encompass the familiar range of auto-parts nuts and bolts, although it is using its new research facilities to try to develop batteries for electric cars in a joint project with a French company. What's different about Magna is Magna itself. Stronach, who is now fifty, recalls how one day back in the 1960s when he was newly arrived from Austria and running a machine shop, his foreman came to him to say he wanted to leave to start up on his own. Realizing he would not merely lose a first-rate foreman but would also gain a competitor, Stronach proposed that he himself bankroll his employee. Out of that kernel of thought developed what is undoubtedly the most highly developed form of intrapreneurship in North America. Magna itself is now a corporate container for more than fifty small plants. Each plant is limited to roughly 100 employees. Plants that expand beyond that size because of sales successes are bifurcated into two new ones. Similarly, groups of these quasi-independent plants are limited to twenty; groups that grow larger are subdivided. Stronach describes this as "the pond and stone principle. If a plant gets too large, the manager will no longer know either his employees or his customers, just as if a pond is too large, the ripples from a stone dropped into it won't reach its centre."

Human behaviour, rather than the textbooks, is also the foundation of Stronach's other organizing principle. The attraction of working for Magna is that "it's the next best thing to owning your own business." All managers receive a cut of the profits made by their plants, and also a cut of the profits of new plants created by subdividing their own original one. All employees receive not merely a share of Magna's profits but Magna shares. "Employees have a moral right, not just to a share of the profits they helped to make but to a share of their company," explains Stronach. "You can never get rich on a salary, only on equity."

Stronach, who's graduated from auto-parts maker to industrial philosopher, is convinced he's defined an industrial role model that most Canadian companies can, and must, copy. (One Magna executive tried to convince Conrad Black to adopt the system as an alternative to selling off Dominion Stores.) His philosophy is in fact carefully grounded in practicality: a benefit of limiting the payrolls of each plant to a maximum of 100 is that union organizers find it impossible to break in. But Stronach believes he has something better to offer labour: "Business has failed to provide the working class with an alternative to our present system of corporate concentration and bureaucracy and then wonders why workers aren't productive. The fact is, people today are too well educated and too accustomed to equality and to individual freedom to be prepared to spend the rest of their lives as wage slaves."

The other place to find a role model for the Canadian economy is in a rather grungy office in an industrial section of Port Moody near Vancouver, in the person of a man who, with his baggy trousers and narrow ties, looks like a storeroom clerk. He's James McFarlane, a Manitoba farmer's son who went into the navy, left as a lieutenant-commander, and started his own company, International Submarine Engineering. McFarlane now is beginning to be thought of in his field of submersibles as sort of a latter-day equivalent to Willy Messerschmidt in the aviation industry. ISE designs and manufactures unmanned, remote-operated submersibles, each with its own robot arms, seeing-eye TV monitor, computerized radio control equipment, seismic devices, and echo sounders. Its seven-functioned or active-jointed remote-controlled feedback arm is easily the most advanced in the world.

According to McFarlane, "submersibles are today at about the stage where the DC-3 once was." As planes used to, these contraptions create markets for themselves, locating and repairing breaks in underwater pipelines and in oil rigs, surveying the sea bottom, recovering practice torpedoes, exploring for undersea minerals such as manganese nodules. ISE is now working with a French firm to build the world's first nuclear-powered commercial submarine. (It will be designed for a crew of thirteen and be able to operate submerged, including beneath ice, for up to three months.) ISE's sales aren't that large, at $10 million, nor is its payroll, at 120; but the calls now come in daily to McFarlane's Port Moody office from London, Houston, Tokyo, Milan, Riyadh, Paris.

The point that Stronach and McFarlane and the others add up to is a straightforward one. If they can make it in Canada, then there is no reason carved in stone why Canadians collectively cannot make it.

The rewards that Stronach and McFarlane and the others have achieved are beyond the reach of most Canadians. "Industrial restructuring" is one of those neutral, abstract words favoured by academic economists. Those whose industries will be restructured by the pressures of the global marketplace will experience pain, at times acute pain. It is noteworthy that while academic economists almost unanimously advocate free trade to spur economic growth, none yet have advocated free trade in academic economists. Without a generous adjustment program to preserve the incomes if not the jobs for those who will be restructured – retraining will be possible for some – the resistance of workers, unions, towns, and regions would bring the process of restructuring to a halt.

Other changes can be suggested, and often have been. Canada's "two solitudes" of universities and businesses will have to become a synergistic whole. In an almost despairing review on the progress elsewhere of research into new materials and in fields such as biotechnology, the Science Council of Canada commented: "Canada is a decade or more behind in these technologies – almost too far to know enough to panic." The adversarial relationship between labour and management has a lingering aura of the 1930s, like a silent movie rerun. (One useful reform, suggested by Donald Daly, would be full corporate financial disclosure; today's secrecy inevitably arouses union suspicions and resistance to change.) Similarly, the solitudes of government and business will have to call off their phony war; the extensive consultation that preceded the May, 1985, budget represented an unprecedented reaching out by government (by far the most imaginative process of pre-budget consultations, including a series of open public seminars, has been that initiated by the government of Saskatchewan starting in 1984).

The real challenge is social and political rather than economic. Inescapably, the ideals of a liberal political culture and the necessities of the global marketplace contradict each other. A market economy demands two leaps of faith that Canadians haven't been prepared to take since the 1950s, nor have they needed to as long as the world needed our resources. The first is the faith that wealth accumulated by those who succeed will eventually be distributed to those who fail: not "trickle-down" economics as such, but a delayed, managed, trickle-down. The second leap of faith is that pain today will bring gain tomorrow; in order to work, Schumpeter's "creative destruction" thesis does require that the creation of the enterprises of tomorrow be preceded by the destruction of today's uneconomic enterprises.

The extent of this challenge can perhaps be best appreciated by casting it in regional terms. A policy, even an unadmitted one, of

229

restructuring regions would touch a national nerve of quite another order from that of a deliberate policy of restructuring industries. It would put to the test the unwritten pact of Confederation itself. Implicitly, by agreeing to join a Confederation that itself made little economic sense, each province took on trust that, in return, it would not have its own economic illogicality challenged beyond some acceptable if undefined point. Regional equalization, or in other words, the redistribution of national wealth to people in the places where they choose to live rather than, as in most countries, redistribution to people in their own right as individuals, has become the contemporary essence of Confederation; "to challenge it is to challenge Confederation itself," as Herschel Hardin has written. National self-interest is embedded in this collective response to regional interests: if Quebecers, say, or Newfoundlanders, face no alternative but to move to Toronto or to Alberta in search of satisfying jobs, then the logic of liberal "equity" cannot deny them the right to move on further, to New York or California, in search of even better jobs. Regional equalization thus is part of the sustaining fabric of the Canadian nation.*

That fabric, though, is already strained by the disappearance of the surplus resource revenue that once underwrote regional subsidies. The strain will be intensified by the pressures of the global marketplace. Even so liberal an economist as Galbraith has written, in *The Nature of Mass Poverty*, that out-migration is the single certain way of ending the "equilibrium" of regional unemployment. Perhaps thinking of his own youth in Elgin County, Ontario, Galbraith wrote: "It selects those who most want help. It is good for the country (or region) to which they go.... What is the perversity in the human soul that causes people to resist so obvious a good?" The perversity, of course, is a sense of place, and in the instance of Quebecers and others, a sense of historical continuity.

The case example of a region that has progressed from industrial destruction to re-creation through out-migration and restructuring is New England. Beginning in the late 1950s, New England underwent a quarter-century of decline as its textile and footwear and furniture plants closed or went south. Today, Massachusetts, New Hampshire,

---

* The Prairies represent the single exception to the unwritten national rule that the preservation of Confederation requires the preservation of regional populations. From the 1930s on, all the Prairie Provinces experienced out-migration, as recently as the early 1970s in the case of Saskatchewan.

230

and Connecticut rank as the top three states in terms of their low rate of unemployment – the phenomenon of Peterborough, New Hampshire, is one reason; Boston's Route 128 circle of high-tech companies is another. Many of the sources of this resurgence cannot be replicated easily: the omnipresence throughout the region of first-class educational institutions; the relative proximity of New York and Boston; the sheer attractiveness of so many New England towns and hamlets (the absence of blacks is one that isn't mentioned publicly). It remains true also that in much of rural New England – Maine as an example – economic decline is deepening rather than reversing.

The challenge for Canada is somehow to hold onto the best of the political culture that we have and yet to take hold of the economic future. The cost of hanging too far back will be a decline into genteel poverty. That of hurrying ahead too fast would be social polarization. To magnify the challenge, every Canadian will be able to look south and measure, by the widening of the cross-border economic gap that has begun to open up, the difference between what is being achieved here and there. This is the ultimate challenge for Canadians: to keep in step with the U.S. economically and still to march to our own very different cultural drummer.

Chapter Sixteen
The Continental Economy:
Seek or Hide

"Go back to your igloo."

Message left by an anonymous worker in the Northern
Telecom plant in Nashville, Tennessee, on a car with
Ontario licence plates.

In the early 1980s, North American economic history turned upside down. For the first time in this century, the economic gap between the United States and Canada widened rather than narrowed. Statistics never tell a full story, but two figures convey a good deal of it: at just under 11 per cent compared to just over 7 per cent, Canada's unemployment rate is half again as high as that of the U.S.; the Canadian dollar is worth less than seventy-five cents.

Almost certainly, the gap will widen further. Since 1982, more than $100 billion worth of foreign investment has poured into the U.S. each year. The payoff from this has yet to be fully felt. "The potential exists for another boom like in the sixties," says the Washington international trade consultant Harald Malmgren. Canada, by contrast, suffered a net loss of capital through to the end of 1984. Many businesses have still to clear off their debts from the Great Recession; they haven't yet modernized their plant and equipment, nor have they "down-sized" to trim their payroll costs. The lack of new foreign investment, even after investors have been reassured they were welcome, has been striking and disturbing: Americans, after all, can get $1.35 worth of investment for each U.S. dollar they move across the border. Even after more than two years of recovery, almost the only motion in the Canadian economy was caused by the back-eddy of U.S. expansion.

"I worry deeply that the gap between us is going to grow larger and larger," says Science Council chairman Stuart Smith. "If that

232

happens, our best and brightest will leave, and in the end we may be left with no alternative but to plead to be allowed in, sort of like Newfoundland joining Confederation."

Some signs exist that this gravitational pull is already happening. The formal immigration flows have changed little. But more and more Canadians are starting to think of the U.S. as the economic future. As hasn't happened since the early 1960s, a growing number of upper-middle-class parents are sending sons and daughters to American universities, for the education, certainly, but also for the career contacts. A senior federal civil servant recounts that his two sons, both entering their teens, "talk all the time about moving to the U.S., not because of the jobs – jobs to them are abstract – but because to them that's where the action is." The economist Carl Beigie reports of the class he teaches at McGill University, "the phrase I hear them use most often is 'green card.' "

As yet, the cross-border gap is a crack rather than a gulf. The best measure of it is provided by the annual comparative analysis done by the U.S. Department of Labour on the basis of "purchasing power parity exchange rates," which attempts to calculate the real purchasing power of wages in each country after allowing for publicly paid services. On this basis, Canadians in 1984 enjoyed a standard of living of 96 per cent of the level of Americans.* This represented a decline from 1976 when Canada was actually ahead, at 102 per cent. The direction matters rather than the degree. If the gap progressively widens – toward, say, the level of around 80 per cent that applied in the 1950s – national cohesion would be corroded. Canada might retain its sovereignty, but it could lose its will to be sovereign.

Perhaps the best description of the relationship between the two economies was provided by MIT economist Lester Thurow at a seminar held in Saskatoon in October, 1984, as part of a public education

---

* This comparison, while not exact, is far more representative of reality than the conventional calculation of average national incomes compared in U.S. dollars, by which measure Canada appeared to have declined to tenth or lower in the international table. According to the U.S. Labour Department, Canadian living standards remain markedly higher than those of major European countries such as West Germany (78 per cent of the U.S. level in 1984), France (76 per cent), and Britain (66 per cent).

series organized by Saskatchewan Finance Minister Bob Andrew in advance of his budget. "Canadians and Americans are like co-passengers on the same aircraft," Thurow told his audience of businessmen, farmers, educators, civil servants. "You can decide whether you want to be in first class, which is where Americans are now sitting, or you can decide to sit in steerage, which is where Canadians are sitting today. The one decision you cannot make is to get off the plane."

Thurow's analysis almost certainly is correct. In comparison to the European Economic Community, even after a quarter-century of formal economic union, Canada and the United States, although quite separate sovereign economies in a legal sense, are incomparably more intimately integrated in terms of the scale of investment held by each country in the other, the volume of two-way trade, the joint ownership of corporations, the cross-border movement of professionals and executives, the commonality of language and social customs and business practices, the interconnection of communication and transportation facilities, the standardization of commercial regulations and environmental and health standards. (Metric is the maverick exception.)

Trade provides the handiest measure of integration. Most provinces – B.C. is an exception – now export more to the U.S. than to the rest of Canada. In all, 75 per cent of Canadian exports go south; except for some "tied-aid" sales, the U.S. provides just about the only international market for Canadian manufactured products. Smith of the Science Council says, "I cannot think of a high-tech manufacturing company that doesn't depend on U.S. sales." Even Quebec furniture makers, almost the archetypal "basketcase industry," now export one-third, or $245 million, of their annual output to the U.S. Some of these sales are a gift created by the cheap Canadian dollar. But happenstance will harden into permanence as Canadian exporters first acquire orders almost wonderingly and then develop sales offices and distribution and service and repair networks, negotiate co-ventures, and later perhaps buy up American companies or set up local subsidiaries of their own.

Since its accession to power, the Mulroney government has taken several major steps toward continental economic integration, quite aside from whatever decision it eventually takes on bilateral free trade. The disbanding of FIRA means that but for a few options held in reserve, a continental capital free market now exists. By the Western

234

Accord of April, 1985, the government established a continental free market for oil and gas; shortly afterward, Washington announced that U.S. oil exports to eastern Canada would now be permitted, opening the way for increased southern sales from Alberta. Most provinces, Manitoba as much as Quebec, are proposing a similar integration of hydro power.

Most of the steps toward continental economic integration are simply a by-product of the routine daily decisions of corporations. As a result of its takeover of the Harris Bank of Chicago, the Bank of Montreal has established an electronic service to transfer funds directly between corporations and their bank accounts in either country; according to a bank press release, the new service "effectively knocks out the barrier to funds transfer between the two countries." As a consequence of deregulation south of the border followed by regulatory reform north of it, major American trucking companies, like Yellowfreight and St. John, have entered the Canadian market for the first time by offering non-stop delivery from points south to points north. Newly deregulated American airlines, such as People's Express, Empire, and Pilgrim, have similarly added Canadian points to their feeder networks. Comments Stephen Blank of MultiNational Strategies, "Most companies act as if the border no longer exists and treat it as just another, and a minor, cost of doing business."

The aspect of continental integration that Canadians have always known about, and against which the nationalists fought for so long, was the northward extension of the U.S. economy in the form of branch plants, capital, technology, and managerial expertise. The far less widely appreciated aspect of continental integration is that the Canadian economy has similarly extended southward. The export of Canadian capital, branch plants, managerial expertise, and, though much less so, technology, is now becoming as significant a force in the creation of an integrated continental economy as was the old, and now slackening, northward flow. For these Canadian companies, the U.S. market has become *their* market and the Canadian market simply a stepping stone to it.

This phenomenon isn't in any way unique to Canadian companies. The U.S. economy now resembles an international bazaar in which everyone hawks his wares, deposits his money, and earns his profits in the most valuable currency in the world. Japanese auto manufacturers, for instance, earn 80 per cent of their total profits in the U.S. While the economies of Southeast Asia may now be the envy

235

of the world, their secret ingredient is that they design their products either for the American market or to American standards and tastes, which then ensures the success of these products throughout the world, including Southeast Asia (and the Soviet Union to the extent they are allowed in).

The familiar manifestations of this phenomenon are the U.S. trade deficit, of $120 billion (U.S.) in 1984 and a potential $140 billion in 1985, and the massive influx of foreign capital that will cause the U.S. to become a net debtor nation sometime in the winter of 1985-86 for the first time since 1914. (High interest rates are an attraction, but a secondary one; the principal attraction is that the U.S. is the best haven, and the most profitable resting place, for capital in the world.) Less well known, even by Americans, is the extent to which so many of the most "American" of U.S. corporations now are owned by foreigners: Carnation Milk, Standard Oil of Ohio (let alone Shell), A & P Stores, Howard Johnson motels, IT & T, Gimbels, and the makers of Brylcreem, Alpo dogfood, Pepsodent, McDonald's hamburgers.

For Canadians, the difference between past and present is that Canadians now are near the head of the pack. According to the U.S. Department of Commerce, the largest holder of foreign assets in the U.S. in 1982 was Holland, followed by Britain, Canada, West Germany, Japan, Switzerland, France. After adjusting for a technicality, this means that Canada now ranks second among foreign holders of U.S. industrial and commercial properties.* Predictably, Canadians didn't know this, or couldn't allow themselves to believe it, until an American pointed it out to them – Andrew Malcolm of the *New York Times* in his 1985 best-seller, *The Canadians*.

Several Canadian observers spotted the phenomenon earlier. Alan Rugman of Dalhousie University's Centre for International Studies has charted the progress of Canadian multinationals since 1980; in a 1984 report co-authored with John McIveen of the Toronto-Dominion Bank, he commented that these companies "are operating in international markets [and] performing in a highly successful manner in the face of fierce competition from U.S., European and Japanese multinationals." University of Toronto economist Ed Saf-

---

* Dutch investment, while considerable in its own right – Shell and Heineken as examples – is overstated because many foreign investors, including Canadians, use a loophole in Dutch tax law to route their investments in the U.S. through Holland.

arian has done the same kind of innovative work. In a 1985 paper for the Ontario Economic Council, he reported that between 1979 and 1984 Canadian investment abroad, most of it in the U.S., had almost doubled, from $20 billion to $39 billion. During the same period, foreign investment within Canada had increased by only one-third, from $54 billion to $73 billion. If these trends continue, Canadian holdings abroad by the turn of the century may be as large as those of foreigners here.*

Malcolm, helped by his calling card as a New York Times correspondent, got the message through to Canadians. He also gave his message a certain "top-spin" as it's known in the reportorial trade. He wrote of "The charge of the Maple Leaf brigade" and that "Canada, the old colonial pussycat, doormat of foreigners plundering resources and profits, is fast becoming a voracious tiger."

Quite a few of the Maple Leafers who have charged south have in fact fallen flat on their faces. Canadian Tire, one of the country's most efficient retail organizations, dropped $55 million on its U.S. chain, White Stores, for which its president, Dean Muncaster, paid the price with his job; People's Jewellers has accumulated a $5 million loss on its southern outlets. Several real estate developers, Daon and Nu-West, bought high and limped back home after selling out low. The Toronto Sun is having no joy with its Houston Post, although less so in that depressed city than Toronto's Leon's Furniture Store, which has had to close its Houston outlet, as has Vancouver's Elephant and Castle chain of restaurants. Rogers Cable is selling off many of its U.S. properties. None of the Canadian oilmen who hurried south to escape the NEP did well, although none did as badly as Hiram Walker Resources, which managed to blow $200 million on a miscalculated takeover. Maislin Trucking's bankruptcy was caused by its takeover of the U.S. company, Gateway, and the Canadian Commercial Bank's bankruptcy was caused by the unrecoverable oil and gas loans it took over in California. Comments Loblaw's president Richard Currie, "Americans love to compete, and they're not as polite about it as Canadians are." Even so, despite the knocks,

---

* According to Safarian's data, Canadian assets abroad as a proportion of foreign assets here amounted to one-quarter in 1974, to one-third in 1979, and to just over one-half in 1984.

Canadians *are* competing.

The real estate developers, back in the early 1970s, were the first in the field. They'd built subdivisions and shopping centres and office complexes all over Canada and pushed on south – Toronto's Cadillac-Fairview as flagship – in search of new worlds to conquer. By the early 1980s a majority of the major commercial developments in Houston and Dallas, and many of the most ambitious in Phoenix – some of the individual homes in one development topped $1.75 million each – were being built by Canadian companies: Trizec, Marathon, Edmonton's Oxford Group, Ottawa's Campeau Corporation, Vancouver's Genstar. Today, Olympia and York, owned by the reclusive Reichmann brothers, Albert and Paul, is the largest commercial landlord in Manhattan and may be the biggest in the world once its $2 billion, four-towered World Financial Centre opens in 1988. With the developers come planners, designers, architects. "Americans realize that our cities are better," comments Colin Stephens of Toronto's Design International. "They love Canada's ambience, and they want to buy it." The Ghermezian brothers of Edmonton, who have built a $1.2 billion shopping mall in Edmonton that was billed as the largest in the world, are now building a bigger one, at $1.5 billion, in Bloomington, Minnesota. Typical of this transfer of Canadian skills to Americans, the World Financial Centre project is being managed by former Toronto Housing Commissioner Michael Dennis.

The brewers came next. Labatt's barrelled south in 1975. Moosehead followed to become a cult among college students, and then Molson. Today, these three rank among the top five foreign beer exporters. Canadian beer, with its suggestion of open-air manliness, has become so popular that the American brewery, Amstel, has opened a plant here to export back its Grizzly brand. (Molson adds a Canada goose to the labels on its export bottles.)

The banks have always been in the south, but they used to be sedate. Today, they are aggressive enough to have attracted criticism from American banks for exploiting a loophole that allows Canadian banks to loan unlimited amounts for "funny-money" corporate takeover bids. All except one of the Canadian banks headquarter their American operations in New York, raise all their money locally, and hire Americans to fill about three-quarters of their positions. (The Royal Bank has moved the headquarters for its Caribbean operations from Montreal to Florida.) The exception is the Bank

238

of Montreal. Its American headquarters is in Chicago; as a result of its 1983 takeover of Chicago's Harris Bank, for $500 million (U.S.), it now ranks as the U.S.'s thirty-third largest bank.

The list runs on and on. Dylex, the agglomeration of women's and men's wear chains, now has 1,000 outlets in Canada and 1,400 in the U.S. Birks, almost a national symbol with its 106 years of history and its "blue box," now earns more than one-third of its revenues from its U.S. stores. Four Seasons Hotels owns or operates twelve upmarket hotels in the U.S., including New York's Pierre, and recently won the contract to operate the La Colinas sports and conference luxury complex midway between Dallas and Fort Worth. Redpath, of Montreal, ranks as one of the largest American sugar refiners. Umberto's of Vancouver this year opened its first branch restaurant in San Francisco. Laidlaw Industries, the Chicago-based subsidiary of Laidlaw Transportation of Hamilton, is the U.S.'s largest school bus operator and its fourth-ranked solid waste management firm. Chicago's classic Second City Theatre is now owned by Torontonian Andrew Alexander.

The principal lure is the obvious one: Canada is small; the U.S. market is just about limitless. "The competition is brutal and Americans are very, very tough businessmen," comments Rogers Cable executive vice-president Phil Lind. "But the business climate is so good that if you are good yourself, and you'd better be, you can do far better than back home."

A more subtle southward tug, but one just as potent, is the fear on the part of many Canadian businessmen that unless they get inside the U.S. market now they may one day be excluded from it by American protectionism. As is true for many Canadian steel companies, the competition from American steelmakers gives the Harris Steel Group few concerns. "They've let their skills atrophy," says president Milton Harris. "Our work force and our technology are far superior." But Harris has bought up four U.S. bar and structural steel fabricating plants, and plans to acquire more: "I'm just not that confident of access," he says. "The best place for me to invest – I've got all the land I need in Milton – would be here; but the market is there."* A 1984 survey by the Canadian Federation of Independent Businesses found that 16 per cent of its medium-sized manufacturers

---

* Harris is one of only two companies in the U.S. northeast that can fabricate and install structural steel. The other is also Canadian, Canron of Toronto.

already had at least one plant in the U.S., while another 25 per cent were actively considering whether to do so.

American protectionism comes in two forms. The first, and probably the most important, is attitudinal. "It isn't the Buy America laws but the Buy America attitudes that worry my members," says small business spokesman John Bulloch. Ian Campbell, president of Wajax, a medium-sized Ottawa manufacturing company, reports that salesmen for his hydraulic cranes have been told by potential customers, particularly in the Deep South, "So we like Canadians better than we like the Japanese. Well, we detest the Japanese." Engineers transferred south by Northern Telecom to its plant in Nashville, Tennessee, have found the paintwork of their cars with Ontario licence plates scratched with stones and, among other blunter messages scrawled in the dust, "Go back to your igloo."

The other brand of protectionism is formal. If no FIRA exists in the U.S., it is because none is needed. More than twenty U.S. federal agencies regulate different aspects of foreign investment and can prohibit it or restrict it in industries that include shipping, aviation, aeronautics, telecommunications, broadcasting, power utilities, banking, insurance, real estate, mining, offshore oil, the merchant marine, and, by far the most important of all, defence, which supports one in three of all American scientists and engineers and can pick and choose its suppliers behind the protective cover-all of "national security."

Probably the most important of the formal protectionist devices is that of the Buy America Acts now in force in forty-six states and embedded in several federal transportation programs. These affect public Canadian companies no differently from private ones. The provincially funded Urban Transportation Development Corporation of Ontario, for instance, is assembling the street cars it has sold to Santa Clara, California, at a local plant.

Supporters of bilateral free trade argue that it could exempt Canada from Buy America Acts and so anchor manufacturing here. The example cited most often is Bombardier of Montreal's assembly plant at Barre, Vermont, with a payroll of 250, established at the same time as Bombardier won a $1 billion order to manufacture subway cars for New York. However, the president of Bombardier's transportation division, Raymond Royer, comments, "Buy America is far less of a problem for Canadian manufacturers than they like to claim because, as they never like to say, many of their components come from the U.S. in the first place, in our case from Westinghouse and GE." The reasons that Royer cites instead for locating the plant at Barre are: "First, to have an American presence. Second, for tax purposes – it saved us about $5 million in duties on each $100 million American order. Third, the Buy America Act." In fact, Bombardier arranged for two American companies, Air Brake and Safety Air Conditioning, to set up plants in Kingston in order to achieve the 60 per cent Canadian content demanded by the Export Development Corporation as its price for financing the sale. Similarly, Ian Campbell of Wajax cites as the benefits of acquiring a fire pump plant in Seattle: "It qualifies us for local content preference, but much more important, it gives us an American presence."

Once in the U.S., therefore, Canadians behave like Americans. Canadians, of course, can do this more easily than can any other outsiders. Even being unmasked as Canadians doesn't necessarily hurt them. In advance of bidding on several U.S. cable franchises, Rogers surveyed the local scenes. The question, "Should your cable system be owned by non-Americans?" attracted an 80+ per cent negative response; the question, "Should your cable system be owned by Canadians?" inspired 60 per cent approval.*

Behaving like Americans means figuring out the best American way of doing things. Bombardier chose to locate its plant in Vermont rather than in New York or Pennsylvania or New Jersey because, as Royer explains, "Vermont gives us two U.S. senators and a governor the same as any other state, and because one plant makes a difference in a small state they are actively on our side." In all its ads in American magazines and newspapers, Bombardier shows a photograph of its Barre plant or of its Manhattan sales office. (The crown corporation, Canadair, does the same; ads for the Challenger jet show it parked outside Canadair's $6 million service centre at Hartford, Connecticut.) "It's a fact of life," says Royer. "Being a Canadian isn't a minus, but neither is it a plus."

The price that Canadians pay collectively for these practical calculations of corporate strategy is invisibility. Except in certain fields – urban planning for example – no image of particular Canadian excellence exists in the U.S., or elsewhere. In contrast to the Japanese,

---

* The one city where being Canadian was a minus was Boston. "Each time the Boston Irish look north they see the Brits," comments Phil Lind of Rogers Cable.

241

the Germans, the Swiss, the Swedes – the slogan "Swedish engineering. Depend on it." is a selling point in the ads for Saab cars – and also unlike the British, the Italians, and the French, Canadians abroad carry with them in their briefcases only their personal and corporate sales pitches.*

The most invisible of all Canadian companies in the U.S. is the one that ranks as the biggest and, by most competitive measures, also as the best. Among manufacturers and designers of telecommunications equipment in North America, Northern Telecom now ranks second in size; in the world, it ranks sixth. In order to tell its story, Northern Telecom took out full-page advertisements in all major U.S. newspapers during the winter of 1984-85. In those ads, the word "Canada" appeared only once, in the sentence: "The SL-10 is used by the West German Bundespost and by corporations, banks and governments in the United Kingdom, Canada, Hong Kong, Switzerland, Portugal, Belgium, Austria and the Republic of Ireland." Northern Telecom's great technological and corporate breakthrough, its switch to all-digital communications systems, the ad copy continued, had been announced in Orlando, Florida, in 1976; readers interested in learning more were asked to write to: "Northern Telecom Inc., Nashville, TN 37228."

"We think of ourselves as a North American company, and abroad we fly whichever flag benefits us the most," says Roy Cottier, Northern Telecom's vice-president. "In Japan, we negotiate as an American company, because the U.S. has more clout, and in Britain as a Canadian one because of the memories of empire." Another Northern Telecom executive, perhaps speaking out of script, describes the company as a "binational multinational."**

Today, Northern Telecom employs just under 21,000 workers in the U.S. and just over 21,300 in Canada. Its chief executive officer, Edmund Fitzgerald, is an American and commutes to Mississauga

---

* One exception: Tilley of Toronto advertises its sports hats in *The New Yorker* as "Made with Canadian persnicketiness."

** Northern Telecom blends into the U.S. background so thoroughly that its executives have appeared before Senate subcommittees to argue against U.S. trade protectionism, but on the grounds that this would hurt North Telecom exports from the U.S. to the countries affected rather than, as would be the case equally, that its exports from Canada to the U.S. would be inhibited.

from his home in Nashville. However, 60 per cent of the senior management of the American company are Canadians, and fast-track managers jump constantly back and forth across the border. The greater part of research and development is still done in Canada, by Bell-Northern's labs in Ottawa, but five major research and development centres are now located in the U.S. By 1990, the company forecasts its total international sales at $8 billion, of which almost two-thirds will be in the U.S., just one-fifth in Canada, and 15 per cent abroad, in Europe and in Asia. Of Northern Telecom's employment in Canada, one-third is created by the company's sales in the U.S.

"It isn't lower wages that has pulled us south; lower wages would pull you right across the Pacific," says Cottier. "The fact is, any company that tried forever to export huge quantities of its products to the U.S. without being present there on the ground would have to be totally naive. To get, you have to give. Americans may talk a free trade game but they're very jingoistic. We have to be seen there as American, that's why we have a ten-man lobbying office in Washington. Also, in our business you have to go where the engineering talent is, in Raleigh, in Dallas, in Silicon Valley, but also in Saskatoon where we've established a fibre optics plant."

Northern Telecom will never move its headquarters across the border, if only because a majority of its shares – 52 per cent – are held by Bell Enterprises, a subsidiary of its parent, Bell Telephone. Of Northern Telecom's publicly traded shares, however, close to two-thirds have at times been held by Americans. Indeed, as a "binational multinational," Northern Telecom now has the best of all possible worlds: in the U.S., it's American enough to qualify for defence contracts; in Canada, it's Canadian enough to qualify for government purchasing preferences. (Not surprisingly, Northern Telecom's Cottier strongly opposes free trade, which would eliminate the company's comparative advantage in Canada.)

A consequence of Canadian corporations behaving like Americans in the U.S. is that, increasingly, back in Canada they also behave as Americans. Perhaps the most dramatic change has occurred among the banks. Once almost the most protectionist-minded of all Canadian industries, the banks have now embraced, if still timidly, the nettle of competitive enterprise. In 1976, pressured by American banks with which they were competing in the U.S., Canadian banks reversed a policy almost as old as Confederation and urged Ottawa to license foreign banks here. Canadian banks now do more than 40 per cent of their total business abroad. The U.S. is their prime territory; some newer banks, like Canadian Commercial and the Bank of British Columbia, earned charters here largely as a licence to operate in the U.S.

Canadian brokers are going the same way as Canadian banks. Following public hearings, the Ontario Securities Commission has recommended that non-residents be allowed to acquire up to 30 per cent of Canadian investment houses. Opinion in the industry is divided, but it is being overtaken by events. In May, 1985, Nesbitt-Thompson became the first Canadian investment dealer to buy up an American company, the small New York brokerage house of Fahnestock. Aside from Northern Telecom, two-thirds of the public shares of many of the most actively traded Canadian companies, such as Alcan, Moore Corporation, Mitel, Dome Petroleum, and Inco, are now traded in the U.S. In an attempt to recapture some of this business, and in the process to integrate cross-border trading, the Montreal exchange has established an electronic trading link with Boston while Toronto has done so with the American Stock Exchange in New York and with Chicago's Midwest Exchange.

The "Americanization" of the Canadian economy that's potentially most significant may be happening in the Canadian media. By 1983, 74 per cent of the total assets of the Thomson Newspapers were in the U.S., along with 52 per cent of Maclean-Hunter; 43 per cent of Torstar; 60 per cent of Rogers Cable; 17 per cent of Southam. Perhaps as a coincidence, although perhaps not, *Maclean's* magazine, once a pulpit for the economic nationalists, is now an advocate of Canada-U.S. free trade. "I'm as Canadian as ever, my spots haven't changed, I wouldn't want to be anything else," says Phil Lind of Rogers Cable. "But to answer your question, yes, it does make a difference. In the seventies we led the charge on Ottawa to require cable systems to delete American commercials running simultaneously on U.S. and Canadian channels. Today, I don't think we'd be leading that charge."

Even stay-at-home Canadian companies are affected the same way. American economics has become Canadian economics, with differences that exist being in degree rather than in kind. But for the occasional half percentage point either way, Canadian interest rates are indistinguishable today from U.S. interest rates. In the spring of 1985, President Reagan undertook a propaganda offensive to sell a flat-rate tax to Congress; among the documents tabled by Finance Minister Wilson along with his May, 1985, budget was a discussion paper proposing a flat 39 per cent corporate income tax.

The aspect of American economics that affects the Canadian economy most radically today is that of deregulation. Here it's happening later: deregulation of airlines began there in 1978, and here in 1984. Transport Minister Don Mazankowski's July, 1985, White Paper will extend deregulation to the entire transportation industry. Important cross-border regulatory differences remain, and always will: the Canadian market lacks "depth"; it is often dominated by public companies (Air Canada accounts for 60 per cent of Canadian air travel); cross-subsidization, through which revenues earned on heavily travelled routes go to support non-economic ones, is part of the political compact of Confederation.

In the U.S. deregulation has produced the pain of corporate bankruptcies and of deep wage cuts. But it has also produced the gain of new and cheaper services. Canadian telephone companies are losing business as customers rent dedicated lines to the nearest point across the border and route all their international and trans-continental calls onward from there. In 1984, an estimated one in ten Canadian air travellers drove or bussed to cross-border points like Buffalo, Seattle, and Plattsburgh and from there went south or east or west on U.S. airlines. Canadian truckers, for the first time, face competition on their home ground, competitors, moreover, whose costs are 25 per cent lower, both because of their scale and because of their market-driven efficiency. One real tidal wave could be gathering in Reagan's plan to deregulate American agriculture, although many doubt he can do it. Should Reagan succeed, he will put in doubt the future of federal and provincial marketing boards that, according to a 1980 estimate by the Economic Council, add $1 billion a year to Canadian food bills but which also safeguard the Canadian family farmer.

Compared to all this, bilateral free trade amounts to scarcely more than an afterthought. If Lester Thurow is right that Canadians and Americans are aboard the same economic plane, even comprehensive free trade might amount at most to the economic equivalent of removing the divider between the passengers in first class and those in steerage. The question, of course, is whether the passengers would then become indistinguishable from each other.

Part Five
Inside the Cave

As the ultimate metropolis, the U.S. has always intimidated as much as it has attracted. Americans themselves, since their New Patriotism has given them a second wind, are again assertive, self-confident, cocky.

Two groups of Canadians know this aspect of America better than most and have to cope with it directly in a way few Canadians do. They are Canada's diplomats and Canada's autoworkers.

The autoworkers have long been the most "Americanized" of all Canadians. They and American autoworkers were indistinguishable, not least because their union was the most tightly-knit and disciplined of all North American unions. They all worked for the same companies, in the same kinds of plants, on the same kinds of jobs, for, with minor differences, the same kinds of wages. Then, abruptly, in the winter of 1984-85, the Canadian autoworkers broke away. The industry hasn't changed, nor have the plants or the jobs, nor, with minor variations, will the wages that those jobs pay. But the autoworkers have found a way to remain North American and yet to become wholly Canadian.

The tasks of the diplomats are, inevitably, more subtle. They are bargaining for their country, not for themselves. No differently, though, they are bargaining with Americans, and in the heart of the U.S. They, too, have had to make a break with their past. Once, the embassy in Washington was staffed with diplomats; today, it's filled up with lobbyists, all selling Canadian lumber and steel and hogs and fishing rights no differently than American lobbyists hustle through Washington selling defence industries or farm foreclosure protection.

In different ways, the diplomats and the autoworkers perform inside the cave. Here's how they do it.

Chapter Seventeen
Mr. Canuck Goes to Washington

"I married you because you were ambitious. You wanted to change things. What are you going to change in Washington?"

A character in *First Lady, Last Lady*, by Sondra Gotlieb

One of the best and certainly one of the most succinct analyses of Washington has been provided by Canadian political scientist Roger Swanson in an article for the *International Journal*. Swanson compared the U.S. government to "a neo-feudal collection of loosely interconnected components each having an organizational life, and sometimes death, all its own." He went on to remark, "It is tempting to conclude that the U.S. government *per se* does not exist."

The first Canadians in public positions who understood what Swanson was getting at, and who were also savvy enough to act upon their understanding, were Adele Hurley and Allan Gotlieb. Neither of them, he as Canadian ambassador, she as a lobbyist for the Canadian Coalition on Acid Rain, changed anything in Washington. Both were too smart to try. Instead, they changed the way Canadians who have interests in Washington approach the intimidating challenge of trying to get what they want. This they accomplished by showing how it could be done, in both instances in exceptionally difficult circumstances. In mid-1981, when Hurley went to Washington, acid rain scarcely measured on any public-interest meter. Through much of Gotlieb's term, from late 1981 to the summer of 1984, when Trudeau retired, Canada, as far as the Reagan government was concerned, was in the doghouse.

Gotlieb defined his *modus operandi* in a speech in November, 1983: "No country inevitably becomes so much engaged in the *domestic process* of another country as does Canada in that of the U.S. This is because Canada is so greatly affected by U.S. domestic legislation and regulations. Thus, a great deal of U.S. foreign policy towards Canada is not really its foreign policy at all, but its domestic policy. And we, whether we like it or not, are drawn into the American domestic process." Hurley describes her method more simply: "I knew I had to get Americans to fight my battles for me." Her ultimate victory was to be invited onto the *Today Show* in early 1983. She sent an American sports fisherman instead: "I wasn't going to waste a spot like that on a Canadian."

Toward the end of *The Ottawa Men*, his study of the civil service mandarins of the 1940s and 1950s, J.L. Granatstein makes a very shrewd point and then throws it away in between parentheses. He notes that in their dealings with their U.S. counterparts during these years, Ottawa officials "usually proved stronger in arguments". He then adds: "(an expertise that allowed them to win battles, but no wars)."

Exactly. One cross-border war "lost" and Canada itself would be lost. Even ordinary commercial "irritants," whether these involve trucking regulations or lumber duties or health standards for beef, matter far more to Canada than to the U.S. The $50 million or so gained by Canadian broadcasters by Ottawa's rule against commercials on U.S. stations is vital to the industry but irrelevant to American broadcasters as a whole – although to complicate matters, the handful of U.S. TV stations actually affected in Seattle, Buffalo, and Plattsburgh can stir up their congressmen who then stir up the entire system in Washington so that an irritant escalates into a war.

The expertise hasn't diminished over the years, although nationalists often sound as if they assume that craven politicians and inept officials will boot away any cross-border war before it even begins. Former Secretary of State Henry Kissinger, in the half page he allotted to Canada among the 1,521 pages of his memoir, *White House Years*, remarked: "Convinced of the necessity of cooperation, impelled by domestic imperatives toward confrontation, Canadian leaders had a narrow margin of maneuver that they exercised with extraordinary skills."

The actual trenches are manned by officials. "The widespread view in Canada of Canada always caving in is totally wrong," Rufus Z. Smith, the State Department's Canadian expert from the late 1950s to the mid-1970s, commented in an interview for this book. "In my own experience, the Canadians bargained very hard and with great skill. They were just better prepared, better briefed, and usually brighter and tougher." He added, "I know that the popular image is that we come to the bargaining table with banks of computers behind us and CIA reports in front of us. In fact, our side was often made up of officials who'd never met before and who had to mug up on the flight to Ottawa."

Smith's use of the word "tougher" may be particularly apt. Canadians assume that Canadian politicians and officials perform when abroad like a troop of Boy Scouts. In fact, when it comes to Washington, the direct opposite is closer to the truth. The status of underdog seems to liberate many Canadians in their dealings with their American counterparts; they act tougher, and better still they act considerably more deviously than Canadians are supposed to act in international forums. The converse is also true. Though many Canadians, nationalists above all, will find it hard to credit, the status of top dog tends to inhibit American officials when they find themselves engaged in cross-border wars. As Charles Doran of Johns Hopkins University remarks, "You constantly see the Americans back off in dealings with Canadians. They just don't want to push too hard; they just aren't willing to take the gloves off."

The spines of Canadian negotiators are stiffened by the knowledge that their country cannot afford to lose a single war, and also by the knowledge that for the sake of their personal careers they cannot be seen to have lost one. Conversely, success or failure in dealing with Canada will neither blight nor advance the career of any senior Washington official. Specific issues aside, like lumber and the rest, the most that Americans demand of their government in its relations with Canada is that it maintain a kind of unfocused amiability. This, for instance, was all Reagan intended by his controversial 1980 proposal for a "North American Accord."*

There was, however, one major defect in the "extraordinary skill"

---

* The actual idea was suggested to Reagan in 1978 by a senior aide, Richard Allen. After Reagan had pronounced it, it came to be seen in Canada, and in Mexico, as a continental energy grab. In fact, all Reagan had in mind was a couple of symbolic gestures such as appointing a new presidential assistant for continental affairs and making pre-inauguration visits to Mexico, as he did, and to Canada, as he didn't because Trudeau was away skiing. The continental energy proposal was lobbed up by Senator Edward Kennedy and by former California Governor Jerry Brown.

described by Kissinger and in the "toughness" described by Smith. These qualities were being applied in 1980 in exactly the same way as they had been in the 1940s and 1950s. But in the meantime the environment in which they were being applied – Washington – had changed utterly.

In October, 1980, External Affairs Minister Mark MacGuigan made one of the sternest statements about Canada-U.S. relations ever made by anyone in his position: "Differences in approach to foreign policy have reached the point where rational management of a crucial binational relationship may no longer be possible." This statement was also one of the dumbest ever made by anyone in that position. It assumed that foreign policy, or indeed almost any policy in Washington, is managed rationally.

The immediate reason for MacGuigan's annoyance was that an East Coast fishery boundary rights treaty, negotiated by the two governments eighteen months earlier, had just been rejected by the U.S. Senate. (Parliament, naturally, had not been asked what it thought about what had been done in its name.) Scarcely any of the senators knew the least bit about fish. The two key senators, Claiborne Pell of Rhode Island and Edward Kennedy of Massachusetts, opposed the treaty because their constituents didn't like it. These two voices, combined with a lot of log-rolling undertaken in exchange for future considerations, was enough to scupper it.*

MacGuigan's angry outburst, understandable enough in itself, represented the last time a Canadian government allowed itself to believe that the American system of government was pretty much like the Canadian system, surface differences aside, or, for that matter, like the systems of most democracies.

Watergate marks the great watershed. Until then, the U.S.'s rough and tumble democracy had been contained by the aura of the imperial presidency. Even before Watergate, the system was undergoing change. Doubts about what had really happened in the Bay of Tonkin, an incident President Johnson had justified in order to send the Marines

---

* The issue was finally settled, quite favourably to Canada, by a decision of the International Court of Justice at The Hague, rendered in October, 1984. This decision to refer disputes jointly to third-party arbitration represents an innovative way of allowing politicians in both countries to escape the blame for making "concessions" that might in fact be entirely justified.

into Da Nang, provoked both the Senate and House to re-assert authority over foreign policy and treaty-making. The Congressional reforms introduced by Senator George McGovern led to the dissolution of the old rule of seniority. Suddenly, everyone had to have a title and some power: the number of committee heads in both houses escalated from sixty-seven to more than 200.

But it was the discovery that the President could be a crook that transferred political legitimacy, and therefore influence, from White House to Capitol Hill. Congress grew into a quasi-independent government with a civil service of 38,000. Prompted both by lobbyists and by their own aides, who increased in number and in ambition, congressmen challenged the President and initiated more and more of their own substantive legislation. Each change reinforced the other changes: the more Congressional subcommittees there were, the more lobbyists there were – 15,000 of them, the princes among them the well-tailored "K Street lawyers." There were also uncounted numbers of public relations consultants, pollsters, speechwriters, entrepreneurial academics, experts for all sides of every subject. To provide the fuel for this machine, there were 3,000 public action committees (PACs), all raising funds and dispensing them to their favourite causes, and sometimes to their favourite politicians. Journalists, particularly the ones who appeared on television, blossomed into superstars after Watergate, courted and cossetted for the sake of a favourable comment.

It was all exuberantly American. It was creative and competitive and democratic. Anyone could get into the game: a majority of the PACs were set up by unions and public interest groups. And it was a game that was open. Americans, unlike Canadians, believe in the political marketplace as well as in the economic marketplace. Adele Hurley brought back from Washington "a reluctant admiration for the Congressional system. Americans take for granted that a letter to their congressman will make a difference, and often it does; Canadians assume it isn't worth the effort to write to their MP, and often it isn't."

But the game was also staggeringly wasteful and awesomely inefficient because most of these diffused power centres spent most of their time preventing anything being done. Often, the accomplishments of the lobbyists and the PACs, for example, all the tax loopholes added to Reagan's 1980 tax cut plan, amounted to a subversion of the general public interest by highly paid special interests. In her book, *Politics and Money*, published in 1983, Elizabeth Drew reviewed the scene and shuddered: "What results is a corrosion of the system, and a new kind of squalor. We have allowed the basic idea of our democratic process – representative government – to slip away."

The merits and demerits of this system are beside the immediate point: this is how politics is played in Washington and how public policy is crafted. Thus, along with the Japanese, the Koreans, the Israelis, and most of the rest of the world, Canada has to play the game and learn how to win it. Canadians, in other words, must play American domestic politics for the sake of Canada's national interests.

Canadian diplomats, however, have never been trained to play these kinds of games. Traditionally, Washington, no differently from London or Paris or for that matter Cairo, meant confidential discussions with State Department officials and with serious-minded journalists like Scotty Reston of the *New York Times*, and contacts comfortably made at the Burning Tree Golf Club.

To underscore the disadvantage, all the way up to the 1980s Canada-U.S. affairs were handled within External Affairs either by everybody, since it was taken for granted that everyone was an expert on the U.S., or by nobody, with cross-border irritants dealt with by whichever "line" department, Transport or Defence or Energy, happened to be involved. In 1980, for instance, the National Energy Policy was drafted and then announced without External Affairs being asked how the Americans might react, and how they might be headed off. Not until 1978 was a separate U.S. branch established within the department – previously it had been part of the Western Hemisphere branch – to focus expertise and information on the subject. This unit, now staffed with some of the department's best minds, has since grown steadily to rank third in size after the European and Asia/Pacific branches. Oddities in the structure remain: we have no consulate in Miami although there are more Canadians there in more need of help, with pensions and so forth, than anywhere else outside Canada; our sixteen consulates in the U.S. are staffed with almost as many tourist officers, thirty-six to thirty-eight, as trade officers. In Washington itself, Canada's embassy ranks only eighth in size of staff, after Russia, China, Japan, Britain, Saudi Arabia, France, and Brazil.

Nor was this lackadaisical laissez-faire attitude toward the U.S.

unique to official Ottawa; almost all Canadians in positions of influence felt the same way.

An earlier chapter quoted Robert Fulford's remark that a lack of original thought about the United States constituted "the great empty space in our thinking." The extent of this emptiness is truly astonishing: Canadians have been at least as guilty, and in context incomparably more so, of taking the U.S. for granted as the reverse about which Canadians complain so constantly. Until the mid-1980s, not a single centre or program of American studies existed at any Canadian university. The first two such centres, at the University of Western Ontario and, on a much more modest scale, at the University of Quebec at Montreal, will open in the fall of 1985. By contrast, centres or institutes of Canadian studies exist at more than twenty American universities; about 450 U.S. universities and colleges offer courses about Canada to some 18,000 students each year.* Similarly, while carping about Canada being ignored by the U.S. media is commonplace, it was not until the fall of 1984 that any Canadian news organization was represented in Washington by more than a single correspondent. With only a couple of exceptions, these reporters covered only the "Canadian angle" of Washington stories, so that most Canadian readers and viewers wanting to understand America had to rely on the American media. As well, not a single Canadian reporter was stationed anywhere in the U.S. outside of Washington.

"We assume we understand the U.S. because we watch so much American TV and read so many American magazines," commented Ambassador Gotlieb in an interview for this book. "In some ways we are behind the Europeans in our understanding of the U.S." As an example, Gotlieb mentioned that it was not until he got to Oxford, after studying at Canadian universities, "that the teachers made me understand how creative American jurisprudence could be."

---

* Standards varied widely, of course. Among the best are those at the Johns Hopkins School for Advanced International Studies, for which French is an entrance requirement, and at Northwestern in Evanston, Illinois. The quarterly published by the Association for Canadian Studies in the U.S. now contains articles of significant scholarly merit.

Through the sixties and seventies an excuse could be found for this lack of perception about the United States; during these years Canadian affairs were exciting and immediate and so absorbed all our attention. Of quite another dimension was the well-known Canadian inferiority complex, the inability to look south with a cool, clear, observing eye. Don Lenz, a Canadian-born vice-president of Goldman Sachs on Wall Street, recalls once arranging a meeting between Stelco and Dofasco executives and their American counterparts. "The Americans were so impressed by and so envious of the technological efficiency of the Canadian mills. But those Canadians acted so awed of the big Americans. They acted, dammit, just like Canadians."

The achievement of Hurley and of Gotlieb was to act in the U.S. the way Americans act – while remaining unrecalcitrant Canadians.

In May, 1981, when Hurley set off on her mission to get Americans to start worrying about acid rain, she was twenty-seven. Her formal credentials comprised a Master's degree in environmental studies and two years' experience as an aide to Stuart Smith, then Opposition Leader in the Ontario legislature. She also possessed flair, quick eyes between huge horn-rimmed glasses, and an even quicker wit.

Hurley was the agent for an idea that had begun in the mind of John Fraser, Minister of the Environment in the Clark government.* Late in 1979, Fraser met privately in Toronto with a group of environmentalists and suggested the way to get action on the critical new issue of acid rain (more than 50 per cent of the amount that falls on Canada originates south of the border) was to send a "white hat" down to Washington, in other words, a public interest lobbyist, to play the political and media angles.

The Canadian Coalition on Acid Rain, a body comprising forty-two individual groups representing tourist, trade, and game-fishing interests and also the concerns of a number of churches and native people's organizations, was quickly set up to provide political and legal cover for the lobbying exercise, and also the money to pay for it. When Hurley arrived in Washington, her first move was to

---

* Though rated by environmentalists as the most effective minister in many years, Fraser, curiously, was appointed Minister of Fisheries in the Mulroney government.

persuade a lawyer-lobbyist to rent her an unused corner of his office, with access to such vital necessities as copying facilities and Congressional reports.

Once set up, she hunkered down. She stayed away from Capitol Hill: "Never go there until you know what you're doing." She stayed away from the media: "I didn't know the rules." Mostly, she spent her time studying Washington by herself. "I got very, very lonely. Whenever I got really depressed, I'd call up a New Englander." Few of her official calls were answered. The secretaries were polite but bemused: "You say you're with who, honey? What kind of rain do y'all have up there in Canada?"

Her break came when some Americans decided she could help them. These were former senior officials in the Carter administration, now carrying on the environmental fight from the outside. She and they met, and she passed their test: "I did know my stuff." A couple of doors opened a crack. The Carter types advised her on how to get properly registered as a lobbyist, plugged her into the network of scientific experts, got her invited to the weekly meeting of the Clean Air Committee at which all the public interest environmental lobbyists trade information and plot joint strategies. Eventually, she managed to get acid rain added to the committee's agenda.

The first calls that mattered came from junior Congressional aides anxious for a quick fix for their bosses' speeches. Operating on the principle that "You never get a second chance to make that first impression," Hurley gave them what they needed not only instantly, but comprehensively: "I never misled them. I always told them about scientific data that put into question our arguments about the effects of acid rain."

Reporters, who'd picked up her name from aides, soon started calling. Two of these were from the *Cleveland Plain Dealer* in the heart of smokestack country, tipped off by the coal lobby that Hurley was a high-paid flack for Canadian hydro companies trying to increase their exports by pushing up the costs of their U.S. competitors. Over dinner she convinced them first of her own innocence, and then of her cause. They went on to write a prize-winning series that ended with a *Plain Dealer* editorial: "Acid Rain *Is* a Hazard."

By now the calls from Congressional offices were starting to come from senior aides, asking for advice on whom to call as witnesses before committee hearings. "The ideal was a Harvard professor, but without a beard," Hurley recalls. In 1982, she herself testified at a Senate hearing. That summer she blitzed the media, "the real media": the TV networks, the *New York Times*, the *Washington Post*. She was invited to appear on the *Today Show*. Later that year, a Lou Harris poll showed that 40 per cent of Americans believed that acid rain was a serious problem.

This accomplishment was by no means only that of Hurley and the Canadian Coalition on Acid Rain. The Canadian government, executing what Willis Armstrong has called "a masterly exercise in statecraft," was in parallel throwing its all into the battle, from flying squads of ministers descending on Washington to "Stop Acid Rain" buttons handed out to tourists crossing the border. Most important of all, Ottawa forged an alliance with the New England states, pitting the weight of those senators and congressmen against those from the Midwest. As further reinforcement, the American environmental movement, a far more formidable force than the Canadian one (by 1985 not a single new nuclear power station was under construction in the U.S.), threw itself into the fray.

To have made a topic of such marginal interest to most Americans into a subject of popular concern constituted an astounding achievement. Yet it remains to this point an achievement without consequence. By the time Adele Hurley left Washington, in mid-1983, nothing had actually been done about the emissions of acid rain by smokestack America. Nor has anything been done about it since.

In Washington, no matter how much power may have been fragmented and decentralized, ultimate power remains with the President. No one can explain with confidence the reasons for Reagan's personal indifference to acid rain. On the face of it Reagan's conservative ideology and his personal love of the outdoors ought to signal an ardent conservationist on the Sierra Club model. The popular explanation for Reagan's indifference is politics: curing acid rain costs money, which the smokestack industries of the Midwest cannot afford. Some apologists argue that Reagan himself genuinely believes that acid rain is not the cause of the destruction attributed to it – 2,000 "dead" lakes in Ontario alone.

Critics respond that anyone who could appoint James Watt as Secretary of Interior cannot possibly care at all for the environment. Perhaps the best explanation for Reagan's indifference has more to do with style than with either politics or ideology. While Governor of California, he apparently became convinced, having encountered a few such environmentalists, that they were all bearded and sandalled weirdos. As has been remarked often, Reagan's range of beliefs isn't large, but those he does espouse, he espouses wholeheartedly.

Whatever its causes, Reagan's personal attitudes have determined those of his administration. During the preceding Carter presidency, in August, 1980, the two countries signed a joint Memorandum of Understanding committing them to negotiate a formal pollution control agreement and to undertake joint research. In June, 1982, however, the Canadian proposal for a joint program to cut sulphur dioxide emissions by 50 per cent by 1990 was rejected. The Memorandum of Understanding was torn up. Nothing has replaced it since but political cosmetics.

Paradoxically, though also predictably, the single substantive result of Hurley's activities in Washington was achieved back in Ottawa. The more attention the subject received there, in newspaper and magazine articles, and in speeches by New England congressmen, the more interested Canadian politicians became in the subject. By the time of the Shamrock Summit in Quebec City in March, 1985, acid rain had come to be regarded as the acid test of whether Prime Minister Mulroney could get as well as give in his new "special relationship" with Ronald Reagan.

Some Canadian protestations about U.S. negligence have, in fact, been firmly grounded in hypocrisy and, in the instance of successive Environment Ministers, in political self-interest. While it is certainly true that, because of wind patterns, more than half the acid rain deposited in Canada originates in the U.S., it is equally true that of the five biggest sulphur dioxide offenders on the continent, four are in Canada, with Inco's smelter at Sudbury at the top of the list.* At the same time, Canadian standards for the emission of nitrogen dioxide by automobiles are one-tenth as stringent as those in the United States. Most hypocritical of all, the principal cause of the devastation of Canadian forests is not acid rain, wherever its origin, but the woodcutting and silviculture practices – or rather, the lack of them – of Canadian lumber companies and governments.

After his first meeting as Prime Minister with Reagan, in September,

---

* Partly, this is just the accident that Canadian sources, being smelters, are large, while U.S. sources, being mostly private power stations, are small. No accident, however, is the fact that Ontario Hydro imports highly pollutant American coal in preference to cleaner but more expensive coal from Alberta.

1984, Mulroney declared that achieving action on acid rain was his "number-one priority." What he actually achieved was mostly more cosmetic touches. At the Shamrock Summit, he and Reagan announced the appointment of "special envoys" – former U.S. Transport Secretary Drew Lewis and former Ontario Premier Bill Davis – who would be charged to come up with a joint action plan and to report back to the two leaders before their next meeting. Even this face-saving formula was accomplished with difficulty: despite a new poll by Lou Harris that revised upward to 75 per cent the number of Americans concerned about acid rain, Reagan's scepticism remained so strong that he agreed to it only a week before the Quebec City meeting.

Nevertheless, all the lobbying in Washington produced an effect. To strengthen his bargaining hand at the summit, Mulroney announced the first major anti-acid rain program in more than half a decade: $150 million in pollution control subsidies (Inco was the first to apply) and U.S.-style emission standards to come into effect beginning with the 1988 model cars. The efforts of Hurley and the Coalition may not have moved the mountain in Washington, but they had budged it in Ottawa.

Beyond any doubt, Allan Gotlieb has been Canada's most effective representative in Washington since we first opened a legation there in 1927 and elevated it to an embassy in 1943. (Pearson, who was ambassador from 1945 to 1946, was certainly as effective, but those were the easy "Good Neighbour" years.)

Much of Gotlieb's effectiveness has been particular to the man. Now fifty-seven, an international lawyer trained at Harvard and as a Rhodes Scholar at Oxford, he is a Renaissance figure with a fine-honed taste in the arts and equally well-honed bureaucratic elbows. A good deal he has owed to his wife, Sondra, a novelist and a political hostess in the manner of Alice Roosevelt Longworth, artlessly outspoken and guilefully outrageous. Within a few months of his arrival in December, 1981, Gotlieb was cited in an insider's guide to the city, Who Runs Washington? "If you were to draw up a list of the brightest men in Washington, you'd quickly put down Allan Gotlieb and then wonder who else to put on the list." Later, he and the veteran Soviet diplomat Anatoly Dobrynin were the only ambassadors singled out with full-page photographs in a coffee-table volume, *Power and People*, assembled by Ronald Reagan's former official photographer. Sondra Gotlieb, meanwhile, made the front page of the *New York Times* with her comment, "When you say 'Canada,' a glaze comes over people's eyes. Maybe we should invade South Dakota." Soon she was hired to write an insightful, irreverent fortnightly column for the *Washington Post*. Between them, the Gotliebs turned the Canadian embassy into what *Vanity Fair* magazine described as "one of the capital's very few salons ... the only social hotspot on Embassy Row."

The glitter concealed the purposefulness. With Canadian-born stars such as Donald Sutherland and Margot Kidder serving as lures, the likes of Kissinger and Paul Volker and George Shultz and Caspar Weinberger, and such press luminaries as Ben Bradlee and Reston, munched their way through Manitoba caviar and maple mousse. "The Canadian taxpayers aren't paying us to entertain charming but ineffectual people," Sondra Gotlieb has remarked. "You have to have people who other people want to meet, because interesting people won't come unless there are other interesting people there." The only way to get Americans who mattered to come, so as to be able to let slip a few words about duties on lumber or trucking regulations in between sips of spritzer, was to invite other Americans who mattered. Probably only the Gotliebs could have figured a way past the Catch-22 contained in this formula for success. In this respect, their accomplishment is unlikely to be repeated by their successors and thus is incidental to this chronicle – except as proof that Canadians can play the Washington social game as well as, if not better than, anyone else.

During Gotlieb's term, a number of cross-border irritants were soothed and various cross-border signals unsnarled, thanks also to the fact that his supporting staff has included some of the ablest to be found within External Affairs. But in the long run, these achievements mattered less than the overall strategy that Gotlieb developed for fighting the cross-border wars. This is the plan that succeeding ambassadors and governments will undoubtedly follow.

Gotlieb began crafting this strategy before he moved to Washington. In the January-February, 1981, issue of *International Perspectives*, as Deputy Minister for External Affairs, he co-authored a long analytic article with a fellow senior officer, Jeremy Kinsman. The pair made a delicate retreat from the Third Option, then nominally still official policy, and then addressed themselves to the cardinal issue of what to do about the U.S. "Canadian policy needs a strategic approach to succeed . . . a coherent approach on the part of government in pursuing Canada's interests vis-à-vis the United States." There had to be a thought-out, coherent policy of managing the U.S. relationship, in other words, rather than the ad hoc dependence on good neighbourliness of the past. Once in Washington, Gotlieb evolved an actual strategy, in part by trial and error.

Gotlieb's strategy begins with the premise that the American political game cannot be played in the usual Canadian way – which is to say, quietly. "There is an element of public diplomacy to diplomacy, and I believe it is an important element," he has said. The next premise is that in order to win, Canada must enlist Americans onto its side. "Our interests will prevail only if they are coincident with the interests of Americans who can prevail." To implement the strategy, Gotlieb and his staff have searched ceaselessly for Americans whose interests coincide with Canada's – for instance, importers of steel and lumber products concerned about import quotas, or municipalities glad to have Canadians bid for cable-TV licences in order to heighten the competition, or New England politicians worried about acid rain. Once these allies were identified, the embassy reinforced them every way it could, by sharing information, by advising on tactics, by direct lobbying with line departments, with Congress, with the White House itself.

Thus, for the first time, Canadian officials burrowed deep down into the vitals of the domestic American political system. One of Gotlieb's cardinal rules, however, was not to overdo it. "If we were advancing a position directly opposed to one the administration had adopted, we would proceed very carefully and keep the officials fully informed." That caveat aside, the Canadian embassy functioned more like a flying squad of lobbyists than a genteel cadre of diplomats. "My worry is very seldom that I am interfering too much in the American domestic process, and rather than I am not getting around to see enough congressmen and senators," Gotlieb remarks. Each item lobbied for, from hogs to fish, was treated as an entity unto itself; deliberately, no attempt was made to trade a gain on one item for a concession on another. "The American system is so diffuse that it just won't work along the classic lines of 'you let in our potatoes if we test your cruise missiles.'" The last rule was perhaps the most demanding: expect no favours to be granted to Canada, simply because it is Canada, a nice neighbour next door. "The fact that a particular policy could do harm to Canada might cause a particular congressman to feel bad," says Gotlieb, "but it wouldn't change the way they voted if they were under pressure from their constituents. The fact is, we have no votes in the U.S."

With this last comment, Gotlieb defined the limits of his own strategy. In contrast to Israel, or to Mexico, or to Ireland and a number of other countries, there are indeed no Canadian votes in the U.S. Canada cannot summon up any divisions to mount pressure on congressmen. Canada therefore has to try harder to find congressmen whose interests happen to be coincident with our own, knowing all the while full well that some of these allies will turn into enemies the moment the discussion shifts from, say, acid rain to the matter of potatoes from P.E.I. underselling potatoes from Maine.

No differently from other countries, Canada can also resort to conventional diplomacy as between sovereign states and in these instances get a message through by the alternate techniques of confidential diplomacy or political pyrotechnics. Canada's ability to get attention paid by these classical techniques is more limited than that of many other countries, however, in a way that is both flattering and frustrating. "Americans don't really think of us as foreigners but as cousins, fellow North Americans," comments Gotlieb. "The paradoxical consequence is that on the one hand this allows us to get special breaks, and on the other hand it causes Americans to react with genuine surprise and hurt when we vociferously oppose some particular American policy. In these instances, they tend to regard us as being, somehow, perverse Americans, and can be unforgiving of such 'aberrant' behaviour."*

Gotlieb's style of high-profile, interventionist strategy does entail risks. The least consequential among these is probably the one most commonly cited: that Americans will get mad. "I don't see why you shouldn't lobby us, everybody does; you should see the Japanese," remarks Senator George Mitchell of Maine. "It's the way we think democracies should work. Anyway, we intervene in the domestic politics of other countries, in Western Europe for instance to gain support for the installation of the missiles."

Intervention in American domestic politics does set a precedent

---

* Rufus Smith recalls Representative John Dingle once denouncing some Canadian criticisms of American policy as "downright un-American."

for U.S. counter-intervention – not that the invitation really needed to be issued. There was at least a tacit alliance between Washington and Alberta during the period of the rows over the NEP. Gotlieb's opposite number in Ottawa, Ambassador Paul Robinson, took it upon himself to lecture Canadians not simply about U.S. interests, such as the NEP and FIRA, but about Canadians' own interests, as in spending more on defence and less on social welfare. (Robinson's outbursts aroused more amusement than annoyance although Americans would have been much less equable had Gotlieb, say, publicly advised the U.S. government to spend less on defence and more on welfare.)

The results justify the risks. Much of Gotlieb's term, from December, 1981, encompassed the most tense period of Canada-U.S. relations since the Second World War. At the same time, the U.S. was struggling with by far the largest trade deficit in its history, to which Canada was the second-largest contributor after Japan. While there were many alarms and mini-crises through to the fall of 1984 when Mulroney created his own cross-border "special relationship," not a single measure discriminating against Canadian trade was enacted. In several instances, such as steel import quotas, Canada secured an exemption from measures applied against other countries but which in similar situations in the past had been imposed across the board. Such long-standing irritants as fishing limits on the East Coast (which once had so exercised MacGuigan) were settled. The value of this kind of record can be measured by comparing it to the kind of irritant that, left untreated, can quickly become an open sore. In 1977, Florida Representative Sam Gibbons, angered at "all the doctors and dentists taking holidays at the taxpayers' expense – I never had Canadians in mind at all," – moved and enacted a little-noticed tax amendment that disallowed for tax purposes expense claims for attending conventions outside of the U.S. To remove the amendment from the statutes took four years, during which Canada's tourist industry lost millions a year because of conventions that stayed home. (Mexico was even harder hit.)

Even the most adroit of ambassadors can accomplish little unless the atmospherics are right. By mid-1982 the worst of the cross-border storm was over, although the tensions revived again during Trudeau's peace initiative of 1983-84. During this period, Shultz and MacEachen initiated the quarterly meetings between foreign ministers continued since by Clark and Shultz. (As a former top executive of the consulting firm Bechtel, Shultz is probably the best-informed about Canada of all Secretaries of State, and also the most sympathetic.) Discussions about possible sectoral trade pacts began late in 1983 between Trade Minister Gerald Regan and his counterpart, Bill Brock, and proceeded with unexpected speed and cordiality. (A key factor was the friendship that developed – they used to take in Super Bowls together – between Brock and Regan's predecessor, Ed Lumley.)

One of Mulroney's first decisions on taking office was to confirm Gotlieb's appointment as ambassador. The speculation is that Gotlieb will remain until 1986 and then be replaced by former Alberta Premier Peter Lougheed. Beyond any question, whoever succeeds Gotlieb will continue the same interventionist strategy, although not necessarily in the same high-profile way.

In the meantime, Mulroney has implemented his own cross-border strategy. It is based on a personal friendship – unequalled since the era of Mackenzie King and Roosevelt – with Ronald Reagan. For all practical purposes, Mulroney rather than External Affairs Minister Joe Clark is the Minister for Canada-U.S. relations. Direct calls between Ottawa and the White House now represent the principal north-south link rather than the salesmanship of embassy staffers among congressmen and industry lobbyists. The "special relationship" between Mulroney and Reagan will be considered in Chapter Twenty. A couple of aspects of it can usefully be mentioned here.

Personal relationships between leaders have always mattered in relationships between nations and always will. Former West German Chancellor Helmut Schmidt played an important part in convincing Trudeau, to whom he was close, to go ahead with the cruise missile tests. Similarly, Reagan's fondness for Mulroney convinced him to agree to appoint the special envoys on acid rain at the Shamrock Summit and to appear on stage with Mulroney at the closing of the gala at Le Grand Theatre and to mouth the words to "When Irish Eyes Are Smiling," although not actually to sing like Mulroney.

The interests of any political leader are always first and last the interests of his own constituents, though. It's an open question how much of his own stock of political credits, held in reserve to push a flat-rate tax scheme through Congress, say, Reagan could afford to expend for the benefit of Canadian economic interests.

The more important qualification to be made about the Mulroney-Reagan relationship is that most of the cross-border relations are defined not by leaders but by objective realities: Canada and the U.S. are trade competitors; the U.S. is a military superpower and Canada is its military dependency; the U.S. has strategic interests around the world it is determined to protect, while Canada, for lack of any such interests, and also because of its liberal political culture, is able to take a more disinterested, more humanitarian approach to foreign policy. Nothing will change these realities. Personal friendships at the top can modify or assuage cross-border frictions but they cannot deal with the root cause of the frictions, which arises out of the distinct, and in part opposed, natures of the two societies.

In one way, the nature of the relations between Ottawa and Washington have never been less important than they are today. "Sovereign to sovereign relations between Canada and the U.S. don't matter that much any more," comments Washington columnist Joseph Kraft. "They have been superseded by thousands and thousands of sub-sovereign commercial and cultural and personal relations."

Yet in another way, those natural, unforced relations, the growing interdependence of the two economies, the multiplying links in communications and transportation, the omnipresence of American popular culture, all combine to make sovereign to sovereign relations more important than they have ever been. Canada has never before been so alike to the United States in its externals, nor, as Europe recedes over the horizon, has Canada ever before been as solitary.

The place at which national distinctions have been drawn has always been at some point along the axis between Washington and Ottawa. It is here that successive Canadian leaders have every now and then drawn a line and said, "No, we are different." So far the Mulroney government hasn't yet found a way to say this; still to be determined is whether it knows what to say.

Chapter Eighteen
Made-in-Canada Cars

"You have to build something, whole cars or pieces of cars, in yen."

Lee Iacocca, Chairman, Chrysler Corporation

Until it happened, Bob White could never bring himself to use, even to himself, the word "break"; he preferred the softer, unspecific "restructuring." The night after it happened he lay awake on his motel bed in Dearborn, Michigan, until four a.m., then dozed off to be wakened at six a.m. by a phone call summoning him to a TV interview. "As I started dressing, I got excited," White recalls. "I knew exactly what had to be done for the next two years. And I knew we'd made the break."

The break of the White-led 125,000 Canadian autoworkers from their parent American union is potentially the most dramatic political event in Canadian labour history since the unionization of the public service in the late 1960s. Although theirs is by no means the first major Canadian union to break away – paperworkers, railway workers, chemical workers, and electrical workers have all done so – the autoworkers are by far and away the largest union to do it, and they are the most likely to break a path that others will follow. Together with the steelworkers, who remain a U.S. union, autoworkers are the kings of organized labour, the highest paid of blue-collar workers, the best organized and the best disciplined. Unlike civil servants and teachers, even though these are now more numerous, the steelworkers and autoworkers are the *real* unions. Their histories go back to epic battles at Sudbury and at Oshawa that are the heart and muscle of Canadian labour history; when the strike order goes out, their members will tighten belts around beer bellies for as long as it's necessary.

Among the core unions, only the steelworkers, the machinists, and the food and allied workers now remain as "international" unions. Within the Canadian Labour Congress the membership of the international unions is down to one in three, from two out of three in the early 1960s. For the first time in its history the Canadian labour movement is standing almost entirely on its own.

So far the political consequences are unclear. It's not yet certain how many international unions will go the way White has gone, either by merging with the Canadian autoworkers (in the case of the rubber workers this is a distinct possibility) or by being compelled by rank-and-file pressure to make the same kind of break. The autoworkers' own future isn't rosy. American auto industry experts believe that by 1990 autoworker membership will be reduced by at least one-third, as companies "down-size" to cope with the competition. Everyone, not just Lee Iacocca, has a yen for Japanese cars, or South Korean cars, or somewhere down the road, cars made in China.

The entire labour movement these days is in retreat. Specific setbacks, such as the crushing of the six-month strike by Eaton's employees in 1984-85, are painful but at least are familiar. Instead, the real "enemy" is everywhere. In the 1980s, the prevailing ideology is neo-conservatism. The global economy is transferring assembly-line jobs to the far side of the Pacific, while the new technology that may anchor production in North America can do this only by eliminating jobs. The market economy is transferring jobs to small companies and to family-owned firms where the word "union" isn't so much anathema as irrelevant.

In this milieu, the leap to independence by Canadian unions could turn out to be a kind of Pyrrhic victory. But then again, maybe not.

Until relatively recently, the idea of Canadian unions being Canadian wasn't so much daring as unthinkable. If they hadn't been American, there would have been no unions in Canada at all. British unions withdrew after the First World War; as the Winnipeg General Strike of 1919 demonstrated, home-grown organizations were too weak to stand on their own.

Up until the late 1950s, American unions "symbolized the American standard of living that most Canadians craved," as John Crispo has written in his definitive study, *International Unionism*. Apart from symbolism, the American unions represented strength, in numbers, in money, in organizing expertise, in leadership. Except for the Winnipeg General Strike and the Asbestos strike of 1949, organized by the Quebec-based CNTU, all of the epic battles of Canadian labour history have involved American unions, from the famous General Motors strike at Oshawa in 1937, through the struggles of northern Ontario gold miners in 1940-41 and of the copper workers at Murdochville in 1952, and on to the epic Newfoundland woodworkers' strike of 1959.

One change over time was that as Canadians in general became more liberal, unions became socially respectable: they no longer needed to fight for their lives, so they less and less needed American strength. Another change was that sentiments of nationalism from the 1960s on influenced unionists no differently from other Canadians. A slowly maturing change was that the differences between the two labour movements, always existent, became progressively more pronounced. By the late 1960s the international ties of Canadian unions, for which there was no equivalent outside North America,* had become not merely an embarrassment but a constraint to their development.

There was also an additional wrinkle. With the exception of a few carbon-copy universities, trade unions are in a certain sense the most British of contemporary Canadian institutions. When postal worker leader Joe Davidson said "To hell with the public," he did so in a broad Scots accent; after Davidson retired, he went back to Scotland. White himself was born in Northern Ireland. Along with this Britishness in personalities has come a Britishness in ideas. Transplanted across the Atlantic, the class system became the adversarial system: labour as "we," management as "they." Canadian unions have been far slower than American unions to adopt co-management remedies for failing companies and incomparably more resistant to employee profit-sharing plans as partial replacements for paycheque increases.

There is also the concept, carried across the Atlantic, that unions are social organizations, not simply economic ones. American unions, overwhelmingly, have been business unions; their creed, defined for

---

* Not quite unique: many Irish unions are subsidiaries of British ones.

269

them by Samuel Gompers, is "More." (This is also the creed of the most Americanized of Canadian unions, the building trades workers.) Canadian unions certainly want more money for their members. But they also want something more for society as a whole. In contrast to American unions, which bargain with whichever politicians happen to be in power, Canadian unions stick by the NDP, or at least their officials do and their members do so indirectly through their unions' financial contributions. The annual presentations to the government by the Canadian Labour Congress say as much about peace and the poor as about wages and working conditions. The alliance with the NDP puts the labour movement at odds with the governing party in power – as was evident during Trudeau's term, though far less so under Mulroney – but this also makes it an integral part of a political party that represents one in five Canadians.

Combined, these changes have turned North American labour history upside down. Today, Canadian unions are stronger than their American cousins. One in three working Canadians is a union member, as against fewer than one in five among American workers. No doubt, the acceptance of collective values here in contrast to the cult of individualism there – socialism has never taken root in America because its core moral precept, that all men are equal, is the essence of the American Dream – made this shift in relative effectiveness inevitable. But the differences are now quite striking. The grinding down of the Solidarity Movement by the B.C. provincial government was at least as severe a setback to organized labour here as was Reagan's defeat of the air traffic controllers' strike south of the border. But the long-term political effects here have proved to be quite different. While Reagan's political dominance dates from that strike, B.C. Premier Bill Bennett went on to record the highest public disapproval rating of any Canadian politician in power, including Trudeau. Canadians don't like to see workers yelling at management. Neither, though, do they approve of managers yelling at workers.

Two factors made the break of the autoworkers not just out of the ordinary but extraordinary. One was that it happened because of a single figure; Bob White commands a personal loyalty from his members for which there are few equivalents in the contemporary

270

North American labour movement. The other factor is that in doing what he did, White was not merely challenging the most powerful corporations in the United States; he was challenging the core ethic of post-war American corporate culture. This ethic isn't so much that "What's good for General Motors is good for America," which, until very recently, was a statement of the obvious. It is that what General Motors and the others *said* was good for business *had* to be good for business because these corporations were such giants: to deny this was to deny everything that had made America what it was. Before White, the solitary challenger of that ethic had been Ralph Nader.

Now that a certain light has penetrated through the shutters, the nearest equivalent to the way the Big Three used to make management decisions would seem to be the Tzarist Court. Far from simply being rigidly centralized, the companies' decision-making process was both claustrophobic and megalomaniac. Top managers lunched together every day in the executive restaurant – "Dover sole flown over from England on a daily basis; you could order anything you wanted from oysters Rockefeller to roast pheasant," recounts Iacocca in *Iacocca*. Once, Henry Ford told Iacocca to get rid of an executive because he was "a fag." When Iacocca protested that the man, a friend, was married with children, Ford ordered, "His pants are too tight. Get rid of him." Iacocca did as he was told. In Iacocca's recollection, multi-billion-dollar business decisions were made no less arbitrarily and, in the instance of Chrysler, quite zanily: the board of directors of the U.S.'s tenth largest corporation governed its affairs without receiving the benefit of financial reports. Until first the energy crisis and then the Japanese broke up the party, sheer size protected the Big Three from themselves. And if arbitrary, their decisions at least were straightforward: everything went from top to bottom without any return flow.

Decisions crossed the border in exactly the same way. In the minds of auto executives, Canada existed as a political fantasy. The first auto head to deliver a public speech in Canada, Roger Smith of GM, did so in January, 1985, to mark the twentieth anniversary of the Auto Pact; he said the Auto Pact was fine. But for the inconsequential Volvo plant in Halifax, all automobiles made in Canada are made by the Big Three or by American Motors. Aside from the safeguards provided by the Auto Pact, plants are located haphazardly on either side of the border as a consequence of corporate convenience – tilting in Canada's favour because of the decline in the value of the Canadian dollar which, by the curious alchemy of foreign exchange, makes Canadian-made cars cheaper the instant they cross the border. In this schema, General Motors of Oshawa, say, had no more to do with the design, engineering, and marketing of the cars it turned out than did the General Motors plant at Freemont, California.

Labour negotiations were almost as unreal as the industry itself. Occasional strikes helped the companies to clear their backlogs of unsold inventories. For the sake of appearances, or perhaps in memory of Walter Reuther, the autoworkers would every now and then complain. But in fact they had nothing much to complain about: their wages were half as high again as the national industrial average, and fringe benefits covered everything from nine "personal holidays" a year to a guarantee of 95 per cent of their salaries for up to a year if they were laid off. Until the Japanese spoiled it by making it impossible for wage settlement costs to be passed on to consumers, bargaining sessions amounted to little more than a show.

In making his move, White had two things going for him. He's a hero to his members. If Canadian unions are going to get across the valley of declining membership and dwindling bargaining power until economic and political circumstances change (if they do), then White is one of two labour leaders – John Fryer, the head of the National Union of Provincial Government Employees is the other – who may be able to find the way across. As a reinforcing asset, White is a hero to the media. Despite all the contemporary union-bashing, few commentators have cared to take a poke at White.

The principal impression White projects is that of coiled confidence. A close associate comments, "Bob's a very secure person. He doesn't have to prove a thing to himself." His parents emigrated from a scrabble-poor farm in Northern Ireland when he was thirteen; he's now fifty but with his slim, boyish looks he gets mistaken for little more than two-thirds that. He dropped out of school and ended up in a woodworking company in Woodstock that happened to be a UAW shop. Against the advice of his father, he became a union activist. At the age of twenty-four White was touched by the legend. He attended a UAW international convention in Atlantic City and was dazzled by Walter Reuther's oratory. Within a year, he'd become a full-time organizer. One of his happiest memories is of being Reuther's gofer, driving him around Toronto on a visit. In 1972, he was picked by UAW head Dennis McDermott for the key post of personal aide; six years later, when McDermott moved on to Ottawa to become president of the CLC, White succeeded him. Once he considered leaving, when Doug Fraser, the president of the UAW, publicly praised him as "just outstanding" and suggested he should run to succeed him. But to do that, White would have had to become an American citizen. He said no.

In some respects, his humour as a conspicuous difference, White resembles Trudeau, whom he admires. He's quick and he's tough. He has Trudeau's ability to look at problems in a detached manner, abstracting himself from them, but he also has the same certitude of superiority and impatience with criticism. The important fact about White's character is the most obvious one: he's a natural leader, and wherever he went the autoworkers were bound to follow.

The first crack in cross-border solidarity appeared in 1980 when Chrysler had to be bailed out by the U.S. government. In return for its $1.5 billion, the U.S. Loan Guarantee Board demanded and got wage concessions from Chrysler's American employees and then sent the same message across the border. White said no. "It wasn't Chrysler that was asking for concessions. It was the U.S. government telling us to make them," he explains. White only went along when Ottawa similarly advanced $200 million in loan guarantees to Chrysler Canada and so stamped the deal with a Maple Leaf.

In 1982 he said no again. Alone among the twenty-six-member UAW international council, White voted against reopening the contracts already signed with GM and Chrysler so that workers could contribute to the industry's recovery by cutting their wages. When Chrysler Canada's contract fell due, White refused Iacocca's demand for a no-increase settlement. A five-week strike produced a $1.14-an-hour increase. Iacocca doesn't mention the incident in his memoir but he flew to Toronto in mid-strike and yelled a lot of "f" words at White, not least because he had to extend the increase to Chrysler's American workers.

By this time White was no longer irritating only the Big Three. At least as much, he was irritating his own union. His obduracy had made the UAW look like patsies. Almost as annoying, White's militancy turned out to have been justified, whether by luck or by prescience. Through 1983 and 1984, the Big Three rolled to record

273

profits, almost entirely because of the quotas imposed on Japanese imports, which added about $2,000 to their prices and equally to the prices the Big Three could stick on their own cars.

White's single-mindedness amounted at times to narrow-mindedness. If the UAW went easy in its negotiations with GM and Ford in 1984, this was because it wanted to avoid a strike that would have hurt its political champion, Democratic candidate Walter Mondale. As well, the new UAW president, Owen Bieber, was still working himself into the job. Within the industry itself, the circumstances on either side of the border were quite different, though. Job security was a major issue there, but not here. GM, for instance, had let go 100,000 workers in the U.S. at the same time as it had increased its payroll in Canada by 6,000. This was due in part to the luck that many of the large models, suddenly back in popular favour, were being made in Canada, but equally to the fact that auto plants in Canada were more productive. The devalued dollar helped; so did the fact that, as McDermott puts it delicately, "We don't have ghetto kids with chips on their shoulders in our plants."

The crisis broke in the strike against General Motors Canada in October, 1984. White in the bargaining that had led up to it had a "cushion" of the $7.50 less than the comparative cross-border rates of pay earned by Canadian autoworkers and, behind him, the pressure of members more interested in improving their salaries than in the job security that had been the UAW's principal concern in its negotiations with Ford and GM in the U.S. Offered the same deal for his own members as American autoworkers had already accepted, White flatly refused.

The thirteen-day strike against GM Canada that resulted also idled 40,000 American autoworkers for lack of parts made in Canada and used in their plants (GM's trim plant in Windsor was its only one in North America). None of the American workers complained, though. Instead, the complaints came from Solidarity House in Detroit. Word was passed to White that he was embarrassing the UAW by holding out for more than it had settled for earlier. Afterwards, Bieber denied press reports that he had once threatened to cut off the strike fund – all the cheques were issued in Detroit – unless White settled. White says himself, "I realized that it's one thing to be bargaining with the company and quite another to be bargaining simultaneously with your own union." The evidence suggests that White's version is correct. Beyond any doubt, some GM executives were in regular touch with Solidarity House officials. Rumours of the possibility of the strike fund being cut off compelled White to tell the GM negotiators at one bargaining session, "Just in case you've heard any rumours, I want you to know I've got in my wallet a $10 million cheque from McDermott. The CLC will raise funds for us as long as we stay out." (In fact, his wallet and the CLC's treasury were bare.)

In its details White's settlement with GM Canada wasn't that different from those negotiated by the UAW in the States. Rather than the profit-sharing the UAW there had agreed to, White got a straight wage increase, which meant both that Canadian autoworkers would be able to count on it and that their base rate at the start of the next negotiations will be proportionately higher. "Profit-sharing creates the illusion that workers are being treated like executives. That's phony," says White. "What's really phony is that if there are no profits to be shared, workers won't blame management but their union." The most important cross-border difference was in the attitude of the autoworkers themselves: the UAW's contract was certified by 57 per cent of its members; White's by 85 per cent.

Right after the settlement, White said publicly that "The days of rubber-stamping U.S. agreements are gone"; either the Canadian union should have complete negotiating automony or be linked to its parent only by "loose fraternal ties." Instead, at a special meeting of the UAW executive council at Solidarity House on December 10, he was given two alternatives: go along or quit. For more than an hour, White addressed his colleagues about the differences, historic and contemporary, between unions in Canada and those in the U.S.; he then asked for authority to bargain independently. After White finished, no one spoke or asked a question.

The actual vote was twenty-five to one (a ballot cast by White himself) to reject his proposals. Only then did the bitterness break into the open, as UAW executives demanded a national vote among Canadian members and White replied they could have a vote if they wanted it but that its result would be certain.

Later, Bieber told reporters, "I don't think it's in the best interests of Canadian workers, but it's their decision to make." Some Canadian autoworkers thought the same way. Jerry Hartford, a retired public relations director, wrote to the *Oshawa Times* accusing White of "leading our members to the bushes at the bottom of the garden." Other unionists were as sorry to see him go, but for quite different

275

reasons. Among a number of American UAW members who wrote to tell White he would be missed because he and his Canadians had been the most politically progressive of the autoworkers was Victor Reuther, the brother of the UAW hero.

The Canadian autoworkers effectively became a separate union on May 1, 1985. Thereafter, their weekly check-off went into a new strike fund in Toronto. By their old standards, this fund was small. On a take-or-leave basis, the UAW had offered the Canadian autoworkers just $30 million out of the $500 million (U.S.) international fund.* Still, the autoworkers' strike fund was easily the largest in Canada. The formal structures and constitution of the new union were to be decided at a founding convention in September.

Once the break was certain, McDermott declared, "It will create a climate that others will have to follow." In fact, no other unions have yet followed the autoworkers into independence, although all the international unions now are under pressure to fulfil the CLC's guidelines on Canadianization by having, for instance, their Canadian executive officers elected by the Canadian members alone rather than, as in the case of the building trades unions, by the international membership at large.

Canadian nationalists cheered. Mulroney, in a question-and-answer period following his December 10, 1984, speech to the Economic Club in New York, disappointed his audience – for the only time on that occasion – by declaring that the autoworkers were "fully entitled to take the decisions they judge to be in their own best interest." Other commentators, including some nationalists, wrung their hands. Patrick Lavelle, president of the Canadian Auto Parts Association, said, "I don't understand what he's trying to do. I don't understand what his motives are." Crispo, a labour expert, wrote that the breakaway "could do immense harm to his [White's] members' well-being as well as that of the Canadian auto industry as a whole."

Implicit in such criticism was the presumption either that White, once independent, would bargain for more than the tariff could bear, or that the auto companies would retaliate by pulling plants out of Canada. The best answer to the second concern was provided

---

* The Canadian autoworkers also received $6 million worth of real estate and other assets.

by GM chairman Roger Smith; "We deal with different unions all around the world. This should not present any insurmountable problems." In an interview for this book, White responded to the first criticism: "Sure I'm out on a limb. Every time a new model is introduced in the U.S. and not here, I'll be blamed. The fact is, I'm not a fool. We're not going to be different just for the sake of being different. The break hasn't changed economic reality. It has changed only one thing. From now on, we are going to be responsible for ourselves, and that changes everything."*

White's economic reality is defined for him by the Auto Pact. When Lyndon Johnson and Lester Pearson signed it on January 16, 1965, both admitted they didn't understand it. Its details are inordinately complicated, but its essentials are straightforward. Canada functions as a kind of industrial park for the Big Three and American Motors. Subject to a commitment to maintain a minimum ratio of production to sales in Canada of about 60 per cent, the auto companies can site their assembly and parts plants wherever they choose and can sell their cars duty-free in either country. The result was the ultimate dream of free-traders: rationalized production throughout a larger market.

Nationalists damned the Auto Pact through most of its history. On the one hand, it narrowed the differences in the prices of automobiles on either side of the border, and, more quickly, it raised pay scales in Canada to virtual parity with those of American autoworkers. But on the other hand, it moved engineering and management jobs across the Detroit River and, after an initial spurt, left Canada with a permanent deficit in cross-border auto trade. Nationalists complained in particular that the pact had pre-empted Canada from ever developing its own independent auto industry, as Sweden had done with its Saabs and Volvos. That often-made comparison with Sweden omits one key comparative detail. Between them, Saab and Volvo turn out about 400,000 models a year. Canada's output, in 1984, was one million.

---

* Since the breakaway, White's future has become a subject of considerable speculation. Guesses range from a bid to become NDP national leader to creating a new, huge, European-style metalworkers' union. White says he will stay on at least until 1986 to conduct the first negotiation with GM. Associates believe his interest thereafter is in going abroad in some foreign aid post.

The dollar made much of the difference, with higher productivity accounting for the rest. Cars made in Canada now cost $500-$600 less than cars made in the U.S. The Big Three realized this in 1980. Since that year, they've invested more than $4 billion in new and retooled plants in Canada; American Motors is putting $760 million into its new plant at Brampton.

Once an economic scapegoat, the Auto Pact has now become the national saviour. In 1984, autos and parts accounted for one of every four dollars of exports to the U.S. By the time of the pact's twentieth anniversary, in January, 1985, the Canadian auto trade deficit had dwindled to $2 billion, and with the annual Canadian surplus now running at more than $5 billion, the cumulative count will tilt in Canada's favour sometime in mid-1985.

More significant has been the performance of the independent Canadian auto parts manufacturers. They are not party to the pact, which is why "after-market" prices, for batteries, tires, and other replacement parts, are 20-25 per cent higher in Canada than in the U.S. But the pact has created a market for these companies by "anchoring" Big Three assembly plants here (the "just-in-time" inventory system puts a premium on the physical proximity of suppliers). The dollar again, but also the sheer competitiveness of companies such as Magna, Tridon, A.G. Simpson, and Epton, has caused Canadian parts manufacturers to increase their share of the Canadian market to 51 per cent today from 36 per cent in 1980. Employment in the fiercely competitive parts industry is now as large, at about 65,000, as in the "captive" assembly industry.

Because of its production safeguards, which would never again be ceded by the U.S.,* the Auto Pact does not represent a model for Canada-U.S. free trade. Its effectiveness is now being undermined by the location of Big Three plants in Mexico and, more dramatically, by the Japanese manufacturers who've set up shop in the U.S. But

---

* The key production safeguards are not those between Canada and the U.S. but those between the Big Three and the Canadian government. Since the potential benefits for the U.S. were always hard to define, guesses as to why Washington agreed to the pact back in 1965 have ranged from fear of an independent Canadian auto industry to a pay-off to Pearson for sending a peace force to Cyprus. In an interview with the author, Philip Tresize, now at the Brookings Institute and one of the U.S. negotiators of the pact, said, "We believed it would be a forerunner to a whole series of bilateral trade pacts that would have benefited both economies."

it does now represent a case model of Canadian industrial competitiveness.

The Auto Pact represents only half, if that, of the economic reality within which White and the autoworkers have to operate. Once the kings of the labour movement, the autoworkers have become in some respects its walking wounded.

In the global economy, most North American automobiles can be made most efficiently outside of North America. By the late 1980s, imports are expected to account for one in three cars sold in Canada and the U.S. The Reagan government's decision to end the quotas on Japanese cars on April 1, 1985, amounted to a conscious refusal to continue forcing consumers to subsidize the profits of the auto companies and the wages of the autoworkers. (The Mulroney government temporarily maintained quotas here to force Japanese companies such as Toyota to invest in local plants.)

Consumer preferences for the quality and costs of imports aren't the only cause of this phenomenon. The Big Three themselves are now leading the import parade. Chrysler, for instance, intends to use the end of the quotas as an opportunity to triple to 250,000 its imports of Mitsubishi cars to be sold under its own brand names. As an encouragement to do this, Chrysler owns 24 per cent of Mitsubishi. Simultaneously, Chrysler will also import models from South Korea's Samsung, of which it owns 50 per cent. To complete the circle, Mitsubishi also owns 15 per cent of Samsung.

The real problem for autoworkers, though, isn't so much what is happening in Southeast Asia as that Southeast Asia now is starting to happen in North America. By the late 1980s, Japanese auto plants in the U.S. (Honda, Nissan, Toyota, Mazda, with Mitsubishi due to become the fifth) will be turning out one million cars annually, as many as Chrysler does now. These plants pay UAW-scale wages, including those at non-unionized Honda and Nissan. Yet they can still out-price the Big Three. "Humanistic management" is one reason. To staff its plant in Smyrna, Tennessee, Nissan interviewed 150,000 applicants for 2,000 positions, selecting workers on the basis of their readiness to accept such transpacific techniques as flexible job classifications, perpetual training and retraining for new tasks, and Quality of Life Circles that replace the familiar and comfortable hierarchy of "we" and "they." Another reason for the success of Japanese plants in the U.S. is the massive use of robots, numerical-controlled tools, and flexible manufacturing systems. A last reason is fanatic attention to quality detail, which demands the utmost both from assembly-line workers and from component suppliers.

These kinds of demands are burdensome for McDermott's "ghetto kids with chips on their shoulders." Revealingly, Japanese companies have located their plants in places like California and Tennessee rather than in Michigan. The most ambitious attempt to determine whether an American auto company can do as well with American workers is GM's "Saturn" project. To try to manufacture a compact that can match the price of imports, GM is planning a high-technology assembly line that will reduce from 200 hours to forty hours the time required to assemble each model. More striking yet, the work rules in the plant are being developed jointly by the company and the UAW.

The Big Three are by no means down and out. They alone manufacture the big cars that Americans like, and which are the most profitable. As permanent assets, GM and Ford and Chrysler can count on cash in the bank accumulated during their bumper years of 1983 and 1984. Nevertheless, by 1990, more than four in ten cars sold in the U.S. are expected to be either imports, from Southeast Asia and Europe, or models manufactured in the U.S. by Japanese and perhaps South Korean companies in order to escape any re-imposition of import quotas. (The Japanese plants create assembly-line jobs but few indirect jobs because 75 per cent of their parts and components are imported from Japan.)

White's solution is "government-to-government agreements to divide up the market, instead of allowing multinationals to decide everyone's living standards." What White doesn't say when he says this is that he is asking Canadian taxpayers and consumers to subsidize indefinitely the profits of the auto companies and the wages of the autoworkers.

The one in ten Canadians now out of work are in effect subsidizing the wages of those Canadians now employed. The new economic gypsies who flit from one short-term job to another, and from one insecure small company to another, are similarly subsidizing the wages of those enjoying tenure in corporate and government bureaucracies. The same is true for young workers during layoffs: the unions' iron rule of seniority means that older workers keep both their jobs and their salaries while newcomers lose everything.

These contrasts represent probably the most acute of all the contradictions between the ideals of the political culture of liberalism and the economic realities of the global marketplace. The U.S. has largely accepted the logic of the marketplace: wages have been cut, but unemployment also has been cut, to 7 per cent. In Canada, the questions of pain-sharing and gain-sharing have scarcely been addressed. Nor are answers readily available that unions will find easy to accept – work-sharing, which requires discarding the rule of seniority; co-management, which merges "we" and "they" into one; profit-sharing and bonuses, both of which are uncertain and which reduce the value of the contract negotiated by the union; "two-tier" contracts by which new workers are paid less than the standard union rate.

One solution, often debated but never implemented, is that of a "social contract" or an incomes policy. In the ideal, as in Austria, in Sweden, in West Germany, in Japan, government and business and labour jointly decide the average wage increases the economy can afford in the face of international competition and then abide by these limits in individual bargaining. "It's the way we're going to have to go," says NUPGE head Fryer. "I believe in the adversarial system, but I believe we have to be prepared to move beyond it. In fact, I believe that some form of social contract is inevitable, and that if we don't accept it we are going to pay a terrible price."

A major obstacle to a national social contract is that, as Fryer points out, "Labour would have to be treated as an equal, a real equal, by government and by business. Neither of them are today prepared to do that." As considerable an obstacle, left unsaid by Fryer, is that the labour movement not merely flatly rejects a social contract or incomes policy, but refuses even to discuss the subject. Most labour leaders prefer the old adversarial system that until now has served them and their members so well. No union leader feels this way more strongly than does White. In public, he and former Saskatchewan Premier Allan Blakeney argued the merits and demerits of an incomes policy at the 1983 NDP national policy convention. In private, he and Art Kube, the head of the B.C. public service union, argued the same issue during a May, 1985, meeting of the executive council of the CLC. That internal debate was significant. It marked the first time that senior Canadian labour leaders have discussed a social contract strategy. The May debate among CLC leaders was an informal one; despite White's objections, a formal debate on the subject has been scheduled for the CLC executive council's meeting in September, 1985.

A decision about a national incomes policy is probably the most important single decision now facing organized labour in Canada. It amounts to making a choice between trying to go with the flow of the global marketplace or trying to resist it. Between past and present there is one significant difference. As White has said, "From now on we are going to be responsible for ourselves. And that changes everything."

Part Six
The Way We Are

Not for a long time has a Canadian government had to deal simultaneously with two decisions of such importance and complexity as Star Wars, whether or not Canada should join the U.S. anti-missile research program, and free trade, whether or not Canada should try to negotiate some form of a comprehensive bilateral pact.

The two issues interconnect. A "no" to Star Wars, or the Strategic Defence Initiative, would make Washington far less willing to negotiate a satisfactory trade pact. But a "yes" on Star Wars would make Canadians far less willing to accept a tight, cross-border economic embrace.

Common to both issues is that their ultimate consequences are unknowable. The most impartial of analysts cannot forecast confidently whether an agreement on Star Wars research would amount to getting onto the back of the Pentagon tiger, or whether free trade would amount to the equivalent of getting into the same cage as a tiger.

The next three chapters try to describe and to analyse these two issues, first of free trade, then of Star Wars, in both their immediate and their long-term perspectives. The concluding chapter suggests some answers.

Chapter Nineteen
Free Trade: Deal or No Deal?

"If it ever happens, it will be the consummation of the longest courtship in the world."

Peter Marici, vice-president, National Planning Association, Washington

Each time Canadians have been asked to say "yes" or "no" to free trade with the United States the answer has come, unvaryingly, "yes *and* no."

The economics of the matter have never been in much doubt. From Governor General Lord Lansdowne in 1887 to the Macdonald Royal Commission on Canadian Economic Union and Development Prospects of 1985, everyone who has examined the matter more or less objectively has concluded that bilateral free trade would make Canadians economically better, healthier, and richer. The Macdonald Commission has calculated the gain in national wealth at between 3 per cent and 8 per cent. There would be losses along with the gains. One estimate puts the unemployment "churn" at 7 per cent of the labour force, meaning that about one worker in fifteen would be moved to a different (often a better) job while some would lose their jobs entirely. Overall, though, access to a larger market would allow Canadian companies to increase their production runs and so to become more efficient; consumers would benefit from a reduction in some consumer prices; total wealth would increase; governments would receive greater revenues.

Nor has the importance of the economics of the matter ever been in the least doubt. The U.S. accounts for three-quarters of all Canadian exports. More important, it accounts for 90 per cent of manufactured exports. Thanks largely to the auto boom, the cross-border trade in these high-value goods is now close to even – $42 billion going southward and $48 billion coming northward in 1984. These statistics don't take account of the value to Canadian companies of sales *in* rather than to the U.S. Tan-Jay of Winnipeg, one of the country's most enterprising clothing manufacturers, sells $50 million worth of sports wear in the U.S. All but $5 million of this is accounted for by clothes finished for Tan-Jay in Los Angeles from fabrics imported from Hong Kong, Taiwan, Italy; but these sales create executive, sales, and design jobs back in Winnipeg.

The catch in the collective Canadian craw always has been the politics of the question. Lansdowne said most of what needs to be said: "The centre of political activity in regard to all commercial questions affecting the North American continent would inevitably be at Washington." Sovereignty, in matters both political and cultural, would remain in legal form; in fact, it could gradually fade away, imperceptibly, like Alice's Cheshire cat, until all that remained was not a smile but a puzzled frown as to how this could have happened.

Past and present are not the same, though. Canada has caught up to the U.S. in its standard of living, although the gap is beginning to widen again. Although a bilateral deal would be something considerably less than a deal between equals, neither would it be a deal between "an elephant and a mouse." The Canadian market is the ninth largest in the world, just after Italy's; fully one-fifth of all U.S. exports go north.

In contrast to the past, this is probably Canada's last chance. A "no" this time probably would be irrevocable. It's hard to imagine the convergence of today's circumstances repeating themselves: a close friendship between the two leaders, both of them at the start of terms in office; a Canadian government committed to "freer" trade as a way to achieve its goal of restructuring the economy. Whether the Mulroney government says "yes" or "no," its decision will be no less either an historic triumph or an historic blunder.

The most important difference between present and past is that Canadians have already made up their minds about the question in the only way they ever could have done – without knowing it or admitting it. For most practical purposes, a Canada-U.S. free trade agreement already exists. The statement that Canada alone among industrial nations lacks guaranteed access to a market of at least 100 million people is repeatedly lobbed up as a kind of bogeyman. It needs to be permanently grounded. For one thing, no nation has that kind of market guarantee except within its own borders; within

Western Europe, a recent EEC study calculated the cost of customs paperwork and regulations at its internal borders as the equivalent of a 15 per cent tariff on all goods.

Much more to the immediate point, Canada today enjoys the equivalent of something like 90 per cent access to the 230-million market that exists next door. Canada enjoys this access because U.S. protectionism is constrained by its international obligations under the General Agreement on Tariffs and Trade (GATT) and because Canada and the U.S. have negotiated mutually advantageous tariff cuts under the umbrella provided by successive multilateral GATT negotiations. By playing with great skill a kind of green light-red light game under the GATT rules, Canada has snuck up into virtual free trade with the U.S. Aside from all of this, Canadian goods cross the border with relative ease because commercial practices on each side of it are so similar. The striking fact about cross-border trade isn't that disputes often occur but that, relative to its scale – about $150 billion – there are so few of them. This isn't free trade in the legal or textbook sense, but it's about as close to it as any two nations anywhere have achieved.

One of the first people to take note of this was Ambassador Bill Brock, the former U.S. Trade Representative, now the Secretary for Labour. In the fall of 1983, following Ottawa's proposal for sectoral free trade talks to which he had responded enthusiastically, Brock suggested at one meeting with his officials that the best way to deal with Canadian political sensitivities might be for the two countries to declare jointly that a free trade area already existed between them. This would have allowed the Trudeau government to escape the opprobrium of actually negotiating a free trade agreement; following this immaculate conception, the two sides could then have got down to practical negotiations about eliminating tariff and other trade barriers still on the books.

Brock never advanced his idea as a serious bargaining proposition. Yet it was in no way far-fetched. By 1987, as a result of tariff-cutting commitments already made as part of the Tokyo Round of GATT,*

---

* These tariff reductions were negotiated by the Trudeau government but announced by the Clark government in July, 1979, exactly 100 years after Macdonald had announced his high-tariff National Policy.

about 80 per cent of Canadian exports will cross the border free of duty. About 95 per cent will carry duties of 5 per cent or less. At that level, tariffs are virtually irrelevant compared to the effect upon selling prices of a shift of a few cents either way in the comparative values of the Canadian and American dollars. As an example, Ian Campbell, president of Ottawa's Wajax Industries, says, "I'm trying to make up my mind whether to put our next plant in York, Pennsylvania, or in Markham. If the dollar goes up to eighty cents it would take $1.5 million out of my bottom line unless I'm already in York. If it stays where it is, then I should be in Markham, which is where I'd rather be."

Unquestionably, some of the tariffs that will continue to apply after 1987 will be high: clothing (25 per cent), footwear (22 per cent), textiles (17 per cent), furniture (14 per cent), chemicals and glassware (7 per cent). Most of these high tariffs, though – petrochemicals as an exception – are designed to protect industries in Canada and the U.S. from imports from third countries rather than from imports from each other.

These exceptions aside, the level of tariffs now in effect between Canada and the U.S. would rank the arrangement as one of the freest between any two countries in the world. Comparisons are difficult, but the best guess of trade officials in Washington is that the existing informal free trade pact between Canada and the United States puts it among the top dozen of the forty-odd official free trade areas recognized by GATT and which range in their extent from the one between Britain and Ireland (93 per cent of trade free of any duties) down to that among Tanzania, Uganda, and Kenya (6 per cent duty-free).

Within the Mulroney government, free trade has become the policy that dares not speak its name. The Prime Minister has told aides he considers that the 1911 Reciprocity Election "settled the matter." Mulroney no doubt also remembers the shot he himself took at John Crosbie's call for a Canada-U.S. "economic partnership" during the 1983 Conservative leadership campaign when he said: "Free trade is terrific until the elephant twitches, and if it ever rolls over, you're a dead man. We will have none of it." Instead, Mulroney and Trade Minister James Kelleher talk determinedly about "freer trade," "enhanced trade," "security of access," and, as a catch-all, "a comprehensive agreement."

This is verbal gamesmanship. In its literal sense, free trade exists nowhere but in textbooks. It doesn't even exist within Canada itself. All provinces discriminate against goods and services from other provinces, through preferential purchasing (a 10 per cent margin for local contractors is common*), through differential taxes for wines and spirits (New Brunswick's Moosehead beer moved into the U.S. because it was blocked from selling in Ontario and Quebec), and through different licensing requirements for everyone from lawyers and doctors to garage mechanics. Even the GATT escape clause, Article 24, which allows member nations to establish free trade areas, refers only to "substantial" free trade among the two or more countries applying for the exemption.

To compound the confusion, the definition of a "comprehensive agreement" set out in Trade Minister Kelleher's Green Paper of January, 1985, is the same as everyone's everyday definition of free trade: "the removal of tariffs and non-tariff barriers on substantially all bilateral trade."

The joint declaration on trade issued by Mulroney and Reagan on March 18, 1985, the last day of the Shamrock Summit, in fact went well beyond free trade in the common usage of that term. The two leaders charged their trade ministers, Kelleher and Brock's replacement, Clayton Yeutter, to come up with specific negotiating proposals on, among other things: "National treatment . . . with respect to government procurement and funding programs . . . standardization, reduction or simplification of regulatory requirements . . . reducing restrictions on petroleum imports and exports, and maintaining and extending open access to each other's energy markets . . . reducing tariff barriers . . . facilitation of travel for business and commercial purposes . . . elimination or reduction of tariff and non-tariff barriers to trade in high-technology goods and related services . . . cooperation to protect intellectual property rights (copyright)."

In anyone's language, all of that adds up to free trade. In any event, since free trade is the term everyone uses, it will be the term used here.

---

* In March, 1985, B.C. became the first province to remove all preferences for local contractors in bids on government contracts.

The fact that for most practical purposes free trade already exists between Canada and the U.S. both diminishes and enhances the value of a formal, bilateral pact. It reduces the economic risks involved in going the rest of the way. But it leaves less economic ground to be gained.

The strongest argument of free trade advocates – by almost all academic economists, by all business organizations, by the C.D. Howe Institute, by the Macdonald Commission, by Kelleher – is that it will increase Canadian exports to the U.S. In fact, this may not happen. The inhibiting factor is that it has already happened. Between 1980 and 1984, Canadian exports to the U.S. almost doubled from $47 billion to $83 billion, one of the fastest rates of increase since the mid-sixties when the Auto Pact provided a temporary boost to Canadian exports. In the last two years, Canada has enjoyed cross-border trade surpluses on a scale never before even approached – $16 billion in 1983; $20 billion in 1984. The 1985 surplus is likely to be at least as large.

This extraordinary performance is in part fortuitous, the result of the cheap Canadian dollar and the slow economic growth here that has inhibited the Canadian demand for American goods. But the surpluses raise some troubling questions. How long, for example, will the U.S. accept a trade deficit with Canada exceeded only by its deficit with Japan? Will U.S. negotiators use the surplus as an excuse to be far more demanding than they would have been a few years ago? Far from least, will Congress now be in an unsympathetic and exigent mood?

A couple of trial balloons have already been floated up. In advance of the Shamrock Summit, the U.S. Treasury Department wanted investment liberalization added to the agenda – this despite the replacement of FIRA by Investment Canada – and had to be talked out of it in the interests of sustaining the smiles. At a Canada-U.S. conference in Toronto in May, 1985, Bill Eberle, a former senior U.S. trade negotiator, now a Washington trade consultant, commented: "The trade issue is not limited to trade. We will have to discuss exchange rates and investment policy." In an interview for this book, Larry Fox, vice-president of the U.S. National Association of Manufacturers, said, "We'd go for a free trade pact provided it didn't have any gimmicks in it. The automobile production-sharing agreement would have to be dropped." Most recently, Trade Secretary Clayton Yeutter has made Canadian limits on its softwood lumber exports a precondition for free trade negotiations. "We can't proceed on the broader relationship if we have sensitive issues like this (lumber) on the side," Yeutter told the Senate Finance Committee during his confirmation hearings in June, 1985.

A certain public bargaining may be involved in all of this. The more troubling question is whether the Mulroney government has oversold – to itself, quite aside from the public – the importance of the agreement it is likely to be able to reach. The government has put an enormous amount of energy into the issue: two official discussion papers, by Kelleher and by External Affairs Minister Clark, coast-to-coast consultations, a year's study by cabinet, endless speeches, a Commons' committee inquiry. All of this could end up not with a bang but with a kind of apologetic cough.

The title of Kelleher's discussion paper of January, 1985, is uncommonly bold: *How to Secure and Enhance Canadian Access to Export Markets.* Since then, Kelleher has used the phrase "secure and enhance" almost like a mantra.

This policy objective is wholly valid. Through 1985, Canadian exports of hogs, strawberries, salt fish, specialty steels, and, by far the most important, softwood lumber were threatened or actually constrained by various U.S. protectionist actions. Threats of protectionism can be as effective as actual protectionist measures: a "chilling" effect inhibits Canadian exporters who, to avoid threatened protectionist measures, may voluntarily limit their exports or postpone scheduled plant expansions.* Some Canadian companies move plants south to get across the drawbridge before it is hauled up; foreign investors worry whether money spent in Canada will pay off in sales to the U.S.

All of this made for alarmist headlines. The fine print beneath them was quite a bit more measured. In the calculation of former senior Canadian trade negotiator Mel Clark, during the half-decade 1978-83, out of 662 petitions for protection against "unfair" imports presented either to Congress or to regulatory agencies and departments, only forty-four concerned Canadian goods and just *six* of these resulted in actual protectionist measures. In 1983, for example,

---

* Protectionist threats can chill in another way. To ward off protectionist proposals in 1983, the Canadian softwood producers spent $4 million on lobbying.

the U.S. International Trade Commission ruled that Canadian potatoes were not being dumped across the border below fair market price and that Canadian softwood lumber exports were not being subsidized by low provincial stumpage fees. Similarly, in September, 1984, Canada was exempted from U.S. steel quotas.

In 1985, the action again centred on softwood lumber. In a new twist, U.S. legislators tried to rewrite the rules. By redefining when countervailing duties could be applied, a bill by influential Florida Congressmen Sam Gibbons threatened more than $3 billion worth of Canadian lumber sales. To a degree, though, Canadian producers were the authors of their own misfortunes. At a time when U.S. producers were hard-hit, they had capitalized on the cheap dollar to flood the southern market, and may have engaged in overcutting; as a consequence, Canadian producers had made little attempt to develop third-country markets that could have absorbed some of their output and so eased the pressure on American producers.

The protectionist mood in Congress is real. Bills have been moved in both the Senate and House to impose an across-the-board 20 per cent surcharge on all imports. How far all of this will get is another matter. The Reaganites are convinced free-traders. American consumers are hooked on cheap imports and count on them to sustain their lifestyle. Many U.S. manufacturers similarly are hooked on cheap components and depend on them to keep their own products competitive.

More to the immediate point, it is open to doubt just how far Canada can go toward achieving "secure access" by even the most comprehensive of trade pacts.

In March, 1985, the U.S. and Israel concluded a free trade agreement that will eliminate all tariffs between the two countries by 1995. Even the formidable Israeli lobby, though, could not convince the U.S. to give up or to limit the applicability of the two most important of all protectionist programs in the U.S., and in all countries – "anti-dumping duties," imposed when goods are dumped onto the U.S. market below their domestic production cost, and "countervailing duties," imposed when the government of the exporting country subsidizes its industries. Two factors were in play here: the concern of U.S. manufacturers that Israeli manufacturers would in effect cheat, and the determination of U.S. congressmen not to yield their right to protect their constituents.

Unless the application of U.S. countervailing and anti-dumping duties, and also of "safeguard" actions (temporary quotas or duties imposed to protect domestic industries threatened with extinction by imports), can be severely curtailed, "secure access" becomes a chimera. "More secure access" is possible, although the actual negotiation of it would be excruciatingly complicated. Both countries might agree to accept more stringent definitions of the occasions when these "contingency protection" duties could be applied. A way might be found to exempt Canada from actions undertaken to deal with imports from third countries. Some new agency – a Joint Economic Commission comparable to the International Joint Commission – might be set up to examine, more or less impartially, complaints by industries in either country about rival cross-border products.

All of this would be useful. But the nirvana of "secure access" would remain far out of reach. Within the EEC, for instance, bickering among member states over trade practices is unremitting despite all the fine print of the Rome Treaty. Lobbyists and lawyers and Congressional legislators will always find loopholes. "Buy American" attitudes matter far more than "Buy American" laws and regulations. Although the Defence Production Sharing Act is exempt from all protectionist measures and from preferences for national contractors, Canada now is running an annual deficit of about $300 million in defence trade: the Pentagon just prefers to keep the business, and jobs, back home.

If free trade cannot achieve "secure access" for Canada, the question about it thus becomes one not so much of whether or not to do a deal as of What's the Big Deal?

If free trade isn't such a big deal, neither can it be a very big risk. The commonest criticism is that bilateral free trade will reduce Canada to an industrial hinterland. In a statement soon after he assumed office in June, 1985, Ontario Premier David Peterson said that "to many, the phrase 'free trade' has become synonymous for work without a future and a future without work." Peterson here was looking backwards, or more likely, was looking at the voters. To argue that Canada cannot compete in a free trade market is to ignore the reality that Canada is already competing in an almost-free trade market – to the extent of that $20 billion surplus.

Some Canadians will indeed be put out of work. As economist Abraham Rotstein points out, "Americans love to talk about a 'level playing field' for trade. What they and free trade supporters forget is that a lot of our players would be sitting on the bench; it's absurd to think that branch plants, which only came here because of high tariffs, would compete with their parents." True. It is true also, though, that branch plants that exist only as tariff factories – most drug companies, for instance – will leave eventually anyway. It is also ironic, if not absurd, for economic nationalists to argue against free trade by arguing for the need to protect branch plants.

The task of compiling a list of Canadian industrial losers to free trade is a good deal more difficult than the alarmists suggest. Everyone's list starts with the small-scale textile, clothing, footwear, and furniture manufactures, principally in Quebec. Yet in a 1984 study for the Ontario Economic Council, economists David Cox and Richard Harris concluded that most of these would do better than other Canadian companies, essentially because access to the U.S. market would allow them to achieve the efficiencies of scale that many other Canadian industries, because unprotected, already have done. Cox and Harris estimated that free trade would cause the clothing industry to increase fivefold in output and threefold in employment; in order, they rank the other principal beneficiaries as textiles, knitting, transportation equipment, and urban transit.

Cox and Harris may be too optimistic. Most companies in these industries are small and are underfinanced. Transition arrangements, perhaps extended to ten years, could soften the shock. More important, a generous program of financial assistance to the workers would be essential, otherwise the resistance to the industrial restructuring would be too fierce for any government to sustain.

In the contemporary economy of the global marketplace, industrial restructuring is inevitable sooner or later. Rejecting Canada-U.S. free trade in the hope of avoiding industrial adjustment is the economic equivalent of closing the back door of a barn while the front one remains wide open.

Another concern of nationalists about free trade can similarly be reduced in scale, although not entirely resolved. This is that such a pact would compel the "harmonization" of Canadian economic and social policies with those of the U.S.

Some harmonization would occur. Government industrial grants and subsidies would be more closely scrutinized. (Only subsidies to companies which export, and which are already forbidden by GATT, would be put into doubt.) Already, though, Canada has no choice but to recalibrate many of its social and economic policies to those initiated in the U.S., as in the instances of deregulation and of a flat-rate income tax. Concern about the applications of U.S. countervailing duties has caused Ottawa to limit its subsidies to the Atlantic fishing industry.

At least conceptually, it is possible that a free trade pact could allow Canada to negotiate the right to maintain various industrial subsidy programs that are now in question. The trade-off here, although American negotiators would never admit it formally, would be with defence spending, which functions in the U.S. as a substitute for regional industrial equalization.

If a free trade or "comprehensive" pact is far less of a big deal than the Mulroney government has implied, why bother with it at all? Whatever economic gains are achieved some economic and political risks will have to be taken.

More secure access isn't negligible. It would thaw out some of the "chilling" effect on Canadian industries and on potential foreign investors. If real, across-the-board free trade was negotiated, all Canadian companies would have an opportunity to increase their production runs (and simultaneously to specialize). Some consumer prices should decline.

The principal benefits of free trade, all of them economic, tend to be second-order ones. Similarly the risks, all of the consequential ones being political, tend to be second order, or unlikely to manifest themselves during the first few years of an agreement.

The first second-order benefit, seldom spelled out because to do so seems to be rude, is that a bilateral pact would give Canada a "comparative advantage" over all other countries trying to sell to the U.S. Opposition to the pact in Western Europe and in Japan has so far been muted, not least because these countries have no target to aim at yet. It's virtually certain that Western Europe at least will argue at GATT that whatever pact is negotiated is illegal. Trying to define Canada-U.S. free trade against the measure of GATT's own non-definition of free trade should keep many lawyers employed for many years.*

A second advantage commonly regarded as quite unmentionable is that a Canada-U.S. pact might provide the first building block (or second after the Caribbean Basin Initiative) for an eventual regional trading bloc that could encompass, as former Secretary of State Henry Kissinger has suggested, the American hemisphere and Australasia. This would be strictly a defensive strategy to be brought into play only if the entire GATT-based international trading system breaks down, as might happen if Western Europe continues its retreat into protectionism or if political pressures within the U.S. push it in the same direction. The collapse of GATT would be a political disaster for Canada, although perhaps not that severe an economic blow. This is why the Mulroney government has supported so strongly a new round of international bargaining to further reduce trade barriers. But if the worst should happen, an Americas-Australasia regional bloc would create an opportunity for Canada to escape being left to survive by its own devices in North America.

The last, and the most considerable, second-order benefit of a free trade deal has nothing to do with trade as such. In one way or another, the Canadian economy has to be restructured. Free trade, by leaving Canadian industries with nowhere to hide, may be the one way to force the restructuring that has to happen anyway. Further, the government could always blame the unpleasantness on the Americans.

Free trade, from this perspective, is not a quick fix. It is not a quick fix from any perspective. But it could function as a "cold shower," administering to Canadian industry a kind of shock treatment. This cure isn't guaranteed. Britain tried to apply it to itself without noticeable effect by joining the European Common Market in 1973. But in Canada, the cry of "the Yankees are coming, the Yankees are coming" just might do the trick.

The critical factor here is that free trade can accomplish little except as part of an integrated industrial strategy. The real economic debate,

---

* Some argue that a Canada-U.S. pact would itself seriously weaken GATT and the international trading system. This is ingenuous, although perhaps also ingenious, as an argument raised against a bilateral pact. In fact, Canada is almost the only GATT member among more than 100 not to have used the Article 24 "escape clause" to negotiate a free trade agreement with one or more GATT members.

which has yet to begin or even to be defined, will have to encompass a wide variety of issues: labour-management relations; the entire educational system; the future of protected industries such as textiles and the rest that are now being carried by Canadian taxpayers and consumers at a fearful cost; competition policy; the "privatization" of crown corporations; deregulation. In the absence of an integrated industrial strategy, free trade amounts to an appetizer with the rest of the meal uncooked – for that matter, still running around on the hoof.

The potential benefits of free trade, short-term or long-term, will apply only if the deal actually involves free trade in the ordinary meaning of that term. Here, the Mulroney government may have placed itself firmly in a cleft stick. It has become skittish about across-the-board free trade because of the effect competition might have on Quebec-based industries like textiles. Its rhetoric has dwindled from a "comprehensive" pact down to an "enhanced trade" pact. But to achieve even "more secure access," let alone its original self-defined objective of "secure access," the government is going to have to give on textiles and the rest in order to get.

Once, the U.S. lusted after Canada's resources. Some annexationists may have lusted after Canada's body politic. Sentiments in Washington today are wholly pragmatic. Brock's original interest in the 1983-84 sectoral free trade proposals was in using a deal with Canada to signal other nations, Japan and Western Europe in particular, that the U.S. was prepared to go its own way unless the world moved toward freer trade. That motivation still applies today, but less so: Japan is making a few gestures toward liberalization; new multinational trade talks – despite the delaying tactics of France – will be held one year or other.

In strict economic terms, U.S. interest in a bilateral pact has always been minimal. Some industries could benefit from continental economic rationalization, but only marginally. A generalized recognition does exist that incessant cross-border trade rows benefit neither country. The last factor in play is Reagan's personal interest in North American amicability, and, more important now, his personal relationship with Mulroney.

Senator Richard Lugar, chairman of the key Senate Foreign Relations Committee, has said, "If the President moves with the spirit of the Canadian government to lessen trade barriers, to move toward free trade, Congress will not block those initiatives." The revisions to the U.S. Trade Act of 1984 as approved by Congress provided specifically for free trade pacts to be negotiated with Israel and Canada. Agreements made with these countries can be given so-called "fast-track" treatment by the two Houses. The right words said at the right time by Reagan would speed the process along.

In the middle of this process, though, there is a large "But." Congressional reaction to a genuine free trade agreement with Canada would be one thing. The notion of rewriting history might seduce congressmen into acting like statesmen. Congressional reaction to a limited pact would be something quite else. Released from the need to act like statesmen, congressmen would perform as representatives of their constituents' interests; in turn, lobbyists would push to the limit the interests of American industries that might be threatened by increased Canadian exports.* It's doubtful Reagan would want to invest much of his political capital on behalf of a minor commercial arrangement.

To get what it wants – a significant improvement in security of access – the Mulroney government may have to give far more than it wants to. But real free trade, even if not all that big a deal economically, is, potentially, a very big deal politically. Not at first, but beginning the day after the deed is done.

In a 1975 study for the Economic Council, political scientist Peyton Lyon reviewed the historical record of free trade arrangements and concluded that, except for the nineteenth-century German *Zollverein*, "there is no significant example of political union being preceded by the removal of barriers to trade."

The circumstances in North America are unique, though. An obvious difference is that just two countries of widely differing size are involved, in contrast to the European economic union. Perhaps more important, the major European powers have had a long experience of accommodating contiguous small neighbours, while

---

* The 1983–84 proposed sectoral trade deals suffered this fate. Despite the best efforts of officials on both sides, industries kept enumerating the losses they might sustain by even the most limited of sectoral pacts. By the fall of 1984, when the government changed, not a single sectoral deal had been agreed to, even in the least contentious of all sectors, that of agricultural equipment.

Canada is the only test case the U.S. has experienced until recently.

Since the circumstances are unique, so are the potential political consequences. Some should be beneficial. To the extent free trade benefited Canada economically, it also would generate extra revenues to underwrite Canadian political independence: social support systems could more easily be maintained, and, similarly, Canadian culture. Just the closing of the cross-border economic gap would strengthen national cohesion; genteel poverty is a recipe for political impotence. Although critics fear that a bilateral pact might cut Canada off commercially from the rest of the world, its more probable effect would be the direct opposite. With the exception of the specialized case of "tied-aid" exports, all Canadian companies selling abroad learn their first lessons in the U.S. and then hopscotch from there to elsewhere.

The most important political benefit of free trade could be to help liberate Canadian foreign policy. The assumption, a reasonable one, has been that any increase in Canada's export dependency on the U.S., now the destination for three-quarters of all Canadian exports, would increase Canada's political dependence on the U.S. The opposite could happen. Until now, Canadian governments have justified their silence by the fear of U.S. economic retaliation. A free trade pact that "tied" the U.S. hands could liberate a Canadian government – provided it really wanted to be liberated.

All of this is reassuring. But much of it is iffy. The central fact about a bilateral pact is that by signing it Canada would be jumping into the elephant's bed. After 200 years of saying "yes and no," Canadians would have said "yes, yes, yes." Bilateral free trade would be irreversible. Once the "leap of faith" had been taken there could be no jumping out of the bed, even if the elephant, in a wholly amiable way, started to roll over.

No doubt the elephant would roll over one year or other. This scarcely is a new experience for Canadians. The real political risk is, instead, a second-order one: that over time the bed itself would shrink. The implacable logic of a Canada-U.S. free trade pact is that it would evolve first into a customs union and eventually into a common market or full continental economic union.

Supporters of free trade always deny this. Yet their denials are curiously cursory. In *Taking the Initiative*, an excellent and balanced study of the issue published by the C.D. Howe Institute in May, 1985, economists Richard Lipsey and Murray Smith devote just one among 183 pages to the possible evolution of a free trade area into more integrated arrangements. They conclude that these would be "unacceptable" to Canadians and thereafter treat the matter as settled.

One way to guess what may happen in the future is to review the past. Up until less than five years ago, free trade itself was "unacceptable" to Canadians.* Today it has become almost the conventional wisdom, espoused by the Macdonald Commission, the C.D. Howe Institute, all the major business organizations from the Business Council on National Issues to the Canadian Manufacturers' Association to the Canadian Chamber of Commerce, the western premiers, the government of Quebec, and a clear majority of federal cabinet ministers. Vocal opposition to free trade is limited to the Ontario government, some unions, a small number of economic nationalists, and *The Toronto Star*. Once free trade was enacted, it is hard to imagine why this same conventional wisdom, by summoning up the same arguments of economic advantage and necessity, would not move on to espouse a customs union and later full economic union. This was Lord Lansdowne's conclusion 100 years ago and that of Mitchell Sharp in his 1972 "Third Option" paper. Nothing has changed since.

This progression isn't preordained. But it would be propelled forward by the logic of economic efficiency. In a customs union Canada and the U.S. would jointly agree on common tariffs to be applied to all other countries. The pressure for this to happen would be intense. If Canadian and American tariffs on third-country products remained widely different, exporters in those countries would route their products to whichever North American market imposed the lower tariffs and then transship them duty-free from there to the other country. As an illustration, in 1985, following the imposition of U.S. quotas on steel, countries such as South Korea and Brazil increased their exports to Canada; to prevent cross-border "leakage" Canada had to require these products to be stamped clearly with their country of origin. Strict customs inspections at the Canada-U.S. border could contain the problem, but this additional paperwork would defeat the purposes of bilateral free trade.

---

* The political "ice" was broken by the Trudeau government's September, 1983, policy paper proposing, very tentatively, possible sectoral deals.

The step beyond a customs union would be full economic union, as in Western Europe. A bilateral pact would extend to all goods and services the virtual free trade that now exists in capital flows (also in energy products). Only free trade in labour would be left to complete the equation. Today, all Canadian and American citizens with means can become citizens of the other country without great difficulty. The logic of keeping unemployed Canadians as "hostages" while corporation executives and professionals can so easily move across the border will be hard to sustain.

No way exists to prove or disprove that a free trade area would lead inexorably to a North American common market, but one harbinger of the future has already appeared. At their annual meeting in Grande Prairie, Alberta, in May, 1985, the premiers of B.C., Alberta, Saskatchewan, and Manitoba approved a resolution that called for a "Canada-U.S. common market" rather than just for free trade. It's probable that the premiers really didn't understand the terminology; but they used it, and they were not greeted by cries of "unthinkable."

If the ultimate consummation happens, it probably wouldn't be until around the turn of the century. By then, the two economies would be so closely integrated that the last yielding would be imperceptible. But today's decision will determine what will happen then.

Free trade thus has the contradictory characteristics of being at one and the same time less of a big deal than is often supposed, and, potentially, the biggest deal of all in Canadian history. Unless implemented as part of an integrated industrial strategy, its economic consequences will be considerably less than its supporters expect; over time, its political consequences are likely to be as great as its opponents fear. To this latter conclusion, one significant qualification must be made: much of the economic integration attributed to free trade is underway already; whether or not a formal pact is negotiated, Canadian companies can only compete with American companies if they are as efficient as them – are very like them, in other words.

By mid-1985, Mulroney had begun to sound increasingly uncertain on the subject. Any kind of a pact, he told reporters just after Parliament had adjourned in July, "would probably meet with an overwhelming degree of ambivalence. You would get six and you would lose half a dozen, in typical Canadian fashion." This uncertainty was shared by the cabinet. Stevens, the most influential of the economic ministers, strongly opposed a comprehensive agreement. Kelleher favoured one but his report to cabinet merely summarized the opinions he had collected across the country rather than advocated any one option. A joint report on a negotiating schedule was due to be completed by Kelleher and Yeutter and presented to the two governments in September, the same month that the Macdonald Commission report, with its call for full free trade, was due to be published.

At the time this is written, the likelihood is that the government will enter into open-ended negotiations late in 1985. If all that emerges is a rather modest commercial pact – some new legalisms to make access "more secure," some shaving of tariffs – then the matter won't have been worth the time and energy expended on it by the government nor all the print used up on the subject, including in this book.

A true free trade pact that would eliminate or substantially reduce most tariff and non-tariff barriers would be another matter. To a considerable extent, it would codify and confirm the near-free trade that already exists. Its essence would be in its exemptions. Continued protection for cultural industries would be the key. Without that, there could be no assurance of Canadian distinctiveness. The negotiations would be tough because Americans quite genuinely don't comprehend why Canada, unlike the U.S., cannot let its cultural industries thrive or shrivel in the marketplace. If that lesson cannot be taught, then no trade pact can even be considered. Equally, an exemption would have to be secured for Canadian economic and social programs, such as regional equalization; the trade-off here, unstated in the fine print, would be with U.S. defence-spending.

At a guess, the Mulroney government is more likely to play it safe than to take the risk of being politically sorry. If so, the entire subject can be shifted to the back pages of the newspapers. Depending on how the negotiations unfold, though, it may decide to seize the historic, and almost certainly last, chance to fulfil economic logic and to restructure the economy by the mechanism of a full free trade pact.

That choice, if it is decided on, should be decided by Canadians and not by the government of the moment, a government moreover that did not seek a free trade mandate during the election campaign. A choice in favour of free trade today would represent, almost certainly, a choice for North American economic union tomorrow. This is the ultimate choice of Canadian history. The cardinal fact about such a choice – perhaps the core of the doubt that caused King to say "no" to his own free trade deal in 1948 – is that the government that made it would not be around to answer for its full consequences; only historians would be able to judge whether the great dare had succeeded or whether the cure had worked economically but the patient had died politically.

It may well be the case that the imperatives of the global marketplace make economic integration inevitable anyway. More important, it may well be the case that Canadians are now politically cohesive enough and self-confident enough to cope with the political pressures that would be generated by continental economic union. A national declaration of a readiness to compete head-to-head with the U.S. would be like the exorcising of the last of Canada's devils. These are calculations of the heart and spirit that only Canadians collectively, and not their political representatives, can and should make.

In their referendum of May, 1980, Quebecers demonstrated their self-confidence in Confederation, and in themselves. If a free trade agreement, rather than some modest commercial pact, is negotiated between Ottawa and Washington, the final choice between "yes" or "no" should be made by Canadians in a national referendum. Canadians then would be rewriting their own history. The decision they took would be theirs to live with.

Chapter Twenty
Good Relations, Super Relations

"As a name for the nation, perhaps Uscan, or Canusa,
or (better?) Namerica."

The Economist, April, 1985

On September 24, 1984, a few days after Brian Mulroney became
Prime Minister, the *Wall Street Journal* published an interview he
had granted to its Ottawa correspondent. Mulroney used the opportunity to tell the audience of American businessmen that he wanted
to reach what he wanted it to hear about Canada's new attitude
toward foreign investment. Midway through, the reporter asked about
Canadian-American relations in general. Mulroney replied: "Good
relations, super relations, with the United States will be the cornerstone of our foreign policy."

Commentators picked up on the phrase "good relations, super
relations" and applauded or tut-tutted according to their own
inclinations. The key word slipped by without remark. This was
the word "cornerstone." No Canadian prime minister had ever said
anything remotely like it. The character of Canadian foreign policy
was being changed more decisively than at any time since the Second
World War.

In interviews, politicians sometimes say more than they intended
under the pressure or the excitement of the moment. In February,
1985, in Kingston, Jamaica, where he was attending his first international conference, of the Commonwealth Caribbean heads of
government, Mulroney confirmed that he had meant what he'd said.
In his set speech, he covered familiar ground by describing how the
Canada-U.S. relationship had been "refurbished" to focus on areas
of agreement rather than on topics of discord. He then continued:
"A more co-operative and clearly defined relationship [with the U.S.]

will provide a solid foundation for the conduct of Canada's global foreign policy."

Whether as its cornerstone or as its foundation, Canadian foreign policy is to be built upon, and to be accommodated to, "good," "super," "co-operative" relations with the U.S. A kind of straight-jacket has been wrapped around Canada's international purposes. It doesn't immobilize us. But it does redefine the ways that Canadians can walk around on the world's stage.

The first observer to recognize the nature of the fundamental change that had been made to the design of Canadian foreign policy was *Globe and Mail* columnist Jeffrey Simpson. In a column written right after the Shamrock Summit between Reagan and Mulroney in March, 1985, Simpson made the crucial distinction between "sovereignty," upon which Mulroney and External Affairs Minister Joe Clark had laid such stress in their public comments during the meeting, and "independence." Sovereignty, in matters such as the new North Warning radar system that Mulroney and Reagan had formally signed during the summit, wasn't at issue, wrote Simpson: "We have yielded none of it." Instead, "The casualty is the independence of our foreign policy." The consequence of "tying ourselves so tightly to American foreign policy ... as an implicit trade-off for better [economic] treatment," he continued, had been "that whatever shreds of cred-ibility we had as an 'honest broker' or 'mediator' have been reduced to nil."

Other observers arrived at the same conclusion, if in different ways. In a glowing cover story about the summit, *Time* concluded that it showed that "Canada was not only the U.S.'s staunchest ally but a strong supporter of American military leadership." A few weeks later, *The Economist* ran an editorial observing that, "No, Brian Mulroney won't turn Canada into Ronald Reagan's 51st state, but shouldn't somebody, someday, somehow?" As names for the new continental nation *The Economist* suggested, "Uscan, or Canusa, or (better?) Namerica."

Press analyses aren't carved in stone. Mulroney took a dig at them in an interview with the *Financial Times* of London in July, 1985. Asked whether Canada was "in the U.S.'s hip pocket," he replied, "That's a product of small minds and of really indolent journalism."

Mulroney indeed has on several occasions exercised his "brief" to defend Canada's sovereign interests with determination and skill. At his first meeting with Reagan, in June, 1984, he brought up the issue of the "extra-territorial" application of U.S. laws to U.S. subsidiaries in Canada and, although as Opposition Leader his views commanded little authority, he made it plain he regarded this as unacceptable treatment of a sovereign nation. In contrast to Trudeau, who never once mentioned acid rain during his meetings with Reagan or with Carter, Mulroney has made action on this issue the "highest priority" in his encounters with Reagan. The North Warning System Agreement will place all the northern radar stations under full Canadian control, unlike the preceding DEW (Distant Early Warning) line system that was fully paid for and managed by the U.S. Defence Department.

Yet a "brief" is just that, the side of a case a lawyer argues because it is the side that benefits his client of the moment. The lawyer himself or herself doesn't necessarily hold any opinions on the merits or otherwise of the matter. As Prime Minister, Mulroney is his own client. He fabricates his brief, as well as argues it. His policy becomes the nation's policy.

Sovereignty is legal form. It is the preoccupation of lawyers. Independence is national substance. It is the stuff of leadership. In the distinction between the two lies Canada's challenge in the 1980s. The question mark that will frame Mulroney's term as Prime Minister is whether he will maintain the appearance while giving up the substance; and, no less, whether Mulroney will do this without realizing that he has done it.

All those who know Mulroney say of him, "What you see is what you get." He is what he is, charming, savvy, pragmatic, with no hidden inner doubts or any hidden inner dreams. He wants to be liked, as is well known. Far less clear is what he wants to do with the power he has pursued for so long and has at last gained.

In his biography, *Mulroney, The Making of the Prime Minister*, L. Ian MacDonald recounts that during a rare quiet moment in January, 1984, while still Opposition Leader, Mulroney described to aides "[what] he would like to be remembered in history for": a constitutional settlement that included Quebec; restructuring of the economy; improved economic and social conditions for native people; and "consolidating a distinctive role for middle powers in the world." Another accounting, and a much more direct one, is provided by

306

one of Mulroney's principal advisers. On more than one occasion since he became Prime Minister, Mulroney has told him, "I want to be remembered in history as a manager. Except by King, this country hasn't been managed since John A. Macdonald."

The two accounts aren't mutually exclusive. The first is a kind of wish list. The second has about it a quality of self-analysis, as if Mulroney had taken the measure of his own strengths, as a negotiator, as a mediator with an exceptional aptitude for gaining the confidence of both parties to a dispute, and had projected these into a national mandate for himself. Except that in the matter of Canada-U.S. relations, Mulroney himself comes to the bargaining table with his own predispositions formed by his own character and experiences.

Of all Canadian prime ministers, Mulroney is the most wholly North American. He likes Americans, he understands them, and he admires unstintingly the American dynamic of egalitarian individualism of which his own climb from Champlain Street in Baie Comeau to 24 Sussex by way of the presidency of Iron Ore of Canada amounts to a shining example. In *Mulroney*, MacDonald provides an insight into the tensions and misunderstandings that exist between Mulroney and Canadian intellectuals, most of whom tend to be nationalists: "They were generally Protestant, high-minded and disapproving about displays of affluence. He was Catholic, upwardly mobile, with no reticence about living at the top of the hill."

Mulroney's liking for Americans doesn't make him that unusual. Pearson, for instance, shared it. Mulroney's distinctiveness among Canadian leaders lies rather in his lack of fear of America itself; it sets off in him neither alarm bells nor self-doubts.

The formative influence here was perhaps not so much Mulroney's boyhood in Baie Comeau, important though that was, as his adult life as a Quebecer. Quebecers have never felt threatened by American political power in the way that English Canadians have. Perhaps more significantly, Mulroney has participated personally in the struggle for survival of two minorities, French Canadians and Anglo-Quebecers. Both were threatened every bit as much as Canada's nationhood may be by the overshadowing omnipresence of the U.S.; and both have survived. As a politician, Mulroney is well aware that Canadian voters become uneasy when the cross-border embrace seems to be too tight. Within himself, he doesn't share that unease, essentially because he himself has wriggled out of tighter embraces, collectively both as a Quebecer and as an Anglo-Quebecer. He knows also that his term as president of a branch plant, the Iron Ore Company, won for him permanent financial self-sufficiency.

Mulroney first made his mark, at the age of seven or eight, singing "Dearie" for Colonel Robert McCormick, owner of the *Chicago Tribune*, in the dining room of the Le Manoir hotel built to provide visiting executives with some of the comforts they'd grown used to in Chicago and New York. Mulroney earned $50 for his performance. He gave the money to his mother, and also all the later tips he earned entertaining the "Colonel" with Irish ballads and French-Canadian folksongs.

Plenty of other Canadians, and Americans, began their careers in the same kind of way and in the same kinds of places – company towns created out of nowhere by absentee capital parachuted down into the hinterland, but creating there jobs and decent houses and adequate schools, and, as a byproduct of all of this, making it possible for some of the children of the workers, those who were nervy enough and energetic enough, eventually to make their way out of the hinterland and into the metropolis.

In the 1984 campaign, the phrase Mulroney used most often in his speeches was "small towns and big dreams." It was a bit corny. But it was pure Mulroney. He himself had dreamt big and had realized his dreams. He believes that every Canadian can do the same. He believes equally that it is irrelevant if the small town where the dreams begin happens to be a company town owned by absentee capital. The magic ingredient is "jobs, jobs, jobs"; once those are created, in whatever way, everything else becomes possible.

Here, Mulroney differs from many others who have made their start in life in the way he did. Often, those who have escaped from company towns carry with them a sense of anger at the dependency they, and their parents, once were trapped in. Even personal success doesn't soften the resentment they still feel at "the mine," "the mill," "the fish plant" that hired and fired, rewarded and punished, on the basis of orders sent along a 1,000-mile telephone line. Mulroney, by contrast, proudly recounted the story of singing for Colonel McCormick to the Economic Club of New York when he spoke there on December 10, 1984.

In their otherwise unrelievedly laudatory biography, *Brian Mulroney*,

Rae Murphy, Robert Chodos, and Nick Auf der Maur relax enough to make a couple of at least implicitly critical comments. Of Mulroney's upbringing in Baie Comeau, they remark, "There is no evidence Mulroney ever saw anything wrong with this scheme." On the broader subject of Canada-U.S. relations, they comment, "Mulroney sees Canada as in firm lockstep with the U.S. It is not making light of the simplicity of his position to suggest that he accepts the Yalta theory of spheres of influence as it applies to Canada."

In Baie Comeau, and equally during his five years as president of the Iron Ore Company of Canada, the lockstep relationship that Mulroney experienced was direct and palpable: orders came along the telephone line from Chicago or Cleveland. The university he first attended, St. Francis Xavier in Antigonish, Nova Scotia, happens to attract more students from across the border than any other in the Maritimes, including many of its best football players. Later, at Laval University, when beginning to emerge as a serious politician, he was deeply moved by and excited by the election of an Irishman as President of the United States; his biographer, L. Ian MacDonald, has commented that Mulroney modelled his sonorous oratory on the rolling rhetoric that Ted Sorensen used to craft for Kennedy. Mulroney almost always holidays in the U.S. He follows American politics almost as closely as he does Canadian, and his encyclopedic knowledge of their system has dazzled politicians and officials in Washington.

None of this makes Mulroney less of a Canadian in any respect. It does, however, make him a certain *kind* of Canadian. He is in a sense a Canadian of the 1950s, a product of the era of "Good Neighbours," when most Canadians aspired to be like Americans. The doubts about the nature of American society that many Canadians came to hold through the 1960s and 1970s never affected Mulroney. He was by then too concerned with his career and also too absorbed by the political excitement and pressures in Montreal. A friend says, "He would like to have the respect of the nationalists, but he genuinely believes they are wrong." So he can at times sound like an echo of an easier, less complicated past.

A couple of examples. At a press conference in December, 1984, after he had given his "Canada is open for business again" speech to the Economic Club of New York, Mulroney was asked if he was concerned about nationalist criticism of his open-door policy. He replied, "I am concerned about the 1.6 million Canadians out of jobs, who are not concerned about nationalism and who are concerned about providing for their families." Earlier, in November, 1983, not long after the U.S. invaded Grenada, he was asked how he would have responded had he been Prime Minister. Daringly, given the widespread criticism in Canada of the invasion, Mulroney replied, "If our friends need the benefit of the doubt from time to time, so be it; I'm going to do it."

There is a postscript to the second incident. In private, Mulroney told aides that he had been shocked by Reagan's failure to advise Trudeau of U.S. intentions. "When I become Prime Minister, we're going to do better than that," he told a close associate. To be consulted is to be paid proper dues as a sovereign nation. The reason Canada wasn't consulted, though, was because Reagan knew that Trudeau's answer would be negative; he knew, in other words, that Canada was independent. The one is form. The other is substance.

During the 1984 election campaign Mulroney said as little as he could, and he has since paid a price for that tactic. He did, however, tell Canadians all they needed to know about what he would do about Canada-U.S. relations. Those relations would be friendly; "we can disagree without being disagreeable." Barriers to trade would come down; investment would be made to feel welcome again. To earn influence in Washington and in other Western capitals, Canada would pay its defence dues: "We are a Western nation, and we share the same democratic values as all the members of the alliance." The one additional element to the cross-border equation that Mulroney did not mention – could not have mentioned because it would have sounded like bragging – was his personal relationship with Ronald Reagan.

Between Mulroney and Reagan there is the comradeship of kin, quite natural and unaffected yet potentially of immense political significance. It happened almost instantaneously, somewhat like the relationship between King and Roosevelt a half-century ago. Within minutes of their first meeting in the White House in June, 1984, Reagan and Mulroney were trading cornball Irish jokes and campaign anecdotes. Today, they phone each other more than once a month and trade notes more frequently. One who has watched them together compares their relationship to "that of a revered uncle and a favoured nephew," adding though that while Mulroney is respectful he never acts awed. No laboured explanation is needed for Mulroney's admiration of Reagan's power and success. Reagan seems to see in Mulroney something of himself from long ago. There is the common Irishness, of course, though with Reagan the connection with Ireland is pretty distant. Both are doers rather than thinkers. Both are native optimists. Both are superb communicators. Both, and perhaps this is the strongest common denominator of all, are political outsiders who feel themselves to be apart from the permanent governing establishment and who rejoice in their distance from it.

"The calls to and from Ottawa get noticed in the White House log and the word goes through the system, 'Mulroney is in,'" comments a Washington official. "This is a power town, and the President is the President." At the first "country review" of Canadian affairs in January, 1985, in advance of the Shamrock Summit, U.S. officials representing more than sixty agencies were present; the best guess is that an equivalent gathering even for Britain would attract no more than twenty-five. More American cabinet ministers scrambled aboard Air Force One to attend the summit than ever have before for any cross-border meeting of leaders.

The summit itself was mostly show-biz hokum, a mix of "photo ops" of the two leaders staring down at the St. Lawrence from the battlements of the Citadel and of astronaut Marc Garneau emerging coyly from a cloud of dry ice in the centre of the stage of Quebec City's Le Grand Theatre. But there was substance as well as symbolism: the North Warning System agreement; a Pacific salmon treaty signed after fifteen years of haggling; and at least a face-saving gesture about acid rain.

The most important illustration of the effect of presidential favour happened before the summit. The U.S. Defence Department has always been the most difficult of Washington agencies for Canadian officials to bargain with, mostly because Canada, in its view, doesn't pull its defence weight. Suddenly, the Pentagon started performing like a lamb. Earlier, it had insisted on retaining complete control over the North Warning System, as in the case of the DEW line, and on paying the full shot. But as the summit loomed, the Pentagon ceded full management control of the new radar network to Canada; in exchange, Canada would pay 60 per cent of the costs, about $760 million. Just as usefully, the Pentagon agreed to reserve the thirty-

311

nine unmanned stations for Canadian suppliers even though it had already awarded Sperry-Rand the contract to develop two prototype stations.

The most dramatic example of presidential favour occurred during the summit itself. In the course of a casual meeting with Mulroney before lunch on the last day, Reagan, to the delight of the Canadians present and to the equal dismay of the American officials, departed from his script to pledge that he would "go to bat" for Canada against trade protectionist measures threatened by Congress or by regulatory agencies. And while it's uncertain just how often Reagan can afford to use up his Congressional credits as a favour to "the other North American Irishman," it is entirely certain that no comparable pledge has been made since 1936 when Roosevelt "went to bat" for King and secured for him the first Canada-U.S. trade deal since Confederation.

As a people politician rather than a politician of ideas, a consensus politician, in other words, rather than a politician of conviction, Mulroney believes that the way to solve problems is by getting on with people. He learned this lesson in labour-management relations and in backroom politics; he is convinced it applies no differently to international affairs. Thus, Mulroney's personal friendship with Reagan is the foundation of his Canada-U.S. policy.

One problem with international friends is that they are busy people, preoccupied most of the time by their own domestic necessities. Although Mulroney let Reagan know he hoped for someone more senior, Reagan yielded to the urgings of Secretary of State Shultz on behalf of a protégé and in June, 1985, appointed as Paul Robinson's successor as U.S. ambassador in Ottawa a career officer, Thomas Niles, the most junior person to be given the post since the Second World War. The day after the summit, Reagan filled a cabinet vacancy by appointing Bill Brock, who had a strong personal interest in negotiating a bilateral trade pact, as Secretary of Labour. If no telephone call went from Washington to Ottawa in advance of the Grenada invasion of 1983, neither did any come in advance of the U.S. trade embargo on Nicaragua in 1985.

Another problem of personal relationships is that they can become a distraction from the real work of diplomacy. Through the summer of 1985, American and Canadian officials worked frantically behind the scenes to head off Congressional protectionist measures against Canadian softwood lumber. This was a genuine payoff for the "special

312

relationship." In the process, though, a lot of Canada's political credit in the bank got used up. The concern in both Ottawa and Washington was less the issue itself than that if Congress blocked Canadian lumber imports, invidious comparisons would be made that back in 1983, even though Trudeau then was Prime Minister, a similar Congressional attack on Canadian softwood lumber failed. For the relationship to be seen to be "special," in other words, had become an end in itself.

Personal relationships certainly do play a part, but often only a bit part in international relationships. The friendship between Kennedy and Pearson made not the slightest difference to the cross-border rows about economic nationalism during 1963; Trudeau got on splendidly with Carter, but concocted the NEP while he was President. Trudeau and Reagan didn't get on at all, yet Trudeau's meeting with Reagan during his peace initiative was as productive as anyone could have anticipated. Objective reality defines the relationship between nations. Cordiality between leaders can put grease on the wheels; the ways in which the wheels themselves spin and the directions in which they turn are determined by the conflicting self-interests and value systems and the relative strengths and weaknesses of the two countries.

Economics dominated the cross-border reality when Mulroney assumed office. To oversimplify, though only barely, Canada needed help. Investment capital was leaving the country; most worryingly, the low value of the Canadian dollar failed to attract American investors. The unemployment rate was half as high again as south of the border. Almost the only economic momentum that existed was being provided by the influence of the U.S. recovery. None of Mulroney's remedies occasioned much surprise. FIRA would be replaced by Investment Canada. The NEP would be dismantled. Cross-border trade would be "secured and enhanced."

Nationalists were disheartened. Still, they ought to have allowed themselves at least one cheer. A government that had scorned economic nationalism while in opposition was within a year becoming subtly converted to that creed: plans were announced to try to increase Canadian ownership of the publishing industry; a major behind-the-scenes effort was made to ensure that Gulf Canada passed into Canadian hands; Industry Minister Sinclair Stevens declared that he hoped to guarantee a permanent share of the Canadian market for

313

threatened industries such as textiles. Except in energy, and to a degree in investment, the Mulroney government gave up relatively few hostages to continental economic reality, no more probably than would have a Liberal government headed by John Turner.

Instead, the aspect of continental reality that has become central is an aspect that Canadians have scarcely even thought about, let alone debated, for almost two decades. Suddenly, defence policy has become synonymous with foreign policy and so has become synonymous with national independence and national identity.

Chapter Twenty-one
Standing on Guard

"Any Canadian proposal for disarmament is, in the end, a proposal that someone else disarm."

Comment attributed to General E.L.M. Burns, former Canadian Ambassador for Disarmament

Among nations, Canada's defence problems have always been unique. This is because Canada has no defence problems, or no real ones. Canada has no natural enemies. Like Australia, the country is protected by water (by even more water than exists in the southwest Pacific); unlike Australia, Canada has the U.S. next door.

As a substitute for enemies of its own, Canada has found them second-hand among the enemies of its friends. The consequence has been a kind of schizophrenia in the nation's attitude toward military affairs. On the one hand, Canada's military efforts during both world wars as a lesser but important member of the Western alliances constituted a vital source of national pride. On the other hand, in between wars and also during them, Canada's military efforts have served as a painful reminder of national dependency: the ultimate decisions about where and how Canada's efforts should be applied are always made in someone else's capital.

Ironically, therefore, Canada's armed forces at one and the same time protect our national sovereignty and quite unintentionally serve to undermine it. In Canada, uniquely, "defence" is almost a misnomer; "paying of dues" might be a more accurate description. Once, Canada had to pay its dues for the benefits of membership in the British Empire by sending a contingent to battle the Boers in South Africa, later to stand in the mud of Flanders, and later still to slip and stumble and fall on the pebbled beach at Dieppe.

Since the 1950s Canada has had to pay its dues by doing its part in the undeclared war against "the evil empire." For more than a quarter of a century, a contingent of Canadian troops has been stationed in the path the Soviet tanks would follow if they ever rolled westward across Europe, as in fact few have seriously expected them to do since NATO's earliest years. But the dues being demanded today are of a quite different order. The Strategic Defence Initiative that everyone but Reagan calls Star Wars may or may not be, as its supporters claim, a potentially workable defensive system against nuclear missiles. It may or may not be, as its critics claim, a necessary element in a new offensive strategy. All that is certain is that the American empire has made up its mind to do it. Certain also is that the empire wants its northern dependency to play its part, as much for political and symbolic reasons as for military and technological ones.

Before describing the Star Wars issue, some background on the broader issue of defence policy may be useful. For about two decades after the Second World War, a national consensus existed that military dependency was normal. Memories of the wartime alliance were fresh; the Soviet threat was accepted as real. As well, a national commitment to NATO existed because of the role Canada had played in helping to create that alliance.

For roughly another two decades, from sometime in the mid-1960s to the early 1980s, the national consensus held that military matters themselves were irrelevant. Trudeau's decision in 1969 to cut back Canada's NATO contribution by half stirred little public debate; thereafter, the armed forces virtually vanished from the public's consciousness, and the politicians in tandem lost interest in spending money on defence.* The notion of a Soviet armed attack on Western Europe lost its credibility. Canada's contribution dwindled to a proportion that was not so much inadequate as futile: 5,000 armed servicemen among two million in Western Europe.

---

* As Canadians are constantly told, Canada's military spending is the lowest among NATO members except for Iceland and Luxembourg. The unstated part of this guilt trip is that this has been the case ever since NATO was created. Stated even less often is that NATO's real problem always has been that Western Europe, despite a larger economy and population than the Warsaw Pact, prefers to rely on the U.S. nuclear shield rather than spend the money needed to defend itself by conventional means.

The catalyst of change was the Falklands War. Just after Canadians had learned that the boilers of their destroyers were cracked, they saw on TV the cruisers and destroyers of the Royal Navy blown apart by the aircraft of a nation no one ranked as militarily advanced. Suddenly, the joke that Canada would have a hard time invading St. Pierre and Miquelon ceased to be funny. Peter Newman uncovered a receptive audience with his 1983 book, *True North, Not Strong and Free*, in which he wrote: "Our military are honourable and intelligent men and women who have given their country more defence than its dollars deserved to buy. It is time to redress the balance."

By the mid-1980s, therefore, Canadians had come to accept that they had let down their own servicemen, and perhaps had also let down their allies. An appreciation developed also that in order to realize any aspirations Canada might have to renewed international activism – to man peacekeeping or observer forces that might be set up in Central America, say, or to contribute more actively to intra-Caribbean defence, or to show the nation's flag around the Pacific Rim – armed forces of a minimum effective size and level of equipment were as necessary as skilled, well-trained diplomats.

Mulroney, while still in opposition, sensed and then expressed this new mood. He committed himself to an increase in defence-spending, and in the size of the armed services, from 82,000 to 90,000. Revealing of a change in the public's mood, during the 1984-85 public debate about how to reduce government spending in order to reduce the budget deficit, the value of this additional expenditure was never questioned. Yet Canadians had changed their minds only in a particular way. No new consensus existed about defence policy itself, as opposed to a national recognition that the effectiveness of the armed services had to be restored. When the call came to join in Star Wars research, Canadians were no readier to answer "Ready, Aye Ready" than during the years of doubt of the 1960s and 1970s. Indeed, they were less ready because Reagan, or his aides, had by then talked about the "winnability" of nuclear war and because Trudeau had shown by his peace initiative what political independence can amount to.

One of the few unscripted events of the two-day Shamrock Summit happened during an early morning CTV interview given by Defence Secretary Caspar Weinberger. The reporter, Craig Oliver, first confirmed that the North Warning System would be able to detect both bombers and cruise missiles. Would the step beyond be an "active defence" that might involve "launchers being placed in Canada?" he then asked. "What we would try to do would be to locate the best places for defences," replied Weinberger. "Some might be here, some might be in the United States, some might be at sea. It just depends on where the most effective technical place would be for them to be put."

Weinberger's answer was sensible and honest: if anti-cruise missile "launchers" were ever developed, they would obviously go wherever they would be most effective, on whichever side of the border. Weinberger's one mistake was to forget that he was not being interviewed in the U.S. At the state dinner that evening, Reagan engaged in much the same kind of amiable geographic forgetfulness. In his speech, he denounced the Russians for breaking international agreements, lauded the "freedom movements arising everywhere," as in Nicaragua, praised the Strategic Defence Initiative as "the most hopeful possibility of the nuclear age," and offered to "share with you, technology that could provide a security shield."

Between them, Reagan and Weinberger had illuminated for Canadians the distinction between national sovereignty and national independence. As a sovereign nation, Canada had the full right to join or not to join in Star Wars research; equally, Canada had the right to accept or to reject anti-cruise missile "launchers," nuclear-armed or otherwise. This was theory. In reality, only a truly independent nation could say "no," a nation, that is to say, prepared to accept the consequences of a "no," such as a withdrawal of economic favours. That choice now confronts Canadians; some background may elucidate its dimension.

The single vital military asset Canada brings to the Western alliance has always been its own geography. A Soviet attack on the U.S. would have to cross some 2,000 miles of Arctic and sub-Arctic wasteland. During that traverse, the attack would be detected and a counter-attack would be launched that would transform the original attack into a suicidal sortie. The guarantee against a global holocaust amounts to the U.S. retaliatory strike forces, the doctrine of Mutual Assured Destruction (MAD), and the empty expanse of Canada.

This triad applied until the late sixties. By then, intercontinental missiles had replaced the bomber as the principal Soviet threat. A defence against a bomber attack had been at least plausible with the American and Canadian interceptors of NORAD and with ground missiles such as the Bomarcs. No defence against ICBMs was imaginable. To forestall them from ever being launched, the capacity of the U.S. to launch a retaliatory strike now became critical; simultaneously, Canadian geography became largely irrelevant. Between the late 1960s and the early 1980s, NORAD's interceptor strength dwindled from 2,600 to 350.* Even the radar stations to track intercontinental missiles were sited in Alaska, in Britain, and in Greenland.

The cruise missile, which can be launched from Soviet bombers, has revalued Canada's real estate. The North Warning System will be able to track these bombers and cruise missiles and so provide enough warning for U.S. retaliatory forces to be launched.** Although it isn't easy to guide a fighter interceptor or a "launcher" onto the flight path of a cruise missile, because they hug the ground, an effective defensive system is certainly foreseeable. Its optimum location – its virtually certain location in fact – would be in Canada's North. (The North Warning System agreement provides for air strips to be built at "selected northern locations ... including missile and ammunition storage.") By itself, though, a defence against cruise missiles would amount to an exercise in futility. Only if intercontinental missiles, the heavyweights in the Soviet armory, could also be knocked down would a cruise-missile defence become worthwhile and indeed essential. Just conceivably, the Strategic Defence Initiative or Star Wars may one day make it possible to knock down intercontinental missiles – one bullet fired against another – by the unimaginably exotic technology of space-based laser beams and ultra high-speed computers.

Ever since Reagan announced the SDI program, in March, 1983, it has been assailed by criticism and doubts. Some sceptics are

---

* At a press conference in March, 1985, Mulroney accused the Trudeau government of putting Canada into a position of "unbecoming subservience" to the
U.S. by allowing the DEW line to run down; in fact, the decision to do this
was taken by the U.S. Defence Department, which paid for the full costs of
the system.

** Since nothing in defence technology is ever simple, it is possible that the North
Warning System will be obsolete by the time it comes into operation in 1992,
so that Canada's real estate will once again be devalued. Theoretically, bombers
and cruise missiles can be tracked most effectively by satellite rather than by
ground stations. The first such prototype satellite, Teal Ruby, is due to be
launched in January, 1986.

convinced it is not so much a military program as a cover for a massive pump-priming of U.S. industry to achieve commercially valuable technological spin-offs. Beyond any doubt Reagan himself believes that Star Wars may one day "outlaw nuclear war" by creating an impregnable defence around both the U.S.'s counter-force missiles and its population. Few experts believe this will be possible. Many worry that Star Wars will both precipitate a new arms race, and, by creating a kind of Maginot Line illusion about the possibility of a defence against missiles, encourage those who during the early Reagan years talked about the "winnability" of nuclear wars. One nightmare is that the Soviets, fearing that the defensive shield would actually work, might strike first before their missiles were rendered useless; the opposite nightmare is that American defence planners might press for a first strike, counting on Star Wars to ward off the reduced Soviet retaliatory strike. All of this is hypothetical. The immediate consequences of Star Wars are twofold: it has convinced the Russians to come to the bargaining table at Geneva; it has turned the first spiral of an entire new arms race that will keep the military-industrial complexes going until well into the twenty-first century.

In April, 1985, during a NATO defence ministers meeting in Brussels, Weinberger invited all the allies to take part in the $26 billion (U.S.) research program. The bait offered was research contracts, commercial spin-offs, and jobs. Britain, Japan, and West Germany, the last somewhat equivocally, said yes: France,* Norway, Denmark, and Australia said no. Canada said nothing. That silence remains unbroken.

Whether or not to join in Star Wars research represented a cruelly difficult decision. Not since 1957, when Diefenbaker, fresh in office, had to deal with the NORAD agreement negotiated by the outgoing St. Laurent government, has a brand new government been faced with an issue of such complexity and long-term importance. The Star Wars issue is not merely difficult to decipher; much of it is unknowable. The system may or may not work; if it does work, it may or may not be deployed and so breach the 1972 ABM (anti-ballistic missiles) Treaty. No way exists to prevent Star Wars-type

---

* France advocated a competing European SDI research program to be called Eureka.

research from being done, and it is being done in Russia. The difference with Reagan's program is one of scale. The scale of the project, some $4 billion worth of spending due in 1985-86 alone, will create a dependent military-industrial complex that will make it virtually impossible for any future president to cancel the program, as for instance Carter did with the neutron bomb. But whether the system will ever actually be deployed, around the turn of the century, with all its potentially fateful consequences for international stability (some Soviet response is inevitable) is today quite indeterminate.

In a much more minor key, many of the potential consequences to Canada cannot be assessed with conviction. The industrial benefits, for instance, are highly debatable. Several firms, such as Northern Telecom, Litton Systems, MacDonald-Dettwiler, and Spar Aerospace, could undertake important bits and pieces of research. The actual employment created might be only around 500 person years over a five-year term, according to a study by the Waterloo University Institute for Peace and Conflict Studies; on the minus side, some scientists would be pulled away from commercial research projects, and the spending itself amounts to what Jane Jacobs has called "transactions of decline." Even if the Mulroney government did say "no," these companies would still be able to bid for contracts, although their prospects would diminish sharply. The public response to an official "yes" or "no" is likewise conjectural. In July, 1985, the Gallup Poll reported that Canadians favoured involvement in Star Wars research by 53 per cent to 40 per cent. To politicians, however, the intensity of voters' feelings on a given issue matters more than quantitative counts: within the first six months of 1985, close to 5,000 individuals wrote to Ottawa about Star Wars. All but six urged the government to say "no."

Entirely understandably, the government for a while sounded mostly confused. In December, 1984, External Affairs Minister Clark declared that he was "worried by the implications" of Star Wars. Right afterwards, then Defence Minister Robert Coates, who had already discussed specific research contracts with top U.S. officials, declared that the program was exactly what was needed. Not until February, 1985, did Mulroney support Star Wars research, *by the United States*, as "prudent and necessary" in the light of comparable Russian research. Coates' successor, Deputy Prime Minister Erik Nielsen, continued to sound like a hawk about Canadian involvement and Clark like a dove. As a response to Weinberger's invitation (he originally set a deadline of sixty days for replies, but then waived it), Mulroney appointed a senior official, Arthur Kroeger, to study the whole issue and to report back to cabinet. Kroeger's confidential report, completed in July, made no recommendations but simply described all the factors involved, from the military and technical to the commercial and political. Separately, following the publication by Clark of a Green Paper on foreign policy, which in fact dealt almost entirely with trade matters, a Commons committee was set up to hold public hearings and to report by the end of August on the comments it had received on Star Wars but not necessarily to make recommendations of its own. This quite creative time-consumer delayed until the fall the moment when the government would have to make up its mind.

Like free trade, Star Wars is a decision about tomorrow that has to be taken today. What is done now will redefine what can and cannot be done in the years to come. Either Canada will click, irrevocably, into lockstep with U.S. defence policy and, therefore, with U.S. foreign policy, or it will break away, but at a cost, and perhaps a considerable one because of the symbolic importance of a "no" by so close an ally. At risk would be the "special relationship" Mulroney has so carefully developed with the U.S., in general, but in particular, personally, with the author of the Star Wars project. And it is this relationship that Mulroney counts on as a guarantee of economic favours.

At the time this is being written, Mulroney has yet to make up his mind. On several occasions he has allowed his anxieties to show. In May, 1985, while in London on his way to the Bonn economic summit, Mulroney told reporters he was "not enthusiastic" about joining a scheme in which "Canada may not be in a position to call the shots." The real decision at stake, though, may not be about Star Wars; it is, rather, about the nature of Canadian foreign policy itself, its purposes and its possibilities.

In their 1983 book, *Canada as a Principal Power*, political scientists John Kirton and David Dewitt argue that "American decline and a diffuse global environment have given Canada an opportunity to attain its true potential as one of the principal powers of the globe," a category in which they rank Britain and France. This surely is overstating the case, not least because reports of America's decline have turned out to be decidedly premature.

But if the international major league – one rung below the super-power league – is redefined as "Principal International Influence-Pedlars," then Canada surely could make a credible claim for membership along with Britain and France and some others such as Japan, China, India, and possibly West Germany, although its history limits its manoeuvring room. As "a regional power without a region," as it often has been called, Canada commands little power in the sense of being able to compel other nations to rearrange their affairs to suit its national interests. (One of the few Canadian exercises of this kind of *real politik* was Trudeau's development of a new aid program to French-speaking West Africa to amass allies to offset France's advocacy of Quebec's international aspirations within *La Francophonie*.)

Yet there are few international influence-pedlars that can match Canada, and certainly none among the other more-or-less comparable middle powers like Sweden, Yugoslavia, Australia, Mexico. Most of the reasons for this are familiar enough. Canada has no natural enemies and so has a reputation, substantially deserved, for being disinterested. Canada belongs to most of the best global clubs: the Western economic summit, NATO, the Commonwealth, *La Francophonie*, and OECD, as well as to all the various North-South gatherings. The "honest broker" label that Canadians have sometimes attached to themselves is thoroughly presumptuous since it implies that Canadians uniquely possess a maturity others lack. "Stand-by mediator" might be more appropriate. As aid donors, Canadians are moderately generous; few other countries are as liberal in their immigration policy or as open in accepting refugees (relative to size of population, the largest number of Indochina refugees came to Canada). Not least, diplomacy itself seems to be an acquired Canadian trait: it's been said, "Canadians make foreign policy like the Danes make furniture."

As international influence-pedlars, Canadians possess one other asset that is less often mentioned: Canada is a North American nation.* Except for that circumstance, Canada's international entrée would be that of a somewhat larger Australia or a more affluent Yugoslavia. Because of it, Canada is a middle power not like the others. Canadians, goes the international assumption, understand Americans as no one

---

* Mexico is of course a North American nation geographically, but not culturally or politically.

else does. Canadians, further, know their way around Washington in a way no one else does and enjoy a "special relationship" with the U.S. even during those periods when the phrase itself is out of vogue. On the one hand, no other country is tied as intimately to the U.S. as is Canada by the NORAD and Defence Production Sharing agreement. On the other hand, Canada got into the annual Western economic summit because U.S. support was strong enough to overcome the opposition of France.

Canada's international influence thus depends to a critical extent on its influence, real or perceived, on *the* international superpower. It's Canada's diplomatic equivalent of a legacy stored away in a bank. The question is, when to draw upon that legacy, for what purpose, and above all *how* to do it.

How to exercise influence most effectively isn't so much a difficult question as a variable and fungible question. By definition, influence itself is undefinable. When it is exercised behind closed doors, no way exists to establish whether it was effective or not, or even whether it was actually exercised at all. When it is exercised in public, no change in policy in the imperial capital will ever be credited to it. As an illustration, the most promising of Trudeau's specific proposals during his peace initiative called for a ban on the development of weapons systems to destroy high-altitude satellites. Through the winter of 1984-85, U.S. officials went out of their way to credit the authorship of this idea to France, and did so until Washington concluded that the idea itself was unacceptable.

Clark provided the Mulroney government's answer to this question not long after he took office. "You can only have influence," he said, "if you are known to be friends." The weak link in this analysis, pointed out to Clark right afterwards by his own departmental consultative committee, is that the common price exerted of friends is silence. In both world wars, for instance, the unstinting loyalty of Canada and other lesser allies earned them no say in the councils of war. The failure of the U.S. to consult about its trade embargo of Nicaragua is a minor illustration of the same theme. Amid the pressures of international decision-making, friends inevitably get taken for granted or are placated by gestures, such as the visit to Ottawa by the U.S. disarmament negotiator, Paul Nitze, in March, 1985, on the eve of the Geneva talks between the U.S. and Russia.

Equally though, nags don't get heard, even though they may be listened to as a diplomatic device to forestall an accusation of not having been listened to. A more subtle "punishment" is the withholding of the essential information without which diplomatic analyses can become mere opinion-mongering. (The reverse is also true: imperial leaders sometimes deliberately pass on selected strategic information to their dependencies to ensure their silence.)

Whether or not Trudeau actually influenced Reagan to moderate his Cold War rhetoric during their meeting at the White House in December, 1983, is impossible to establish. Beyond question, though, he established the right of lesser powers to identify independently their foreign policy views, and then to express them out loud in international forums. During his peace initiative Trudeau in fact never broke ranks with Western strategic policies; but he did break the "lockstep" of silence.

Trudeau not only said what he wanted to say, but he played to America's greatest strength. It is a competitive society, competing passionately within itself no less in political ideas and values than in commercial products. There is something absurd, pusillanimous even, in the argument that a political culture that could cope with Vietnam War demonstrators, the Chicago Seven, Daniel Ellsberg releasing the Pentagon Papers, let alone with Democratic presidential candidate Walter Mondale advocating the same nuclear weapons freeze that Canada, in November, 1984, voted against at the United Nations, could not cope with Trudeau, or his successor, talking about peace.

The notion of Canada as a competitor to the U.S. in foreign policy ideas might seem to be preposterous. About a decade ago, though, it would have seemed equally preposterous that a significant number of Canadian companies could be competing successfully in the home market of the greatest economic power in the world – as they are today.

Such a competition would always have to be of a very particular kind. Plainly and simply, Canadians and Americans like each other, and despite the occasional inevitable conflicts of self-interest, they trust each other. Some of the differences in foreign policy outlook are entirely circumstantial. Canada today is in many respects what the U.S. was a half-century ago before it acquired international strategic interests and responsibilities and so became involuntarily entrapped by the often brutal necessities of power. A world policeman simply cannot afford to behave as can an international scorekeeper, and at times a referee. Some of the differences are integral to the natures of the two societies. Canada uniquely is a liberal political culture. Canadians look out at the world through that prism. They see international affairs not as a contest between winners and losers but as an exercise in problem-solving; as a quest, if not for peace then for tolerably amicable relationships, and not as a winner-take-all competition.

A paradox about Canadian foreign policy is that although we put an uncommon amount of effort into it, few Canadian national interests exist abroad, even in trade (beyond the North American continent), that can be advanced by even the most adroit Canadian diplomacy. Instead, it is foreign policy itself that has become the expression of national interest. The Pearsonian myth still has a hold on the Canadian consciousness. Foreign policy is the way Canadians inform the world of the kind of people they are, and perhaps also repay part of the debt they owe to someone – God or nature – for the benign luck of their national circumstances.

At a press conference on February 4, 1985, Mulroney was questioned about his support for Star Wars research, by the U.S., which he had just announced. He replied, "We are not neutrals in regard to fundamental concepts of freedom and justice. We believe in democracy and we believe in the collective assertion of that by the West." In private, Mulroney has been less ornate: "If you act like a neutral, you get treated like a neutral." Perhaps most expressive is the phrase he uses often both in public and in private. "Ya dance with the lady that brung ya." But there is all the difference in the world between an evening of dances and a lifetime of living as one.

Some signs exist that Mulroney is trying to carve out an independent foreign policy. The appointment of former Ontario NDP leader Stephen Lewis as Ambassador to the United Nations is one of them. The development of a stricter policy toward South Africa is another. Foreign aid programs for Nicaragua are being expanded, and External Affairs Minister Clark has allowed his scepticism about Star Wars to show on several occasions. Clark is also engaged in an attempt to develop "counterweights" to Canada's isolation on the North American continent by greater involvement in organizations such as the Commonwealth and La Francophonie.

These initiatives are useful. They employ the instruments of foreign policy to confirm the Canadian character. But that character itself is defined by the crucible of the relationship, inescapably intimate,

326

irrevocably one-sided, between Canada and the United States. The empire now is waiting for an answer on Star Wars. If the reply is "yes," the character of Canadian foreign policy for the balance of this century will be compromised. We will have traded "secure access," in some form or other, for secure support. It's a trade that would turn the nation back into a colony.

Chapter Twenty-two
The Way We Might Go

"But now we are all quite
grown up and fir-
mly agreed to assert our right
not to be Amer-
icans perhaps
though on the other hand
not ever to be
unamerican.

Earle Birney, "Can. Hist."

In 1944, with the end of the war in sight, George Orwell wrote one of the most famous of his essays, "The English People." He tried to foresee the kind of world that would emerge from the holocaust of the war and to define a role that Britain, its strength sapped, might still play. "In the coming world of power politics, the English would ultimately dwindle to a satellite people, and the special thing that is in their power to contribute might be lost," Orwell wrote. "The outstanding – and by contemporary standards – highly original quality of the English, is their habit of not killing each other." Orwell described the cosy humaneness of British life and suggested that the society "could provide the much-needed alternative to Russian authoritarianism on the one hand and American materialism on the other."

Much of Orwell's analysis can be applied, with only a slight wrench and without too much wishful thinking, to contemporary Canada. The domestic agenda is just about complete for the time being. In a way it hasn't been able to do since the 1940s and 1950s, Canada can turn its creative energies outward, and southward. For the balance of this century, Canada's mission may be to find itself outside of itself.

To a point, this isn't new. The late Barbara Ward once described Canada as "the world's first international nation." She had in mind Canada's contributions to peacekeeping and foreign aid. Indeed, before that, Canada derived its substance from the outside, from the umbilical cords that attached it first to the British empire, then to the American empire. At the end of those cords was a society filled with self-doubt and uncertain whether it really could stand on its own feet. This was always the weakness in Ward's description, however flattering. If in some respects through the 1960s and 1970s, and more affirmatively during the "golden years" of Pearsonian diplomacy, Canada could claim to be an international nation, the claim was ill-founded because Canada itself was not a nation.

It is now. The Quebec referendum of 1980 and the constitutional patriation of 1982 and, as the last part of a triad, the 1985 settling of energy accounts with the West, even though it lacks the same quality of drama, certainly haven't created a New Jerusalem here. They have created instead a community that knows how to live with itself.

The timing of political developments can be uncanny, even if fluky. Canada has found itself at the very moment when it had to do so because all its umbilical cords have dropped away. Western Europe, long a psychological counterweight to U.S. predominance even if it has long since ceased to be a political or economic one, is receding over the horizon, turned inward in an almost desperate search for a cure for "Eurosclerosis," its seemingly endemic economic stagnation. At a guess, if and when Western Europe does turn outward again, it will turn eastward in an historic *Ostpolitik* or rapprochement with the "lost" half of the European subcontinent.

Canada's implicit "American option," never uttered out loud but present beneath the skin, has also vanished. Worries about annexation never amounted to much more than a way for Canadians to reassure themselves that the U.S. was interested in them. Today, the U.S. has lost its strategic interest in Canada's natural resources; it doesn't need any of them to build a Star Wars defence. The stake of the multinationals here has begun to dwindle. Most important, Americans have begun to reject actively the idea of continental union because it would "upset the political balance in a way that would mean the rewriting of American politics," as George Ball, the former Under-secretary of State, commented in 1984. In short, too many bleeding-heart liberals would be added to the republican mix.

329

Some see in the Pacific Rim a kind of alternative Third Option. This is an illusion. Canada's economic, political, and military presence there will always be marginal. Canada could function as a kind of human and cultural bridge between East and West. It speaks the two great languages of the West, and people from all over the West are here. So, too, are a growing number from Asia, their knowledge little capitalized upon. Canada has as well at least a window on the Pacific, in Vancouver, shared only by the U.S. and Australia among Western nations.

A more urgent challenge is for Canada to become at long last an American nation in the literal meaning of that term. Canada's non-involvement in its own hemisphere has always been justified by the need to avoid confrontations with the U.S. Instead, avoidance of conflicts with the U.S. – an argument always easy to sell in Canada – has itself been used to justify a certain genteel racism, a distaste for getting involved with unpredictable, undemocratic, Latin Americans. Canada's prolonged quasi-isolationism within the Americas mocks its pretentions to internationalism elsewhere. (There is an intriguing parallel between Canada's hankering to tilt away from the hemisphere and toward Europe and the similar stance adopted by its polar-opposite nation, Argentina.)

Of all the horizons that now beckon, the most expansive is the one that lies immediately to the south. The time is long overdue for Canadians, in Fulford's phrase, to fill up "the great empty space in our thinking." People who know themselves, as Canadians do now, can afford to get involved with anyone else, on any terms. The answer to Atwood's question, "After Survival, what?", may be found in the terms Kroker laid out, "A sustained and intensive reflection on the meaning of the technological experience *is* the Canadian discourse."

In the research, and more particularly in the writing, when vague impressions and half-formed instincts had to be fixed into the shape they would actually take in cold print, this book has taken a turn from its original line of progression. At the start, free trade seemed to be the central continental issue about which Canadians would have to make an historic decision.

That the Mulroney government will probably scale down its ambitions to that of a routine commercial pact is neither here nor there. What matters instead is that free trade itself, when considered carefully, turns out to be a good deal less than the big deal it is commonly presented as being. Virtual free trade already exists: "secure access" is a chimera. Free trade could still be consequential, but as a means of restructuring the economy if applied as part of an overall industrial strategy, rather than as a means of securing and enhancing trade. The fix, in other words, won't be quick, and if it is to work at all it will have to come as a comprehensive package. The attention given to free trade by the government has been grossly disproportionate to the comparative economic value of a real national debate about reform of the education system, say (alone among Western nations, Canada has never had such a debate), or about an overhaul of labour-management relations.

If the Mulroney government does gather up its nerve to seize what will be almost certainly Canada's last chance to negotiate a bilateral pact, the ultimate "yes" or "no" must be uttered by Canadians collectively rather than by their government of the moment. As economist Carl Beigie has remarked, bilateral free trade amounts to "sovereignty-association." The first step therefore would be the negotiation of an actual pact; exemptions for cultural industries would be essential, but the inclusion of "sunset" industries such as textiles would be as essential (subject only to transition arrangements) since otherwise the shock value of the exercise would be lost. Once negotiated, the pact should be put before Canadians in a national referendum, just as the British rewrote their own history in 1973 when they voted to join the European Common Market. The debate during the referendum campaign would be angry, exigent, educational, all the qualities that Canadian politics needs.

I would vote for free trade myself. Not easily, because free trade will almost certainly evolve into economic union. But most of the economic dislocations attributed to free trade are inevitable anyway; so, no less, is much of the impending, and already manifest, erosion of national economic sovereignty. In the global economy, money and technology and industrial know-how have become universal properties in the way that brute labour has always been. In the economic marketplace, people sustain themselves instead of being maintained by their governments. The global economic marketplace cannot be denied, or can be denied only at the cost of a regression to genteel poverty. With or without free trade, Canadians from now on will have to get by on their wits. To pretend otherwise is witless.

A free trade pact would entail considerable political risks. Its potential political benefits are directly proportional to those risks. A national vote in favour of bilateral free trade would represent the ultimate declaration by Canadians of self-confidence in themselves, confidence both in their ability to compete and in their ability to continue as a distinct political and social unit.

I would vote against Star Wars, although this isn't a fit subject for a referendum. The real question about Star Wars isn't whether the government eventually will say "yes" or "no" but why it did not say "no" immediately, in April, 1985, as Australia, Denmark, and Norway all did. (France also, though here the determinant may have been domestic political advantage.)

At stake are two separate issues: the structure of Canada-U.S. relations; the structure of Canadian foreign policy.

A "no" to joining the Star Wars research program would of course put in jeopardy the "special relationship" with the U.S. that Mulroney has revived since it was formally interred by Nixon in 1972. But this special relationship is founded on an illusion. Relations between Canada and the U.S. are special anyway because no two countries in the world are more alike nor are there any whose citizens more unaffectedly like each other. Yet Canadians, without realizing it, have undergone a collective rite of passage in the last few years. By the National Energy Policy and his peace initiative, Trudeau got the message through to American opinion-makers that a different kind of people live across the border – not just a different leader but a different people, who after all elected him. In the famous phrase of former Social Credit leader Robert Thompson, "Americans are our best friends whether we like it or not." Equally, Americans now recognize that Canadians are different, no matter whether Canadians like it or not and would at times prefer to return to the womb of the "special relationship." Henceforth, the cross-border relationship will be "special" only when the national self-interests happen to coincide.

Certainly, it makes a difference when the two leaders are personal friends. Amicability at the top works its way down the system at Washington, both within the administration and within Congress. Mulroney has used his political credits to mount a major attempt to head off Congressional protectionist measures against lumber and to ensure that the U.S. Coast Guard vessel *Polar Sea* abided by Canadian environmental rules as it butted its way through the Northwest Passage in August, 1985. But to expand good personal relations into a comprehensive "special relationship" is to envelop Canadian politics in a subtle straightjacket. In the months preceding the *Polar Sea* voyage, Mulroney deliberately avoided any public protest because to have done so would have enabled his critics to claim that the "special relationship" was valueless. The care and feeding of the special relationship, in other words, becomes a political end in itself. Rather than on "special" relations, or on "good" ones or "super" ones, Canadian dealings with the U.S. should surely be founded on normal relations, it being to both countries great benefit that, normally, these normal relations will be exceedingly good.

For Canada, in the mid-1980s, to return to the old "special relationship," paternalist on the one hand and adolescent on the other, amounts to a renewal of vows of dependency. More to the immediate point, it amounts to an attempt to trade economic favours for a Canadian foreign policy reorganized on the "cornerstone," the "foundation," of good political relations with the U.S. Because of that bargain, a decision about Star Wars puts at issue the entire structure of Canadian foreign policy.

Star Wars illuminates the paradox of the 49th parallel. Because of the integration of the two economies, and in particular of the two defence industries, a "yes" to Star Wars research would bring Canada proportionately more benefits than any other Western country, certainly when related to its comparative level of scientific and technological expertise. The Pentagon could allocate contracts in Canada with almost the same confidence it could allocate them within the U.S. At the same time, because of this integration, a "no" would expose Canada to a degree of possible economic retaliation that would not be true for other nay-saying allies, such as Australia.

The converse is equally true. Because the two countries are already so close, a "yes" would bind Canada to U.S. foreign and defence policy in a way that would not be true for Britain, say, or for Japan. But a "no" would represent a dramatic expression of independence in a way no other ally could achieve by the same hands-off policy.

All of these implications sort out into a simple equation: the greater the benefits, the greater the risks, either way. The risks, which are real, would magnify the benefit of a "no." Their existence would make it a clear signal sent southward and across the oceans of the kind of society that Canadians have created for themselves and intend to preserve.

The answer has to be "no." As the two economies become more integrated, as they inevitably will, free trade aside, the independent character of Canada's foreign policy will become the source of its particularity, its breathing hole through the ice; if that outlet is closed, the society within will suffocate. Some jobs may be lost; some technological expertise may be missed out on. But any other answer, including no answer at all as some in the government advise, would amount to saying "no" to the nature of Canada, to a denial of its distinctiveness and of its at least potential purposefulness.

Within North America, Canadians are distinct in two ways, one that they have created for themselves, the other the consequence of circumstance. Canada is unique on the continent because it is a liberal political culture. Also uniquely, but by happenstance, it is a middle power rather than a superpower.

The distinctive Canadian liberal political culture was born relatively easily, although by no means inevitably, out of post-war affluence. By devices such as colour-free immigration and regional equalization, a level of liberalism has been achieved in Canada for which there are very few if any equals anywhere. This accomplishment is being tested by harsher times, of which the almost inevitable consequence, as in Britain, is social polarization. When, and if, economic good times return, an inherent contradiction will remain between the new economy of the marketplace and the political culture of liberalism. The former is concerned with efficiency and with creating spaces in which winners can flourish, if necessary at the expense of losers; the latter is concerned with equity and with protecting losers, even at the cost of inhibiting winners. No grand intellectual schema exists to resolve this contradiction. But many of the inherited and acquired Canadian characteristics will now come in handy: pragmatism, civility, an aptitude for compromise, the ability to find a balance between the needs of the collectivity and those of minorities and individuals. Above all, liberalism preserved can preserve Canada's characteristic quality as a society in a state of *becoming*, a society, in short, with its future still reshaping its present.

As a middle power rather than a superpower, Canada is in some ways an America before the fall. It does not have to cope with the temptations that come naturally to superpowers, nor equally to the responsibilities that superpowers cannot escape. Canadian diplomats are not kidnapped, nor are Canadians abroad hijacked. We do not have to calculate whether the Soviet Union really is or is not ahead in some aspect of military deployment or technology. One temptation is to moralize. A more potent temptation was described by the former diplomat John Holmes in a 1973 article for *The Toronto Star*: "Unlike the Americans, our besetting sin has been avoiding rather than exaggerating our international responsibilities. If we want to replace a Pax Americana with something more multi-lateral, we have to take on some unpleasant assignments ourselves."

Defence is one such assignment that Canadians have looked squeamishly away from. One lesson taught by the Grenada affair had nothing to do with the lack of consultation. Rather, when the eastern Caribbean islands became genuinely concerned about their security it never occurred to them to look to their northern Commonwealth partner for help. Canada's diplomatic voice will be hollow unless there is behind it, not as a menace but as a known fact, a sufficiency of armed strength.

That this strength should be conventional is self-evident. Among the qualities of Canadian international distinctiveness, none is more critical than that this country should have voluntarily chosen not to develop nuclear weapons, although it possessed the ability to do so, and that it should have given up nuclear weapons after it had acquired them, mostly involuntarily. To abandon that distinctiveness for the sake of a few thousand Star Wars research jobs and some highly speculative technological spin-offs would represent a denial of the nature of the Canadian international character.

A good deal of that character is the product of sheer blind luck. Secure from invasion, snugly protected by the U.S. nuclear umbrella, distant from terrorism – although not out of its reach as shown by the destruction of the Air-India 747 – Canada has it made. This luck gives Canada no right to point the path to virtue to others. Starting off with so many talents, Canada equally has no right but to follow its own path on issues such as Star Wars and Central America.

Canada can no more avoid its luck than it can avoid forever expending energy on defining a national identity that most people have had defined for them by their ancestors. Canada is what it is. The question is what it will do from now on with what it is.

The notion that Canada could play an activist role in international

335

affairs may seem to be presumptuous. It is presumptuous, but no more presumptuous than the notion of the 50,000 Loyalists that they could create a separate nation above the Great Lakes, or the notion of Macdonald that he could extend a colony across a continent. Nor, moving nearer to our own times and context, the notion of that very small band of diplomats around Pearson that they could perform as interlocutor between the U.S. and Western Europe and as a catalyst in the creation of international institutions.

One reason for supposing that Canadians may once again be able to play an active role in international affairs is that they haven't done so now for almost a quarter of a century. Since around 1960, the nation's best and brightest have applied their energies and talents inward. One of that breed, Stephen Lewis, has now chosen to become Ambassador at the United Nations. Such things don't happen in isolation. A harbinger of change appeared in 1982-83. Out of nowhere a peace movement emerged. Suddenly, tens of thousands of Canadians were talking about the world rather than about themselves; later, they cheered a prime ministerial peace initiative that most knew perfectly well could accomplish little. Another illustration was the impassioned response to the Ethiopian famine. Another is the way so many Canadians now are trying to unravel and to master the complexities of the subject of Star Wars.

The nation's long winter of quasi-isolation is over. Any spring can be rife with deceptions and disappointments. But the temper of the season is different. It's a time for renewal, for striking out on long journeys, for taking risks. It's the time when people rediscover themselves. For two centuries, Canadians have used the 49th parallel as a shield, mostly against the U.S. but also to a degree against reality. The border now is available to be used as a springboard for Canadians to reach out beyond their own tight society, including into the United States. This we can do as an international nation that is, within itself, a real nation at last.

Appendix A

DRAFT OUTLINE OF
FREE TRADE PACT BETWEEN U.S. AND CANADA

General Provisions

I Preamble

II Provisions for Free Trade

(1) IMPORTS
    (a) Immediate removal of all customs duties.
    (b) Prohibition of restrictions of any kind on merchandise imports:[1]
        Provided:
        (i) U.S. may transform existing tariff quotas on certain products (i.e., cattle, calves, seed potatoes, table potatoes, groundfish fillets, milk, cream and butter), to absolute transitional (5-year period) quotas, such absolute quotas to be greater than the tariff quotas accorded under the Geneva Agreement and to be increased progressively during the 5-year period.
        (ii) Canada may maintain absolute transitional (5-year period) quotas on specified products (principally those products now subject to balance-of-payments restrictions). Provision would be made for improvement over the present treatment through immediate abolition of all existing balance-of-payments prohibitions and for progressive increase in quotas during the 5-year period.

---

1 Each country, by agreeing not to impose restrictions of any kind on merchandise trade, would thereby forego any unilateral right (or such rights as exist under the IMF or the ITO Charter) to impose such restrictions (quotas, exchange restrictions, etc.) for balance-of-payments or any other reasons, except after consultation with and agreement by the other country. The treaty would make no provisions with respect to transactions other than merchandise trade, and each country would continue to be governed by the provisions of the IMF with respect to exchange rates and treatment of other transactions, such as invisible trade and financial transfers.

(iii) U.S. reserves right to impose absolute quotas on imports of wheat and wheat flour.[2]

(iv) Canada reserves right to impose absolute quotas on imports of certain fresh fruits and vegetables on a seasonal basis.[3]

(2) EXPORTS

(a) Prohibition of all restrictions on taxes or merchandise exports: Provided that export controls may be imposed in connection with the movement of products in short supply, but such controls shall be imposed only after consultation and the principle of equal treatment to consumers in both countries shall be observed.

III Trade Relations with Third Countries

Since the removal of restrictions on merchandise imports would apply only between the U.S. and Canada and then only to the products the origin of each of these countries, provision would be made for exception to the most-favored-nation principle. With respect to third countries, the U.S. and Canada would continue their separate tariff structures, retaining freedom of action as to tariffs and other import restrictions as they apply to such third countries.[4]

IV Customs Administration

(a) No impediments or formalities would be imposed by the customs administrations of the two countries except as required for statistical purposes and for the administration of certificates of origin. Such certificates would determine eligibility for treatment accorded on the basis of "content requirement" to be specified in the treaty.[5]

(b) Anti-dumping or countervailing duties would be applicable only in

---

2 This reservation would be effected through a Protocol which would specify the conditions to govern imports of wheat and wheat flour into the U.S. from Canada, and would take cognizance of commitments made under the International Wheat Agreement.

3 This reservation would be effected through a Protocol which would permit the imposition by Canada of quantitative restrictions on a seasonal basis for periods not to exceed those applicable to certain fresh fruits and vegetables under the Geneva Agreement.

4 It is the intention of Canada to offer simultaneously to the United Kingdom a free trade arrangement substantially similar to that proposed between the U.S. and Canada.

5 For example, goods having less than the required content would be subject to duties or other treatment applicable to imports from third countries, with the understanding that "content" would be Canadian content or U.S. content or both.

established cases of dumping or subsidization. Thus, the circumstances under which such duties could be applied would be carefully circumscribed to prevent abuse and to prevent the use of such duties as an indirect device for restricting the flow of goods between the two countries.

(c) Provision would be made for reciprocal arrangements respecting tourist purchases whether or not wholly or partially of third-country origin.

V Consultation

(a) Provision would be made for free and close consultation with respect to any matters arising out of the operation of the treaty.

In particular, the Governments of the two countries would agree that, in the event of the adoption by either country of domestic programs designed to maintain prices and regulate production and marketing of primary agricultural products, they shall recognize as basic objectives of such programs the increase in consumption and trade in such products in the two countries. They would further agree to consult with a view to avoiding measures under such programs which might have the effect of defeating the objectives set forth in the preceding sentence.

In addition, the Governments of the two countries would agree that, in the event that, in the opinion of either country, the imposition of quantitative restrictions on imports appears to be necessary in order to protect its balance-of-payments, they shall consult; and would agree further that such measures would not be taken except after agreement between the two countries.

(b) The treaty would not specify the formal machinery for consultation, but would leave the two Governments free to determine procedures for consultation.

It is left for further consideration whether the treaty should provide for arbitration of disputes and special procedure for interpretation.

VI General Exceptions

Exceptions would be allowed for measures:
(a) necessary to protect public morals;
(b) necessary to protect human, animal or plant life or health;
(c) relating to the importation or exportation of gold or silver;
(d) necessary to secure compliance with laws or regulations which are not inconsistent with the provisions of this treaty, including those relating to customs enforcement, the enforcement of monopolies, the protection of patents, trade-marks and copyrights, and the prevention of deceptive practices;

(e) relating to the products of prison labor;
(f) imposed for the protection of national treasures of artistic, historic or archaeological value;
(g) undertaken in pursuance of obligations under intergovernmental commodity agreements;
(h) necessary to the application of standards or regulations for the classification, grading, or marketing of commodities in international trade.

VII Security Provisions

Provisions relating to national security appropriate to this treaty, and exceptions thereto, would be determined after consideration by the appropriate authorities of the two countries. These provisions might appropriately include arrangements for continued free access by each country to the production of the other in the event of attack.

VIII Relation to General Agreement on Tariffs and Trade (Geneva)

(a) Both countries would be governed by provisions of the Geneva Agreement with respect to the following:
1) National Treatment on Internal Taxation and Regulation
2) Freedom of Transit
3) Publication and Administration of Trade Regulations
4) Subsidies
5) Non-discriminatory treatment on the part of state-trading enterprises
6) Inter-governmental Commodity Agreements

IX Termination and Ratification

(a) The treaty would have a term of 25 years and would be subject to termination by either Government only at the end of that term and then on three years' notice.
(b) Ratifications would be exchanged as agreed after further consideration.

X Territorial Application

(a) The treaty would apply to the customs territories of the two countries. (In the case of the U.S. this would include the continental U.S., Alaska, Hawaii, and Puerto Rico.)

Bibliographic Notes

The sources for this book were the conventional ones of interviews – with more than 100 individuals – most of them conducted in person but some conducted over the telephone, and of newspaper and magazine articles, government reports, and books. All my requests for interviews were granted except by Prime Minister Brian Mulroney, a failure to make contact with the top rung of the ladder that I also experienced in an earlier work on another prime minister.

Whatever else may be lacking in the Canada-U.S. relationship, a sufficiency of printed words is not one of them. Those readers who want to survey the material in detail should review the excellent bibliographies provided in *Canada and the U.S.*, edited by R.P. Bowles *et al.* (Prentice-Hall, 1973), and in E. Mahant and G. Mount, *An Introduction to Canadian-American Relations* (Methuen, 1984). For the benefit of readers who may be interested in tracing back the sources of some of my own ideas, or of recreating the social, political, and economic contexts from which they were derived, a summary description of the printed material I relied on follows. To avoid repetition, two works to which I referred repeatedly should be mentioned here: Lawrence Martin's agreeably readable *The Presidents and the Prime Ministers* (Doubleday, 1982) and Stephen Clarkson's partial but thoroughly professional *Canada and the Reagan Challenge* (2nd ed., Lorimer, 1985).

Chapter One. Yanks and Tories. The Loyalists are coming back into fashion, or at least into notice. The basic historical information is provided in Christopher Moore's *The Loyalists* (Macmillan, 1984). Thereafter a reader is urged to turn to Dennis Duffy's elegant *Gardens, Covenants, Exiles* (University of Toronto Press, 1982). A lively viewpoint is presented by David Bell's essay, "The Loyalist Tradition in Canada," contained in *Canadian History Before Confederation*, edited by J.F. Bumsted (Irwin-Dorsey, 1972). William Kilbourn's biography of William Lyon Mackenzie, *The Firebrand* (Toronto, 1956), remains a classic account of the revolutionary temper among the counter-revolutionaries.

Chapter Two. The Flag and the Plume. For their own sakes, readers should turn to Donald Creighton's majestic two-volume biography of Macdonald, *The Young Politician* and *The Old Chieftain* (Macmillan, 1952-55). Joseph Schull's *Laurier* (Macmillan, 1968) is a workmanlike counterpoint. Two excellent sources of material about political attitudes in those times are P.B. Waite's *Life and Times of Confederation* (Toronto, 1962) and *Canada, 1896-1921, A Nation Transformed* by Robert Craig Brown and Ramsay Cook (McClelland and Stewart, 1974). For material about the debates about Reciprocity vs. Commercial Union, and about the annexationist movement, see Robert Craig Brown's *Canada's National Policy, 1883-1900* (Princeton University Press, 1964), and, of course, Goldwin Smith's *Canada and the Canadian Question* (Macmillan, 1891). A useful analysis of the effect of the National Policy on Canada's economic development is contained in Glen Williams, *Not For Export* (McClelland and Stewart, 1983).

Chapter Three. No Fences Makes Good Neighbours. No way exists to understand Mackenzie King other than to read his diaries. A delightful introduction to them is C.P. Stacey's *A Very Double Life* (Macmillan, 1976). Stacey's *Mackenzie King and the North American Triangle* (Macmillan, 1976) uses King's diaries to try to decipher the meanings behind his wartime and post-war policies toward Britain and the U.S. The same ground is covered more solidly in two books by Robert Cuff and J.L. Granatstein, *Canadian-American Relations in Wartime* (Hakkert, 1975) and *American Dollars, Canadian Prosperity, 1945-50* (Samuel-Stevens, 1978), and also in John Holmes, *Canada and the U.S. Political and Security Issues* (CIIA, 1970). The American historian J. Bartlett Brebner's seminal 1945 book, *The North Atlantic Triangle*, was reprinted by McClelland and Stewart in 1961. Granatstein's *The Ottawa Men* (Oxford, 1982) is a superb description of the mandarinate of the 1940s and 1950s, in myth and in reality. Some of the best passages in Martin's *The Presidents and the Prime Ministers* describe the relationship between King and Roosevelt. For an expression of early intellectual nationalism, see Harold Innis's *The Strategy of Culture* (Toronto, 1952) and *Essays in Canadian Economic History*; the most eloquent of the early intellectual continentalists was Frank Underhill, whose ideas are gathered together in the excellent *In Search of Canadian Liberalism* (Macmillan, 1960). A good example of Canada-U.S. economic analysis untroubled by nationalist issues, the last such example available, is the Duke University Press's 1959 volume, *The American Economic Impact on Canada*.

Chapter Four. Gentle Patriotism. Denis Smith's *Gentle Patriot* (Hurtig, 1973) is a worthy biography of Walter Gordon, and Gordon's own memoirs (McClelland and Stewart, 1977) provide a few new insights. *C.D. Howe* by Robert Bothwell and William Kilbourn (McClelland and Stewart, 1979) covers the other side of the story. Although Peter C. Newman's *Renegade in Power* (McClelland and Stewart, 1963) is a bit overheated and is out of date, it remains the best description of Diefenbaker's years in power; Newman's chronicle of the Pearson years, *Distemper of Our Times* (McClelland and Stewart, 1968), is again a bit overtaken by subsequent information; yet it is still an invaluable chronicle of the period. Diefenbaker's own memoirs are well worth reading but should not be taken too literally. George Grant's *Lament for a Nation* (McClelland and Stewart, 1965) is, of course, the foundation document of modern Canadian nationalism.

Chapter Five. Passionate Patriotism. Those who want to follow the development of post-1968 Canadian economic nationalist thought will come upon more material available than all but the most diligent could cope with. A reading sample ought to include Abraham Rotstein's elegant collection of essays, *The Precarious Homestead* (New Press, 1973); *Getting it Back*, ed. by Rotstein and Gary Lax for the Committee for an Independent Canada (Clarke, Irwin, 1974); John Hutcheson's *Dominance and Dependency* (McClelland and Stewart, 1978); Ian Lumsden's *Close the 49th Parallel* (University of Toronto, 1970); Dave Godfrey's *Gordon to Watkins to You* (New Press, 1970). The issue of foreign ownership is examined in detail in Wallace Clement's *Continental Power* (McClelland and Stewart, 1977) and in Patricia Marchak's *In Whose Interests* (McClelland and Stewart, 1979). Essential reading because of its quality of sustained originality is Herschel Hardin's *A Nation Unaware* (J.J. Douglas, 1974). The source book for Waffle thought is *Canada Ltd. The Political Economy of Dependency*, ed. Robert Laxer (McClelland and Stewart, 1973). The opinions of leftist nationalists can be tracked most handily in the issues of *This Magazine* and also in Philip Resnick's *The Land of Cain: Class and Nationalism in English-Canada* (New Star, 1977).

A good corrective to all this indignant nationalism is Ramsay Cook's counter-nationalist *The Maple Leaf Forever* (Macmillan, 1971).

Chapter Six. Oil Wars. The source document on the cross-border infighting over the NEP is Stephen Clarkson's *Canada and the Reagan Challenge*. The NEP itself is well covered by three books, David Crane's *Controlling Interest* (McClelland and Stewart, 1982), Bruce Doern and Glen Toner's *The Politics of Energy* (Methuen, 1985), and James Laxer's *Oil and Gas* (Lorimer, 1983). The oil industry's perspective is described vividly, if a bit extravagantly, in Peter Foster's *The Sorcerer's Apprentices* (Collins, 1982). No published study has been done on FIRA; basic data is contained in Jack Layton's doctoral thesis, "Capital and the Canadian State." Eric Kierans' 1984 Massey lectures, *Globalism and the Nation-State*, have been published by CBC Enterprises, Toronto.

Chapter Seven. Diplomatic Distinctions, 1957-1968. The Diefenbaker period is covered by the sources already mentioned, and by Lawrence Martin. The same is true for the Pearson period, with the important addition of Pearson's memoirs, of which Volume Three, *Mike* (Toronto, 1975), was published posthumously. A useful supplement is Peter Stursberg's *Lester Pearson and the American Dilemma* (Doubleday, 1980), based on taped interviews with most of the principals. A staunchly nationalist perspective is provided by *An Independent Foreign Policy for Canada* (McClelland and Stewart, 1968), a collection of essays edited by Stephen Clarkson. The specific question of Canada's role, and non-role, in Vietnam, is covered, critically, by James Eayrs in his monumental, multi-volume *In Defence of Canada* (Toronto, 1965-80), by Charles Taylor in *Canada and the U.S. in Vietnam* (Anansi, 1974), and, in a challenge to this now conventional critical interpretation, by Douglas Ross, *In the Interests of Peace: Canada and Vietnam, 1954-73* (Toronto, 1984).

Chapter Eight. Diplomatic Distinctions, 1968-1984. My own biography of Trudeau, *The Northern Magus* (McClelland and Stewart, 1980), contains, revealingly if a bit embarrassingly, just one chapter on Trudeau's foreign policy, within which Canada-U.S. affairs are disposed of in a few paragraphs. Clarkson's *Canada and the Reagan Challenge* gives the subject matter more of the space it deserves. A somewhat abstract but still worthwhile review of Trudeau's foreign policy is contained in David Dewitt and John Kirton's *Canada as a Principal Power* (John Wiley, 1983). An early book, but a valuable one, is Peter Dobell's *Canada's Search for New Roles* (Oxford, 1972). Rather heavy going but certainly worthy is *Canada's Foreign Policy: Analysis and Trends*, edited by B. Tomlin (Methuen, 1978).

Chapter Nine. From Massey to Masse. The two pillars upon which any analysis of Canadian cultural nationalism must be founded are *The New Romans*, edited by Al Purdy (Hurtig, 1968), and Margaret Atwood's *Survival* (Anansi, 1972). As important is *A Guide to the Peaceable Kingdom*, a collection of essays edited by William Kilbourn (Macmillan, 1970). The most useful additions thereafter are Rick Salutin's *Marginal Notes* (Lester & Orpen Dennys, 1984), and, in a somewhat convoluted attempt to make anti-Americanism into a common denominator between Quebec and English Canada, Susan Crean and Marcel Rioux's *Two Nations* (Lorimer, 1983). When the shift is made from Canadian cultural nationalism to Canadian culture, the range of the reading material widens beyond the possibility of summary. For instance, no comprehension of Canadian literature can begin except with a reading of Frye's two collections of essays, *The Bush Garden* (Anansi, 1971) and *Divisions on a Ground* (Anansi, 1982), nor, equally, Robert Fulford's essays in *Saturday Night* magazine. Bruce Powe's *A Climate Charged* (Mosaic Press, 1984) represents a bracingly iconoclastic interpretation of Canadian literature. For basic statistics, an invaluable source if now a bit out of date is Paul Audley's *Canada's Cultural Industries* (Lorimer, 1983). This chapter will have fulfilled its function if it inspires a number of readers to turn to Arthur Kroker's *Technology and the Canadian Mind* (New World Perspectives, 1984). Kroker's work provides the necessary references to the works of Innis, McLuhan, and Grant. Neil Compton's brilliant essay, "In Defence of Canadian Culture," is included in the volume *On Canada*, ed. Norman Penlington (University of Toronto Press, 1971).

Chapter Ten. Nationalism: Elegy and Epilogue. This is a look back at all that has gone before.

Chapter Eleven. The Culture of Liberalism, the Politics of Red Tories. Louis Hartz's epochal analysis was set out in his *The Liberal Tradition in America*, but perhaps his most relevant work, because it includes a chapter on Canada by Kenneth McRae, is *The Founding of New Societies* (Harcourt Brace, 1964). Gad Horowitz's heretical counter-analysis is contained in *Canadian Labour in Politics*

(University of Toronto Press, 1968). The debate between Rod Preece and Horowitz over whether or not Red Tories exist is contained in the Spring/Summer and Fall, 1977, issues of *The Canadian Journal of Political and Social Theory*. The Red Tories get a second inning, and score a lot of runs, in Charles Taylor's *Radical Tories* (Anansi, 1982). A lively and highly critical review of Canada's political culture, or lack of one, is contained in David Bell and Lorne Tepperman's *The Roots of Disunity* (McClelland and Stewart, 1979), which also contains an excellent bibliography of the entire subject. An excellent review of such ideology as does exist in this country is contained in William Christian and Colin Campbell's *Political Parties and Ideology in Canada* (2nd ed. McGraw Hill-Ryerson, 1983). Seymour Lipset's most recent review of Canada-U.S. sociocultural differences is included in the proceedings of the American Assembly's seminar where he presented his lengthy and quite brilliant paper: *Canada and the United States*, ed. Charles Doran and John Sigler (Prentice-Hall, 1985).

Chapter Twelve. La Différence. Joel Garreau's *Nine Nations of North America* (Houghton-Mifflin, 1981) is great fun to read in its own right. Edgar Friedenberg's *Deference to Authority* (M.E. Sharpe, 1980) is filled with insights, at times about the author himself. For Canadians needing a quick mug-up on the States, few better sources exist than Richard Reeves' recreation of de Tocqueville's travels, *American Journey* (Simon and Schuster, 1982). Andrew Malcolm's *The Canadians* (Time Books; Fitzhenry and Whiteside, 1985) provides an American's view of the differences.

Chapter Thirteen. The Canadian Identity, Eh? W.L. Morton's *The Canadian Identity* (University of Toronto Press, 1961, 1972) is dated and yet was the first of its kind. A colloquial attempt is Pierre Berton's *Why We Act Like Canadians* (McClelland and Stewart, 1982). A much more thoughtful one is Abraham Rotstein's *Precarious Homestead*. Hardin's *A Nation Unaware* is essential reading here. Another useful source is George Woodcock's *The Canadians* (Fitzhenry and Whiteside, 1979). William Kilbourn provides an elegant introduction to the subject in his own introduction to *A Guide to the Peaceable Kingdom*.

Chapters Fourteen to Sixteen. The Economic Imperative. Here, the daily business pages provide a better guide to what's going on than government reports and long-winded studies. The subject is moving so quickly, and is changing so constantly, that all that can be achieved are occasional wing shots. Paul Hawken's *The Next Economy* is, appropriately, available in paperback (Ballantine, 1984). A lively and anecdotal account is provided by Richard Louw's *America II* (Penguin, 1983). Fernand Braudel's *The Perspective of the World* is an awesome exercise in scholarship; his period is the fifteenth to the eighteenth centuries, but in the last chapter he turns his eye to the present. Malcolm's *The Canadians* takes American readers through a quick, jaunty walk across the frontier. Jane Jacob's *Cities and the Wealth of Nations* (Random House, 1984) is both demanding and inspiring.

Chapter Seventeen. Mr. Canuck Goes to Washington. Seminars and colloquia on Canada-U.S. relations have grown into a flourishing cottage industry. Among the more useful of the collections of speeches delivered at these sessions are those of the American Assembly already cited, and of the Atlantic Council, *Divergence and Dependence* (Ballinger, 1982). An excellent review of intergovernmental issues is contained in Charles Doran's *Forgotten Partnership* (Johns Hopkins, 1984), and, now getting a bit out of date, Roger Swanson's *Inter-Governmental Perspectives on the Canada-U.S. Relationship* (New York University Press, 1978). A different perspective, because it provides a view of Brazil, Mexico, and Australia as well as of Canada, is Annette Baker Fox's *The Politics of Attraction: Four Middle Powers and the U.S.* (Columbia, 1977). On the specific topic of acid rain, the most comprehensive source is John Carroll's *Acid Rain: An Issue in Canadian-American Relations* (Canadian-American Committee, 1982).

Chapter Eighteen. Made-in-Canada Cars. Lee Iacocca's *Iacocca* (Bantam, 1984) hardly needs any more publicity. A comprehensive review of the auto industry and of where it might go is provided by the MIT-organized study, *The Future of the Automobile* (MIT Press, 1984). The best account of the role of American unions in Canada is contained in John Crispo's *International Unionism* (McGraw-Hill, 1966); the story is updated in Jack Williams, *The Story of Unions in Canada* (J.M. Dent, 1975).

Chapter Nineteen. Free Trade: Deal or No Deal. The most up-to-date and comprehensive analysis will be presented in the report of the Royal Commission on Canada's Economic Union and Development Prospects (due to be published in September, 1985). A very thorough analysis is contained in the C.D. Howe Institute study, *Taking the Initiative*, by Richard Lipsey and Murray Smith (C.D. Howe Institute, No. 27, 1985). Official opinion, although pretty general and deliberately bland, is set out in the two Green Papers, *How to Secure and Enhance Canadian Access to Export Markets* (Hon. James Kelleher, January 1985), and *Competitiveness and Security* (Hon. Joe Clark, May, 1985). A good outside view is presented in Peter Morici's *The Global Competitive Struggle: Challenges to the United States and Canada* (National Planning Association, Washington, 1984). One other useful general background report is Frank Stone's *Canada, the GATT and the International Trade System* (Institute for Research on Public Policy, 1984). Among seminars on the subject, the collected speeches of the Brookings Institute meeting of April, 1984, represent a useful introduction to the topic.

Chapters Twenty to Twenty-Two. The two biographies of Brian Mulroney both benefited from considerable co-operation from the subject and suffered from a suspension of their authors' critical faculties. These are: Rae Murphy, Robert Chodos, and Nick Auf der Maur's *Brian Mulroney: The Boy from Baie Comeau* (Lorimer, 1984) and L. Ian MacDonald's *Mulroney, The Making of the Prime Minister* (McClelland and Stewart, 1984). Clarkson's updated edition of *Canada and the Reagan Challenge* covers Mulroney's term to the end of 1984, and *Canada Among Nations, 1984*, ed. Brian Tomlin and Maureen Molot (Lorimer, 1985), similarly provides background on the transition between the Trudeau and Mulroney policy approaches. On the subject of defence, Peter Newman's polemic *True North Not Strong and Free* (McClelland and Stewart, 1983), if now a little bit out of date, provides valuable background information; a good, more recent summary is contained in Albert Legault's essay, "The Defence Dimension," in the American Assembly report.

Acknowledgements

This book began as a five-part series of articles on the Canadian and American economies published in *The Toronto Star* in May, 1984. I worked intermittently on the subject through the balance of the year and began full-time work in January, 1985, on a leave of absence from *The Star*. I conducted interviews in Ottawa, Toronto, Montreal, Vancouver, and Calgary, and, thanks to a grant from the Canada Council, extended at arm's length, in Washington, New York, Chicago, and San Francisco. The writing was completed in mid-July, 1985.

My wife Sandra was my critic, my confidante, and my editor, as she has been for my three previous books. She unsnarled my sentences and sharpened my thoughts.

Several persons read one or more chapters in draft. The careers of some might be retarded if they were mentioned. Those who can be thanked, but simultaneously must be absolved of any blame for the finished product, are Robert Fulford, Edythe Goodridge, Michael Phelps, and Alastair Sweeny, who also provided some inspired assistance with the historical research. Among those who were especially helpful in allowing me to argue out ideas with them I would like to thank in particular Abraham Rotstein.

Nancy Colbert provided me with the most important service a literary agent can provide a writer: she suggested that the original articles should be expanded into a book. Through the labour itself, my editor, Jan Walter, was at all times supportive, and even better, was at all times calm. My copy editor, Dick Tallman, was quick and deft.

I owe a particular debt to *The Star*'s managing editor, Ray Timson, for crafting out a six-month leave of absence in between assignments and for sending me on more southern sorties than was perhaps strictly necessary to fulfil my duties as Ottawa columnist. The staff of the Parliamentary Library combined efficiency with equability, as did Brenda Brady of the U.S. Information Service in Ottawa; they made much of the research a positive pleasure.

Index

351

Freedom of Information Act, 127
Free trade, 16, 24, 27, 29-33, 36, 40,
52, 53, 66, 68n, 125, 126, 149, 150,
152, 197, 209, 229, 234, 240, 243-
45, 277, 278, 283, 285-303, 322,
330, 331, 332, 334
Free trade pact (1947-48), 52, 302
French Revolution, 18
Friedenburg, Edgar, 161, 166, 190
Frye, Northrop, 133, 134, 136, 137,
140, 150, 182
Fryer, John, 272, 281
Fulbright, William, 115
Fulford, Robert, 54, 74, 137-38, 139,
140, 255, 330
Fulton, Davie, 86

Galbraith, John Kenneth, 46, 221, 230
Gallagher, Jack, 93, 95, 222
Gallup Poll, 78-79, 100, 150, 178, 321
Gamble, John, 169
Garneau, Marc, 311
Garner, Hugh, 139
Garreau, Joel, 176
Gaucher, Yves, 135
General Agreement on Tariffs and
Trade (GATT), 42, 99, 108, 287,
288, 289, 295, 296
General Motors, 271, 272, 273, 274,
275, 277, 278, 279
General Motors (Canada), 274, 275
Genstar, 238
George, Henry, 29
George III, 19
George V, 38
Georgia Straight, 139
Gerry, Peter and Robert, 46
Ghermezian brothers, 238
Gibbons, Sam, 264, 292
Gibbons, Roger, 169
Gillespie, Alastair, 77
Gilmour, Jim, 216
Ginsberg, Allan, 139
Gladstone, William, 24
Glen, Lenny, 186
Globe and Mail, 190, 191, 305
Godfrey, Dave, 147

Goldwater, Barry, 168
Gompers, Samuel, 270
Gorbachev, Mikhail, 71
Gordon, Alison, 175
Gordon, Walter, 57, 61-71, 76, 77,
115
Gotlieb, Allan, 130, 249, 255, 256,
260-65
Gotlieb, Sondra, 249, 260, 261
Gould, Glenn, 133, 145
Gould, Jay, 35
Graham, Billy, 181
Grain Growers' Guide, 39
Granatstein, J.L., 53n, 110n, 112n,
250
Grant, George, 22, 25, 42, 66, 146,
157, 166, 194
Gray, Herb, 69, 77, 80, 83, 87, 91, 99
Gray, John, 138
Great Recession of 1981-82, 223, 232
Green, Don, 224
Green, Howard, 110, 113, 163
Gregg, Allan, 165
Grey, Governor General Earl, 36
Grierson, John, 142, 145
Griffith Laboratories, 217
Group of Seven, 133, 145, 182
GSR Company, 225
Gulf Canada, 91, 101, 152, 313
Gwyn, Sandra, 24n, 129n

Haig, Alexander, 98, 125
Haliburton, Robert, 22
Hamilton, Alvin, 66
Hardin, Herschel, 76, 164, 195, 230
Harkness, Douglas, 113
Harper's magazine, 222
Harris, Lou (poll), 258, 260
Harris, Milton, 239
Harris, Richard, 294
Harrison, Fred, 175
Hartford, Jerry, 275
Hartz, Louis, 158, 162, 165, 166, 169,
170
Hatfield, Richard, 126
Hawken, Paul, 199, 200, 202
Hayden, Melissa, 145

110, 114n, 115
Martin, Paul, 71, 116
Martin, Samuel A., 166n
Masse, Marcel, 135, 143, 152
Massey, Vincent, 44, 141, 188
Massey Commission on the Arts, Letters and Sciences (1951), 44, 45, 65
Mathieson, Bob, 186
Matthews, Robin, 75, 137
Matthews, Terry, 93
Mazankowski, Don, 207, 245
McCall, Christina, 164, 172
McCall's magazine, 43
McCarthy, Joseph, 44, 108
McCharles, D.C., 90
McClelland, Jack, 69
McCormick, Colonel Robert, 308
McDermott, Dennis, 273, 275, 276, 280
McFarlane, James, 228
McGovern, George, 253
McIveen, John, 236
McIvor, Donald, 102
McKinley tariff (1890), 34
McKinnon, Hector, 53
McLeod, Young, Weir, 221
McLuhan, Marshall, 137, 138, 141, 147
McNamara, Robert, 111
Medicare, 144, 158, 164, 178, 180, 192
Mercantile Bank, 69
Merchant, Livingston, 115
Merrill Lynch, 205
Middlekauff, Robert, 19
Mirus, Rolf, 201
Mitchell, George, 263
Mitel, 93, 201, 244
Mitsubishi, 279
Mitterand, François, 207
Mobil Oil, 88, 90, 91, 102, 208
Molson's, 238
Mondale, Walter, 274, 325
Montreal Gazette, 82, 127
Montreal Symphony Orchestra, 143
Moore, Christopher, 20n
Moore Corporation, 244

Morris, Jan, 184
Morton, W.L., 194
Mowat, Farley, 139
Mukherjee, Bharati, 190n
Mulroney, Brian, 41, 42, 50, 81, 85, 86, 91n, 97, 101, 104, 105, 107, 116, 126, 130, 132, 143n, 152, 157, 163, 165, 169, 170, 171, 189, 197, 209, 214, 223, 234, 259, 260, 264, 265, 266, 270, 276, 279, 286, 288, 289, 291, 295, 296, 297, 298, 302, 304-14, 317, 319n, 321, 322, 324, 326, 331, 332, 333
Multiculturalism, 74, 158, 190
Multinationals, 61, 65, 67, 78, 81, 86, 89, 90-97, 100, 102, 105, 216, 221, 236, 242, 280, 329
Muncaster, Dean, 237
Mundell, Robert, 177
Munro, Alice, 134, 136
Murphy, Rae, 309
Mutual Assured Destruction (MAD), 318

Nader, Ralph, 271
Nash, Knowlton, 110
National Arts Centre, 135, 143
National Ballet, 141
National Continental Union League, 35
National debt (Canada), 216, 217, 219, 223
National Energy Board, 66
National Energy Policy (NEP), 57, 62, 78, 80, 82, 85, 86, 88-105, 124, 128, 149, 150, 220, 237, 254, 264, 313, 332; "back-in" provision, 95, 97, 99; Petroleum and Gas Revenue Tax (PGRT), 95n, 100; Petroleum Incentive Program (PIP grants), 95, 99, 100
National Film Board, 142, 143, 145
National Gallery, 141
National Oil Policy (1961), 66
National Policy, 16, 27, 29, 30, 31, 32, 33, 287
NATO, 107, 108, 110, 111, 113, 120, 124, 131, 316, 320, 323